Hafiz Boboyorov

Collective Identities and Patronage Networks in Southern Tajikistan

ZEF Development Studies

edited by

Solvay Gerke and Hans-Dieter Evers

Volume 24

Center for Development Research (ZEF)
University of Bonn
www.zef.de

LIT

Hafiz Boboyorov

Collective Identities and Patronage Networks in Southern Tajikistan

LIT

This dissertation has been accepted by the Philosophical Faculty of the University of Bonn.

First Supervisor: PD Dr. Conrad Schetter
Second Supervisor: Prof. Dr. Stephan Conermann
Date of oral exam: 06. 12. 2011

Bibliographic information published by the Deutsche Nationalbibliothek
The Deutsche Nationalbibliothek lists this publication in the Deutsche Nationalbibliografie; detailed bibliographic data are available in the Internet at http://dnb.d-nb.de.

ISBN 978-3-643-90382-2
Zugl.: Bonn, Univ., Diss., 2011

A catalogue record for this book is available from the British Library

Klosbachstr. 107
CH-8032 Zürich
Tel. +41 (0) 44-251 75 05
Fax +41 (0) 44-251 75 06
E-Mail: zuerich@lit-verlag.ch
http://www.lit-verlag.ch

LIT VERLAG Dr. W. Hopf
Berlin 2013
Fresnostr. 2
D-48159 Münster
Tel. +49 (0) 2 51-62 03 20
Fax +49 (0) 2 51-23 19 72
E-Mail: lit@lit-verlag.de
http://www.lit-verlag.de

Distribution:

In Germany: LIT Verlag Fresnostr. 2, D-48159 Münster
Tel. +49 (0) 2 51-620 32 22, Fax +49 (0) 2 51-922 60 99, E-mail: vertrieb@lit-verlag.de

In Austria: Medienlogistik Pichler-ÖBZ, e-mail: mlo@medien-logistik.at
In Switzerland: B + M Buch- und Medienvertrieb, e-mail: order@buch-medien.ch
In the UK: Global Book Marketing, e-mail: mo@centralbooks.com
In North America: International Specialized Book Services, e-mail: orders@isbs.com
e-books are available at www.litwebshop.de

TABLE OF CONTENTS

ACKNOWLEDGMENTS

In our world, we achieve nothing without mutual trust and collective effort. The current PhD work, which also talks about collective bonds, fates and endeavours in one part of this world, is no exception. If I have met the expectations of this research project, it should not be regarded as a result of my exceptional efforts alone.

I give especial thanks to the personal support, devotion and self-sacrifice of my mentor and first supervisor, Dr. habil. Conrad Schetter. On a regular basis, when in Bonn on weekly and sometimes daily basis, he devoted his time, knowledge and library to establish and improve this work. In the early stages we stayed together and shared our preliminary field impressions during a regional seminar in Kunduz and Farkhar, Afghanistan, and Kulab and Dushanbe, Tajikistan. To help me to shape my research focus he visited my study region during my field research. I express sincere gratitude for all his efforts and devotion to helping me finally fulfill this research project.

I am also thankful to my supervisor Professor Stephan Conermann, who found time to personally arrange my affiliation with the Philosophical Faculty of Bonn University. My colleagues and friends in our research project, "Local Governance and Statehood in Amudarya Borderland Region," at the Center for Development Research (Bonn University) did not spare their support for my practical and study orientation in the German environment. I am therefore indebted to Janosch Prinz, Katja Mielke, Andreas Wilde, Henrik Poos, Bernd Kuzmits, Andreas Mandler and Sarah Dusend for their critical and productive remarks on the early and later versions of my dissertation, and especially for their kind and warm relations with my family.

Without my family this work would lack a good deal of personal experience and reflection. In Tajikistan, my family is part of the whole social structure which is necessary to compare and reflect upon the cases from the field. In Germany, daily talks and advice from my brave wife, Robia, accompanied by our daughter and son, Mehrofar and Nurbakhsh, regarding their socialisation – and especially to the nice Spielplätze in the friendly municipality of Bonn – encouraged and inspired me to win against unexpected disappointments.

I am grateful for the financial and institutional support of DAAD (German Service for Academic Exchange), which opens the doors of German universities to many foreign students. Such a unique exchange is indeed a most effective means to improve our life and world by creating for them deserving meanings and a future. DAAD generously funded my life and research activities over three years and provided family allowances when we stayed in Bonn, Germany. I also express my gratitude for the financial, institutional and advisory support of the Center for Development Research, and personally to Ms. Rosemarie Zabel, Dr. Günther Manske and others. The Center funded my field research during fifteen months in Tajikistan. The supplementary grant of the Network Scholarship Programmes of the Open Society Foundation in London (Soros Foundations Network) and the endowment of Katholische Hochschulgemeine Bonn were also vital in helping me to continue my incessant work on the dissertation. I am thankful for the trusted financial contributions of these charitable organisations.

I pass cordial thanks to my field research informants and assistants, as well as to my colleagues and friends in the Institute of Philosophy of the Academy of Sciences of Tajikistan. Especially, the regular seminars of the Colloquium "Jahoni andesha" and the circle of its members since 1993 have helped me to shape my intellectual orientation.

To the memory of my mother

PREFACE

This PhD thesis, entitled "Kinship and Islam: The Role of Collective Identities in Shaping the Institutional Order of Patronage in Southern Tajikistan," is part of the research project "Local Governance and Statehood in the Amudarya Borderland Region," which has been ongoing since 2006 at Center for Development Research (ZEF), Bonn University. The project aims to compare particular and transboundary cases from the Amudarya Borderland region (Afghanistan, Tajikistan and Uzbekistan). My contribution to the research project discusses cases of rural settlements in the borderland region situated in the Khatlon province of Tajikistan.

The social-anthropological field research conducted between March 2007 and May 2008 analyses the mainstream processes of local governance in the rural settlements of five districts of the province, including the Shuroobod and Mu'minobod districts in the Kulob region and the Shahritus, Qabodiyon and Nosiri Khusrav districts in the Qabodiyon oasis. To represent both breadth and depth, I have collected and compared empirical data from different socio-economic contexts in the study region, such as mountainous vs. lowland geographies, subsistence-based vs. cotton-growing economies, ethnically homogenous vs. ethnically heterogeneous communities, small-size vs. large-size settlements, elite-dominated and contested vs. hierarchically representative and integrative political structures and intensively involved vs. provisionally intervened localities by external (state and international development) agencies.

The study considers the role of collective identities, including kinship and Islam, in shaping institutional arrangements at the local level of human interactions. The theoretical approach of this study suggests that local governance involves the political organisation of social order in a local context, which reflects interactions of different actors through historically and culturally embedded institutions of power structures and networks. The central institutions of local governance have been identified as the reciprocal and patron-client norms and principles of political and economic relations.

Through my theoretical and empirical discussions I have classified three mainstream aspects of local governance, including (1) the commitment of local people to differentiated power structures, (2) the legitimation of political and economic claims and the rights of individual actors and (3) the stabilisation of contested socio-political situations.

In the case of the mountainous village of Shuroobod district, as result of a highly contested political and economic environment and the intensive intervention in the community by development agencies, collective identities serve mainly two aspects of local governance. These aspects are (1) the legitimation of political and economic claims and (2) the stabilisation of the contested boundaries of social order. Specific cases discuss the stabilisation function of reciprocal practices of extended families and neighbourhoods, social welfare programmes, resource mobilisation for 'common wellbeing', dispute settlement and development programmes.

In the cotton-growing community of Shahritus district, the next in-depth case study, I observed the integrated boundaries of social order. Political actors, including state authorities and their local allies, use collective identities to establish and integrate the 'cotton-growing communities' of kinship and neighbourhood networks. This is the main aspect of local governance in the cotton-growing community which, unlike the mountainous community, enforces the representative and integrative – although hierarchical – political and economic structures of the mahalla committee and *dehqan* farms. The other important aspect of local governance in this community was identified as the stabilisation of socio-political situations, which again serve to endure the cotton economy. The discussion involves cases of inheritance and religious claims, network-based political and economic representation, reciprocal means and resources of stability, especially resource mobilisation for the cotton economy.

The thesis concludes that collective identities may serve the different purposes of political actors in different contexts and thereby shape different aspects of local governance. In the mountainous, subsistence-based, ethnically homogenous and small community, reference to collective identities seeks to legitimise the privileged access of the elites to political and economic structures and resources. In the lowland, cotton-growing, ethnically heterogeneous and large community, however, the cotton sector and socio-political stability are core concerns for the elites. Generally, I conclude that collective identities express and enforce the normative structures and backbones of local governance and thus build trust, commitment and networks among different actors.

LIST OF TABLES, FIGURES, MAPS AND PICTURES

List of Tables

List of Figures

List of Maps

List of Pictures

GLOSSARY OF LOCAL TERMS

Aga Khan	(Taj.)	The present Imam of Ismaili followers in the world, including most of the population of the Badakhshan province in Tajikistan
Agat	(Uzb.)	The bed of a cotton field
Ariza	(Taj.)	Formal letter of complaint to the state and court
Avlod	(Taj.)	Patrilineal extended family
Basmachi	(Uzb.)	Local guerilla groups in Central Asia which fought against the Bolsheviks during the 1920s-1930s
Begigari	(Taj.)	The second-level administrative unit under the pre-Soviet Bukhara Emirate
Beg	(Taj.)	The head of *Begigari*
Brigada	(Taj.)	The team for collective work since the Soviet Union
Brigadir	(Taj.)	The head of a brigada
Bulabacha	(Taj.)	Cousin from the paternal line
Charoghjoy	(Taj.)	A household-related shrine or healing site
Choykhona	(Taj.)	Literally means 'tea-house', but here it is a neighbourhood- or kinship-related mosque
Davlat	(Taj.)	State; wealth
Dehqan	(Taj.)	Peasant, farmer
Dehqan Farm	(Taj.-Eng.)	Enterprise for agricultural products
Dehqon	(Taj.)	See *Dehqan*
Dekhkan	(Rus.)	See *Dehqan*
Dogovor	(Rus.)	Contract
Elkheshi	(Uzb.)	Extended family
Eshon	(Taj.)	Religious saint and usually the leader of Sufi *tariqa* in a region; he inherits his status from his

		descent group, which is sometimes claimed to be related to the Islamic prophet Muhammad
Etnos	(Rus.)	Ethnic group or community; any group with clearcut boundaries
Fermeri	(Taj.-Rus.)	Related to a *dehqan* farm
Fyucherist	(Rus.)	Futures or investment company in the cotton sector
Guzar	(Taj.)	Neighbourhood based on the geographical structure of a mountainous village
Hajj	(Taj.)	Islamic pilgrimage
Hanafi	(Taj.)	One of the Sunni legal (Sharia) schools widely practiced in Central Asia, including Tajikistan
Hashar	(Taj.)	Collective mobilisation of labour, material and financial resources
Haji(s)	(Taj.)	Islamic pilgrim(s)
Hukumat	(Taj.)	District or city government administration
Imam Khatib	(Taj.)	The officially recognised leading mullah in the village
Ismaili	(Taj.)	A Shia school in Islam
Jamoa	(Taj.)	Community; public (e.g. public prayer or mosque)
Jamoat	(Taj.)	A jamoat is a primary government entity which represents several villages geographically and economically located in the same area
Kelin	(Uzb.-Taj.)	Daughter-in-law
Kenja	(Uzb.-Taj.)	The most junior son
Khatm	(Taj.)	(Re-)initiation ceremony
Khayriya	(Taj.)	Individual donation through a mosque or other religious setting
Klan	(Rus.)	Clan
Klient	(Rus.)	Client

Kolkhoz	(Rus.)	Abbreviation for '*kollektivnoe khoziaistvo*', i.e. collective farm
Kolkhozi	(Taj.)	Related to kolkhoz
Kucha	(Taj.)	Street, larger neighbourhood in a rural settlement
Kuhistoni	(Taj.)	Related to '*kuhiston*' ('mountainous region'); people from mountainous regions resettled in the cotton districts during the time of the Soviet Union
Mahalla	(Taj.)	A unit of rural or urban residence; neighbourhood
Mahalla	(Taj.-Eng.)	Also Mahalla Committee; a primary unit of a semi-official and self-governing political structure
Mahalli	(Taj.)	Local, native; related to a local or native
Mahram	(Taj.)	According to Islam, men who have the right to face-to-face relations with women; close relatives, including father, uncle, brother and husband
Militsi(y)a	(Rus.-Taj.)	Police officer; police
Mintaqa	(Taj.)	Geographical or administrative region
Mullo	(Taj.)	Mullah
Mutavvali	(Taj.)	A guard who inherits a sacred site, like a shrine
Naqshbandiya	(Taj.)	The most widely spread Sufi order in Tajikistan
Nikoh	(Taj.)	Islamic betrothal
Nomahram	(Taj.)	Men who are not *mahram* for women
Norma	(Rus.)	Quota
Oqsaqol	(Uzb.)	Elder and any respected man
Plan	(Rus.)	State- or elite-set tariff for agricultural production

Presidenti	(Taj.)	Literally: 'related to President'; here supports land plots for individual families for their food security
Qabila	(Taj.)	Tribe; kinship group
Qadiriyyah	(Taj.)	The second largest Sufi order in Tajikistan
Qawm	(Taj.)	Descent or ethnic group; kinship group
Qawmdori	(Taj.)	The manners to manage the affairs of related people (kinsmen, co-villagers, etc.)
Qawmiyat	(Taj.)	Related to descent, ethnic or kinship group
Qishloqdori	(Taj.)	The manners to manage village affairs
Rais	(Taj.)	Chief
Rod	(Rus.)	Kin, clan
Sadaqa	(Taj.)	The practice of supporting the poor and beggars
Sahmdor	(Taj.)	Shareholder
Sahmdori	(Taj.)	Shareholding
Sarkhatib	(Taj.)	*Imam-khatib* of the district *jamoa* (public) mosque
Sayyid	(Taj.)	Descent group of the Islamic prophet
Selsovet	(Rus.)	'Sel'skiy sovet', i.e. village council or jamoat
Shahid	(Taj.)	Literally: 'martyr'; here the shrine of an unknown martyr
Shajaranoma	(Taj.)	Generation or genealogical book
Shanbegi	(Taj.)	The Sovietised mobilisation of labour resources; similar to *hashar*
Shaykh/shekh	(Taj./Uzb.)	The inherited and religiously sanctified guard and possessor of sacred assets, such as a shrine, mosque or healing site
Shia	(Taj.)	Political and legal division in Islam which recognises Ali Ibn Abu Talib and his descendents (*Imams*) as the legitimate successor of the Islamic prophet

Shokh	(Taj.)	Neighbourhood based on irrigation canals
Sotikh	(Rus.-Taj.)	0.10 hectare
Sotsium	(Rus.)	Any group or society with clearcut boundaries
Sovkhoz	(Rus.)	Abbreviation for *sovetskoe khoziaistvo*, 'Soviet' or 'state' farm
Sufism or *Sufi*	(Taj.)	The common name for mystical orders and schools in Islam
Sufi	(Taj.)	The follower of Sufism
Sufi Halqa	(Taj.)	A Sufi circle, order or network
Sunni	(Taj.)	Political and legal division in Islam which recognises four companions of the Islamic prophet (Abubakr, Omar, Osman and Ali ibn Abu Talib) as his legitimate successors
Taloq	(Taj.)	Islamic practice of divorce
Tamarqa	(Uzb.)	A household-related land plot
Tarbiya	(Taj.)	Moral upbringing
Tariqa	(Taj.)	Sufi sect or order
Tinji	(Taj.)	Peace, quietness
Uchastkovyy	(Rus.)	The chief police officer of a jamoat
Urugh	(Uzb.)	Kin, kinship group
Ushr	(Taj.)	Islamic taxation from peasantry distributed mainly among relatives
Usto	(Taj.)	Master
Vakil	(Taj.)	'Representative', i.e. the head of a mahalla committee
Vasiyat	(Taj.)	The last will for patrimonial inheritance
Vedomost'	(Rus.)	Payroll
Veteran	(Rus.)	Veteran; a person with a long service record and reputation in state structures

Zakot	(Taj.)	Islamic taxation institution for private goods, including domestic animals and real estate which generate regular economic profits
Zveno	(Rus.)	A small working team or unit under a *brigada*

ABBREVIATIONS AND ACRONYMS

CDD	Community Driven Development
CDU	Community Development Unit (of MSDSP)
DFID (UK)	Department for International Development of the United Kingdom
DVO	Devdor Village Organisation
INGO	International Non-Governmental Organisation
JRC	Jamoat Resource Centre
LDC	Local Development Committee
MSDSP	Mountainous Societies Development Support Programme of Aga Khan Development Network
NGO	Non-Governmental Organisation
NIE	Neo-Institutionalist Economics
PRA	Participatory Rural Appraisal
PRSP	Poverty Reduction Strategy Paper
SCN	Social Constructionist Neo-Institutionalism
TASS	The Futures Company in Qabodiyon oasis
TJ Somoni	Tajik Somoni – monetary unit of Tajikistan
UNDP	United Nations Development Programme
USAID	United States Agency for International Development
USD	US Dollar
VO	Village Organisation
VSC	Village Support Centre (of Save the Children)
ZEF	Zentrum für Entwicklungsforschung (Center for Development Research at Bonn University, Germany)

INTRODUCTION

During the first weeks of my field stay in the southern districts of Khatlon province, I visited provincial and district governments several times to gain permission for anthropological research. The last time I returned to the ideological department of the Provincial Government in Qurghonteppa city to pick up a permission letter, the chairman of the department asked me to wait in his office while the deputy governor issued the letter. There I witnessed his long telephone conversation with a saint (*eshon*), the most respected religious notable of a provincial subordination. He explained to the saint the aim and use of the new president's law on *Tanzim* (literally: '*re*-ordering') (2007) and insisted on his mediation. As he expressed, "[y]ou are a respected man among your people and it is the personal request of our president [of Tajikistan] and governor [of the province] to help us to realise the decree [the law]."[1]

The law on *Tanzim* (2007) was adopted "due to the need to develop society" and therefore "re-orders traditions, celebrations and customs, protects the original values of the national culture [and] improves social and economic… life of the citizens of the Republic of Tajikistan" (1). The state and local authorities have been instructed to sanction and punish people for excessive expenditure on 'backward' and 'superstitious' traditions, festivities and customs, "in order to stimulate reduction of poverty level… and to maintain public order" (ibid.). In the first place, the '*re*-ordering' norms and regulations of the new law must maintain contested political and economic 'stability' and order.

On the way back to Shahritus town, with the permission letter in hand, my first 'field' impression was that the Soviet-originated state apparatus, and its relative monopoly of physical and symbolic violence, also serves to maintain the existing social order. It integrates and adapts both indigenous and external, such as religious and development, agencies. Therefore, these agencies take on desirable images and functions while mediating the *appropriate* claims and needs of political elites. Otherwise, followers and implementers would be under strict surveillance throughout their daily lives. All these contradictions reflect the contested integrity of the social order, while in turn local governance seems to be a day-to-day *project* to enforce this integrity.

---

[1] Personal observation; Qurghonteppa City (Notebook No 1-1, April 2, 2007: pages 38-39).

Background and context

This thesis discusses the role of local people's collective identities, including kinship and Islam, in shaping the institutionalised environment of local governance. Herein, local governance is defined as the political organisation of social order or the institutional arrangements of power relations at the primary level of human interactions. This thesis analyses the roles collective identities play to enforce the contested structures and boundaries of power relations. From this angle, it departs from both actor-oriented and structural-functionalistic models of explanation and assumes instead that political actors invest heavily in material and immaterial resources, such as political and economic incentives, military pressure and collective norms and identities, in order to sustain these contested power structures.

The empirical data collected through anthropological study in southern borderland districts of Khatlon province between March 2007 and May 2008 illustrate the discussion. One in-breadth and two in-depth cases about local governance norms and instruments estimate the comparative value of collective identities in different rural contexts.

Map 1: Map of Tajikistan, with an emphasis on the sites of field research[2]

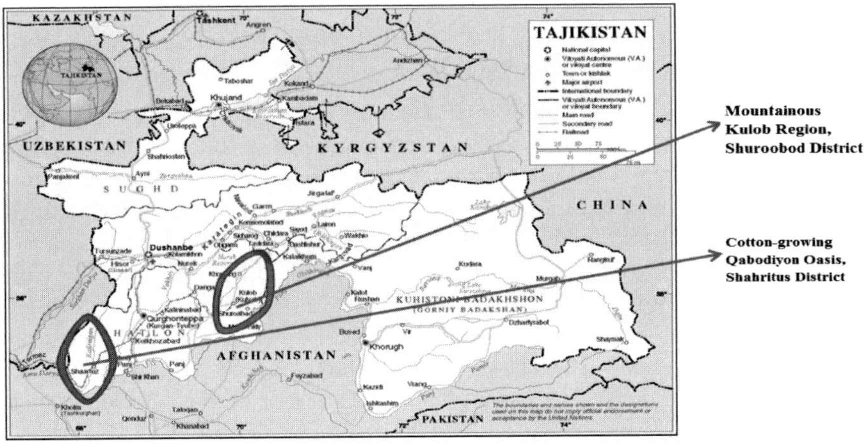

2 Source: the website of United Nations (http://www.un.org/Depts/Cartographic/map/profile/tajikist.pdf), accessed May 7, 2011 (modified).

Before the Bolshevik invasion in the 1920s, the territory of Khatlon province was divided up into separate second-tier administrative units (*Begigari*) under direct subordination to the Emirate of Bukhara.[3] At the same time, separate *begs* (heads of *Begigaris*) claimed and exercised authority over the territory of their adjacent *Begigaris* as well as over the southern borderland territory of Amudarya River. The Bukhara Emir expressed his solidarity especially with the more powerful *begs*, who were more successful in collecting taxes from the population, as the payment of taxes expressed the *begs'* personal or cliental loyalty to the central authority (Logofet' 1909, 1911; Mirzaev 1954; Bartol'd 1965; Donish 1967; Nadzhafova 1967).

The Soviets considered that the Emirate's political-economic systems would not allow for the expansion of central state institutions at the local level and in borderland areas, so they replaced them with ethno-national administrations up until the late 1920s (Martin 2001). The territorial administrations of *Begigaris* were integrated into newly established provinces and districts for both political and economic reasons. Until that point, many lowland regions in contemporary Khatlon province were unpopulated due to several circumstances, including the Bukhara taxation system (i.e. personal attribution of taxes), nomadic and semi-nomadic lifestyles, the frequent raids of nomadic bands and a poor and limited irrigation infrastructure (Bartol'd 1965). The new governors understood the destabilising effects of the old systems, especially for their collectivisation project, when, for example, the disastrous harvest of 1925 led to 26 percent of central Asians flying to Afghanistan (Akiner 2001).

The newly introduced economic system required expansive irrigation infrastructure and additional manpower for cotton plantations throughout Tajikistan, including Khatlon province. The nomadic Uzbeks and mountainous Tajiks were forcedly relocated to these plantations, which nestled near to 'native' communities. The relocation project was temporarily interrupted during World War II but intensified in the late 1940s. Gradually, Khatlon province turned into a central region, which grew the highest proportion of cotton and other agricultural products in Tajikistan. The province was also politically sensitive due to the forced relocation of different ethnic groups. Today the majority of rural settlements consist of the different ethnic groups, such as 'native' Tajiks, Arabs, Sayyids, 'mountainous' Tajiks from different

[3] These local administrations in current Khatlon province involve *Begigari* of Qabodiyon (the current districts of Qabodiyon oasis), *Begigari* of Qurghonteppa (the current districts of Vakhsh valley), *Begigari* of Kulob (the current lowland districts of Kulob region) and *Begigari* of Baljuvon (the current mountainous districts of Kulob region) (Logofet' 1911).

mountainous regions of Tajikistan and Uzbek tribes from different parts of Tajikistan and Uzbekistan. Only a few mountainous districts in the eastern part of the province consisted mainly of *Kulobi* Tajiks.

The integration of Soviet political and economic systems was incomplete and could not entirely change pre-Soviet governance institutions. After the collapse of the Soviet Union, Tajikistan descended into civil war. Today, scholars (e.g. the review and study of Heathershaw 2007) agree that the Tajik Civil War (1992-1997) was not a conflict between two worldviews or the ideologies of Communism and Islamic fundamentalism or Islamic democracy; between the contradictory beliefs about and interests in political and economic course that the nation must have taken, as the leaders of the rival groups claimed. It was due rather to rival political elites, who could not share the positions and resources of the central state and consequently mobilised their local supporters and international allies. Within a short period of time, the central regions of the country – and subsequently for a longer period the ethnically heterogeneous communities of Khatlon province – were the epicentres of the conflict. The open and intensive discord, which mobilised local populations against each other during late 1992 and early 1993, had disastrous outcomes: more than 40,000 people lost their lives and about 1 million survivors fled to other regions of the country and to other neighbouring nations, including Afghanistan, Kyrgyzstan, Kazakhstan, Russia and Turkmenistan. Guerilla warfare continued until the 1997 Peace Reconciliation between the Tajik Government and its Opposition Forces, negotiated under the auspices of the UN and several foreign countries (Matveeva 2009; Heathershaw 2007).

Re-ordering social order: the central assumption, hypothesis and question of the study

In the post-civil war period, core institutional features and practices have been preserved through the local governance processes. In part, Soviet political and economic structures and actors[4] have still persisted, in spite of radical breakthroughs and especially the sub-dividing of the kolkhozes or sovkhozes into *dehqan* farms and mahalla committees (hereinafter mahalla)[5] since 1997.

[4] In this study I define these political elites at the local level as '*kolkhozi* elites'. They relied on both traditional and modern structures to dominate Soviet political and economic organisations (such as kolkhozes), and they integrated and adapted pre-Soviet local political allegiances and collective identities into the Soviet kolkhoz system.

[5] A mahalla, or a mahalla committee, is officially defined and regulated by the Law on Local Self-Governance (2008) as the self-governance structure of rural settlements.

Many studies[6] also assert this core feature while discussing recent, post-Soviet developments and shifts, including privatising the public goods of kolkhozes or sovkhozes, shareholding of land and other strategic resources, the decentralisation of local state structures and the integration of international development programmes.

My basic assumption for this study is that the integration and adaptation of the post-Soviet developments and shifts has been neither easy nor straightforward. Furthermore, integration and adaptation have not been logically linear, if we take into account contestations over the distribution of positions and resources. Thus, I have assumed in my hypothesis that:

- *Political actors need enforcement mechanisms, including collective norms and identities, to integrate and adapt post-Soviet developments and shifts into local governance structures.*

From this hypothesis, I have formulated the central question for this study:

- *What was/is the role of collective identities, among other cognitive constructs and social structures, of local people in shaping the mainstream processes and institutions of local governance?*

In this study I define local governance as the political organisation of social order in a local context, which reflects different actors' interactions through historically and culturally embedded institutions. Local governance institutions include the normative principles and instructive schemata driven by different sources, such as statutory laws, religious norms and other socio-cognitive constructs of the local people.

Scope, significance and expected use of the study

This PhD thesis is part of the research project 'Local Governance and Statehood in the Amudarya Borderland Region', which has been implemented since 2006 at the Center for Development Research (ZEF) of Bonn University.

Informally it is also subject to the state structure at inter-village level, which is jamoat, and implements state orders at the village level. For this purpose, the organisation uses both local people's resources and bureaucratic and military means of the state.

[6] Including Abdullaev (2004), Atkin (1997, 1999), Babajanian (2006), Collins (2002, 2003), Dadmehr (2003), De Martino (2004), Dudoignon (2004), Duncan (2000), Falkingham (2000), Freizer (2004), Gretski (1995), Heathershaw (2005, 2007), International Crisis Group (2005), Idiev (2003, 2006), Luong (2000, 2002), Matveeva (2009), Nissen (2004), Nourzhanov (1996, 2005), Roy (1997, 1999, 2000), Tadjbakhsh (2008) and Verdery (2004).

The project aims to compare particular and transboundary cases from the Amudarya Borderland region, which is currently divided up between the three independent states of Afghanistan, Tajikistan and Uzbekistan. My contribution to the research project discusses cases from rural settlements within the region situated in Tajikistan. These settlements are administered by the borderland districts of Khatlon province, which I define here as '(the region of) southern Khatlon'.

This study, however, is not beholden to actor-oriented and rational-choice approaches in order to explain political and economic processes. Local governance is not merely a normative and positivist concept employed to reflect the simple, linear and rational-choice causality "if A, then B," or if we invest some incentives, political actors change their behaviours and preferences to head in a certain direction. My investment in this study is to explore what is between A and B that political actors are not able or do not wish to change, even if they have incentives provided by, for example, development agencies.

The following discussion considers the role of collective identities, including kinship and Islam, in shaping the choices and preferences of political actors in response to what external agencies offer for the sake of structural change or adjustment. The analysis of the empirical data is illumined by my understanding that the categorical (e.g. group or class) division between political elites and the poor is a simulative and politically biased approach. The impoverishment and marginalisation of 'the poor' is, to a greater extent, the production of development discourses. Empirical cases show that 'the poor', including women, participate in local politics at least through their concessive agreement and cliental justification of taken decisions. This means that the way from A to B, the way from decisions taken by some actors to the ultimate implementation of these decisions, is not just simple and linear but occurs through cognitive and cultural patterns and incentives that serve to fill the contested space in-between.

Whilst I do not expect that policymakers will be able to draw direct and comprehensive instructions from my empirical findings and conclusions, I hope I can share my understanding and experience of 'local governance', 'social networks' and 'political actors'. Although the study is not a policy-oriented and policy-devoted exercise, it frequently makes explicit and implicit reference to core development concepts such as 'trust', 'commitment', 'network' and 'participation'. The cases discuss the intermediary but necessary conditions and incentives, including collective identities, which build trust, commitment and networks among political actors and shape their participatory capacities.

Selection and comparative analysis of the cases

To represent both breadth and depth, my study compares data from different socio-economic contexts in southern Khatlon, such as mountainous vs. lowland geographies, subsistence-based vs. cotton-growing economies, ethnically homogenous vs. ethnically heterogeneous communities, small-size vs. large-size resettlements, elite-dominated and contested vs. hierarchically representative and integrative rural structures and intensively involved vs. provisionally intervened localities by external (such as state and international development) agencies. The thesis analyses cases based on separate villages located in the five borderland districts of the region of southern Khatlon, including the Shuroobod and Mu'minobod districts in the Kulob region and the Shahritus, Qubodiyon and Nosiri Khusrav districts in the Qabodiyon oasis. These data, which I discuss in Chapter Two on the southern Khatlon region, represent their comparable value for my in-depth case studies in two villages – one in the mountainous Shuroobod district and the other in the cotton-growing Shahritus district – presented in Chapters Three and Four.

Table 1: Comparable cases in the region of southern Khatlon

Cases	Differences in independent variables	Similarities in independent and dependent variables
Devdor village in the Shuroobod district	- mountainous area - land abundance for subsistence economy and pasture - water scarcity for drinking and irrigation - income sources of households: subsistence agriculture and cattle-breeding - private and contested distribution of resources - ethnically homogenous - smaller size of village population - less differentiated, elite-dominated but contested political structures - objective limits of external communication - village-level and intensively integrated developmental organisation	-hierarchy of local government -reciprocal and patron-client support practices and networks -kinship and patron-client networking across ethnic groups -state-provided administrative system of the village -local authorities -rural organisations -social infrastructure -developmental programmes
Sayyod village in the Shahritus district	- lowland area - land scarcity for subsistence economy - water abundance for drinking and irrigation - income sources of households: subsistence agriculture, cotton, labour migration - monopoly of land resources by state elites for cotton economy - ethnically heterogeneous - large size of village population - hierarchically differentiated but representative and integrative political structures - no objective limits of external communication - Jamoat[7]-level and provisionally integrated developmental organisation	

[7] A jamoat is a primary government entity which represents several villages geographically and economically located in the same area. The chairman of the jamoat is appointed directly by the district governor. The chairman, in turn, appoints his subordinate employees in the jamoat administration. He also appoints the mahalla heads of the subject villages, who are mostly advised by family elders and religious notables of the villages. The mahalla heads also represent their villages in the representation council of the jamoat.

A case which is under a scientific investigation is not merely a particular historical event but a class of interrelated events that occur in a specific socio-economic environment and reflect an aspect of a development path. The particular case can be a social revolution, a governance system or a development intervention, and it explains interrelated events by identifying their independent variables which simultaneously characterise the case (George and Bennett 2005: 22).

Already Gluckman (1958), among other social anthropologists, recognised the "limitations and essentially static quality inherent in structural-functional models" and therefore developed 'situational analysis' (in: Kuper 2003: 248). Situational analysis in the anthropological tradition is based on the methods of network analysis and extended case study, which break down big events or phenomena into small but causally connected events and phenomena. This approach focuses less on the structural and functional laws and regularities of a society or a group and more on process-tracing within a particular 'social field' (Tilly 1995: 1602). Whilst structural-functionalist models are strictly guided by theoretical assumptions which ignore internal dynamics, case study is open to new theories and hypotheses. The latter consider the crucial role of intervening variables (such as collective identities in the current study) and contextual conditions which allow more than one outcome.

The cases can be compared and thereby we can draw comparative conclusions, if we have some points to infer about the intervening variables. Therefore, my strategy to select comparable cases was based on identifying the intervening variables (collective identities) which played their role in different contexts. Comparative analysis of the role of collective identities in different contexts was thus the central task of this study. Such an approach was necessary in order to acquire a more or less representative picture of the study region of southern Khatlon.

Table 2 below illustrates my choice of distinctive and comparable cases in cotton-growing and subsistence-based communities within the study region. I did not emphasise the first type [1] – most similar cases in adjacent types due to their low probability. As George and Bennett (2005) assert, "It is generally extremely difficult to find two cases that resemble each other in every respect but one…" (152). To compare cases of the same type [2], the study aimed to understand the role collective identities play in shaping local governance processes in different contexts. I compared particular processes, such as the cotton economy in the cotton-growing village, community-driven development in the subsistence-based settlement and the self-governance structure of mahalla in both villages. To generalise individual cases, the current study compares different processes or types in similar environments, for example similar economic activity or ethnic composition. This strategy helped me to extend the representativeness of each case in its particular environment, and to test if they were crucial cases [3].

Notably, the comparative logic of representativeness barely reaches statistical accuracy (George and Bennett 2005; Barron et al. 2004; Bierschenk and de Sardan 2003; Harriss 2002). The criterion of representativeness is to a possible extent necessary, but its shortcomings do not substantially affect the result of comparative study. Tilly (1995) also mentions that the purpose of research is to explain variability among comparable structures and processes, rather than identifying structural similarities between comparable cases (1602). From this angle, I do not compare two village communities as a whole; rather, I identify internal structures and processes (e.g. property rights, political structure of mahalla, resource mobilisation and development intervention) in one case and compare them with the relevant structures and processes of the other case. This typological logic (George and Bennett 2005: 7) allows one to compare possibly representative cases in two different contexts within the same region [4].

Table 2: Selection of comparable cases

#	Comparable cases	Independent variables	Dependent variables
1	Most similar cases in adjacent types	Differing in only one independent variable and its dependent variable	- Difference in outcomes due to the variables; for this purpose, process-tracing is used
2	Cases in the same type	Similar independent variables	- Similar outcomes - Different outcomes
3	Most likely, least likely and crucial cases	A single representative variable; the extreme variable	- Strongly determine a particular outcome; if not, the variables are impugned
4	Least similar case comparison	Cases differing on all but one independent variable	- Similar in outcomes; via process-tracing to test which independent variable results in similar outcomes

Adapted by Hafiz Boboyorov from the text of George and Bennett (2005: 251-3)

Institutional analysis of comparable cases

The anthropological field research was necessary to understand the institutional setup of local governance or the political organisation of local social order. While observing the interactions of political actors in different settings and situations, the central aim was to understand the governing rules of these interactions. I also studied the reasons, contexts and agents which influenced the continuation or change of the observed rules. My conceptual framework for field research and data analysis also emphasised the perceptions and responses of the actors to institutional persistence or change.

To understand institutional persistence or change I employed the method of process-tracing cognitive and intervening variables (collective identities and norms). These variables can explain better any consistency or change in a particular causal process or institutional setup (George and Bennett 2005; Bierschenk and de Sardan 2003; Mehta et al. 1999). Hence, my study, as I elaborate its theoretical bases in Chapter One, focuses on local people's collective identities as cognitive and intervening variables. I discuss the role these variables play in committing the local people to existing power structures, legitimising the political and economic claims and rights of the elites and maintaining socio-political stability at the local level. From this point, I analyse how these mechanisms enforce, modify or change particular institutions of power relations, resource distribution and stability maintenance. Institutions are tools that actors use to achieve certain goals, rather than functionalist structures or 'absolute rules of the game'. Process-tracing of negotiations and conflicts is therefore necessary to understand how institutions persist or change and which intervening mechanisms influence the outcomes.

Structure of the thesis

This PhD thesis consists of six chapters. Chapter One discusses my theoretical framework, which reveals collective identities as enforcement mechanisms of the local governance institutions or the principal rules and norms of political and economic relations at the local level. Individuals articulate, reinterpret and adapt to or change their collective identities in order to enable or constrain certain institutional rules and practices. Such a reflexive context, however, does not suggest that individuals are strategic or rational when shaping the positivistic environment of institutional change and identity politics. Rather, their behaviours and choices depend heavily on their social structures and cognitive constructs. This chapter classifies and discusses collective identities as the enforcement mechanisms of three mainstream aspects of local governance. These aspects are: (1) commitment to differentiated power structures, (2) the legitimation of political and economic claims and rights of individual actors and (3) the stabilisation of contested socio-political situations.

To test such a role of collective identities, Chapter Two introduces the general and broad but in-depth overview and analysis of the southern Khatlon region. Local Islamic, ethnic and kinship networks and ties are important immaterial mechanisms in sustaining political structures and the political economy of local social order. I discuss this notion in the cases of legitimation sources of political and economic claims, the practices of dispute settlement, reciprocal networks and the mobilisation and adaptation of internal and external resources. These cases also have comparative value for two in-depth village studies of the region, which are discussed comprehensively in Chapters Three and Four.

Chapter Three discusses the important aspects of local governance in a mountainous, subsistence-based, ethnically homogenous and elite-dominated village in the Shuroobod district. In this highly contested political and economic environment, and in a community intensively intervened in by development structures, religious, kinship and village identities serve mainly two aspects of local governance, namely (1) the legitimation of elites' political and economic claims and (2) the stabilisation of the contested boundaries of social order. Specific cases discuss the sources and practices of legitimation. The chapter also discusses the stabilisation function of the reciprocal practices of extended families and neighbourhoods, social welfare programmes, the practices of 'common wellbeing', dispute settlement and development programmes.

Chapter Four discusses the integrated boundaries of social order in the example of a lowland, cotton-growing and ethnically heterogeneous village in the Shahritus district. The roles of ethnic, kinship, village and Islamic identities are examined in line with three important aspects of local governance: (1) the legitimation of elites' political and economic rights, (2) the enforcement of representative and integrative political structures and (3) the stabilisation of socio-political and economic situations. The discussion involves cases of inheritance and religious claims, network-based political and economic representation, reciprocal means and resources of stability and especially resource mobilisation for the cotton economy.

Chapter Five draws comparative and general conclusions for the thesis. In different contexts, collective identities may serve different purposes and thereby shape the mainstream aspects and institutional environments of local governance. Generally, I conclude that collective identities express and enforce the socio-cognitive constructs and backbone of local governance, such as indigenous meanings and practices of commitment, trust and networking.

THEORETICAL FRAMEWORK:

Collective identities as the socio-cognitive boundaries of individuals

This theoretical chapter reveals and frames the role of collective identities in shaping political and economic processes at the primary level of human interactions. I refer to several theoretical concepts within anthropological and social-psychological traditions to build on and elaborate my framework. The thesis is built upon the understanding that local governance reflects the political organisation of the institutionalised environment of local politics. Such a definition, which will be explained in subchapter one, also introduces local governance institutions as the core principles of political organisation at the local level. Subchapter two discusses the interrelation of social institutions and collective rationality, which means that collective norms and identities are among some of the most important tools for enforcing social institutions. This is a subject of discussion in subchapter three.

Local governance of social order

The discussion in this subchapter reveals the contrasting approaches of the development community and the academic world to local governance. The following sections outline these approaches separately and define my understanding of local governance as the political organisation of social order at the primary level of human interactions. Subchapters two and three discuss the analytical components of this understanding, including social order, social institutions and collective identities.

Expectations from 'good' local governance

Since the early 1990s, the term 'good local governance' has reflected development expectations about meeting 'local' and 'global' communities in developing countries. Development agencies introduce the neoliberal concepts and structures of local governance, and they shape the understanding of what constitutes a 'local community', which is routinely perceived and approached as a primary geographical and administrative unit, such as a rural settlement. According to leading development agencies, including the World Bank and UNDP, 'good' local governance involves broader 'community participation' or the involvement of different local actors "in management and decision-making" processes (Burde 2004: 75).

The World Bank emphasises the political decentralisation of decision-making structures along a territorial-administrative line as the core principle of 'good' local governance (World Bank 2000: 121). Often, this and other development agencies enforce Community Driven Development (CDD) structures in order to give control over decisions and resources to local communities and governments. CDD must be devoted to poor people and their institutions as assets and partners by investing in the empowerment of their traditional structures. Here, empowerment pillars include inclusive access to information, the accountability of transactions, demand-responsiveness, enhanced local capacity and administrative autonomy (World Bank 2004).

To justify expectations about 'good' local governance, the development community borrows such concepts as 'institutional capacity' and 'social capital' (e.g. Coleman 1988; Putnam 1993). These concepts suggest that local actors have historically and culturally shaped capacities "such as trust, norms and networks that can improve the efficiency of society by facilitating coordinated actions" (Putnam 1993: 167). Further models of coordinated action or governance (e.g. PRA designed by Chambers 1994, *inter alia*) regard participatory mechanisms as communicative bases for shaping the shared interests, preferences and needs of various actors, including both elites and so-defined 'marginalised' and 'excluded groups'.

Critique of the developmental concepts of local governance

The scholarly review of 'good' local governance concepts and their practical outcomes suggests that, so far, it has been difficult to achieve the 'genuine' participation of broader communities, despite the intensive efforts of development agencies. The World Bank, for example, neglects socio-cultural issues while drawing on economistic and technocratic models for local development (Mehta 2001, in Bretton Woods Project 2002: 2). Like other funding institutions, it tries to improve the investment environment for one group at the expense of impoverishing others. Here, the developmental agenda on structural shift or decentralisation overestimates the role of partnership with local elites and therefore invests in existing differentiated power structures (Reidun 2006: 50; also Williams 2004).

In this case, participation is less about the decision-making power of the wider population and more about the legitimation and enforcement of existing power structures. The brokers and members of 'development networks' manipulate the *master narratives* of development (such as democracy, grass-roots, accountability and gender balance) to boost their own power (Bierschenk and de Sardan 2003: 145). External aid and development resources are therefore mostly invested to empower local interests or strategic groups of elites. In such conditions the metaphor of 'social change', propagated and implemented by Chambers' PRA framework (1994), is mainly valuable as faith, as faith in 'religious salvation' (Henkel and Stirrat 2001, in: Williams 2004: 561). Adversely, constant efforts cannot significantly change the situation of fragmented and repressive structures. The target categories of development efforts, such as women and marginalised groups, remain silent. Their related NGOs disappear following any decrease in funding or the withdrawal of donors (Burde 2004: 77-80). Some may argue that such conditions are inherent in any countries in transition, but "[i]n fact they may not be moving at all...," as Thomas Carothers suggests, with "the end of the transition paradigm" (in: Collins 2002: 141).

Academic understanding has further been illuminated by findings from different 'fields', including the developing intersection of local and global communities. Contrary to the 'localised' projection of the development community, academics define 'local governance' as crosscutting processes and interactions at different levels, which at the same time shape local politics (e.g. Mielke and Schetter 2007: 80). It reflects the political strategies of local and translocal actors concerned with controlling and distributing local resources (Koehler and Zuercher 2003). Actors in local governance are both individual (local, private, public, state and international) agents which not only possess strategic resources but also enforce governance tools and structures in order to sustain certain patterns of resource use and distribution. They shape a heterogeneous social arena where multiple 'communities of action' integrate their governance strategies to achieve their own ends. In such a political environment of power struggle, actors negotiate and exploit their strategies and policies, even though they primarily invest them, for example, in development 'fields'.

Actors' interactions are neither spontaneous nor strategic in evolutionary or rational choice terms. Rather, they are shaped by differential power relations and structures which maintain the strategies of the unequal distribution of scarce material and immaterial resources such as land, water, position and reputation. The very nature of power relations and structures, as scholars (such as Harriss 2002, Bachman 1998, Seligman 1997 and Gambetta (ed.) 1988) suggest, casts doubt on the classic and developmental notion of 'trust', which is believed to favour 'social capital' by negotiating the "risk occasioned by the freedom of others" (Hart 1988: 191; as well as Giddens 1990). Instead, as

Harris (2002) asserts, "the language of 'trust' frequently conceals, or seeks to conceal, relationships of power" (2). Trust is a type of reward for loyalty, deference and the acceptable performance of subordinates in the context of highly structured and hierarchical power relations (Bachman 1998: 313).

The institutional arrangements of local social order

The theoretical framework in this study is embedded in the general theoretical discussion on 'social order', expounded by my colleagues from the Center for Development Research (Mielke et al. 2011). The analytical concept of social order "that is not normatively biased" (ibid. 7) is "a structuring and structured characteristic of social interactions" (ibid. 8). Existing societal structures and processes reflect socio-cognitive characteristics of people and thereby organise their society or community even in the contexts of 'failure' or 'anarchy'. In regard to the repeated notice on 'state failure', for example, Hardin (1995: 30-31) says that "[i]t is generally quite orderly. If there is great disorder, it is often introduced by the state [as well as by other powerful actors] in the effort to rout the orderly resisters."

Notably, the concept of social order is not also state-centrist but rather regards the state as one among other organisational structures of social order. The analytical emphasis on the concept is the human being who reproduces social order "in the course of his ongoing externalization" (Berger and Luckmann 1984 [1967]: 69-70). The human does not make rational choices nor take action without considering his socio-cultural environment. To understand human behaviour in this environment, therefore, the concept of social order introduces socio-cognitive patterns (habitus, norms and values) as analytical tools. These patterns are central to shaping and enforcing social institutions which are the core principles of social order.

Institutions as typified and active rules of social order

Part one of this section defines institutions as the core principles of human behaviour and social interactions. As elaborated in part two, I do not draw a principal division between so-called 'formal' and 'informal' institutions. Rather, the discussion on dominant institutions in part three shows that they embed the behaviours and interactions of political actors. Therefore, in part four, which concludes the current section, I discuss the relevance of social institutions to the socio-cognitive characteristics of local people. Consequently, I pave the way to the next section on collective identities as the enforcement mechanisms of institutions.

Definitions of social institutions

North's (1990: 3) classical definition states that institutions are "constraints that human beings impose on themselves," prohibiting, permitting or requiring specific types of action that are important for reducing transaction costs, improving information flow and defining and enforcing property rights. Thus, institutions can be norms, rules, procedural devices and regulatory frameworks which constrain and enable human interactions (Juetting 2003: 35). In a broader sense, historical events and external influences which dramatically change societal structures are understood as institutions as well. The reason for such divergent definitions, as Juetting (2003: 9) suggests, is a search for "the impact of institutions on development outcomes" through historical, political and socio-economic areas of analysis.

In this study, however, I will not reduce the function of social institutions to 'development outcomes', which is a normatively biased definition. Contrary to rational choice theory and Neo-Institutionalism Economics (NIE), the core functioning mechanism of institutions is not reduced to their enabling and constraining power to attain optimal outcomes in terms of the economic calculation of transaction costs.

I agree with Barron et al. (2004: 13) and Christophe (2003: 199), who define institutions as "inherently guiding principles for action" and "the abstract and impersonal character of the underlying rules," respectively. Any institutions, even if they generate unequal outcomes and consequent contestations and conflicts, are by origin regulatory mechanisms of the existing social order (Knight 1992: 40). Institutions are decision-making rules and guiding constructs which enable and constrain the choices and preferences of actors for control, negotiation and contestation over allocative[8] and distributive[9] activities towards resources and people (DiMaggio and Powell 1991). For my theoretical framework I integrate some points from sociological institutionalism, which is

---

[8] Giddens defines allocative resources as "Material resources involved in the generation of power, including the natural environment and physical artefacts; allocative resources derive from human domination over nature" (1984: 372).

[9] Again, Giddens defines authoritative resources as "Non-material resources involved in the generation of power, deriving from the capability of harnessing the activities of human beings; authoritative resources result from the domination of some actors over others" (1984: 372).

distinctive from rational choice institutionalism and historical institutionalism. Sociological institutionalism emphasises power relations and networks which are embedded in the socio-cultural context rather than in rational choice incentives and in the path or evolutionary dependency of action. Hence, institutions are externalised structures of "beliefs, values and cognitive scripts" which are shared by most of people and therefore shape their incentives and paths for action (Orrnert 2006: 450-451).

Types of social institutions

Institutions are often classified as formal or statutory and informal or socially embedded rules and norms. Formal institutions involve any rules and regulations adopted and enforced by state structures, including constitutions, laws, charters, bylaws and their enforcement mechanisms, which are expected to regulate human interactions through everyday life. Often, economic neo-institutionalist approaches, such as Rational-Action Neoinstitutionalism (RAN), focus on formal institutions, such as rational action rules, by employing game theory, evolutionary modelling and transaction-cost analysis.

However, both formal and 'rational economic' institutions have faced criticism, since they tend to view actors as coherent and strategic and their interests as stable and exogenous (DiMaggio 1998; Sen 1985). Rather, the current thesis follows the concept of Social-Constructionist Institutionalism (SCN), which "argues that all the elements of rational-action models – actors, interests, and preferences – are 'socially constructed' and therefore endogenous and variable (Meyer and Scott [1983], White [1995])" (in: DiMaggio 1998: 697). SCN explains (social) institutions as the historical and cultural constraints and boundaries of actions and actors. They are both socially sanctioned norms of behaviour (customs, taboos, etc.) and internally enforced standards of conduct as well as extensions, adaptations and modifications of formal institutions (Juetting 2003: 11). Hence, I do not make a principal distinction between formal and informal institutions while both state and non-state actors use them. So-called 'informal' institutions integrate and adapt 'formal' ones via *bricolage* or forum means.

In anthropological tradition, the notion of *bricolage* reflects the fact that actors use and manipulate institutions and structures as symbolic resources. That is, the imposed external structures and contents are adapted into indigenous boundaries as their new media and vehicles through the process of syncretism, "a process in which new and old were synthesized into an idiom more consonant with indigenous culture" (Cohen 1985: 37). Other scholars also explain the process as 'institution shopping' (Bierschenk and de Sardan 2003) or 'forum shopping' (Benda-Beckman 1981, in: Bierschenk and de Sardan 2003: 159). As Bierschenk and de Sardan (2003) define, the institutional context of local-level politics is diffuse due to different political institutions 'sedimented' at different times, which in turn creates an action space for 'institution shopping' (159).

Social institutions, which also integrate and adapt formal rules and laws, are not easy to change. Hence, institutional change is mostly about the adaptive integration of new rules and organisations by both external and local actors. The claim about a "parallel system" (Juetting 2003: 30, 36), therefore, does not stand analytically, which is based on the belief that the enforcement of local institutions through external incentives (e.g. development aid) may improve their responsiveness to local development. Since informal institutions are more effective, Orrnert (2006: 452-453) therefore argues that development agencies must use them as a "building block" for introducing formal rules. This claim goes further to suggest that the Soviet and post-Soviet systems and organisations at the local level neglected traditional norms and conventions and consequently gave rise to an 'institutional vacuum'. Hence, scholars (e.g. Evans 2004 and Lecours 2005, in: Orrnert 2006: 451-452) claim the eminence of 'institutional monocropping', which relies on institutional change made by externally-led structural adjustment projects.

Conversely, social institutions are embedded in customs, traditions and codes of conduct which are historically constructed into people's socio-cognitive structures. Actors routinely refer to their socio-cognitive sources, such as beliefs and identities, which set criteria for evaluating the transaction costs of their preferences and choices. This collective rationality, or commitment to the experiences and value standards of others, thus reduces distributive preferences and decision-making options to existing institutions.

Institutional embeddedness of political actors

From the angle of power relations, scholars (e.g. Nugent 2004, Cohen 1994 and Foucault 1991) have questioned normative boundaries which seek to mark distinctive authorities and institutions of political entities such as local, state and international agents. The state, for example, is no longer considered as "a centralised entity that taxes, conscripts, and monopolises legitimate violence within a given territory" (Nugent 2004: 198). It is not a unitary actor which stands above and beyond society and which exercises neutral and disinterested authority over 'locales' and their structures. More exactly, state authorities, like other actors, represent fragmented, interdependent and intertwined interests and structures which are incoherent and illogical if we compare them with the formal and essentialist definition of their authority. The boundary between state and non-state institutions is blurred while state authorities – beyond formal state structures – use informal techniques of power relations. Also, the more 'brutal' political actors, such as the Mafia and warlords, may generate the same institutional instruments and methods as the state does, in order to control and handle information, administer violence and cultivate reputations via indigenous networks of interaction and support. As such, the Weberian typology of authority or legitimate power is irrelevant, which suggests that different actors refer to different sources of legitimacy in order to sustain their influence and power.

The authority of actors 'fails'[10] only if their actions and claims are not compatible with indigenous institutional arrangements (such as reciprocity and patron-clientism). Here, traditional authorities, such as elders and religious notables, cooperate with the state and other external actors hand in hand to maintain social order already at the primary level of human interactions. They enforce indigenous institutional arrangements to regulate local political structures, control access to land and provide socio-political stability, and they also refer to indigenous sources of legitimacy which often contradict the principles set by formal sources such as laws: "In traditional leadership, legitimacy is rooted in history and culture, often combined with religious/divine or sacred references" (Lutz and Linder 2004: 13). Since traditional legitimacy is closely related to the beliefs or cognitive structures of the subject people, traditional authorities therefore have greater mobilisation capacity than any other external actors have. In this regard, formal state authorities as well as development agencies often rely on the traditional actors and structures of mobilisation. As a result, these local actors and structures adapt and absorb the external contents of development (Bierschenk and de Sardan 2003: 148-150).

Consequently, developmentalist contents, or "core properties of ['good'] governance," including participation, accountability and decentralisation, remain mainly as narrations about 'community development' and add to local power configurations without triggering any radical transformation (Bierschenk and de Sardan 2003). Rather, 'field' researchers and reviewers (Bierschenk and de Sardan 2003; Burde 2004; Williams 2006; *inter alia*) show the repetitive

---

[10] The discussion on 'state failure' is based on the belief in the prescriptive authority of the state and thus focuses on "the basic functions of the state [which] are no longer performed" (Francois and Sud 2006:142).

'failure' of the development community in integrating external contents and structures into the local forms.

Collective rationality of social institutions

In sociological or social institutionalism[11] the discussion on rationality is not reduced to the economic or rational choices of individuals, but rather emphasises their social and cognitive capacities to integrate or adapt any cultural and developmental contents (Hardin 1995: 46-47). Other scholars also emphasise this approach by employing such concepts as habitus (Bourdieu 1984), unconscious mental structures (Levi-Strauss 1963, in: Low and Lawrence-Zuniga 2003: 9), shared mental models (Denzau and North 1994), identity and habit (Orrnert 2006) and worldviews (Mielke et al. 2011).

The cornerstones of collective rationality, including habitus, norms and values, distinguish institutions from other categories of agency such as interests, motivations and strategies (DiMaggio and Powell 1991). These collective categories are the doxic or taken-for-granted elements of action which reproduce social structure and explain how and why strategically-oriented agents chronically reproduce and acquiesce to a social structure which may not be in their interests (Bourdieu 1984). As habitual frameworks of action, social institutions, such as 'taken-for-granted' scripts, rules and classifications, enable or constrain the interests, preferences and networks of individual actors in relation to socio-culturally available choices. Even economically suboptimal institutions may persist in reducing the risk of social exclusion and increasing positive material and immaterial returns (Powell and DiMaggio 1991). For example, vertical (such as patron-client) networks of interaction, which maintain the core principles for power relations, optimise unequal resource distribution.

In the context of the former Soviet Union, including Central Asian societies, scholars have discussed the overarching power of reciprocal and patron-client institutions. Lommitz (1988) defines patron-client relations as "a form of reciprocity, where benefits to subordinates are traded against loyalty and power" (45). In such an asymmetrical reciprocal network, the more powerful partner becomes patron and the less powerful one a client. Both partners have something valuable to exchange: the patron provides political and economic

[11] Social institutionalism is one branch of neoinstitutionalism, along with economic neoinstitutionalism and political institutionalism, mostly inspired by sociology of knowledge (Berger and Luckman), ethnomethodology (Garfinkel) and practical action theory (Bourdieu) (DiMaggio 1998).

protection and rewards while the client serves with either material or immaterial returns, such as service, loyalty or bribery. Soviet 'institutional change' incorporated pre-exiting structures which in turn adapted Soviet institutions into the logic of patron-clientism. My empirical discussion also follows this direction and suggests that reciprocity and patron-clientism still remain the overarching local governance institutions.

The other relevance of institutions to collective rationality is suggested as the need to typify institutional order, while individuals are not responsible enough for such order, in part due to their "sluggish and forgetful" memory (Berger and Luckman 1984 [1967]: 87). Typification maintains "orientation and conduct in everyday life" (ibid. 194), which in turn produces and is based on socio-cognitive structures. Therefore, social institutions are typified collective strategies for "a 'permanent' solution to a 'permanent' problem of the given collectivity" (ibid. 87). This perspective is also expressed by Natural Resource Management Institutionalism (NRMI), in that institutions are collective strategies for ecological, livelihood and knowledge uncertainties "about how to deal with risks and hazards" (Mehta et al. 1999: 5).

These strategies derive from cognitive patterns or mental models which are "... internal representations that individual cognitive systems create to interpret the environment" (Denzau and North 1994: 2). As discussed in Mielke et al. (2011), individual behaviour therefore takes the path of collective rationality to select a desirable pattern of manifestation. Here, scholars (Mielke et al. 2011; DiMaggio 1998; *inter alia*) doubt the view which regards strategic choice in rational-choice terms. Rather, strategic choice is limited to culturally specific repertoires and socio-political conditions. The question is not to ask "*whether* people act strategically, but rather under what conditions and how they do so" (DiMaggio 1998: 701). It is thus important to pay attention to "context-triggered schemata (entailing, *inter alia*, modes of rationality) that constitute action repertoires for members of particular societies...[and which] lead to structured schemata variation based on variation of mental models (or 'logics of action')" (North 1998, in: DiMaggio 1998: 701).

Coordination and enforcement mechanisms of social order

Social institutions are performed in an "unreflective, routine, taken-for-granted" (DiMaggio and Powell 1991: 14) manner until they are capable of reducing uncertainty and insecurity. The contested typified and taken-for-granted institutions are therefore enforced by material (such as cooptation), coercive (such as military) and discursive (such as identity) means. Different cultures and political regimes provide different means deriving from their collective rationality (Dobbin 1994a and Brinton and Nee 1998, in: DiMaggio 1998: 698). In this sense, collective rationality is 'constructed' in a way whereby specific political contexts require specific cognitive constructs (DiMaggio 1998: 700). In terms of uncertainty and insecurity, cognitive and cultural factors, such as collective norms which stimulate cooptation, coercion, exclusion, extermination and identification, reinforce the contested institutions.

In order to enforce the contested institutions, powerful actors seek especially to commit their subjects to certain normative practices. Otherwise, as North (1990: 4) also notes, institutions lose their social and political value and people start distrusting and deconstructing them accordingly because, from the rational choice viewpoint, the transaction cost of these institutions is substantially high. Hardin (1995: 27-29, 36, 44-45) suggests that "coordination of power" solves this central deficiency of "the logic of collective action." The enforcement mechanisms of cooptation, coercion and identification are necessary to reproduce a certain type of power and legitimacy. As he clearly refers to the role of collective identities in the process, "[i]n many – but not all – instances, the coordinations will depend on the use of institutions to manipulate identification of individuals with relevant groups" (ibid. 45).

In the following subchapters I reveal the role of collective identities as the enforcement mechanisms of institutions within a specific social and political environment. Before I discuss the issue, in the following subchapter I define my theoretical understanding of collective identities.

Collective identities as enforcement mechanisms of social order

In this subchapter I refer to social-psychological and social-anthropological sources to establish the nexus between collective identities and social and political processes. Section one defines collective identities as individuals' socio-cognitive boundaries, which ascribe and prescribe the meaningful commitment of individuals to the social and political environments, which will be discussed in section two.

Definition of collective identities

I shape my theoretical framework on the basis of the concepts of 'collective self' in social anthropology (Cohen 1994), the 'multidimensional framework of collective identities' (Ashmore et al. 2004) and Self-Categorisation Theory (Hogg et al. 2004) in social psychology. Accordingly, collective identity is the self-concept of the human 'self' or an individual actor with regard to his or her relations with the multiple collectivities he or she encounters in the social world. Collective identities express internalised or cognitive patterns and mental characteristics of behaviour (including norms, values and habitus), which are consequently externalised in institutions. Collective identities are socio-cognitive and contextual boundaries of individuals rather than those of groups and categories.[12] These human individuals' boundaries express their perceptions, habitual behaviours, norms and discourses about their group or categorical affiliations.

Part one below discusses the fundamental and cognitive needs of human beings to identify with groups or categories. Part two suggests that each individual identifies him- or herself with more than one group or category. Thus, group or categorical identity does not imply 'stable' ties and affiliations but rather reflects the cognitive boundaries and contextual preferences of each individual.

Fundamental and cognitive bases of collective identities

A number of psychological experiments assert that human beings have 'automatic' cognitive tendency to *accentuation*, i.e. a predilection for culturally closer groups or categories (Hogg et al. 2004), and to *introjection*, i.e. extending or merging their individual self with socially present and informed groups or categories (Ashmore et al. 2004). For example, one's kinship or ethnic group is more attractive than any other similar group. The experimental theory of the Reaction Time Procedure (Smith et al. 1999, in: Ashmore et al. 2004) asserts the confusion of self-descriptive traits with typical and stereotypical in-group traits in favour of the latter. From this perspective, collective identity is an extension of the self to include relevant social groups or categories and, in part, to ascribe their material properties and immaterial attributes as his or her qualifiers.

The collective tendencies of accentuation and introjection derive from basic human motives. These motives are (1) strive for uncertainty reduction and (2) the search for self-enhancement and the protection of self-esteem – both of which are related to the existential security of human beings (Hogg et al. 2004: 255). Berger and Luckmann (1984 [1967]) and Giddens (1990), inter alia, have

---

[12] Brubaker and Cooper (2000) distinguish between *relational* and *categorical* modes of identification, that is, between groups and categories. Accordingly, group or *relational* web includes kinship, friendship, patron-client ties, teacher-student relations, etc. and category or *categorical* membership classifies persons in accordance with their sharing categorical attributes, such as race, ethnicity, language, nationality, citizenship, gender, sexual orientation, etc. (15).

already suggested the existential need for the reduction of uncertainty and insecurity. Human beings institutionalise their everyday life in order to reduce, in the words of Giddens (1990), their "ontological anxieties," which they experience due to the discontinuity of their surrounding social world (92). For this reason, they employ cultural tropes, including collective identities against 'inchoate' uncertainty, disorder and chaos (Fernandez 1982, in: Cohen 1994). Tajfel (1974) also mentions such a subjective need for order and meaning, which then produces behavioural and inter-group differentiations (75). Several psychological schools (such as cognitive consistency of Abelson et al. (1968), attribution of Harvey and Smith (1977), and social cognition of Fiske and Taylor (1984)) support this explanation (in: Hogg et al. 2004).

The first response to uncertainty and insecurity is a quest for 'sameness' or identification on which people psychologically 'place considerable value' on security from childhood (James 1993: 141, in: Cohen 1994). Hence, behaviour is a means to express the "acute need for visibility and attention," while "being neglected [is] more unbearable than disgrace." Individuals "struggle for self-esteem," that is, to be visible, attached and thus safeguarded by surrounding categories and networks (Myerhoff 1978: 10, in: Cohen 1994: 103). Their need to identify with a collectivity derives from their "shared perceptions and feelings of a common cause, threat, or fate" and consequently generates their collective agency (Snow 2001: 4).

Social-psychological investigations show that protecting self-esteem is a powerful self-motive, especially if it is threatened by *others* (Ashmore et al. 2004: 98-100). In a certain context, therefore, people strive to achieve their satisfactory self-concepts as members of separate groups or categories. However, satisfactory self-concepts are not sought as bases for social comparison with out-groups. In other words, groups or categories are not the subjects of comparison and evaluation, as earlier suggested by some scholars (e.g. Festinger 1954, in: Tajfel 1974: 68). Instead, individuals shape their group or categorical boundaries in order to promote and protect their own status and prestige, since the evaluation of a group or category assumes self-evaluation in a given context. Furthermore, differentiation into social groups or categories is a generally acceptable way to introduce normative standards and prototypes for reducing subjective uncertainty and insecurity about the image, role and place of human beings in their social world (Hogg et al. 2004: 256).

From 'stable' types and modes to cognitive and contextual boundaries

My theoretical approach to collective identities does not reject any types or modes of identification. However, it broadens the prospects of the collective self as the agent who identifies him- or herself with different groups or categories in different contexts. His or her choices from the 'repertoire' of collective identities depend on both his or her cognitive capacities and the structural and contextual conditions of his or her social world. Hence, socio-cognitive boundaries do not draw absolute divisions between groups and categories, although 'institutional regimes' may be designed for such a purpose. Boundaries are 'liminal' in the sense that individual actors traverse and move cognitively across their dividing but 'amorphous and ambiguous' lines. They are "boundaries of minds and consciousness" which individual actors continuously reflect and re-draw (Cohen 1994: 129).

From the social-psychological perspective (e.g. "the problem of secure social identity" by Tajfel 1974: 77), the *otherness* or distinctiveness of people due to their group or categorical affiliation is only a by-product of their search and struggle for sameness and commonality. Social-psychological findings (e.g. by Huddy 2001; Mohr and Fassinger 2000; Stryker and Serpe 1994, in: Ashmore et al. 2004: 85-88) assert that in a neutral environment people experience subjective uncertainty about their identities; they categorise them only when they fear *others*. Instead, people in a particular context may generalise and essentialise their families, tribes, castes or ethnic groups or categories vis-à-vis other groups or categories. Nevertheless, in a different context the same generalisation does not stand analytically, since people may search for other contextually responsive identities. Snow (2001) notes that "... the emergence and operation of collective identities means that other social identities have subsided in relevance and salience for the time being" (4).

Anthropological findings also suggest that identity boundaries are meaningful in relation to each other and within certain ritual and political contexts. Group or categorical boundaries are thus porous and ambiguous, since connections among co-members are contingent, transitory and interest-driven (Tilly 1995: 1595). Any individual has a repertoire of self-concepts referring to his affinity, belonging, commitment and membership to different and even contradictory social groups or categories. These references therefore reflect fluid, multivocal and overlapping identities that establish a 'multidimensional self' in response to various contexts. In addition, the importance of collective identities and their symbolic attributes does not picture a stable hierarchical structure but rather varies in relation to certain contexts (Hogg et al. 1995; Cohen 1985). For example, *the past* is selectively constructed by some actors to legitimise their own and contest others' claims (Cohen 1985: 99). In anthropological studies this selective construction of collective identities is called *bricolage*, as already discussed in the case of 'institution shopping'.

Socio-political contexts are important to articulate certain collective identities. Sometimes contexts can also be overlapping, which then entails merged or overlapping identities. Ashmore et al. (2004) defines a context as "the *general and continuing* multilayered and interwoven set of material realities, social structures, patterns of social relations, and shared belief systems" (103). In a context, one or some or a merged mosaic of collective identities become salient and pervasive. The concepts of *identity salience* and *identity pervasiveness* suggest that collective identities and their attributes (such as thought, feeling and behaviour) can quickly change in response to contextual conditions: "Salience refers to the relative importance of an identity in relation to other identities… [and] pervasiveness or comprehensiveness refers to the situational relevance…" (Snow 2001: 6).

Moreover, the social and political meanings and commitments that collective identities generate are context-dependent. Therefore, the commitment of individuals, even to their small groups, is not stable. The pictorial measure of OSIO – Overlap of Self, In-Group and Out-Group (Schubert and Otten 2002) – asserts "that the meaning of being a member in a given in-group varies as a function of the relationships between in-group and out-group" (in: Ashmore et al. 2004: 100). This finding was proved by the social-psychological *Bristol Experiment* of Tajfel (1974). Group identity, or in-group vs. out-group, which is about the positively valued distinctiveness of groups from each other, depends substantially on social and political context.

The above discussion has defined that human beings necessarily identify themselves with certain collectivities (groups or categories). Such a motive derives from their existential need for the reduction of uncertainty and insecurity and the protection of self-esteem before fellows and *others*. The other important point suggested is that the agent of collective identities is the human individual rather than a group or category (such as a descent group, an ethnic group or a group based on sexual orientation). From this viewpoint, collective identity is the self-concept of the human individual regarding his or her relations with the multiple collectivities he or she encounters in the social world. Thus, collective identity is a socio-cognitive boundary between individuals rather than between groups or categories. Boundaries between groups or categories are fluid and ambiguous in the sense that subject individuals shape, change and cross-cut them. Their behaviour of switching from one identity to the other depends on contexts they encounter in everyday life. Therefore, I have mentioned context as an important dimension of collective identities. The multiple identities of individuals do not mean that they prefer all of them at the same time, but their choice of a particular identity does depend on the relevant context. My reference to the social-psychological concept of accentuation suggests another important point: human beings employ cognitive preferences in order to identify with socio-culturally closer groups or categories, which is why they do not quickly accept unknown groups or categories and simultaneously reject the inclusion of *others* in their own circle.

The role of collective identities in local politics

Collective identities shape the orientation and commitment of people to collectivities and collective actions, and from the stance taken in this thesis, they are significant for political analysis. Political scientists, anthropologists and social psychologists affirm that collective identities link social structure with individual action (e.g. Ashmore et al. 2004: 81; Hardin 1995: 7; Hogg et al. 1995: 257; Tilly 1993: 31). Collective identities are legitimate means, so their agent, i.e. the collective self, refers to the structured social world in order to re-structure his or her own social environment. Different concepts, such as 'solidarity groups' (Polleta and Jaspers 2001: 291) and 'symbolic community' (Cohen 1985), explore the role of collective identities in such (re-)structuring processes. Evans-Pitchard (1940) and Barth (1969), in their studies of tribal societies, showed that collective identities are means used by individuals 'for acting and networking' within the socially and cognitively structured environments of their societies. Collective identities maintain norms of social cohesion and collective mobilisation, and they legitimise certain institutions which, in turn, shape the actions and decisions of individuals.

The following discussion, in three parts of this section, elaborates the role of collective identities in three aspects of the local social order. As discussed in part one, the first aspect suggests that collective identities commit people to certain institutions of power relations, and they serve especially to sustain differentiated positions and statuses of individual actors and to shape their choices and preferences for political action. Part two is devoted to the second aspect, which examines the role collective identities play in mobilising the people's concerns and resources and thereby maintain socio-political stability at the local level. Part three unfolds the last aspect, which shows how individual actors use collective identities to legitimise their own and to delegitimise others' political and economic claims and rights.

Commitment to the institutionalised environment of power relations

Collective identities commit people to a certain institutional environment or order via legitimising power structures and sustaining differentiated positions, roles and statuses of individual actors. Berger and Luckman (1984 [1967]) and Somers (e.g. 1992), inter alia, suggest that both the social world and social actors are 'storied' or constructed realities. There are destabilising dimensions, such as *time*, *space* and *relationality* which endanger the continuity of these realities and their routinised or institutional order. Hence, people use collective identities to ensure the continuity and stability of their constructed individualities and social worlds. The reference to collective identities generates the commitment of individuals to certain rules of political behaviour and organisation. The social-psychological literature tells how they internalise the normative standards of certain socio-political environment.

For example, the social psychological experimental study of 'correlations between private regard and attachment' (Tropp and Wright 2001, in: Ashmore et al. 2004: 100) suggests that it is possible to convince people of the high value of their group or category and thereby commit them to achieve and sustain such image. In this case, the image includes common perceptions and beliefs about the place of the related group or category, especially vis-à-vis *other* groups or categories. Since individuals feel affiliated to more than one group or category, they therefore have multilayered images as well. The multilayered group or categorical images shape and instrumentalise collective representations in human behaviours.

Figure 1: Collective representations of the collective self

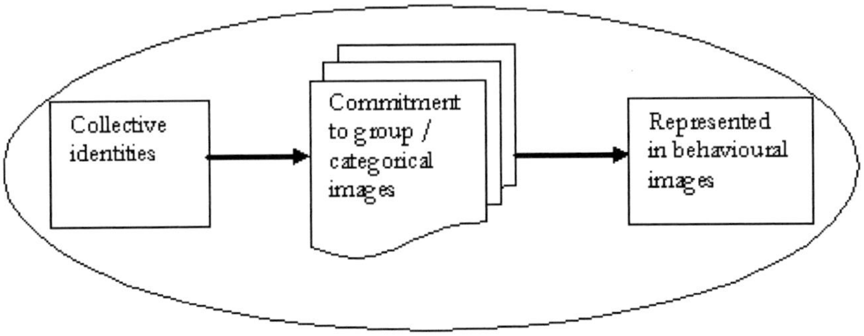

In Figure 1 above, I summarise social-psychological concepts, including Attachment Theory, Social Comparison, Accentuation and the Hierarchical Classification Method (as discussed in Ashmore et al. 2004 and Hogg et al. 2004). Accordingly, collective representations reflect the socio-cognitive characteristics and processes of commitment generated through highlighting collective identities and represented in behaviours via group or categorical images. These behavioural images are not meaningless but rather internalise and prioritise certain collective norms and values for individuals. Commitment reflects the attribution of norms and values to collective identities which individuals expressively manifest in their preferences and actions.

Selected norms and values are embedded into and, in turn, enforce the structures and networks of power relations. Cognitive studies (e.g. Stets and Burker 2000, Stryker and Serpe 1994, Stryker 1980, in: Ashmore et al. 2004) also suggest this social or structural embeddedness of collective identities as the commitment of the individuals to power structures and networks: "Social embeddedness is the degree to which a particular collective identity is implicated in the person's everyday ongoing social relationships" (Ashmore et al. 2004: 92).

Moreover, the social embeddedness of collective identities means that they commit individuals to certain institutional practices by relating these practices to indigenous moral norms. The degree of enforcement, for example, of a particular law depends on its reflection of existing moral codes (Hardin 1995: 43), which explains why people ignore and passively or actively disobey some institutional systems and practices, or they "do not know their own rights and responsibilities," according to these systems and practices. For example, "the presence of codes of honour and shame in hierarchical gender relations" undermines the role of civic laws and structures which struggle to cultivate gender balance (Passaro 1997: 149).

Internalisation and prioritisation of collective norms and values suggest their prototypic or normative representations. These behavioural representations commit individuals to specific roles and statuses deriving from contextually salient groups or categories (Ashmore et al. 2004; Hogg et al. 2004; Cohen 1994).

Figure 2: Prototypic (normative) roles and statuses of the collective self

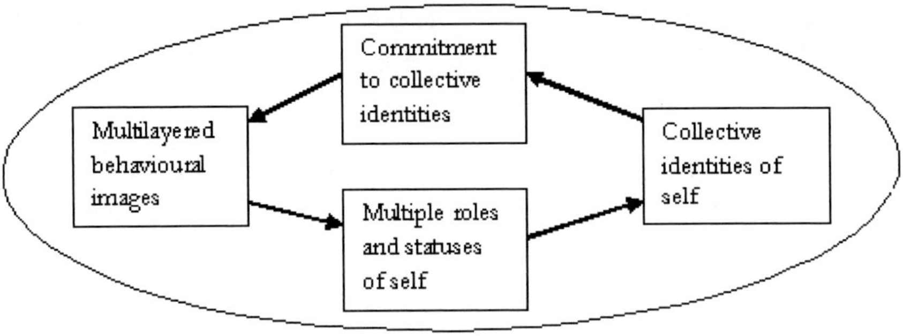

The prototypic representations of roles and statuses are self-descriptive for individuals, that is, they determine their social positions in certain contexts. Therefore, they feel affectively committed (based on honour, shame and pride) to internalise, express and protect self-descriptive norms vis-à-vis the declared *others*. Prototypes, which represent the typical membership of people in a given context, therefore serve to quickly identify individuals with these norms, which are socio-cognitive constructs that describe the entitativity (the extent of integrity) of a group or a category and shape the commitment of members to perform their entitativity roles (Hogg et al. 2004: 253-254).

Individuals conform to contextually specific roles and statuses, not necessarily due to their private preferences but mainly due to their mutually expected commitment to power structures. Since the status quo is not always stable and taken-for-granted, collective identities are highlighted to maintain the stability and legitimacy of separate status relations and differentiated power structures. Hogg et al. (1995) explain this "social psychological process that links identity to behavior via depersonalisation and conformity" (263). There are mainly two means of depersonalisation: 1) normative and evaluative commitment to roles and statuses on the bases of prototypes and stereotypes and 2) affective commitment via the internalised processes of introjection and 'extended identity'.

Collective identities serve as means to depersonalise and thus conform to the agency of individual actors to the collective norms of behaviour. The processes of depersonalising and internalising collective norms are reflected in the socio-culturally stable patterns of personality and positions, i.e. roles and statuses. Socio-cognitive studies list a number of underlying phenomena, such as social stereotyping, shared norms of social cohesion and pressure and emotional contagion and empathy, which people employ to depersonalise themselves and others (Hogg et al. 1995: 263; Hogg et al. 2004: 254). Similar anthropological observations suggest that initiation and healing rituals transform the identities of individuals during critical periods of their life-circles (Cohen 1985, 1994). Furthermore, depersonalisation adapts the perceptions, feelings and choices of individual actors to socially and culturally available meanings and institutions.

The process of adaptation, in part, is mediated through the interpretation of historical experiences. Committed individuals admit them as their own collective experiences and hence shape their preferences and choices. The other similar function of collective identities is to shape the mutually expected preferences and choices of individuals. Hardin (1995: 53) suggests that these preferences and choices are "exogenous," that is, constructed as socio-cultural patterns of commitment to a certain status.

Status is an individual boundary enacted through the tacit recognition of hierarchical differences and power relations, which "may often be translated informally into influence and authority" (Cohen 1985: 34). As Barth (1969) observes as well, status is a political resource for action when it is established as a reference to categorical affiliation and therefore to committed behaviour in intra-group and inter-group relations (28-31). Normative attributes are sought to ascribe and thus to commit individuals to specific power structures and relations (such as political networks based on hierarchical statuses). Here, collective identities are means to prescribe these attributes as parts of individuals' self-concepts, as their status quo. They need to acquiesce in their status, "because challenging their status quo raises self-conceptual uncertainty to unacceptable levels" (Hogg et al. 2004: 256). Since the status quo is not always stable and taken-for-granted, collective identities are therefore highlighted to maintain the stability and legitimacy of separate status relations and thereby differentiated power structures.

Moreover, the socio-cognitive concept of *introjection* and the symbolic anthropological concept of 'extended identity' suggest the deeply internalised or affective and evaluative commitment to depersonalisation in the form of status. Hence, prototypic roles and statuses are not only typified representations but also positive conformity to contextually salient collective identities and their related norms. According to Attachment Theory and the concepts of Accentuation and Social Comparison, the possession and manifestation of the collective norms by individuals enhance their positive recognition and prestige among other people (Ashmore et al. 2004: 90).

Status relations commit individuals both to their own images and to the statuses or prototypic images of other individuals. 'Related' people pressurise each other by evaluating and prioritising their indigenous networks and relations as attributes of their collective identities. They positively evaluate and symbolically reward those who occupy prototypic and responsive roles, maximise *their* positive identities more than those of *others* and stigmatise or ostracise those who do not obey networking norms. In this case, collective identities serve to provide consensual social attraction to and acknowledgment of rewards (recognition, prestige, position and material good) and punishments (sanction, dishonour, stigma, ostracism and exclusion from favours).

Cohen (1994) and Hardin (1995) define these networking norms and their enforcement power as 'ethnic norms', 'community norms' or 'community boundaries', none of which marks or enforces the boundaries of an ethnic group or a geographic community as such; rather, these boundaries serve to shape and enforce political and economic networks within and through different groups and communities. Boundary norms are effective, since they refer to the indigenous (such as kinship and religious) mechanisms of reward, sanction and exclusion. The cognitive processes of accentuation and social comparison suggest that deviance from these norms may categorise people to the degree of the *total other* (like enemies, dirties and pollutants) via the rituals and practices of ostracism and stigma. As far as subject people internalise and prioritise these mechanisms, there is no special need for coercive and materially expensive means of enforcement, as they not only believe in and support these mechanisms individually but also use them to subjugate each other. Hardin (1995: 103) affirms that such "enforcement comes directly from the relevant group members," which is both normatively motivated and economically and politically stimulated.

Mobilisation for collective action

As suggested above, collective identities depersonalise the choices and preferences of human individuals. This condition is also necessary to achieve their trust and solidarity for collective action. According to the social-psychological concept of depersonalisation (Ashmore et al. 2004: 94; Hogg et al. 2004: 254), collective identities generate certain stereotypes such as commonalities based on descent, ethnic or religious origins, belief in one's power, rights and resources. At the same time, these commonalities stress the difference of *others.* Notably, these stereotypes are hardly adequate for the reality or even differentiated power relations. Rather, they are means that political actors seek to mobilise people for collective action which mainly favours them. Stereotypes are knowledge forms that individuals easily take to import relevant socio-cultural meanings and thereby enact their agency. These meanings, in turn, shape the mutual expectations of the members of the 'category of action' regarding their commitment and conformity to normative demands for collective action.

In order to generate relevant stereotypes, political actors circulate claims and narratives about the collective identities of the 'category of action'. In this way, they try to persuade affected people about their group or categorical (such as descent, ethnic or religious) commonalities. Modified myths and historical events serve to sensitise honour and pride on the basis of descent, ethnic or religious common origins and shared norms. Political studies are familiar with such practices, defined as 'group consciousness' and 'national self-determination'. Such ideologised 'identity politics' describes and invokes the beliefs of group members in their privileged rights and resources (Tilly 1993, in: Ashmore et al. 2004: 94; Barron et al. 2004). The narratives teach members about their *higher* position, especially in relation to *other* groups, about the differences in and even the lower status of *others*. This position describes their group or categorical attributes as normative demands for collective action (Polletta and Jaspers 2001: 284). A similar discussion in social psychology, about 'ideologised positions' (Fisherman 1968, in: Tajfel 1974: 75), also suggests that distinctive attributes of different groups or categories are part of a political project to endow political claims for collective action with normative and emotional commitment.

Besides stereotypes, the already mentioned socio-cognitive process of introjection[13] plays an affective or emotional role in depersonalising individuals. The term, introduced by Rosenberg (1979, in: Ashmore et al. 2004: 92), suggests that individuals devote and sacrifice themselves to some collective or joint actions. Here, introjection "refers to the adoption of externals (the related persons or objects) into the self, so as to have a sense of oneness with them and to feel personally affected by what happens to them" (in: Ashmore et al. 2004: 92). In such a social-psychological environment, the fate of the group or category is experienced as the fate of the self, which then invokes solidarity and 'bounded groupness' as necessary conditions for the survival of the self. This is the reason why individuals make 'colossal sacrifices', as Hardin (1995: 23) answers the question raised by Benedict Anderson.

However, collective action is organised neither in favour of the 'category of action' nor for the sake of the highlighted collective identity. Instead, collective identities are sought and in the process adapted to shape solidarity groups and

---

[13] The similar concept in symbolic anthropology is called 'extended identity' (Cohen 1985).

collective movements for the sake of political alliances and networks. For example, attachment to a locality generates solidarity, not necessarily due to common interests but especially due to the goals of individual actors who may confront those of their fellows. Locality, like other references, is the "point [...] of orientation," the point which has different meaning and significance for different actors (Kuper 2003: 247). It is an inscribed space that holds past memories which are simultaneously interpreted differently by different actors (Low and Lawrence-Zuniga 2003: 13).

Prototypic leaders serve as mobilisers of the (labour, financial and material) resources of subject peoples for collective action. They refer to collective identities to interpret their own images and behaviours as prototypic or exemplary to the highlighted groups or categories. These prototypic leaders thus claim that they represent and protect both the sacred and mundane interests of their groups or categories. Consequently, they legitimise their claims by acquiring the trust of the subject group or categorical fellows (Hogg et al. 2004: 242, 246, 259; also Ashmore et al. 2004: 90-91), and they also commit their subject people to the norms of collective action. Hardin (1995) defines these norms as the "norms of identification," which are exclusively based on the 'coordination power' of leaders.

Legitimation of the political and economic claims of individual actors

Empirically established anthropological concepts such as 'symbolic community' and 'networking boundaries' (Cohen 1985; Polletta and Jasper 2001) suggest that collective identities serve to shape and change group or categorical boundaries along the alliance (e.g. marriage, friendship or patron-client) networks of claimants. Hence, for instance, communities are not 'geo-social' categories but rather their boundaries are frequently re-drawn due to the alliance and networking strategies of individual actors. These communities are not egalitarian, parochial, stable, face-to-face and conformist, as suggested in traditional anthropology and as Cohen (1985: 50-53) observes as well. Due to their political function their bonds and boundaries are fluid, relational and emerging out of the particular political and economic interests of individual actors.

As one can see, individual actors refer to collective identities to legitimise their own political and economic interests and privileges. In the same way, the social-psychological concepts of 'ethnic pluralism' (Tajfel 1974: 75) and 'work groups' (Knippenberg and Schie 2000) suggest that reference to collective identities interprets these interests and privileges as necessary needs and conditions of the people who are considered members of related groups or categories. These collective identities, in turn, serve as a means to highlight collective norms which generate the commitment or loyalty of the subject people to these interests and privileges, which mainly favour only some of them. As already mentioned, Hardin (1995) defines these highlighted norms by reference to collective identities as the 'norms of identification'.

In anthropological tradition, group- or category-related positions and resources are defined as 'symbolic goods', of which there are two categories: 1) symbolic means and 2) symbolic resources. Symbolic means include, as Snow (2001) suggests, "the interpretative frameworks (or frames), avowed and imputed names, and dramaturgical codes of expression and demeanor (e.g. particularistic styles of storytelling, dress, adornment, and music) that are generated and employed during the course of a collectivity's efforts to distinguish itself from one or more other collectivities" (7). Symbolic resources can be any important material resources such as land, water, sacred places and professions (Cohen 1994). Symbolic goods are means through which one can seek the legitimacy of power structures and resource allocation. As the figure below (Figure 3: The circle of symbolic legitimacy) illustrates, individual actors refer to collective identities in order to seek their privileged personal relation to symbolic goods.

Figure 3: The circle of symbolic legitimacy

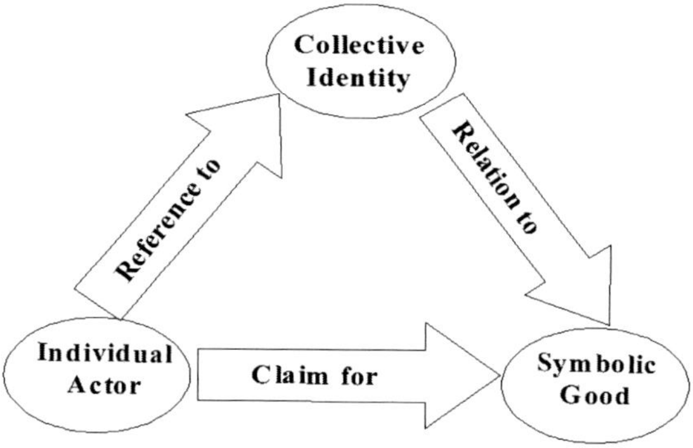

Symbolic goods maintain oral, written and inscribed memories about the political and economic privileges of related individuals, and they especially inform such privileges of some over others while compensating political and economic inequality by means of the exchanges of moral values and obligations. The practice of morally compensating differentiated access to symbolic goods is one important source of legitimacy. Narratives are also another source of legitimacy which are generated through reference to certain symbols and signs of symbolic goods. Myths, memories and experiences about the group's origin, history and its relationship to important resources (including land and water) seek to inform and justify the claims of individual actors. Notably, these claims do not imply recognising the rights and benefits of each group member, but they are linguistic means that favourably placed actors manipulate for their own purposes. Even separate members of a particular group have different stories about their groupness, thus reflecting their different political and economic claims, which is how powerful actors craft *master narratives* to bolster existing 'status and power differentials' through their economic and political networks (Ashmore et al. 2004: 97, 104). For example, the historical interpretation of symbolic goods hardly serves to tell the truth about the latter. Rather, 'history' "can be not only a catalogue of chronological events with distinctive political and institutional consequences but a powerful biographical narrative that group elites deploy to legitimize their status and actions…" (Barron et al. 2004: 23).

Individual actors also use collective identities to reduce the influence of their challengers on subject people by framing (e.g. stigmatising) them in accordance with collective norms (Polletta and Jasper 2001: 290, 295). Barron et al. (2004) define such a function as 'identity manipulation' when candidates mobilise their voters based on their place of origin. The claim on the place of origin is legitimate and effective, although such a form of collective identity might not have been salient previously: "Geographically-defined groups would see their collective pride as threatened if a candidate from another area won. Pride then had to be defended through a violent clash" (ibid. 25).

Again, individual actors refer to their relation to certain (symbolic) goods, and they claim that contested land or a shrine belongs to 'their group'. Such a claim does not reflect their concern about protecting the common good of the 'group' and is rather about defeating their own opponents. Claimants mobilise loyalty and, if necessary, the body of their 'group' members to insist on their own agendas and rights.

Lommitz (1988) and Verdery (2004) show such a symbolic relation of goods to individuals in the cases of the Soviet and post-Soviet economic systems. According to Lommitz (1988: 53), "personal networks of reciprocity or clientelism" of the Soviet system functioned on the rationale of norms and values related to separate collective identities. Verdery (2004) also observes such principles of property rights during and after socialism. In the (post-) socialist context, property is a set of political, economic, cultural and social constructs and relationships through which persons are related to one another by means of things and their non-economic values. Cultural idioms, including identities, have an important role in defining and linking people to one another and to the properties. Thus, property is about boundary-making: it sets inclusions and exclusions, "belongings," such as what "belongs" to whom, and who belongs to or has affinities with some larger entity that has a relation with specific values or things (Verdery 2004: 22-23). For example, public property rights are no more than the 'administrative' or privileged rights of state administers. The latter have privileged rights over things and people in order to shape networks and institutions that control and mobilise resources (ibid. 30).

It is necessary at this point to mention the prevailing discussion about property rights offered by Ostrom and her associates within the framework of Common Property Regimes (CPR). This discussion of property rights is worthy because it distinguishes between five types of property rights, including access, withdrawal, management, exclusion and alienation, which vary among individuals and in different contexts, drawing from their personal claims and collective affiliations (Schlager and Ostrom 1992). However, the main point from this perspective, with which my theoretical framework does not match, is understanding what is meant by a 'community of users'.

This approach highlights demarked groups as coherent actors of power relations which have distinctive boundaries (collective identities) and political and economic interests separate from one another. According to Ostrom (2000), a 'community of users' consists of members of a clearly demarked group who "share contracts" and thereby have the legal right to include or exclude non-members from using a resource (332). Proprietors or user groups refer to collective identities, in part, to develop strict boundary and authority rules in order to sanction and exclude those who do not contribute to the maintenance of existing property relations (ibid. 341).

Chapter conclusion

This theoretical framework has referred to various anthropological and social-psychological concepts to understand the role collective identities play in maintaining greatly needed but highly contested local governance institutions. The framework has been based upon a theoretical discussion of 'social order', which defines local governance as a political organisation of order and stability at the primary level of human interactions. This approach seeks the interplay between the institutional principles of local governance and the collective identities of local populations. Institutions are externalised principles and routines of behaviour, and their interactions are regularly observed in the everyday lives of people and in the course of their political and economic exchanges. Collective identities, like other normative structures, are internalised, cognitive patterns of behaviour and interaction (like norms and values) which are consequently externalised in institutions.

Different experimental (social-psychological) and field (anthropological) studies have been applied to define collective identities as the cognitive and contextual boundaries of individuals. Individuals have multiple identities, i.e. they identify with different groups or categories. However, they choose, highlight and protect one of them or an overlapping image of two or more identities in a particular context. Such human behaviour suggests that different contexts of human interactions require different identities. The last discussion on the theoretical framework enquired into the political use of collective identities. I found basically three aspects, so individual actors refer to collective identities to legitimise and persist three types of local governance institutions:

(1) Institutions of power structures: this aspect suggests that collective identities commit people to a certain structured environment of power relations. They especially serve to sustain the differentiated positions and statuses of individual actors and to shape actors' choices and preferences for political action.

(2) Institutions of collective mobilisation: this aspect discusses the role of collective identities in mobilising local people's concerns and resources in order to maintain political or economic stability at the local level.

(3) Institutions of property rights: this aspect shows how individual actors use collective identities to legitimise their own and to delegitimise others' political and economic rights and claims.

The case studies from the southern Khatlon region of Tajikistan, set out in the following empirical chapters, discuss the role of certain collective identities in maintaining these institutional aspects of local governance.

LOCAL GOVERNANCE OF SOCIAL ORDER IN SOUTHERN KHATLON, TAJIKISTAN

The empirical data show how, in different socio-economic contexts, collective identities (especially kinship and Islam) shape the institutions of local governance or the political organisation of local social order. To strengthen the comparative value of the research, I collected data from different villages within the region of southern Khatlon, i.e. the borderland districts of Khatlon province in Tajikistan. Before discussing two in-depth village case studies in Chapters Three and Four, in the current chapter I discuss the broader context of five districts in the region. This is an important step, as it draws a more or less representative picture of the region and then compares two village case studies against this background.

Subchapters one and two in this chapter briefly introduce the southern Khatlon region and its political and economic settings, conditions and ongoing processes. Subchapter three describes and discusses the collective identities in the region which are emphasised through the whole study. These identities include (1) ethnicity, (2) kinship networks and ties and (3) local Islam. Notably, this study is less concerned with interethnic interactions, which mainly take place on the intermediary and national levels of political processes. The focus is rather limited to local politics in rural settlements where the majority of people are affiliated to the same ethnic groups. Subchapter four discusses the role of collective identities, especially kinship (including village, descent, family and neighbourhood) and Islamic affiliations, in shaping local governance processes. The subchapter is divided up into three sections, each of which discusses separately (1) political organisation, (2) (de-)stabilising factors and (3) the political economy of social order.

Short overview of the southern Khatlon region

Khatlon province was established in 1992 after merging the former Kulob and Qurghonteppa provinces. Today, the province consists of 24 districts and more than 2 million people making up the most ethnically diverse groups in the country (Abdullaev 2004: 10). Khatlon province comprises the higher proportion of three-quarters of the Tajik population living in rural areas (Government of Tajikistan 2002a: 15). Both national and international surveys (e.g. UNDP 2003a, 2003b) suggest that the economic indicators of the province are the worst in the country, although recent evaluations do not emphasise such regional differentiations (e.g. Government of Tajikistan 2005). The common perception about the region's poorer social and economic standards has been shaped by major conflicts and the displacement of local people, which took place in the central and southern districts of Khatlon province during the civil war (1992-1994) (World Bank 2000: 27).

Currently, Khatlon province is divided up into the Kulob and Qurghonteppa regions (*mintaqa*). Kulob City is the regional centre of Kulob districts while Qurghonteppa city is the centre of both the province and the districts of Qurghonteppa region. These regions also differ from each other due to their geographic, economic and socio-cultural conditions and characteristics. Kulob region is situated to the east of the province, consisting of both lowland cotton-growing and mountainous subsistence-based districts. The eastern districts of Kulob region, where I conducted one main part of my field research, are unique within the province due to their mountainous conditions of ecological, economic and, to a greater extent, ethnic homogeneity.

Political and economic settings of the southern Khatlon region

Local governance reflects the political and economic relations of different actors at the local level. From this point, the thesis does not follow the developmental or state-centristic approaches to local governance which blame the central executive power for encouraging a monopoly and thus the malfunctioning of local political structures in Tajikistan (e.g. De Martino 2004). Rather, I assert the argument of researchers (like Idiev 2006: 7 and Matveeva 2009: 22) about the combination of 'tradition' and 'modernity', or 'old' and 'new'. The political and economic exchanges of actors are based on locally practiced cultural norms and social institutions, which shape relatively stable and enduring patterns and structures of interactions, that is, social order. The local social order is therefore maintained in the course of interactions among traditional, so-called 'local' authorities, state officials at different levels and their international 'partners'. They not only take over local government and development offices but also shape traditional, including religious, structures. The similar construction of power structures at the local level has been observed in other parts of the world as well (e.g. in African Benin by Bierschenk and de Sardan 2003: 153-154).

Jamoats, collective farms and mahallas, are the core political and economic structures at the local level. Since Soviet times, kolkhoz or sovkhoz were formally economic institutions at an administrative level equal to the village council (currently replaced by jamoats), the latter being the delegation authority of the state and local people for the political and social governance of the subject villages. In fact, the existing power structures and networks integrated informally into and through kolkhoz or sovkhoz adapted their political and economic functions as well as those of post-Soviet substitutes – jamoats, collective and private *dehqan* farms and mahallas.

Jamoats especially have taken over most of the political and economic functions of the former village council and kolkhoz or sovkhoz at the inter-village level. A jamoat, which is a second-level primary state organisation, is defined as a player in 'local government' in the Law of the Republic of Tajikistan 'On Self-Governance Institutions of Town and Village' (Law on Local Self-Governance 2007[1994]). It is in charge of tax collection and socio-political stability as well as economic activities (e.g. cotton-growing and harvest) in cotton-growing districts.

Mahallas were inherited from the pre-Soviet system of local governance, although with a few modifications and the enforcement of its mediation role to bring together local (so-called *kolkhozi*) and state elites and their indigenous mediators (like elders and religious notables) at village level. Adopted in 2008, the Law on Local Self-Governance (2008) seeks to formalise this network of various actors through mahallas. Local government structures, such as jamoats and interior (police) departments (at the jamoat and district levels), enforce such a mediation role of the mahalla. Mediation is provided to both endure socio-political stability and implement fixed economic targets (e.g. tax collection and cotton harvest), which again favour the prevailing patron-client network of the elites.

In the last two decades, mainly through 1997-2005, a range of multilateral legal, fiscal and technical investments have targeted the decentralisation of local political and economic structures and the redistribution of political and economic resources. The revised Law of the Republic of Tajikistan 'On *Dehqan* (*Fermeri*) Farms' (*Dehqan* Farms 2002) established *dehqan* farms as the legal entities of individual families or a group of families. The law and its further amendments, including the Decree of the Government of the Republic of Tajikistan No 385 from 1 October 2002 (Government of Tajikistan 2002b),[14] introduced the institutions of family inheritance and shareholding (*sahmdori* or *hissagi*) as the proprietorship rights of individual shareholders (*sahmdor*) to private and public goods.[15] Despite the involvement of a multilateral delegation

---

[14] Cf. USAID (2004); also see an expert interview with the chairman of the collective farm of Devdor village (Notebook No 1-2, June 7, 2007: pages 96-97).

[15] According to the Law on *Dehqan* Farms (*Dehqan* Farms 2002) and its further amendments (cf. USAID 2004), all rural inhabitants, both men and women, have

assigned to monitor especially shareholding redistribution campaigns, for example in Shuroobod district in 2005, established *dehqan* farms enforced the subsistence institution of family inheritance, which mostly benefited powerful local elites. In cotton-growing (such as Shahritus and Nosiri Khusrav) districts most of the cotton farms register local people as shareholders, but the farm leaders mainly benefit from economic activities. Less favoured people, who constitute the majority of the population in both the cotton and mountainous districts, maintain their livelihoods from different sources, including subsistence agriculture, livestock and labour migration.

Similarly, the patron-client network of the elites, in most cases, markedly dominates the locally integrated community-driven development (CDD) structures and programmes of INGOs. Since 1994, INGOs were first involved in the Qurghonteppa region, the worst affected area during the civil war, to support politically and economically the return of refugees from neighbouring countries. After the Peace Reconciliation (1997), some INGOs remained in the Qurghonteppa region, in part in the Qabodiyon oasis, and shifted their focus from economic support to CDD programmes. Among them, UNDP Shahritus Area Office implemented its CDD programmes through related jamoat-level structures, i.e. Jamoat Resource Centres (JRCs). There are structures similar to JRCs in the studied mountainous districts of Kulob region, including in the Mu'minobod and Shuroobod districts. In addition, the Local Development Committee (LDC) of Mu'minobod district and the Mountainous Societies Development Support Programme (MSDSP) in both the Mu'minobod and Shuroobod districts represent CDD structures and programmes involving more than 20 international development agencies.

Collective identities in the southern Khatlon region

Both domestic and foreign scholars have discussed the political and institutional role of collective identities at the national and local levels of Tajikistan. Their conceptual approaches, including 'sotsium' or 'etnos', '*kolkhozi* identity', 'clan identity' and 'communal identity', are worthwhile discussing here in section one. In the next sections – two, three and four – I mainly focus on collective identities, including ethnicity, kinship ties and Islam, as contextually relevant cognitive boundaries for individual actors. In contrast to some of the abovementioned conceptual approaches, collective identities in the southern Khatlon region do not reflect stable, invariant, clear-cut and institutionalised

---

proprietorship rights to an equal amount of land and other resources, including the public properties of former kolkhoz or sovkhoz.

boundaries among local people. Rather, collective identities extend beyond the territorial notions of rural settlements, fragment their inclusive scopes into sub-village categories and sometimes crosscut each other and other collective identities to shape overlapping and merged boundaries. In a sense, multidimensional and context-responsive references, in part, of kinship and Islam serve to shape indigenous political and economic (reciprocal and patron-client) networks.

Conceptual approaches to the political role of collective identities

This section reviews some of the more dominant concepts formulated by domestic and foreign scholars about the political role of collective identities. Part one of the section talks about Soviet concepts (such as 'sotsium' or 'etnos') which still find their proponents among domestic scholars. These concepts equate identities with groups and categories and thus draw clear-cut institutional boundaries between different (ethnic and local) groups and categories. Part two discusses recent concepts (including *kolkhozi* identity, clan identity and communal identity), which also bear similar primordialist and structuralist traces.

Collective identities as 'epistemic groups'

Mostly domestic and Russian scholars (including Idiev 2006; Nourzhanov 2005; Shozimov 2003; Olimova 2000; Kulchik et al. 1996; and Niyazi 1998) refer to collective identities as 'epistemic groups'. Accordingly, certain institutions and networks represent distinctive boundaries of certain ethnic or other local groups. These 'epistemic groups' are made up of homogenous groups of individuals who seek to achieve the historical 'ideal types' of their groups. Scholars define such groups as 'sotsium' or 'etnos', referring to the ethnocentric concept of the Soviet scholar Gumilev (1967).

According to this approach, not only cultural monuments but also social and political institutions are the attributes of group or categorical (e.g. ethnic, urban vs. rural and class) boundaries. Certain integrated mindsets and institutional mechanisms shape the isolated political structures of certain groups, which are not shared by other groups. For example, Idiev (2006: 15) talks about the epistemic units of Turkmen, Laqay, Qunghurot and Gharmi ethnic groups who dwell in some districts (Jilikul, Kolkhozobod and Qumsangir of Vakhsh oasis) of Khatlon province, as well as of Maschohi and Isfaragi groups in the northern districts of Sughd province (Maschoi Kuhna, Maschoi Nav and Isfara).

Idiev (2006) suggests that the settled Tajiks do not construe their boundaries in the materialised form, as Uzbeks do through their sacred sites. The settled 'Tajik sotsium' is more 'mobile' and thus more able to adapt to modernisation processes than the 'mountainous' Tajiks and Uzbek tribes (e.g. Laqay and Qunghurot) who inhabit the political and cultural 'peripheries' of Tajikistan. The communal structure of the mountainous communities and Uzbek tribes is stable and closed, while urban and settled Tajiks adequately support 'the demands of modernisation'. Urban and lowland environments dissolve the hierarchical structures and descent principles of social status, while kinship networks and communalism are dominant on the periphery. Settled Tajiks are more loyal to formal, centralised institutions of the state than other groups. Conversely, 'immobile' and 'backward' groups are attached to their 'tribalist' and 'paternalist' structures of clan, regionalism and patronage networks (ibid. 15-54).

The similar approach of 'institutional primordialism', which ascribes certain norms and institutions to certain groups, has also been suggested by other mentioned scholars; of course, not always in favour of the same groups. Kulchik et al. (1996) are among many Russian writers who claim that the intellectual and mental capabilities of Central Asian Russians favoured them to forerun other ethnic groups during and after the Soviet Union: in part, to dominate urban settlements, to lead an industrial sector and to integrate democratic and market institutions. Olimova (1999) and Niyazi (1998) continue the argumentation that Central Asian settled and urban (both Tajik and Uzbek) groups welcomed the modernisation processes of the Soviet Union, while the peripheral and mountainous groups confronted them by 'ruralising' cities, developing 'black markets', practicing parallel and radical forms of Islam and supplying the 1990s civil war in Tajikistan with unemployed and unprofessional fighters.

Certainly, such a claim does not represent the empirical reality when contradictory histories and stories circulate, not only between different groups but also within the same groups. In their interpretations, Idiev (2006), Olimova (1999) and others do not consider the factor of power relations, which destroys groups as everlasting epistemic units and their ideal types. Rather, the historical and normative ideal types themselves are subject to multilayered interpretation according to different individuals and contexts. Not only between but also within the same groups we find different stories about the single 'monument' reflecting the often contradictory claims of individual actors. For example, 'woven' stories about acquiring the status of 'haji' (Islamic pilgrim) without pilgrimage, about the dreamt mission of organising a Sufi circle (*halqa*) and claims about ancestral purity via *shajaranoma*[16] reflect power relations.

Kolkhozi identity

Some scholars (Roy 1997, 2000; Tadjbakhsh 2008) propose and support the concept of a '*kolkhozi* identity', namely the 'old identities' of regionalism and localism which were inherited from pre-Soviet Central Asia. Accordingly, Roy (1997, 2000) develops the concept of '*kolkhozi* identity' by highlighting modified local affiliations through Soviet structures such as territorial-administrative and economic units: "A kolkhoze is either the expression of a solidarity group, old or new; or the object of a power struggle between rival groups, who are thus inclined to identify themselves with ethnic or political oppositions conceptualized somewhere else" (Roy 1997: 137-138). Thus, this concept overestimates the role of solidarity or rival groups in shaping the distinctive collective identities and political networks of the regions.

To assert their suggestion, the proponents of this concept refer mostly to post-Soviet changes in Tajikistan, including the civil war in the 1990s, when the ideals and ideologies of communism, democracy, nationalism or Islamism were used as pretexts for power struggles among regional elites. These ideals and ideologies were "brandished as labels in the attempt to legitimize the different regional clashes" (Tadjbakhsh 2008: 9). Similarly, Roy (2000) claims that existing political parties in Tajikistan represented different regions. For example, the communists were mainly from the northern region, while most of the opposition forces came from the south-eastern regions of the country.

To a certain degree, the explanation based on '*kolkhozi* identity' is reasonable enough, but it cannot answer some important questions, for example related to the regional affiliation of political actors. Not only people from the south-eastern regions of Tajikistan but also the representatives of other regions substantially shaped opposition movements in the 1990s. Also, today, the ruling elites of different regional origins have replaced the old communist elites.

Clan identity

Collins (2002, 2003) and De Martino (2004) are among the architects of 'clan identity' in the case of Tajikistan. They consider the historical legacy of Central

---

[16] '*Shajaranoma*' is genealogical book. It consists of two root words of '*shajara*' (an Arabic word for 'tree') and '*noma*' (a Tajik-Persian word for 'letter' or 'book').

Asian political and economic networks built on the basis of 'politicised' kinship groups. They argue that these networks adapted and modified Soviet and post-Soviet local governance structures, such as kolkhoz, sovkhoz and mahalla. New ideological references, such as ethnonationalism, political Islam or communism, serve as boundaries separating distinct clans.

Thus, Collins (2003) offers the concept of 'clan identity', which should serve "as the critical unit of analysis in Central Asia," in part, to understand stability, conflict and transition (171). According to the author, clan identity is a permanently salient and overarching identity which shapes political networks and collective actions. The clan (and its indigenous equivalents such as 'klan', 'avlod', 'urugh' and 'rod') is based on notional or actual kinship, which is quite different from ethnic, religious and cliental affiliations. This is a way, Collins (2003) suggests, by which we can overcome essentialist views of regionalist, Islamic or ethnic identities.

From this angle, Collins (2003) and De Martino (2004) argue that ethnonational discourses and affiliations reflect kinship ties of local population. The Soviet model of ethnonationalism seeks to impose and legitimise local and central political and economic networks and regimes by adapting ethnic symbols into localist loyalties. Movements, which have traditionally been explained as ethnonational and religious mobilisation, are thus dominated by clan groups. Likewise, *Hanafi* and *Sufi* Islamic schools are not monolithic in Tajikistan. Instead, they represent 'rural' or clan networks of people, and they differ not only among different regions but also within the same regions due to the variety of kinship and regional networks. Due to dispersed networks, as well as to religious and Sufi practices, Islam therefore lacks an integrated political structure. These scholars, however, neglect the role of political actors in subjugating and re-interpreting Islam – and thereby re-shaping its political forms.

Adherents to the concept of 'clan identity' also suggest the role of the clan in distributing resources and thus in legitimising the claims of individual actors. According to Collins (2002), clan affiliation serves as an egalitarian principle of resource distribution: "They [powerful men] provide political, social, and economic opportunities to the members of their respective networks, and in return count on these members' personal loyalty and respect to maintain their status" (Collins 2002: 142).

Some other scholars (e.g. Nourzhanov 2005; Abdullaev 2004; and Freizer 2004) idealise the similar concept of *avlod*. They regard *avlod*, or "an ascent patriarchal extended family," as both a salient identity and a dominant institution which shapes local politics and economic networks. *Avlod* maintains mental structures which isolate 'individual consciousness' from the exclusive 'world' of the kinsmen. This holy world shapes the categories of historical memory, social structure and political-economic relations. The members of *avlod* are duty-bound to remember and glorify their ancestors across seven generations. Naturally, each *avlod* is attached to a locality and dominates certain political and economic structures at different levels of society (such as brigadas and local and central state structures). Therefore, the argument goes that trust and solidarity networks are exclusively built on clans. The oldest male members run such networks, while the age and gender norms of 'relatedness' and 'exclusion' shape vertical access to people and resources. The core of this normative order is *nang* (*avlod*-related dignity), which defines the needs and preferences of individual members.

Communal identity

Some studies also discuss the role of 'communal identity' in shaping local political and economic structures. Analyses have been provided in the cases of other Central Asian states, including Uzbekistan (Stevens 2005; Rasanayagam 2002) and Kyrgyzstan (Radnitz 2005). Other observations (by Freizer 2004; Abdullaev 2004; and Falkingham 2000) are devoted to Tajikistan but without any in-depth case studies. They define 'community' or the primary administrative unit of rural residence as an encapsulated and isolated world set apart from both society and state. Community members develop clear-cut boundaries and networks based on their relational ties, which disconnects them from other communities as well as from the state.

In the case of Aksu political mobilisation in Kyrgyzstan, Radnitz (2005) suggests that the state is virtually absent in the everyday lives of the local population. Communal members base their isolated networks on egalitarian norms which express their solidarity with the holistic entity of their community. Community members struggle to maintain their 'good reputation' by obeying their collective rules and norms, and they also mutually control their conformity to communal norms by maintaining an informal information system or through the medium of gossip. Furthermore, being included in these political and economic networks serves as a reward for obedient members. 'Good access' to communal networks and resources, such as *hashar*, is considered fair recompense for conformity to and solidarity with communal norms and institutions.

As the above overview suggests, there are three important conceptual and methodological challenges that are required in order to understand the political role of collective identities in Tajikistan. These are as follows:

(a) The abundant research on collective identities rarely shows the latter's role in enforcing existing institutions, but rather it manifests them as the exclusively instrumental means of political actors. Social institutions are considered apart from the socio-cognitive world of the people.

(b) Most scholars consider social institutions as self-sufficient and taken-for-granted structures of particular (ethnic, regional, clan or communal) groups, which principally have no need for enforcement mechanisms.

(c) The discussion on both collective identities and institutions mostly refers to cases of national and Central Asian political and economic processes – cases which took place in the past and were collected from secondary sources.

Before I discuss the role of collective identities in local politics, the following sections illuminate ethnic composition, kinship networks and ties and local forms of Islam in the southern Khatlon region.

Ethnic composition of the southern Khatlon region

The regions of Kulob and Qurghonteppa are distinct from each other due to their geographical situations, economic conditions and ethnic compositions. The mountainous districts of Kulob region (including Shuroobod and Mu'minobod) have ethnically homogenous Tajik communities, whilst the lowland, cotton-growing districts of both Kulob and Qurghonteppa regions are populated by different ethnic groups.

Similar to other places in the Qurghonteppa region, the Qabodiyon oasis is home to the ethnically heterogeneous communities of Shahritus, Qabodiyon and Nosiri Khusrav districts. *Mahalli*[17] people, as they define themselves, have inhabited the oasis since pre-Soviet times and internally categorise themselves as Tajiks, Arabs and Sayyids[18] or Shaykhs.[19] Before or during Soviet Union rule,

---

[17] '*Mahalli*' literally means 'local' or 'native'. It also refers to the inhabitants of lowland areas.

[18] Sayyids*:* The plural form for '*Sayyid*', which refers to the descent origins of people who claim they are direct descendants of the Islamic prophet Muhammad through his grandsons, Hasan ibn Ali and Husayn ibn Ali, who were the sons of his daughter, Fatima Zahra, and cousin and son-in-law, Ali Ibn Abu Talib. Today, especially since Soviet rule, Sayyids are no longer a distinct descent group. Rather, they claim such

the Arab population of Hisor valley and Uzbek (including Durman and Qunghurot) tribes from other parts of Tajikistan, as well as from Uzbekistan, resettled in the oasis. They were eventually identified as '*mahalli*' as a result of an increase in their kinship ties with the *mahalli* people. From the 1950s, the Soviet government evicted *kuhistoni*[20] Tajiks, mostly from the Hisor and Rasht valleys in central and central-eastern Tajikistan, to supply cotton-growing plantations with manpower. As well as *kulobi* Tajiks from the mountainous districts of the Kulob region were deported to lowland areas. Like other groups, the resettled Tajiks either developed separate neighbourhoods in the *mahalli* and Uzbek settlements or organised distinct villages. Apart from the others, however, the *kuhistoni* people have less developed kinship relations with the *mahalli* people in the oasis.

Since Independence (1991), central state elites have mobilised their ethnic and regional co-members to struggle for state power. Consequently, the central and south-western parts of Khatlon province were conflict epicentres. In 1994, state elites took over central state power and exiled their rivals to adjacent countries until the General Agreement on the Establishment of Peace and National Accord signed in 1997 between the Tajik Government and the United Tajik Opposition.

---

status and start compiling their *shajaranoma* (genealogical book) to legitimise their privileged access to political and economic resources.

19 '*Shaykh*' is an Arabic word for 'old man'; here, it means the claimants or owners of sacred sites.

20 '*Kuhistoni*' literally means 'mountainous', i.e. people who primary lived in the mountainous areas of Tajikistan and were not identified with the *mahalli* people, i.e. the native inhabitants of lowland areas.

Map 2: Ethnic map of Tajikistan[21]

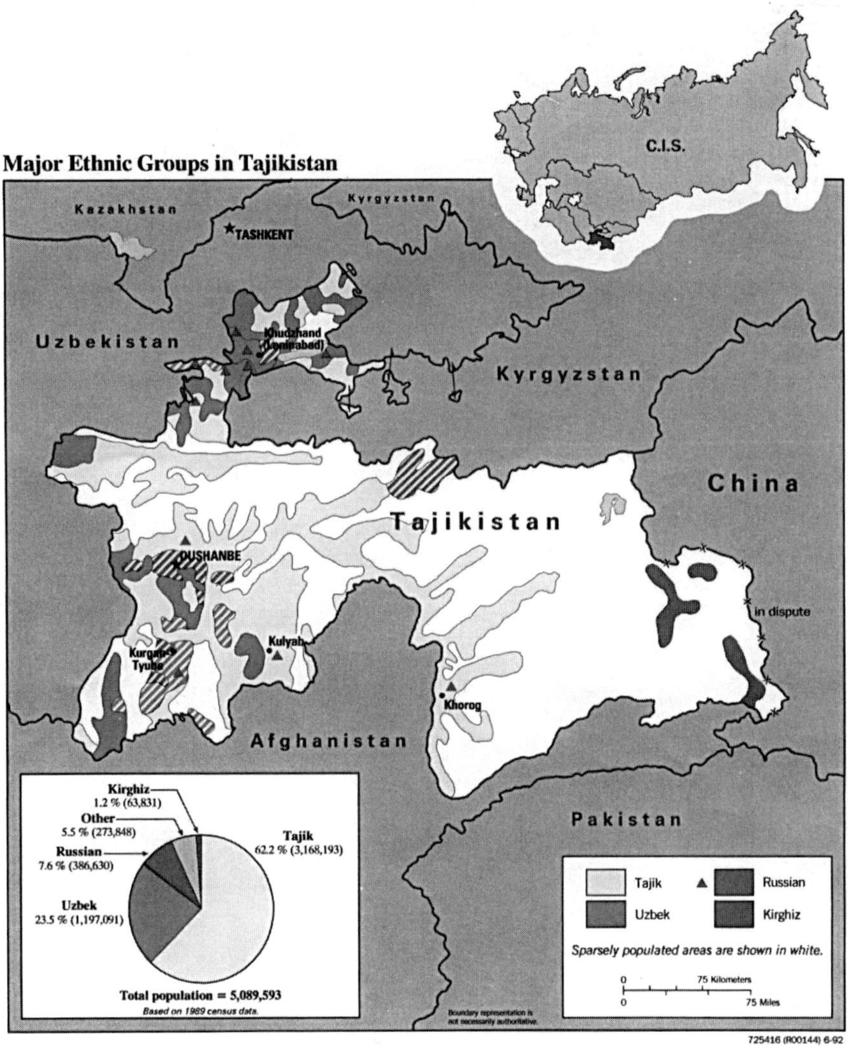

[21] Source: the website of the University of Texas, Austin: (http://www.lib.utexas.edu/maps/commonwealth/tajikistan_ethnic_92.jpg) (accessed January 22, 2011)

Because of the scope of this study, which emphasises political and economic relations at the local level, only a few cases discuss ethnic identity. Nevertheless, I share the understanding that in many instances ethnicity legitimises political regimes which seek the support of wider ethnic groups (Heathershaw 2005; Nourzhanov 2001; Roy 2000; and Smith et al. 1998). For this purpose, intellectual elites of ethnic nationalism use the Soviet-invented "rules for historiography" to interpret historical events and heroes (Smith et al. 1998: 71-72). The intellectual interpretation of history and national and religious feasts, such as Nawruz or Ramadan, celebrate and enforce differentiated classes and loyalties. The political elevation of symbolic categories (including titular languages) to state status seeks to enhance the reputation of political elites among titular categories. In addition, political elites use ethnonational discourses to discredit and prevent claims and mass mobilisations against their political regimes by manipulating such discourses to generate political and moral cohesion within their own fragmented and highly divided structure.

Kinship networks and ties

In the surveyed villages of southern Khatlon, references to various kinship, residential and neighbourhood affiliations and networks are sought to commit people to existing socio-political and economic order and stability. Among these references, *qawmdori*[22], or village identity, is more inclusive and refers to the inclusive commitment of villagers as a whole vis-à-vis 'outsiders'. These outsiders are, first of all, other known villages, peoples and at the same time 'strangers', especially other ethnic and kinship groups or categories, among the villagers. This villagers' boundary-making practice influences their expectations about the representation of their kinship (family and descent) groups and networks to power structures. Local authorities use especially family and religious ceremonies, including weddings, funerals and holidays, to actualise the normative aspects of this boundary.[23]

---

[22] *Qawmdori* or *qishloqdori* literally means 'to govern a people' or 'to maintain village wellbeing', which can be interpreted in different ways, including as a reference to the broader group or categorical (kinship, religious or ethnic) connections of a particular village to other villages and peoples. It also can be viewed as village affiliation and commitment vis-à-vis any other villages. Sub-village references can also be claimed as *qawmdori*. Elites and their mediators use all references, in part, to maintain socio-political and economic order and stability.

[23] Only rarely in the case of a single mountainous ethnic Tajik (*Gharmi* people in Jam'iyati dehqon and Birlyash villages of Shahritus district) did I observe ceremonies which serve to enforce the Islamic community.

The *qawmdori* reference to 'village honour' shapes indigenous and modified practices of collective action and resource mobilisation, thus enabling elites to reshape indigenous institutions (such as *hashar*,[24] *shanbegi*[25], *khayriya*,[26] and *ushr*[27]) which would otherwise be limited to extended family networks. By reflecting the honourable affiliation to village communities through kinship networks, *qawmdori* symbolises joint activities, such as cotton harvesting in cotton-growing villages, as its attributes.

The other reference to village identity is *mahaldori*, which commits local people to maintaining an honourable image of their villages through their subordination to local authorities. *Mahaldori* categorises local people and subsequently commits them to sub-village kinship and neighbourhood groups, especially in large and heterogeneous cotton-growing villages. The governance of political and economic structures is contested and inefficient without such institutionalisation of sub-village groups. Despite weak and fluid boundaries among these groups, they are split up into extended families (*avlod* or *elkheshi*), *qawm* (descent) groups,[28] and sub-village neighbourhoods (*kucha* – street, *shokh* – irrigation divisions, *guzar* – larger neighbourhoods, etc.). Such categorisation is a necessary tool in cotton-growing villages, in order to generate distinctive group identities and thereby shape their political and economic structures, including cotton farms. The elders, *oqsaqols*[29] or *kucha* leaders and mullahs of these groups govern these political and economic structures. The related ceremonies of food-sharing at the beginning of the sowing season (e.g. *oshi kucha*, *darveshi*, *chorshanbegi* and *sumanakpazi*) serve to shape the sub-village cotton-growing 'communities', i.e. cotton farms.

---

[24] *Hashar* is primarily a practice of labour mobilisation among indigenous networks such as extended families.

[25] *Shanbegi* is a Sovietised *hashar* used for state projects.

[26] *Khayriya* is a financial donation made by individual families, primarily organised during Friday and holiday prayers by religious and mahalla authorities.

[27] *Ushr* is an Islamic tax which is practiced as reciprocal exchange among kinsmen. Usually, wealthier men give a certain amount of their harvest to their poor kinsmen.

[28] To name descent groups, the interchangeable terms of *qawm, qabila, avlod,* etc. are used. See also the footnote below about *qawmdori*. Old men in the Shahritus district remember that in the past the principle of 'bone' (an Uzbek word '*suyak*') was decisive in constructing kinship and economic networks: "Today the 'document' ('*hujjat*') is not the 'bone' anymore" (Sufikhuja Begakov – Notebook No 1-5, December 8, 2007: page 27) but rather a consideration of the potential of networking with any group.

[29] *Oqsaqol* is Uzbek word which literally means 'white beard'. *Oqsaqol* is a powerful and respected man of his family or neighbourhood.

In the cotton-growing districts, another term, *qawmdori*,[30] refers to the proper relation of a particular family to broader (e.g. reciprocal and religious) networks or groups embedded in a particular village. Elites and their mediators highlight '*qawmdori* honour' ('*nangi qawmdori*') to actualise 'group integrity' through the mobilisation of co-members for cotton growing and harvesting. Certain institutions of cotton-growing activities, such as *agat* (the Uzbek word for 'a bed of cotton') and *norma* (a Russian word for 'quota'), are prescribed as the affective (honour) commitments of each family as a part of its association with such networks and groups. At the same time, '*qawmdori* honour' seeks to invoke *elkheshi* and *qawm*-related commitment to enforce social and political stability, in part, by stigmatising court appeals and disputes and by strengthening the role of religious and customary institutions involved in dispute settlement.

Sub-village categories are not properly institutionalised in smaller villages of mountainous districts; instead, the patron-client ties of *kolkhozi* elites are central to shaping power structures, which may explain increasing conflicts over power resources. *Qawmdori* is thus a prevailing discourse in such villages, and it seeks to justify the claims of competitors for power resources and to mobilise their supporters.

Local Islam

Like kinship and village affiliations, Islamic identity is not monolithic and invariant in local, everyday social interactions. Steinberger (2003), among other scholars, observes that this nonmonolithic Islam "is, to some extent, malleable to the dictates of political necessity" (236). Islam does not necessarily shape distinctive religious communities but rather serves political and economic elites to legitimise their regimes and claims. Historically, the *Hanafi* legal school and *Sufi* orders[31] have subjugated people to the ruling elites and their local allies (Sagdeev 2000). Islam is used "primarily to interpret secular politics, which in any Muslim country requires a clerical blessing. Almost every purely secular act of a social or political nature is accompanied by an appropriate explanation from the position of Islam" (Malashenko 2000: 160). Steinberger (2003) and Sagdeev (2000) also show that after the collapse of the Soviet regime the main challenge for the political elites was to recover their religious image. For this

[30] *Qawmdori* literally means 'to maintain one's *qawm*' and *qawm* refers to multiple affiliations, including kinship group, descent group, villagers and so like, who are related through a broader network or category comprising a particular village.

[31] Especially the notable *Naqshbandiya* brotherhood, whose founder was Bahouddin Naqshband (d. 1390), had strong ties with political elites (Arabov 2004).

purpose, they go to Hajj (Islamic pilgrimage), swear on the Koran and participate in religious ceremonies to heighten their reputation and legitimise their privileges. Politically 'moderate' or depoliticised Islam has replaced communism as an ideological source that national states use when seeking the mobilisation of wider support. Moreover, state elites use Islam to respond to their political and economic challengers.

At the level of the individual village communities, I observed multilayered Islamic references as well. Without the re-invention of Islamic boundaries by religious authorities, however, Islam reflects the contestations of individual actors over political and economic resources. People attach different religious meanings and histories to their villages, sacred sites, spiritual saints and their own selves, and they refer to these distinctive meanings and histories in order to legitimise their political and economic claims and privileges.

The other use of Islamic identity is to integrate the contested boundaries of social order, that is, to integrate peoples and to mobilise their resources for particular political and economic projects. In this respect, one important reference is *qawmdori*, which reflects a merged village, kinship and Islamic identity. Local mediators basically allude to this reference to commit subject people to existing power structures, including mahalla. For this purpose, in many studied rural settlements, eshons (saints), hajis,[32] imam-khatibs[33] and mullahs, as well as *kucha* mullahs in larger settlements, are among the leading members of mahalla who serve as mediators for elites. They represent village mosques and organise religious ceremonies and holidays to ritualise decision-making boundaries and hierarchies. Also, in larger rural settlements, there are *kucha* mosques which serve as settings whereby religious and other traditional authorities consolidate sub-village neighbourhoods under mahalla. In the smaller, mostly mountainous, settlements there are only village mosques, which are limited to the patron-client networks of *kolkhozi* elites.

Religious ceremonies, including funerals and feasts, serve as settings to mobilise resources for some institutional practices by interpreting the latter as the Islamic commitment of people. Especially, the religious authorities of mahalla commit the subject people to taking care of the 'poor' ('*bechora*'), those marginalised families whose discontent may destabilise the political and economic situations. Indigenous institutions, such as *sadaqa*,[34] are thus modified

---

32 '*Hajis*' is the plural form of '*haji*', i.e. an Islamic pilgrim.

33 *Imam-khatib:* an officially state-recognised village mullah who is responsible for religious arrangements.

34 *Sadaqa:* mostly food support for poor families, which is provided during religious and customary ceremonies such as weddings and funerals. Since indigenous practice is

for this purpose. Also, Islamic identity represented by central and sub-village mosques is sought to enforce the stability of interactions in the everyday lives of local people. It commits the residents of sub-village neighbourhoods to reciprocal exchanges. In this respect, the degree of religiosity of one neighbourhood as a whole is evaluated vis-à-vis the 'good examples' of other neighbourhoods.

Religious authorities, such as eshons and hajis, mediate in order to modify the scopes of the indigenous institutions of resource mobilisation, otherwise practiced exclusively within their indigenous (e.g. extended family) networks. For this purpose, they announce and personally initiate *hashar* in religious settings to invoke overlapping village honour and religious commitment. Similarly, mahalla leaders and mediators, and their state allies, use religious taxation institutions, such as *zakot*[35] and *ushr*, and support practices such as *sadaqa* and *khayriya* through mahalla and state religious departments. These institutions symbolise overlapping *qawmdori* or village, kinship and religious identities vis-à-vis their *others*, such as other village inhabitants and 'infidels' (non-Muslims).

The role of collective identities in the political organisation of social order in the southern Khatlon region

The current subchapter discusses cases about the role of collective identities, especially kinship (including village, descent, family and neighbourhood) and Islamic affiliations, in shaping the core institutions of local governance in the southern Khatlon region. The subchapter is divided into three sections which discuss political organisation, (de-)stabilising factors and the political economy of social order.

---

limited to the religiously recognised 'poor', mahalla authorities therefore mediate to redistribute related resources to other families whom they see as poor families. Also, *sadaqa* has negative connotations among people, including the poor, which is considered as begging if it is accepted from strangers. *Sadaqa* is also a practice of devotion and sacrifice for sacred sites.

[35] *Zakot* (from the Arabic word '*zakah*') is one of the Five Pillars of Islam. It is a religious tax required from especially wealthier Muslims, who must pay 2.5 percent of their wealth, such as livestock, a private house, transportation and goods for trade, as well as 5-10 percent of agricultural products depending on irrigation.

Political organisation of social order

Local elites, their mahalla mediators and state allies refer to kinship networks, village and neighbourhood 'communities' and Islamic identity to shape local political and economic structures. However, the situation differs from place to place, especially between cotton-growing and subsistence-based, ethnically heterogeneous and ethnically homogenous and large and small villages. In cotton-growing villages, which are usually large in size and heterogeneous in ethno-lingual compositions, the local representatives of state elites participate directly in shaping the political and economic structures of mahallas and *dehqan* farms. Here, local state functionaries also mediate to shape a mahalla as an inclusive structure for the most powerful villagers. A mahalla consists of the head of the mahalla or vakil (literally: 'authorised representative'), an imam-khatib (an officially recognised mullah), assistants and heads of *kuchas* (neighbourhoods) in larger villages, assistants and heads of *kuchas* in smaller villages and powerful farmers. Among these actors, vakil and imam-khatib mediate between local authorities and state and religious elites at upper levels. In most politically stable mahallas, regardless of the size of the respective villages, a vakil represents powerful and respected men and an imam-khatib is the most respected religious leader, especially due to his personal ties with upstanding religious authorities.

Especially in lowland communities, where state elites have an economic interest in maintaining the cotton sector, the integration of all indigenous authorities, including religious notables, family and neighbourhood *oqsaqols* (elders), is the prevailing principle employed to mould political structures. Therefore, religious notables (hajis and imam-khatibs, as well as *kucha* mullahs of sub-residential units in larger villages) are among the mahalla's leading members. They use village mosques and religious feasts as core decision-making settings and means to ritualise and thereby enforce the political role of elites.[36]

These settings and means are used to isolate women and to deviate men away from elites and notables. The latter isolate themselves, not only to encircle the decision-making setting but also to maintain their reputation by avoiding inconvenient encounters. I witnessed a case when a former teacher, who entered into a hot dispute with a *domullo* (elite mullah) about the dubious

---

[36] Personal observations in the villages of Qahramon (*elkhudoi* – March 20, 2007), Birlyash (*elkhudoi* – March 23, 2007), Jam'iyati dehqon (*wedding* – April 16, 2007), Ayvoj (funeral – April 19, 2007), Sayyod (*khatm* – March 25, 2007), Ayvoj (funeral – April 21, 2007) in Shahritus district and Okhundboboev (funeral – March 26, 2007) in Qabodiyon district (Notebook No 1-1)

personality of religious notables, was forced by a vakil to move to another space.[37]

The observation about the political function of religious and customary ceremonies in different districts[38] shows that these ceremonies also sustain solidarity among villagers or separate sub-village neighbourhoods. These ceremonies serve as settings which highlight the kinship, village and Islamic identities of the subject people in order to commit them to their mahalla authorities. In part, the village-level seasonal and religious ceremonies of food-sharing (*elkhudoi* or *nawruzi*, funerals and feasts), organised by individual households, separate wealthy men, farmers or villagers, serve to bring people under the authority of the mahalla. These practices also generate differentiation between senior and junior and between male and female villagers. Thereby they adapt the political functions and institutions of not only state organisations but also the newly integrated international development structures of the UNDP and MSDSP in the studied (Shahritus, Mu'minobod and Shuroobod) districts.[39]

In 2007, the district branch of MSDSP in the Mu'minobod district planned to establish VOs in most villages. The staff of the Community Development Unit (CDU) organised participatory village mapping, a PRA exercise that introduces and shapes the development goals of the MSDSP and its CDD programme at community level. In six villages, which I visited during the mapping activities in April-May 2007, CDU employees and mahalla leaders decided to conduct meetings during evening prayer in the village mosques, a good reason for gathering men but excluding women. The representatives of the MSDSP, especially the head of the CDU, who steered the introduction process of VOs, prayed together with the villagers in order to hold ground for an after-prayer discussion about the Islamic commitment of the villagers to 'common wellbeing'. In this way, mosques served as settings to ritualise the PRA mapping exercises and thereby to legitimise VOs as the 'community' of male prayers.

---

37 Personal observation in Ayvoj village (Notebook No 1-1, April 21, 2007: pages 82-85)

38 E.g. the villages of Zulmobod, Doghiston, Darai ob in Shuroobod district and villages of Ayvoj, Jam'iyati dehqon, Qizilaskar, Sayyod, Qahramon, Qumshokh, Birlyash in Shahritus district

39 E.g. in the villages of Shahbacha (May 7, 2007) and Yakkachinor (May 10, 2007) (Notebook No 1-1)

Picture 1: A PRA meeting after evening prayer in a village mosque

Representation of extended families (*elkheshi* or *avlod* groups) to a mahalla is successfully applied to some large and heterogeneous villages in the Shahritus district, which at the same time boosts the political economy of their cotton-growing networks. In both Shahritus and Shuroobod districts, separate *kucha* neighbourhoods of the larger villages use mosques to consolidate related neighbourhoods under the authority of their mahalla representatives. In Sayyod, a village in the Shahritus district (where I conducted one of my in-depth case studies), apart from the recently opened village mosque, there are traditional *choykhonas* (literally 'tea-houses') or mosques of separate *mahallas*[40] which consolidate the commitment of, at least, *qawm* co-members. Smaller and some larger but ethnically homogenous villages have unrecognised sub-village mosques or guesthouses where people gather for extended family prayers, while

[40] In this case, in Sayyod village, *mahalla* also refers to three descent groups which traditionally inhabited separate *kuchas* (streets). But especially after Soviet-initiated household planning (*tamarqa*) in the 1970s, the kolkhoz merged their distinctive borders and located new households to different descent groups in shared spaces.

village mosques, being the subject structures of mahallas, are dominated by powerful villagers.[41]

For the same reason, mahalla authorities and their state mediators draw socio-geographical boundaries, which are shaped along irrigation canals (*shokh*) and sub-village neighbourhoods (*kucha* or *guzar*), in order to commit neighbours to their 'invented' identities. Reference to these neighbourhood identities enforces the authority of their mahalla representatives, such as *kucha* leaders or *oqsaqols*. During the 1970s, Soviet kolkhozes and sovkhozes started to establish *kucha* neighbourhoods based on the irrigation canals created inside cotton-growing and larger subsistence-based villages. In such villages, *oqsaqols* are in charge for intensive *mahaldori*[42] activities among co-residents. They invoke the villagers' sub-village or neighbourhood affiliations for collective mobilisation. Also, local notables and state elites sustain the *mahaldori* authority of *oqsaqols* by inventing and practicing sub-residential boundaries.

The significance of the mahalla as an integrative structure is obvious in the ethnically homogenous (Qizilaskar and Jam'iyati dehqon) villages of Shahritus district. In these cotton-growing villages, mahallas and mosques do not represent every patrilineal extended family (*avlod*), because of both the contested and weak authority of the mahalla leaders. For example, at the time of my field study visit, a mahalla formally existed in Qizilaskar village, but the dismissed vakil had not been replaced for two years.[43] In this situation the villagers are split into distinct religious communities as well. My informant told that "[t]here is no single public place in the village; the mosques are divided up into different *avlods*. Each *avlod* ['s members] pray in a separate place, mostly in their kinsman's home. The common mosque only serves for [religious] feasts."[44] In Jam'iyati dehqon village, half of the fourteen farmers, who are the most powerful and respected men among their extended families, do not represent and thus do not recognise mahallas.[45]

---

41 E.g. in the Devdor and Darai villages of Shuroobod district and the Sayyod and Qizilaskar villages of Shahritus district.

42 '*Mahaldori*' literally means 'to govern *mahal*', and here '*mahal*' refers to the territorial-administrative unit of a village. However, the notion has different meanings in different contexts, as the thesis further demonstrates.

43 Personal interview; Qizilaskar village; Shahritus district (Notebook No 1-1, April 15, 2007: pages 61-64).

44 Ibid.

45 Personal interview; Jam'iyati dehqon village; Shahritus district (Notebook No 1-1, April 10, 2007: pages 53-54).

The political structure of the sub-village neighbourhoods (mostly unirrigated *kuchas* or *guzars*) of smaller villages (e.g. less than 100 households) in mostly mountainous areas are shaped by the patron-client network of the village elites. In these villages, a vakil is appointed by the elites and supported by their state allies. This is one of the central reasons why powerful villagers contest strategic positions and resources in small villages, even those with only perhaps 10 households (e.g. Busholak village in Shuroobod district).

In several villages in Shuroobod district, state authorities, powerful men and ordinary villagers are not content with the current 'order of things' created in the aftermath of land reforms between 1997 and 2005, or with the institutional intervention of INGOs. For example, since 2002, the MSDSP has established VOs in most villages of the district, whose presence in some cases has challenged the political role of the *kolkhozi* elites. In the surveyed Devdor and Kaftar villages, the new organisation is mainly reduced to those who do not represent traditional structures such as mahallas and collective farms. Not only do elites categorise the leaders of VOs at best as 'teachers', i.e. incompetent in *qawmdori*, but also most of the subject populations refer to a *qawmdori* as a boundary which is undermined by the contested VOs. They do not recognise any political role for VOs, since leadership, according to them, is a privilege of a man who represents indigenous patron-client networks, and who "is wealthy and has access to [state and international] offices… in order to serve his people."[46]

To reduce the contested boundary of a *qawmdori*, for example, the government of Shuroobod district has recently taken the 'experience of Mu'minobod', an adjacent mountainous district, which 'has succeeded' in the integrated political organisation of village communities, in part by adapting development structures into indigenous institutions. The governor of Mu'minobod district directly participates in shaping and supporting the political leaders of rural organisations on the basis of district-wide patron-client networking. For this purpose, he and his office personally interfere in the activities of numerous (more than 10) INGOs under the umbrella of LDC. A deputy governor of Mu'minobod district explained this involvement, which eventually integrated CDD programmes and structures of INGOs into mahallas, as political concern "in order to prevent twofold-power [Russian word: *dvoevlastie*] and threefold-power

---

[46] Personal interview; Darai ob village; Shuroobod district (Notebook No 1-2, June 12, 2007: pages 7-10).

[Russian word: *troevlastie*]…" of vakils, the head of the village organisation and brigadir.[47]

In Shuroobod district, both district governmental authorities and MSDSP representatives have come to the conclusion that VOs must not be the 'oil in the water', expressing their reliance on local notables and mediators: "Now the government is unifying mahallas and village organisations. It understands that leadership [*kaloni*] should be [limited] to the same person," as a mahalla and a VO leader recounted.[48]

Integration of the 'foreigner' into the local social order

A strategic tool of elites is the 'foreigner' ('*khoriji*') discourse, which categorises and transforms international development actors and programmes into indigenous structures. In both Mu'minobod and Shuroobod districts, the MSDSP, the most intensively integrated INGO at village level, is usually labelled as the 'Aga Khan', which hints at its non-Muslim ('Western') and religiously stigmatised ('*Ismaili*') origins. It is a widespread rumour among the local people that Aga Khan may have 'hidden' (i.e., anti-Islamic) intention to establish VOs. Nonetheless, they console themselves that the MSDSP, like any other INGO, will leave their villages after 'the poor' have gained enough wealth.

In this manner, a public outreach manager in the MSDSP, who is closely related to the local elites' patron-client network, completes his dual job. When he visits villages for the first time, to introduce the development structure in the mosques, he first mentions the dubious image of Aga Khan as a Westernised *Ismaili* and then rejects this 'slander' by manifesting a detailed *shajaranoma* (genealogical book) about "Aga Khan, who is not only *Ismaili* but also a direct Sayyid, the great-grandson of the Islamic prophet… who came at the appeal of our government to help the poor." The genealogical book (below picture) has been shown and advertised in order to convince local people of the religious purity and superiority of Aga Khan.[49] This is a way in which local and state elites link 'foreigners' to their networks and thus shape the scope and trajectory of their agency.

---

[47] Personal interview with the deputy governor of Mu'minobod district (Notebook No 1-1, May 3, 2007: page 97).

[48] Personal interview; Roghiyon village; Shuroobod district (Notebook No 1-1, May 13, 2007: page 148).

[49] Personal observation; Mu'minobod district (Notebook No 1-1, May 5, 2007: pages 104)

Picture 2: *Shajaranoma* of Aga Khan

Simultaneously, local elites categorise and discredit the non-related leaders of INGOs' integrated structures, such as VOs, as "servants of the foreigners."[50] In such cases, elites contest not only the leaders and their organisations but also the development projects, even after they have been technically implemented. Rather, any 'foreigner' is acceptable, but only if elites endorse their presence and especially if they represent them.

In Mu'minobod district, for example, the state-run LDC is an umbrella organisation for all international agencies, including the MSDSP and its jamoat- and village-level structures. The government and MSDSP office in Shuroobod district make a similar effort to bring all VOs of the district under the auspices of jamoat-level umbrella organisations – SUDVOs – and the latter under the auspices of a district umbrella organisation – SdDC. Similarly, in Mu'minobod,

[50] Frequent personal interviews with the head of Devdor Village Organisation (Notebook No 1-2 and 1-3, June-September, 2007)

Shuroobod and Shahritus district jamoats represent and directly shape the decision-making body of the UNDP-established JRC.

State and local elites dominate the political structures of integrated INGOs and shape the prioritised aspects of their activities. In all subject villages of Sayyod Jamoat, the staff members of JRC 'Khoja Mashhad', jamoat employees and mahalla authorities identified prioritised problems and implemented related development projects.[51] By implementing these projects at village level, the 'Planned Scheme of Prioritised Problems' (JRC Sayyod 2004) has become a supportive institution which, in part, consolidates power resources through the jamoat.

In Mu'minobod district, the LDC has shifted the primary focuses of INGOs in favour of the political and economic priorities of district government elites. The personal concern of the district governor, who is at the same time the head of the LDC, actualises 'state objectives' as those of the LDC by individually issuing his decree defining the targets and contents of development projects. In a regular meeting of the LDC, his strong and expressive statement suggested social and political activities of INGOs as exceeding their competency and diminishing their reputation. Stevens (2005) observed a similar situation in Uzbekistan when development agencies are welcomed, principally due to their economic resources and nonpolitical activities. These development 'partners' are thus "... more concerned with building beautiful toilet blocks than challenging the power structures..." (ibid. 292). In the global context, development aid is a power resource which mainly empowers development brokers and their local clients (Bierschenk et al. 2002: 3).

In the periodical meeting of the LDC, the governor of Mu'minobod district stressed that "[n]o project should have political relevance; they should have technical purpose. Today, the improvement of economic conditions and infrastructure is of paramount importance."[52] In the same meeting he signed the implementation phase paperwork for 15 infrastructure development projects run by different INGOs, but he postponed a project for Qipchoq village "due to the unsatisfied condition of the pasture and herding of livestock in the village." The governor established a commission consisting of the chairman of the related jamoat, a related people's delegate (*deputat*) and a project

---

[51] Problems such as potable water, telephone lines, electricity, irrigation canals, drains and ditches, schools, medical aid, hospitals, lack of financial resources and economic enterprises.

[52] Personal observation; Mu'minobod district (Notebook No 1-1, May 3, 2007: pages 98-102).

member to check if the villagers had met his 'order', and then to 'grant' the project.

Stabilisation of social order

As already depicted above, a mahalla is a central structure that *kolkhozi* elites dominate and use to stabilise political and economic relations at the village level. Not only do they enjoy the political and economic support of the state and development agencies to enforce this structure, but they also refer to the collective identities and norms of local people to govern social and political life. In most surveyed villages, both Islamic references and sub-village neighbourhoods (such as *kucha* or *guzar*) and descent groups, sometimes centred around separate mosques in larger villages, as well as *elkheshi* and *qawm* affiliations, are sought to sustain the stability of social order.

The following parts discuss the role of collective identities in legitimising the political and economic claims of individual actors (part one) and in resolving disputes which arise from these claims (part two).

Contested boundaries of social order

The Government of the Republic of Tajikistan admits that some conditions worsen "fair access to land, in particular for the rural poor" (Government of Tajikistan 2002a: 24). These conditions include (a) costly and complex bureaucratic procedures, (b) imperfect legislation and the absence of legal assistance, and (c) scarce agricultural resources while for example, "arable land totals 0.7 million ha or 0.11 ha per capita" (ibid).

To improve equal access to land and other agricultural resources, the Tajik Government adopted shareholding (*sahmdori*) regulations which re-allocated land and other assets of the former kolkhozes and sovkhozes to their subject employees (Government of Tajikistan 2002b; *Dehqan* Farms 2002). According to the shareholding rules, "[o]nce these shares have been allocated, shareholders become the primary right holders of the property. They may devise their shares to their children, lease them out to the former Kolkhoz/Sovkhoz, lease them out to private farmers, contribute them for use to the charter capital of the former Kolkhoz/Sovkhoz, contribute them permanently to the charter capital of the former Kolkhoz/Sovkhoz, or withdraw the share to farm privately. The important point is that each individual member may decide what to do with his or her share" (Duncan 2000: 2).

However, only a few people, particularly *kolkhozi* elites and some of their local clients, benefited from the land reform campaign during the early 2000s. The Action against Hunger (Great Britain)'s report from October 2003 asserts that the reorganisation and redistribution of farms in the cotton-growing regions of Khatlon province was "a success only on paper." From 1,000 interviewed households in 50 villages, the report revealed that only 3.5 percent of the farmers obtained land and independent farms, while 92.2 percent of ordinary people did not know how to apply for and use their shares (in: Nissen 2004: 5; see also International Crisis Group 2005).

Through the field research, as the two in-depth studies will also show in detail, I observed the increasing discontent of the majority of the local populations, who suffer from extreme economic and political inequality. In this situation, elites refer to collective identities to legitimise their access to strategic positions, professions and properties. Whilst even old men cannot properly remember historical events that have occurred during their lifetime, elites re-invent the histories of their ancestors, descent groups and villages, as well as stories about their personal lives and deeds. As a part of this strategy, they ascribe to their names, statuses and assets and initiate ceremonies, including *khatm*,[53] to seek public acknowledgment of their sacred and inherited rights. Although the Soviet Union destroyed and muddied the waters concerning inherited rights, the claim for inheritance remains a strong source of legitimacy.

The claim about privileged access to resources stresses and revives Islamic and other local affiliations in both cotton-growing and subsistence-based villages. The claimants refer to saints' blessings ('*dasti pir giriftan*'), sacred endowments or preeminent inheritance as the right to a sacred resource (e.g. water spring) or profession.[54] I witnessed several cases where claimants referred to their dream of 'a saint's blessing' as a reason for legitimising privileged access to resources (including land and water). This is especially the case for resources which have not been privatised or integrated as public goods due to unclear and complex legal regulations. For instance, a 'Sufi' from Kulob city came to Busholak village and settled on about 1 hectare of land in order to lead a "cloistered life." He claimed that he had dreamt about his saint, who was originally from this village, and ordered him to return to his "grandfather's land" and "enlighten his grave." While not all local people condoned his presence or claim, he sought additional

---

53 *Khatm* literally means 'to finish reading' the Koran as a sacred practice. In this context *khatm* is a sacred food-sharing celebration which seeks the public acknowledgment of privileged rights, claims and boundaries.

54 Such as a blacksmith, circumcision master, construction master, healer and mullah.

legitimacy by providing them with religious services voluntarily and often free of charge.[55]

The religious reference is vital for legitimising one's claim to not only religious assets but also other important goods, such as land and water because, first of all, these assets and goods have symbolic and sacred meanings, and often they have spiritual and religious values that predetermine who must own them. Without a religious reputation, many would not have legitimate access to such resources. Hence, the pursuit of a religious way of life, including religious practices, knowledge and pilgrimage (Hajj), legitimises wealth and improves connections with powerful men.

The other legitimation source is referencing superior descent origins (such as Sayyids) and personal ties with and blessings from past saints. This reference seeks privileged rights to religious assets, including mosques and shrines. Powerful men try to 'restore' their *shajaranoma* (genealogical book) to claim descent purity and privilege regarding property rights. Some 'Sayyids' of Qumshokh village in the Qabodiyon oasis claimed that their 'descent purity' stems from both paternal and maternal lineages, which reflects their contestation with the current shaykh (the inherited owner) of Chiluchor-Chashma shrine, the most visited and therefore economically profitable sacred site in the Qabodiyon oasis. Another claimant from Sverdlovsk village argued that until his grand-grandfather came to Chiluchor-Chashma village during the Bukhara Emirate's reign, "the local people did not practice Islam in a proper way." He argued that his descent group originates from an Islamic scholar of Bukhara, Abdulloi Nonkattai Bukhoroi (perhaps an idealised personality), who in turn was related to Abdulkadir Gilani, the founder of the Kadiriyyah order:[56] "We come from the ancestral group of Abdulkadir Gilani, who was grand-grandson of *Rasululloh* [i.e. the Islamic prophet Muhammad]. Originally, we were Sayyids, but these [Chiluchor-Chashma shaykhs] think they are."[57]

Although even old men cannot properly remember historical events which have occurred during their lifetime, the claimants re-invent stories about themselves as well as about related symbolic goods. Such contradictory stories result from the political and economic contestations of powerful men, for example in the

---

[55] Personal observation; Shuroobod district (Notebook No 1-3, August 27, 2007: page 14; also tape recording No 53-55).

[56] The Sufi brotherhood, Kadiriyyah, was founded by Abdulkadir Gilani (d. 1166) in Baghdad and spread to Khorasan and Central Asia during the 12th century (Arabov 2004).

[57] Personal interview; Shahritus district (Notebook No 1-1, April 4, 2007: pages 43-46; also tape recording No A-05).

surveyed villages of Shahritus district. A powerful man in Birlyash village, Norburi, assured me that his grandfather resettled the village in 1903 before the Durman tribe arrived from Urganj (currently in Uzbekistan) during the 1930s. He claimed that, thanks to faithful service, his grandfather established kinship ties with his lord (*boy*), the most powerful lord of the village, Mavlon-*boy*. While this man made his claim based on a kinship tie with a powerful *mahalli* man, the Durman claimant, Ergash, who is the *kucha* head and brigadir at the same time, re-told the village's history in his own words. Accordingly, he stemmed from Nuron-*boy*'s descent group, who came from Urganj and resettled in the village in the 16th century, obviously a few hundred years before Mavlon-*boy*, which he backed up by referring to the old village mosque which was built during this time.

Picture 3: The old village mosque

Similarly, the principal mullah of Qahramon village claimed that he built the village mosque in 1987 and thus perpetuated his name by inscribing 'his composed verse' on the door of its storage room.[58] This claim flies in the face of the clear memory of villagers, who assured me that they built the mosque during 1989-90 via a *hashar*.

For the same purpose, in the mountainous communities of Shuroobod district, powerful actors tell individual and descent stories in relation to their villages; the imagined historical events of the villages seek to legitimise their own or delegitimise others' property rights. There is an increasing prevalence of powerful men inventing stories and organising ceremonies to claim inheritances and privileged rights to strategic properties such as land and water resources, gardens, mosques and shrines as well as economically important professions. The open support local state officials lend to *kolkhozi* elites persuade local people that state offices and resources are elites' private properties. Furthermore, local people consider state bureaucratic services, wages and other material forms of support as patronage favours and gifts from elites.

In addition, they acknowledge the inherited privileges of *kolkhozi* elites over properties and positions as former kolkhozes and sovkhozes. Elites, who dominate power structures and resources in the studied villages of Shuroobod district, try to protect their privileges by discrediting rivals as 'provocateurs' and 'strangers' who undermine *qawmdori*. *Qawmdori* is a reference to the merged kinship and Islamic identities of the villagers, which seeks their commitment to peace and stability in the face of increasing political and economic inequalities.

Dispute settlement

In the face of increasing political and economic contestations at the local level, elites search for local means of dispute settlement and conflict prevention. Local people also agree with the elites, in that "the best thing about local self-governance [mahalla] is that problems are settled 'on-site' [Tajik: *'dar joyash'* as well as Russian: '*na mestakh*']."[59] These means of dispute settlement include the moral norms of local people regarding hierarchical relations and collective honour. These norms maintain hierarchical relations between local elites and the subject people, as well as between men and women. The collective honour of the people commits them to these hierarchical relations as attributes of their

[58] The following verse, which I observed in another case, with a slight difference:
Man navishtam dar in makon yagona,
Bimonad az mani miskin nishona [Literal translation: 'I wrote in [built] this place alone, It remains from this poor a token'] (Notebook No 1-1, March 20, 2007: page 3).

[59] Personal interview with the deputy chairman of Dashtijum Jamoat and of JRC 'Dashtijum'; Shuroobod district (Notebook No 1-2, June 13, 2007: pages 11-12).

kinship and religious identities. Mahalla mediators prevent and resolve disputes and complaints by discrediting 'strangers'. Barron et al. (2004) observe a similar response to disputes and conflicts in the case of Indonesian communities, where authorities do not prefer legal means of dispute settlement but rather refer to 'stalemate', that is, the refutation and neglect of powerless disputants.

The mahalla relies on hierarchical practices and institutions inside nuclear and extended families and within religious and neighbourhood circles. My field research affirms that mahalla authorities regulate the behaviour of juniors through their parents (Idiev 2006: 62) as well as through other family seniors and school teachers, which is why the authorities worry about the increasing number of children who remain 'ill-bred' (*betarbiya*) due to the labour migration of their fathers. The presence of mothers, they assure, is not effective, since 'the male awe' (*haybati mard*) is necessary to frighten children into compliance. Besides institutionalising fear, authorities support the family-related religious institution of *vasiyat* (the last will of the father), which ensures the hierarchical subordination and rights of family members. *Vasiyat* is not practiced solely just before the father dies but usually during his old age. This institution enforces the role of the father or the privileged brother as the representative of other family members to the mahalla. Mahalla authorities or elites and their mediators also refer to Islamic identity to intervene in marriage and family relations as the institutional measure of internal control. For this purpose, they pressurise parents to marry off their sons and daughters 'at the proper age for marriage'.

Religious practices, such as public (*jamoa*) prayers, funerals and feasts, also serve to strengthen the hierarchical relations of people. The power of religious notables, who are key members of mahalla authorities, is partly related to the belief of the subject people in their piety and sacredness. They believe and fear that mullahs – and especially eshons (saints) – are capable of calling up and using supernatural forces. In most other cases, however, the authority of religious notables springs from the fear of the people that they will be excluded from the religious community and services. I often witnessed religious authorities frightening the subject people by threatening not to serve (pray) at the funerals of disloyal men. According to common belief, the funeral prayer saves and extends a dead person's soul. Such a struggle for salvation also makes 'the dead slaves', in order to defer to reputable relatives who are at the same time mahalla authorities: "Everyone wants to sit in the heart of his senior, who is the only person to protect his esteem [during his funeral]."

Local institutional bodies, including mosques, *choykhonas* (literally 'tea-houses' – neighbourhood mosques in larger villages) and public schools, serve to reproduce and reinforce hierarchical structures and relations. In part, a *choykhona* reproduces and spreads socially important information and the experiences of mahalla authorities to the younger generation, thus serving to reproduce indigenous practices and the norms of hierarchical interactions. Today, it is also the religious centre of sub-village neighbourhood and kinship communities. In a similar way, village schools and teachers serve to implant the moral norms of hierarchical obedience from an early age. Earnest teachers particularly are reputable among parents, as they ease the burden of child upbringing (*tarbiya*). In turn, mahalla authorities elevate the reputation of teachers and turn public schools into the institutions of moral and physical correction.

These institutional practices shape the mahalla as an internal and hidden structure of social cohesion and control, which sometimes impresses observers as a result of the "unconflictual structure of relations between people" (Idiev 2006: 90). A mahalla is not a state-centristic entity and does not intensively and overwhelmingly govern the body and mind of community members. Instead, *kolkhozi* elites repeatedly refer to collective norms and identities to establish the mahalla as an internal power structure. Similarly, state structures are perceived and integrated as the source of the elites' power. The subject people do not spoil their relations with elites, while the state is perceived as a network used to perpetuate elites' extended influence.

Any disputes, especially when contesting the position and wealth of elites and which are not resolved 'on-site', are claimed to be 'village secrets', so 'strangers' must not know about them at all. This claim usually refers to state structures, including the courts, which have jurisdiction to hear and settle disputes. Also according to common belief, those who publicise their disputes via court betray to the solidarity among the community members, and this internalised norm is so strong that even those who are suffering tend not to divulge their 'secrets'. An old teacher in Qumshokh village in the Shahritus district was angry with the illegal seizure of his land plot by mahalla authorities, but at the same time he was proud of his behaviour, in that that "[he had] never written an *ariza* [complaint letter] against anybody in [his] lifetime,"[60] which was certainly one of the reasons why he eventually withdrew his court appeal.

Collins (2003: 178) explains the avoidance of court deals due to clan identity amongst local populations. My observation goes further and suggests that clan commitment is often enforced by pressure from both traditional and state authorities. Mahalla authorities pressurise people into solving, or dissolving,

[60] Personal interview; Shahritus district (Notebook No 1-1, March 22, 2007: pages 11-13)

their problems by referring to their kinship, village and Islamic norms and honour. Falkingham (2000: 22) also notes that distrust in courts and other state structures plays a critical role in the withdrawal of complaints and disputes.

State authorities, including military officers (chief jamoat interior officers and district interior servants), not only prevent villagers from disputing and solving conflicts through the court system, but they also support mahalla mediators, including religious notables, in discrediting any court deals. They especially highlight shared kinship and the village and Islamic identities of local people reflected in the moral norm of '*qawmdori* honour', or 'village unity'. For the same purpose, although the courts might retain cases unsettled via formal regulations, they will pressurise claimants to dissolve them via religious practices. In this instance, disputes over the distribution of resources (such as land and water) especially are neglected, stigmatised, forcedly suppressed and punished.

A district-level NGO, Arbitrazh, in Shahritus district represents an arbitration (non-state and mediatory) court (*sudi hakamavi*), so both educated lawyers and traditional mediators, including old and religious men as well as some respected women, mediate in disputes. The arbitration courts were established through the support of DFID (UK) on the basis of nine legal advice NGOs set up in nine regional centres of the country, including Shahritus district for the Qabodiyon oasis. Their primary goal was to mediate in disputes and conflicts related to property rights, and in this way to support small enterprises run by especially less favoured people (Arbitrazh 2007). However, as a representative of the NGO 'Arbitrazh' recounted, so far only 5 percent of the appeals have dealt with disputes over agricultural resources (such as land) and small economic enterprises, and the less favoured disputants are very much in the minority. Most of the deals, however, are related to market traders and their creditors in town and district centres.[61]

Political economy of social order

Political economy is an important aspect of local governance, as it enforces the institutional setup of local social order by reproducing economic relations. The following discussion shows how local and state elites use indigenous and external norms, practices and resources to sustain political economy. The subsections below discuss the role of collective identities in enforcing these norms, practices and resources through reciprocal exchanges of families (part

---

[61] Personal interview; Shahritus district (Notebook No 1-7, March 13, 2008: pages 121-122).

one), through the political and economic subjugation of women (part two) and through mobilising the resources of local people, the central state and development programmes (parts three and four).

Reciprocal networks

Reciprocal practices within and beyond extended families are important in maintaining political and economic stability at the local level in the face of increasing inequality. However, in both the mountainous and cotton-growing villages of southern Khatlon, reciprocal networks are mainly reduced to extended families. This condition of socio-economic interaction is first of all connected to the fact that in the region, as in the whole country, "[t]he majority of Tajiks continue to live in large extended families… According to the recent UNDP-World Bank Tajikistan Living Standards Survey (TLSS), two thirds of the population live in a household with three or more adults and children, and mean household size varies between 5.2 in Dushanbe to 8.3 in Regions of Republican Subordination (RRS), with households averaging 7.0 people in GBAO [Badakhshan], 6.1 in Leninabad [Sughd], and 7.7 in Khatlon" (Falkingham 2000: 15).

Extended family members support each other during economic hardship and share resources and means for conducting economic and political activities. Distrust ensuing from indigenous moral norms does not allow people to shape reciprocal exchanges beyond their extended families. A common example is *hashar* (sharing a labour force and some material goods), which is practiced exclusively within single extended families. Family members work together to construct and repair houses, complete agricultural activities and organise group-related ceremonies.

The inclusive *hashar*, which may involve more than one extended family, is organised by mahalla and state authorities. In many cases, though, the reciprocal practices of extended families are not harmonious; therefore, mahalla authorities refer to collective norms and identities to enforce them accordingly. Islamic and kinship affiliations highlight reciprocal norms and institutions such as indebtedness, inheritance and marriage.

Islamic and kinship identities enforce mutual indebtedness between family seniors and juniors, especially parents and their children as well as senior brothers and their more junior brothers. In this regard, parents regard them as 'slaves of their children' and have to feed them, train them in local traditions, transfer their professions to them and marry them off 'at the proper age', all in accordance with indigenous collective norms. In turn, male juniors especially are indebted to serve and take care of their family elders. In common language, 'son' and 'wealth' (*'davlat'*) are synonymous words for junior male members who provide not only labour but also care for family members in their dotage. According to collective norms and practice, care in old age (insurance) is called 'old-age wealth' (*'davlati piri'*). In reciprocation, the 'debt' of the son is not only taken for granted but also is reproduced through everyday discourses and moral pressures. Many family elders and their mahalla mediators would echo an informant, who informed me that "I discharged my debts before them and now it is their turn to return. What you have done, you gain it back. My father took care of his mother."[62] Due to its significance as far as stability is concerned, mahalla mediators also meddle in the public ostracisation of male juniors who do not take care of their older relatives. The discredited and distrusted juniors are thus alienated from important political and social networks and events, including religious ceremonies.

Reference to Islamic and kinship identities also reproduces the reciprocal institutions of the last will (*vasiyat*), patrimonial inheritance, initiation or socialisation celebrations (e.g. *khatm*), marriage and the everyday exchange of food and goods. Mahalla authorities, including extended family elders, commit subject people by interpreting the reciprocal institutions of extended families as Islamic and kinship commitments. Such moral pressure is an effective means of preventing the escalation of family disputes over privileged access to and inheritance of patrimonial (household) goods. Local state officials also arrange inheritance documents according to the local norms of patrimonial inheritance.

The institution of *khatm*, a religious gathering of members of the same extended families, not only ensures the sharing of food and other material goods but also dedicates religious faith and feelings to the initiation or re-initiation of the family members. This measure is especially useful in stabilising challenged kinship relations and thus enforcing solidarity among family members. One of my key informants, a 25-year-old man, had already exceeded 'the proper age' of marriage and therefore not generated any economic income for his family. Moral and psychological forms of pressure were imposed upon him by family members, neighbours, the *kucha* mullah and a female healer. The main concern of his father and other senior members of the extended family was that he may develop a friendship with other unemployed young men due to their collective hobby of dove-breeding. As a result of this pressure, both the young man and his family members believed that wizardry had harmed him and therefore he was experiencing a 'Muslim illness', leaving him without a 'warm hand' to work

---

[62] Personal interview; Shuroobod district (Notebook No 1-2, June 12, 2007: pages 7-10).

for his household and without a 'warm heart' to be married. As such, the healer told him he had to be 'cured', but that this should be done without coercion or pressure from others; rather, attention and inclusion by family members, neighbours, elders and mullahs would 'return' him.

As one of the most effective reciprocal institutions, marriage commits young couples to their extended families. Young men must marry 'Muslim' women who serve their seniors, bring up children and thereby ensure care for elderly relatives. People do not trust women who do not belong to their kinship networks and who may have 'different mores' and 'different ways of life'. Love is thus considered a plight which weakens the courage of men and alienates them from their reciprocal network. Labour migration to Russia hardly changes such perceptions and practices but rather enforces them.

Hence, in order to reduce uncertainties and insecurities for kinship and religious networks around labour migration, *khatm* is increasingly devoted to labour migrants before and after their travel to and from Russia. The (re-)initiation ceremony of *khatm* sanctifies the migrants' family commitment, checks their trustworthiness and religious fidelity and thereby mobilises their financial resources to maintain reciprocal exchanges within the family and sometimes beyond. Today, labour migration invests in the kinship and religious networks of local people, as "[o]ne migrant provides up-keep for between three to ten relatives" (Matveeva 2009: 17). The contribution of this source of income is substantial, since "... each year nearly 10% of the population leaves Tajikistan to seek employment opportunities abroad. Remittances sent home account for more than a 1/3 of national GDP..." (International Organisation for Migration 2011).

Domination over the bodies and minds of women

Domination over the bodies and minds of women is a necessary function of local governance structures, since they make up a prevailing and inexpensive labour force for both subsistence and cotton farms. Practices and discourses shape the female image and work as the 'family face' and honour of related men. If they do not work for their households, including for cotton-growing farms, women are publicly dishonoured and stigmatised, which also dishonours men because it appears that they are being suppressed by their women. Here, several factors are important, including self-perception and collective perceptions about women, the habitus of shame, religious institutions, discourses about female honour and the practices of stigma, as roughly illustrated in Figure 4 below.

Figure 4: Domination over the bodies and minds of women

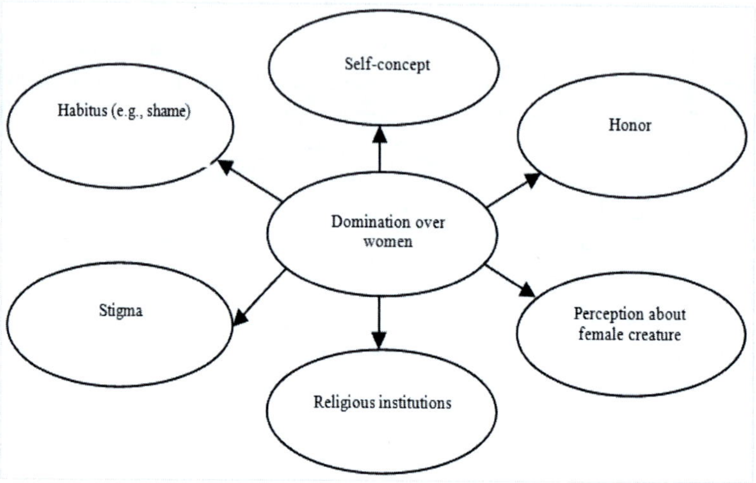

Women are obliged to accept their inferior status within their families and communities. Their emotional preferences and choices regarding family life are a matter of habitus, since they may fall in love with anyone to whom they are betrothed by adult relatives. They must also obey their male adult relatives regarding limited or family-oriented public and economic activities. Falkingham (2000: 7) also observes the difference between male and female status, the latter measured in terms of collectively perceived female functions, especially childbearing and housekeeping. As my research also reveals, the employment of women in public organisations, such as schools, hospitals and *dehqan* farms, is legitimate only when it complements 'household work'. Religious divisions between related (*mahram*) and unrelated (*nomahram*) men enforce this norm by imposing emotional and moral sanctions against face-to-face interactions between women and unrelated males.

Farmers, who especially need women to work on their farms, frequently refer to the Islamic norm whereby women must not independently run public offices or economic enterprises. A woman who has no serious reason why she holds a public position or runs a private business is deemed 'licentious'. Serious reasons include having no male family members of working age (such as a father, husband, brother or son) or disabled male family members.

Such institutionalisation of Islamic norms in post-Soviet Tajikistan gives rise to women's withdrawal from public life and their seclusion in the family circle. Religious norms and discourses that divide men and women include role and status differentiation as well as differences between seniors and juniors. This situation has been observed in the gender gap caused by poor female enrolment in the educational sector: "School enrolments have dropped and there is evidence of a growing gender gap. A recent survey found that 89 percent of boys aged 12-16 in urban areas were enrolled compared with 75 percent of girls; and in rural areas the enrolment rate was 90 percent for boys compared with 80 percent of girls" (Falkingham 2000: xv). Notably, the coercive measures of the Tajik government and the Ministry of Education in recent years have significantly prevented this growing gender gap. However, the differentiated role of women in society is also reflected in the "clear pattern of subject segregation between the sexes, with girls much more likely to study subjects related to health care and education, while boys are more likely to study industry, agriculture, and business related subjects" (ibid. xvi).

The Jamoat Resource Centres (JRCs) of the UNDP, the VOs of the MSDSP and Save the Children are among international development agencies which aim to improve the political and economic status of women. According to the CDD concept of the UNDP, any JRC-related programmes, including microcredit programmes, should involve people at the individual level. The individual involvement of women especially in these programmes should be prioritised over efforts aimed at group representation and mediation (e.g. through family senior members). In fact, 'clients' ('*klients*') of microcredit programmes are mostly senior male family members who serve as contracted debtors and ensure compliance with debt pledges. Female and junior family members are only considered if their male seniors authorise them as contracted debtors or they are in a position to personally ensure the pledges themselves (in the latter case, this applies mostly to widowed women). Alternatively, they serve as mediators for their male seniors if the development programmes require their personal participation. Furthermore, the Islamic institution of *mahramiyat* or division between the related and the unrelated men of women plays a significant role in preventing women from taking the lead in negotiating development programmes dedicated to them. The female informants asserted that any face-to-face interactions with male-dominated programmes would invoke the suspicion of fellow villagers about their distorted engagement.

As well as *mahramiyat* and women's inferior access to patrimonial goods play crucial role in indigenizing developmental design of other economic activities of women. For example, in 2007, a JRC launched a sewing workshop for 20 seamstresses in Sayyod village as a way of improving their economic and political roles. However, for women, sewing has a completely different meaning: it represents the secluded family status of mainly unmarried girls who are 'searching for their luck'. Also, traditionally, seamstresses can usually only offer their services to members of their reciprocal networks, to so-called 'familiar' ('*donista*') people, including kinswomen, friends and friendly neighbours. Therefore, a sewing workshop is not an attractive proposition for women,[63] and is in direct opposition to the notion that a female *kolkhozi* elite member, the head of the women's council ruling a collective farm, monopolises all work and the flow of other development resources.

The day of 14th December 2007 heralded the opening of an enterprise building in the village, which was visited by representatives from the local office and the Dushanbe headquarters of the donor organisation. Before the 'guests' arrived, people responsible for the project, including the head of a JRC and the head of the women's council, explained to twenty female stakeholders what was involved in the 'project'. They explained a few accountability 'secrets', in that "If the *foreigners* [meaning international representatives of the donor organisation] ask, you must tell that we know the budget of the project, which is 8,000 USD, and you must tell them that our contribution is 30 percent of this amount." This measure is used to prepare for accountability questions that an international delegation usually asks 'stakeholders' about.[64]

Not only did family-secluded seamstresses dislike the monopoly of their profession by an elites workshop, but also the location of the enterprise troubled the male prayers, including the mahalla authorities, who felt that the presence of women would "spoil a sacred site." The workshop was situated inside the new village mosque, which was formerly a cultural club under the Soviet kolkhoz. The jamoat mediated to assign one corner of the building to the workshop.

---

63 Personal interview with a private seamstress; Sayyod village; Shahritus district (Notebook No 1-5, December 25, 2007: pages 120-121).

64 Personal observation; Sayyod village; Shahritus district (Notebook No 1-5, December 14, 2007: pages 108-110).

Picture 4: Opening ceremony for the female workshop and preparation of the male community for a Kurban holiday in the same building

On the day of the opening ceremony, both parts of the building were full of workers: women (in the room on the left-hand side) waited for their guests, in order to represent their 'development' *project*, and men worked in other rooms (on the right-hand side) to prepare the new mosque for the upcoming Kurban feast. The elders (sitting and observing in front) were furious about some women 'trampling' over their [men's] sacred site and therefore sought how to avoid from them:

> Elder 1 (to Elder 2 and Elder 3): Women should not come and go here… I said to you before: the sewing workshop should not have been placed here, it is the mosque, people [men] come to prayer, what do women do here?! Some of them are *benamoz* ['dirty'; according to the religious norm relating to menstruating women]!
>
> Elder 2: Benefaction is good [he means the room repaired by the donor organisation for sewing]. One person [he means the donor organisation] comes from a different place [foreign country] and builds something, so it is good. Finally he leaves, and the place remains in good repaired order. Let them have

> the workshop for now; later, we will find a solution [he means to move them to another place and integrate the room as a part of the mosque].
>
> Elder 1: Let them have the "Tojikmatlubot" shop [a small shopping centre built during Soviet rule and currently unused while the former shopkeeper claims for it], not the mosque![65]

Other areas of female employment and development programmes also face similar challenges. The public employment of women is based on the differentiation between the two 'worlds' of men and women (see Table 3 below: Male and female distribution of wage labour).

---

[65] Personal observation of a talk between Elder 1 (Mahkam Boyakov), Elder 2 (Shoniyoz Eshniyozov) and Elder 3 (Ochil Teshaev) (Notebook No 1-5, December 14, 2007: pages 108-110; also tape recordings No DS 300242-244). As I observed during my recent field visit on April 7-12, 2012, the sewing workshop was removed from this public place and privatised by the female elite member. The room designated and repaired for the workshop was privatised by Elder 1's son, who at the same time was the mosque's muezzin (clergyman calling people to prayer).

Table 3: Male and female distribution of wage labour

#	State, international and private employment	Number of workers	Female workers	Average monthly salary
1	Cotton *dehqan* farms and *brigadas*	278	251	10
2	Petty trade of agricultural harvests (fruits and vegetables etc.)	34	22	70
3	Schools	46	19	110
4	Hospitals and medical centres	21	14	45
5	Bazaars, shops and stalls	15	8	150
6	District and Jamoat governments	7	3	130
7	Shahritus cotton plant	65	2	200
8	District fire station	6	1	130
9	District trucking company	1	0	24
10	State security office	3	0	70
11	Water technical centre UNKOS-PMK-24	10	0	90
12	Hired construction worker (in Qabodiyon oasis)	23	0	100
13	District electricity company	4	0	150
14	Horse transport (*asparoba*)	3	0	150
15	Railway	29	0	250
16	Private entrepreneurship workshops	2	0	250
17	Taxi	20	0	370
18	INGOs	4	0	550
19	Professional masters (masters of truck, construction workers, traditional masters, etc.)	8	0	600

Source: Personal survey (October 2007 – March 2008)

In contrast to male employment, female employment in public offices is related to family status as a housekeeper. Their work is perceived and interpreted as part of their family duties, while individual economic income is regarded as 'dangerous'. Women are not expected to generate or possess economic wealth or have their say on the economic and political choices of their families. My male informants were also concerned that emancipated women may 'damage' their superior status.

Some 'emancipated' women (e.g. a widowed female labour migrant and some petty traders who refused to work in the cotton fields) were stigmatised publicly, which further complicated their individual generation of economic wealth. Stigmatisation also sanctions women's economic and political participation beyond kinship networks. For example, in 2004, the international development agency Save the Children established a village support centre (VSC) for Sayyod village in an attempt to encourage the broader political representation of women. The VSC aimed to mobilise monthly fees received from the villagers to implement social programmes dedicated to the wellbeing of women. Family adults were selected as VSC members, while female members ran the organisation. Each family was represented by two male and female members, who together paid 40 diram[66] per month. The members paid fees until Save the Children, in 2005, distributed aid and grants for the rural population and public projects. After Save the Children left the district, the head of the VSC attempted in vain to collect fees again and save the centre. Some people, however, complained that "she begs from home to home, even for a few dirams." Finally, before the VSC was disintegrated, its remaining fund of 80 TJ Somoni[67] was allocated to a pregnant woman whose husband was working in Russia. When her neighbours refused to carry the pregnant woman to the district hospital 6 km faraway, the head of the VSC hired a taxi and took her to the hospital. At the price of the short-lived organisation she saved the life of woman and her newborn child.

Indigenous and external (state and development) support schemes

Elites and their mahalla mediators (re-)distribute indigenous and external (state and development) support schemes in order to maintain social and political cohesion and control over local people. Redistribution practices organised especially through religious and customary ceremonies (including funerals and feasts) serve this purpose. Through these settings, mahalla authorities express and actualise their concerns and agendas for socio-political stability in their communities. Here, the '*tinji*' discourse (literally 'tranquility' or 'peace')[68] is crucial, as it generates fear through recollections of the recent civil war (see also Heathershaw 2007). Elites' abusive spread of the idea of *tinji* endures the highly contested social and normative structures of Tajik society. The *tinji* discourse

---

[66] 100 dirams are equal to 1 TJ Somoni. During 2006-2007, 1 USD was equal to 3.4 TJ Somoni, and 40 dirams were equal to about 0.12 USD or 12 USD cents.

[67] During 2006-2007, 1 USD was equal to 3.4 TJ Somoni.

[68] The claim for '*tinji*' implies the 'peace' or 'stability' of reciprocal and patron-client patterns of kinship ties and political and economic (including bureaucratic) relations.

actualises collective 'norms of identification' (as defined by Hardin 1995), such as *qawmdori* (shared village, kinship and Islamic identity), '*qawmdori* honour' (i.e. honour of descent or kinship affiliation) and 'good neighbourhoods' (*hamsoyadori*).[69] These collective norms of identification with village, kinship or descent groups and neighbourhoods commit people to support each other through their indigenous reciprocal practices and networks.

However, not all, especially so-defined 'poor' ('*bechora*'), people are involved in the indigenous support networks of extended families and neighbourhoods. Therefore, both state elites and their mahalla mediators redesign and reshape (*tanzim*) indigenous support practices and networks as well as "redistribute state and local resources in favour of tranquillity and peace of the people."[70] To modify networks and redistribute resources, they refer to *qawmdori* which commits local people to 'tranquillity and peace'. The Law on *Tanzim* was adopted in 2007 to legalise such stabilisation efforts and the activities of local authorities.

State support schemes are integrated and interpreted in a way which broadens the increasing division between elites and marginalised people. Thus, 'welfare' schemes (e.g. retirement pensions, poverty allowances, mahalla funds, etc.) and modified indigenous institutions (e.g. *sadaqa*) serve to categorise and thereby control those recognised as 'poor' such as orphans, widowed women, the handicapped and old men without aid.[71]

According to state categorisation within the framework of the World Bank-run Poverty Reduction Strategy Paper (PRSP), poverty is a politically sensitive issue. The officially accepted Tajik term for 'poverty', '*kambizoati*', refers to those "layers of the population in Tajikistan" who need economic support. The discourse rejects the term '*qashshoqi*', which in popular understanding means 'poverty', thus implying a category of people devoid of any economic opportunities. Hence, the terms 'poor' and 'poverty' are translated as '*kambizoat*' and '*kambizoati*' to suggest that Tajik society is not impoverished to such a point

---

[69] *Hamsoyadori:* 'a good neighbourhood' – a normative standard which is the attribute of both village and religious identities highlighted vis-à-vis other sub-village neighbourhoods.

[70] Personal observation; Chairman of the ideological department of the Government of Khatlon province, Qurghonteppa City (Notebook No 1-1, April 2, 2007: page 39).

[71] The President's message to the joint sitting of the lower and higher chambers of the Parliament of Tajikistan (broadcast on 20th April 2011 on the Tajik 1st Channel at 20:00-21:30) emphasised the further institutionalisation of such practices through government structures.

that would legitimise the claims of opponents at any level (see for comparison Babajanian 2006; Government of Tajikistan 2002a; Falkingham 2000).

Rather, aid and development resources are mobilised and redistributed according to local "perceptions of what is meant by poverty" (Falkingham 2000: 85). The Tajik Government (Government of Tajikistan 2002a: 20) and the World Bank (2001, in Bretton Woods Project 2002: 3) also admit that in practical local terms dealing with poverty is rather more complicated and multidimensional than the formal identification of vulnerable groups (such as women, invalids and orphans) implies. Due to a misunderstanding of local realities, these 'vulnerable groups' are isolated from other segments of society. Hence, support schemes, including Cash Compensation Programmes (CCPs) of the state and the aid programmes of international agencies, do not significantly improve, as expected, local reality despite the fact that both state and international support schemes and resources involve almost all 'vulnerable groups' (Nygaard et al. 2005: 2).

Resource mobilisation for collective action

Elites and mahalla mediators use indigenous and modified practices of resource mobilisation to maintain their political and economic structures and infrastructure for very low economic outlay. At the same time, the wellbeing of important assets, such as public and economic infrastructure and sacred goods (e.g. mosque and shrine), improves their mediatory reputation and thereby legitimises political and economic privileges. In order to commit subject people to such practices, they highlight *qawmdori* i.e. village identity and its multivocal and merged references to religious and kinship boundaries.

State policy instigated by central state elites, including the president, publicly encourages district governors to follow the 'examples' of Shahritus and Mu'minobod districts. The governors of these 'exemplary' districts personally engage with mobilising internal resources, including through *hashar* and *khayriya* in villages. Indeed, during my field stay in these districts, district and jamoat government officials intensively and effectively organised *hashar* in many villages to repair and construct new schools, religious buildings, roads and bridges, to clean irrigation infrastructure and to plant trees. Financial, material and labour resources were mobilised from different sources, including individual households, wealthy men, farmers, economic enterprises, mahalla and mosque funds, local and international NGOs and state departments.

Without reference to collective identities, however, people do not participate very readily in so-called 'common wellbeing' activities. For this reason, *kolkhozi* elites use the mediation role of their local mediators and clients, such as elders, *oqsaqols*, veterans (former state elites) and religious notables and saints (including eshons and hajis). These mediators reshape the scope of indigenous institutions involved in resource mobilisation, which are otherwise practiced exclusively within their indigenous (mainly family) networks. This applied to village-level *hashars* in many villages in which I did my field observation and survey. Authorities and notables refer to collective identities and norms to generate collective commitment and to compensate for the lack of solidarity among rural inhabitants. For example, in Jam'iyati dehqon village in the Shahritus district, the decision of the mahalla and jamoat authorities to establish a 'communal wellbeing fund' failed, since they could not mobilise the mediation of some notables.[72] In most villages, labour migrants provide financial support to maintain mosques, shrines and other assets which symbolise their sub-village group or categorical (such as extended family, descent group and ethnicity) identities.

Through the mediation of local notables, the 'successful' Shahritus government reshaped *hashar* to clean irrigation infrastructure and to harvest raw cotton in its cotton-growing villages. To invoke the merged or overlapping sense of village honour and religious commitment, veterans, pilgrims and Qabodiyon Eshon[73] announce and personally initiate *hashar* in religious settings. Mahalla mediators modify the collection and distribution practices of *khayriya* (individual donations, mostly on a Friday, and other public prayers during religious feasts), which are used primarily to maintain sacred assets. Similarly, state elites, local mahalla and religious authorities collect and redistribute religious taxes (such as *zakot* and *ushr*) and support the practice of *sadaqa*, which is collected and distributed through the limited religious networks of kinsmen especially.

In addition, the functional capacity of external (such as development) programmes on 'common wellbeing' and 'local entrepreneurship' depends on their adaptation to the indigenous practices of resource mobilisation. Reference to collective identities interprets and thereby adapts programmes into the collective norms of local people. For instance, microcredit programmes of JRCs in Shahritus and Shuroobod districts could not achieve their primary goal "to organise the class of local entrepreneurs, in part from among female traders."[74]

---

[72] Personal interview with the imam-khatib and deputy vakil of Jam'iyati dehqon village; Shahritus district (Notebook No 1-1, April 10, 2007: pages 53-54).

[73] Qabodiyon Eshon (Eshon-i Abdulhamidkhon) is the most respected spiritual Sufi leader of the *mahalli* people (*mahalli* Tajiks, Uzbek tribes, other Uzbek groups and Arabs) of the Qabodiyon oasis. Only *kuhistoni* Tajiks do not acknowledge him as their spiritual leader.

[74] Personal interview with the deputy chairman of JRC 'Dashtijum', Dashtijum Jamoat; Shuroobod district (Notebook No 1-2, June 13, 2007: pages 11-12).

In fact, the 'class' consists of the indigenous reciprocal networks of families and neighbours while accommodating female entrepreneurs in their inferior patrimonial status.

The head of a VO shared his experience of the MSDSP-organised workshop set up by development brokers: "[I]t is impossible to convince people that their 'debt to God' can be paid off if they give their *zakot* to village organisations."[75] People contribute their *sadaqa* and *khayriya*, which act in part as cash support for the poor and those suffering as a result of natural disasters, but only if their village and religious identities are highlighted in relation to *others*, including other villages and 'infidels'. An illustrative case was the mobilisation of financial means to support the families of an adjacent village who suffered from a spring flood. The jamoat committed the vakil of a subject village, who was also the head of the VO, to collect 3 TJ Somoni (about 0.8 USD) from each household. An old man refused to contribute, instead blaming the suffering families for their 'careless' settlement on a flood-prone zone. While they talked on a newly constructed bridge, the vakil sought to convince him to contribute by highlighting his Islamic identity. He said that "*a foreign state* has collected 15,000 [USD] *khayriya* from its people and built the bridge on which we now stand. The infidels are doing *khayriya*. But we are Muslims!" The old man immediately took 10 TJ Somoni from his pocket and told him: "I have borrowed it, [take it], both my own and my son's [contributions]."[76]

In this way the development brokers advised to adapt the development activities into indigenous moral norms and institutional practices.

The case of cotton growing and harvest

State (cotton) and *kolkhozi* elites and their local mediators effectively mobilise local populations to carry out intensive but underpaid work in the cotton fields. I observed similar processes in Sayyod, Budyon, Leninobod, Ayvoj, Jam'iyati dehqon and Birlyash villages in the Shahritus district as well as Komsomol village in the Nosiri Khusrav district. Elites favour and enable local clients and mediators, powerful men and mahalla authorities, to run privileged *dehqan* farms. These "Soviet-style working units" (Christophe 2003: 198; Nissen 2004: 5) are effective ways of committing related family and *qawm* co-members to cotton-growing activities. Elites personally visit the cotton fields and family ceremonies of their cliental farmers, and during the sowing and harvest seasons

---

[75] Personal observation; MSDSP Workshop in Doghiston village; Shuroobod district (Notebook 1-2, June 7, 2007: pages 1-3).
[76] Ibid.

they reward them with material and symbolic goods. As one of the farmers, the holder of countless Soviet awards, told me, "I am old and suffer from blood pressure problems. But the district governor came to my birthday and asked me to get additional land and promised to register it for free and to provide me with technical facilities."[77]

Elites also 'ask' for the mediation of veterans, respected elders and religious notables, including Qabodiyon Eshon, to ensure an intensive cotton harvest. Their initiation of the harvest *hashar* symbolises it as both a '*qawmdori* good' and the 'religious debt' of 'their people'. Seasonal and religious ceremonies during the early sowing season (e.g. food-share rituals of *oshi kucha*, *darveshi*, *chorshanbegi* and *sumanakpazi*) articulate the distinct identity of larger neighbourhoods (*kucha*) and thereby enforce their cotton-growing 'communities' or farms.

Farmers and their mediators also highlight family honour, descent and ethnic identities in order to sustain the institution of *agat* (an Uzbek word for 'bed of cotton'). An *agat* is a unit the physical size of a cotton field, which is interpreted as a symbolic good of individual families. Commitment to this size manifests in subject families' deference to their *qawm* (descent or ethnic) and *qawmdori* honours and norms. Family members work in a designated *agat* during the cotton-growing season, which runs from December through to August.

The so-called '*agat* regime' was invented by an Arab brigadir in Budyon village in 1967.[78] The Arabs were relocated to the cotton-growing plantations of Budyon village in Shahritus district from their home, Qizilkedman village, in the desert area of Beshkent (currently Nosiri Khusrav district). The Arab population collectively refused to live and work for the cotton plantations and attempted to return to their home village, following which the kolkhoz and jamoat chairpersons coercively convinced the Arabs to stay in their new abode. The Arab elders, who mediated in favour of the elites, selected a new brigadier, who, in the second year of the job, introduced the '*agat regime*'. This practice divided up the cotton fields equally between households, measured by *agat* (the cotton bed), as their *qawm* and *qawmdori* committed them to work through the entire cotton-growing season, except the cotton harvesting period. Being more than an economic incentive, this successful institution highlighted the Arabs' local identities vis-à-vis other descent and ethnic groups. Thus, the commitment of Arab households was generated to work in the cotton plantations of Budyon village. Later, this practice was inculcated by the then

---

[77] Personal interview with the heroic female farmer; Budyon village; Shahritus district (Notebook No 1-7, March 14, 2008: pages 123-124).

[78] Personal interview; Budyon village; Shahritus district (Notebook No 1-7, March 14, 2008: page 124; also tape recording No DS 300313).

kolkhoz chairman, 'Cotton Hero', in other villages, which led to 'heroic' status throughout the Soviet Union.

The similarly adapted institution of cotton harvesting is *norma* (a Russian word for 'quota'), which commits individual families to a certain size of cotton harvest. Its performance also praises the moral qualities of the committed families and their loyalty to their ethnic, village and family identities. A case from Ayvoj village illustrates the interplay between local identities and the institutional practice of *norma* in the cotton harvest. The chairman of the Ayvoj collective farm could not find a brigadir for 57 hectares (out of 300 hectares of total land). Then, the chairman of the jamoat, the head of the mahalla and Qabodiyon Eshon, gathered the villagers to select a brigadir. Even the threat of the chairman to mobilise his interior officers could not solve the problem: nobody wanted to take on the burden of the brigada. Next day, immediately after Friday prayer in the village mosque, local elites and notables discussed the problem with those who had attended prayer and negotiated to equally distribute the remaining hectares to every household, according to the *norma* system. The negotiations were achieved partly due to the equal commitment of all village families to their *norma* and partly due to the pressuring rumour that the Qabodiyon Eshon "was offended by some men due to their doubt in God [*shakkoki*]" at the previous meeting. Here, disobedience to the saint was interpreted as the highest sin (*shakkoki*, i.e. doubt in the omnipresent and omnipotent God), and consequently *norma* gained sacred status.[79]

Without reference to collective identities, including Islam, descent and kinship affiliations, *kolkhozi* elites could not sustain the cotton sector, which generates only a small economic income for the majority of cotton workers. Rather, most working age men withdraw from the cotton farms and migrate to Russia to look for better opportunities,[80] thus leaving the cotton sector almost exclusively under the responsibility of women and children (see also International Crisis Group 2005: 19). Female and junior cotton workers are paid miserable salaries, which have less economic but more material value, as their involvement in cotton-growing 'communities' (i.e. farms) ensures their inclusion in reciprocal

---

[79] Personal observation; Ayvoj village; Shahritus district (Notebook No 1-1, April 19-24, 2007: pages 77-90).

[80] For example, 70 percent of young men from Qumshokh village, 30 percent from Qahramon village, 90 percent from the *mahalla* (neighbourhood) of *kuhistoni* Tajiks in Birlyash village, about 300 men from 280 households of Jam'iyati dehqon, more than 600 men from 480 households of Sayyod village, most of the young men from Qizilaskar village in the Shahritus district, most of the young men of Okhundboboev village in the Qabodiyon district and of Sangonel village of Dashtijum Jamoat in the Shuroobod district (Personal survey; March 2007 – April 2008).

networks. According to reciprocal practices and related moral norms, salaries for women and juniors are not desirable. Many senior informants believe that salary or cash payment makes women and juniors arrogant – and thus alien to their families. These informants believe that women and young men do not always spend their salaries on their households but rather engage in 'dangerous' deeds as they have financial means.

To work in the cotton fields without any exclusive demands, such as a salary, is interpreted as a necessary quality of a woman, as it acts as the manifestation of her industrious attitude to housekeeping and loyalty to her family. Here, different local terms (such as 'kolkhoz worker', 'housekeeper', 'unemployed' and so on) therefore describe the same traits of female workers from the cotton farms. The parallel use of these terms is reasonable, since none of them implies any form of individual economic income (see also Falkingham 2000: xv). As women have no actual right to land or other agricultural resources, the situation enslaves them, not only in favour of their families (Nissen 2004: 6) but also especially in favour of the cotton sector. This observation also criticises the assumption that the cotton sector improves women's access to educational and professional fields of the society (e.g. Idiev 2006: 60).

Chapter conclusion

In this chapter I have identified three mainstream aspects of local governance in the southern Khatlon region. These aspects, as summarised in the sections below, are (1) inclusive and elite-dominated political structures, (2) the legitimation and mediation of property rights and (3) the stabilisation of socio-political and economic situations at the local level.

Inclusive and elite-dominated political organisation of social order

As observed, there are two different types of political organisation relating to local social order in the southern Khatlon communities of Tajikistan. These are (1) the inclusive structure of mahallas in cotton-growing rural communities and (2) the elite-dominated structure of mahallas in subsistence-based villages.

In the cotton-growing (Qabodiyon, Shahritus and Nosiri Khusrav) districts of the Qabodiyon oasis, most of the political actors, including elders, *oqsaqols*, religious notables, powerful men, farmers and state functionaries of the jamoat, participate in the decision-making activities of mahallas. The collective identities of local people (including village identity, sub-village and kinship affiliations and Islam), therefore have an integrative function in rural communities which are typically heterogeneous in ethnic composition and large in population size. Everyday religious practices, regular ceremonies and neighbourhood seasonal food-sharing activities (such as prayer, weddings, funerals, religious and seasonal feasts of Ramadan, Kurban, *khatm*, *elkhudoi*, *nawruzi*, etc.) serve to highlight this function of collective identities. Reference to these identities also commits local people to obey their mahalla authorities, including elders, *oqsaqols* and powerful men from extended families and *qawm* (descent) groups, mullahs of the *kucha* neighbourhoods and other local notables. Mahallas were dysfunctional in the cases of Jam'iyati dehqon and Qizilaskar villages in Shahritus district, where they did not represent all family and religious notables. Local elites and notables seek to maintain the integrative structure and function of the mahalla in order to achieve solidarity amongst cotton workers through family ties, descent groups and neighbourhood cotton farms.

State elites do not exercise a monopoly over economic activities in the mountainous, subsistence-based rural communities of Shuroobod and Mu'minobod districts. Additionally, many of these communities are ethnically homogenous and small in population size. These are basic conditions that the state officials do not see necessary for shaping integrative political structures in mountainous communities, so only a few powerful men, so-called *kolkhozi* elites, who rely on their patron-client network with the local state and religious authorities, represent the mahalla's political structure. Here, collective identities, including *qawmdori* (the shared notion of village, kinship and religious identities), are not used to bring villagers under the authority of the mahalla. Rather, elites and their competitors use them to claim privileged political positions and economic rights. In such a context, I therefore talk about contested boundaries rather than about integrated boundaries, the latter observed in cotton-growing communities.

Likewise, newly introduced development structures, including VOs of the MSDSP in the studied districts, have been integrated into mahallas and consequently dominated by elites. We have observed desperate contestations in cases where VOs have not been dominated by elites. To reduce the contested boundaries of *qawmdori*, for example, the government of Shuroobod district has recently taken into consideration 'the experience of Mu'minobod', the adjacent district. Mu'minobod's governor 'succeeded' in the integrative political organisation of subject villages and thus in adapting development structures and programmes into mahallas and other local institutions.

The 'success' of Mu'minobod district depended substantially on frequent reference to local people's collective norms and identities. Participatory village mapping, which mobilises local people to map out the future programmes of

VOs in individual villages, introduced them as an Islamic institution of 'common wellbeing'. The reference to Islam committed the villagers to this institution and the mosque served as a setting that ritualises mapping exercises and thereby legitimises VOs as male worshippers' networks. The adapted development structures of VOs as well as JRCs differentiate between senior and junior and between male and female members.

Contrary to male employment, female employment binds women to their status as housekeepers. Their work is perceived and interpreted as being part of their household tasks, while any individual economic income is regarded as 'dangerous'. This norm adapts female-dedicated development programmes, which aim to improve the women's political and economic status, into male-dominated economic activities. Furthermore, 'emancipated' women are publicly stigmatised to prevent any attempt to generate individual sources of economic income or to establish female-run public organisations relating to common wellbeing and resource mobilisation.

Recipients also adapt the development programmes of 'common wellbeing' and 'local entrepreneurship' into their indigenous practices and networks of resource exchange. One example is microcredit programmes of JRCs, which could not organise the 'class' of local entrepreneurs, in part, from among female traders. The 'class' consists of family and neighbourhood networks while subjugating female entrepreneurs to their patrimonial status. A strategic tool of the state and local authorities is the discourse about 'foreigners' categorising and adapting development structures. Consequently, state and local elites not only dominate the power structures of integrated INGOs but also shape the prioritised aspects of their activities. Furthermore, they mediate to distribute development 'projects' to their clients, to those who obey 'orders' in rural communities.

Legitimation and mediation of individual actors' property rights

In both the mountainous and lowland districts of the study region, increasing economic and political inequality intensifies the discontents of local people. Here, elites refer to people's collective identities to legitimise their privileged access to strategic positions, professions and properties. While even old men do not properly remember historical events that have occurred during their lifetime, powerful men nevertheless re-invent histories of their ancestors, descent groups and villages and tell far-fetched stories about their personal lives and deeds. As part of this strategy, they endow status and assets to their names and initiate sacred ceremonies (like *khatm*) to seek the public acknowledgment of their inheritance rights. The claimants refer to saints' blessings, sacred endowments or preeminent inheritance for important resources and professions. Often, these resources and professions have spiritual and religious values that predetermine who has the right to own them. Without religious reputation, many powerful men are barely able to legitimise privileged access to such resources. Hence, the pursuit of a religious way of life, including religious practices, pilgrimage (Hajj) and the possession of relevant knowledge, are necessary to improve one's religious reputation.

The other legitimation source is reference to superior (such as Sayyid) descent origins and personal ties with and blessings from past saints. Such references seek privileged rights to religious assets such as mosques and shrines. Hence, claimants recover genealogical books (*shajaranoma*) 'destroyed' by the 'infidel' Soviet state, which indicate their inherited property rights. These books re-invent stories which tell how the claimants are related to assets to which they claim ownership. In the same village each claimant retells the history of the village in his own version while contradicting others' stories. Religious ceremonies, especially *khatm*, also serve the same purpose in proclaiming inherited rights to strategic properties such as land plots, water sources, gardens, mosques and shrines as well as to profitable professions.

Mainly in the subsistence-based communities of mountainous districts, *kolkhozi* elites dominate political and economic structures and resources. They maintain their domination by discrediting their rivals as 'provocateurs' and 'strangers' who thus undermine *qawmdori*. *Qawmdori* is reference to the merged kinship and Islamic identities of villagers in order to seek solidarity with and loyalty to elites.

In response to increasing disputes, state and local authorities use indigenous or 'on-site' mechanisms of dispute settlement in both mountainous and cotton-growing communities. Local people also agree with the authorities that "the best thing about local self-governance [mahalla] is that problems are resolved 'on-site'." Such institutional practices shape mahalla as an internal and hidden mediatory structure of social cohesion and control, which sometimes presses home to observers "the unconflictual structure of relations between people."

Indigenous means of dispute settlement involve the moral norms of local people about hierarchical relations and collective honour. These relations differentiate between elites and the subject people and between men and women. In order to sustain and justify these highly contested norms, authorities refer to Islam and kinship-related (locality, village, *qawm*) identities of the subject people. In many cases, subordination to mahalla authorities is interpreted as 'village honour' vis-à-vis 'strangers'. Reference to 'family honour' regulates the behaviour of juniors through parents and senior family members and enforces the institutions of patrimonial inheritance which ensure the political and economic inferiority of women and juniors to senior family members. Elites thus involve older family members in dispute settlement within and beyond individual families.

Reference to religious identity also shapes the hierarchical subordination of local people to religious authorities, which subsequently generates fear of the spiritual power of saints and mullahs to disturb the peace and to provoke God's anger through exclusion from religious communities and services. Mosques and public schools also serve to reproduce the indigenous practices and norms of hierarchical structures and relations. Mahalla and religious authorities raise the reputation of teachers and turn public schools into institutions of moral and physical punishment.

Any disputes which especially contest the position and wealth of *kolkhozi* elites and do not find a solution 'on-site' are categorised as 'village secrets'. 'Strangers' (e.g. inhabitants of adjacent villages and guests from other regions, including researchers) must not know about them. In such cases, court deals are discredited as distorted behaviour and as a betrayal to 'village honour', and this internalised norm is so strong that even suffering men shun openly discussing these 'secrets'. Mahalla authorities pressurise people into solving problems and conflicts (e.g. over resource distribution) by reference to their kinship, village and Islamic norms and honours. Elites support their mahalla mediators in preventing court deals and neglecting, stigmatising and finally resolving disputes through 'on-site' or indigenous means. They especially highlight merged kinship, village and Islamic identities, thus committing villagers to the norms of subordination and loyalty.

Political and economic stabilisation of social order

The reproduction and modification of the reciprocal goods and practices of mutual support and 'common wellbeing' maintain political and economic stability at the village level. In both mountainous and cotton-growing villages of the study region, reciprocal practices (such as mutual support during economic hardship and *hashar*) are limited mainly to extended families. Distrust and indigenous moral norms do not allow people to extend these reciprocal exchanges beyond their extended families. Also, within extended families, senior members have to refer to 'family honour' to mobilise juniors in reciprocal practices, including *hashar*, parental commitment to children and junior members' commitment to caring for older relatives. Reference to Islamic and kinship identities is also sought to reproduce the reciprocal institutions of patrimonial inheritance, initiation or socialisation celebrations, marriages and the everyday exchange of food and goods. These practices, especially the (re-)initiation ceremony of *khatm*, serve to maintain solidarity among family members and to ostracise disloyal members. *Khatm*, in part, reminds labour migrants of their religious commitment to their families, checks trustfulness and religious fidelity by redistributing financial means through reciprocal practices and fixes patrimonial status during labour migration and after reintegration into their home communities. Mahalla authorities refer to collective norms and identities to commit the villagers to these reciprocal institutions of political and economic stabilisation.

State elites and their mahalla mediators (re-)distribute internal and external (state and development) support schemes to enforce the indigenous networks of extended families, descent groups and neighbourhoods. As these support schemes are insufficient, authorities distribute the discourse of '*tinji*' (tranquility and peace) to commit villagers to the networks of political subordination and economic exchange. References to the collective norms and identities of *qawmdori* (shared village, kinship and religious identities), '*qawmdori* honour' (honour of descent group) and 'good neighbourhoods' actualise this discourse. Since indigenous support networks do not involve some poor families, mahalla and state authorities mediate to redistribute support resources. Here, they refer to *qawmdori* to modify indigenous support practices and networks. Also, in 2007, the central government adopted the Law on *Tanzim* (2007) to underpin this modification through the formal means of the state.

State 'welfare' schemes additionally strengthen the hierarchical differentiation between elites and subject people at the local level. These schemes include retirement pensions, poverty allowances, mahalla funds and the modified indigenous institutions of *khayriya* and *sadaqa*. They serve to categorise and thereby subjugate politically recognised 'unsafe' 'poor' people, especially orphans, widowed women, handicapped and old men without aid.

The indigenous and modified practices of resource mobilisation are also used to maintain the wellbeing of political and economic structures and infrastructure in villages at low economic cost. These institutional practices include *hashar*, *shanbegi* and *khayriya* which mobilise financial, in-kind and labour resources to repair and construct schools, religious assets, roads and bridges, to clean irrigation infrastructure and to harvest raw cotton. Other modified institutions include the reciprocal practices of mutual support (such as modified *khayriya*, *sadaqa* and religious taxation institutions of *zakot* and *ushr*) which improve the reputation and material power of elites and their mahalla mediators.

As the state lacks the resources to intervene, mahalla mediators therefore commit subject people to such practices by highlighting their collective identities (such as *qawmdori* as a shared village, kinship and religious affiliation). By reference to the shared notions of *qawmdori*, mediators, such as family elders, *oqsaqols*, state veterans and religious notables, extend the scopes of the indigenous institutions of resource mobilisation, otherwise practiced mainly within limited (especially family) networks. Such mediation is also necessary to mobilise labour migrants' financial resources for practices involved in 'common wellbeing'.

In cotton-growing communities, state and mahalla authorities mobilise the labour resources of local people for cotton-growing activities. *Kolkhozi* elites favour and oblige clients and mediators, who are powerful and respectable men in their communities, to run cotton farms. Such political organisation of the farms is an effective means of committing relatives, *qawm* and neighbourhood co-members to cotton-growing activities. The intensive cotton harvest is also organised through the mediation of the mahalla authorities, including elders, veterans and religious notables. These mediators interpret the cotton harvest as a symbolic attribute of people's kinship and Islamic 'good' and 'debt'. Seasonal and religious ceremonies, including food-sharing rituals, highlight the distinctive identities of kinship and residential groups and thereby enforce their members' commitment to related farms.

Two other widely practiced institutions – *agat* and *norma* – are effective means of organising the political economy of the cotton sector at the local level. The so-called '*agat* regime' obliges individual families to a certain size of cotton field to work on through the entire cotton-growing period. Reference to 'family honour' and descent and ethnic identities commits individual families to the *agat* size, while the latter is symbolised as a materially measured symbolic good of families and *qawms* (descent or ethnic groups). Similarly, the institution of *norma* ('quota') sets the amount of cotton individual families can take from the harvest. *Norma* is interpreted as materialised form of loyalty of the individual families to their *qawm*, village and religious categories.

The majority of cotton workers, who are women and children, are underpaid or not paid at all. In order to commit them to such intensive but underpaid work, mediators refer to the indigenous norms that salary or cash payments render women and juniors arrogant and thus alien to their families. Cotton-growing activities, which are interpreted as the necessary and acceptable qualities of women, thus improve their reputation as industrious housekeepers and as being loyal to their senior family members. 'Family honour' not only commits them to the inferior cotton work but also limits their opportunities for political and economic activities.

As observed in this chapter, the mainstream aspects of local governance, including political structures, property rights and the stabilisation of contested political and economic relations, are common to the entire southern Khatlon region. At the same time, they characterise distinctive features in different contexts. In mountainous, subsistence-based, small and ethnically homogenous communities, *kolkhozi* elites dominate political and economic structures. In these communities, collective identities reflect *contested* boundaries due to disputes over elites' privileged access to public positions and economic resources. In the lowland, cotton-growing, large and ethnically heterogeneous settlements we witness the *integrative* or representative structures of the mahalla and cotton farms. In these communities, collective identities serve to integrate and enforce the indigenous networks of extended families, descent groups and residential neighbourhoods, which simultaneously shape cotton farms. The following two in-depth case studies discuss these *contested* and *integrated* boundaries in view of these contexts.

THE CONTESTED BOUNDARIES OF SOCIAL ORDER: The case of Devdor village in the mountainous area

This chapter discusses the contested boundaries of social order in a mountainous, subsistence-based, ethnically homogenous and relatively small village community. This means that a few powerful villagers or *kolkhozi* elites dominate key political organisations and economic assets at the local level. They have close personal relations with local and central state elites and involve mahalla mediators, including family elders and religious notables, in their patron-client network and thereby influence other people. Also, some powerful men, who are excluded from the patron-client network, contest *kolkhozi* elites' political and economic privileges. In such a context, individual actors use collective identities either to legitimise their own or to delegitimise others' rights and claims. Thus, collective identities serve mainly as means of contestation, coercion and punishment, which therefore serve as core means to maintain social and political stability and order at the local level.

Subchapter one briefly introduces a number of social and economic characteristics and conditions found in Shuroobod district. Next, subchapters two and three introduce the case of Devdor village and its contested political and economic contexts. Subchapter four describes the villagers' collective identities, including Islam, kinship (*avlod*, *qabila* and *qawmiyat*) affiliations, village (*Devdori*) identity and *qawmdori*. Subchapter five discusses how individual actors use these collective identities to legitimise their own and delegitimise others' political and economic privileges and claims. Subchapter six examines the role that collective identities play in maintaining socio-political stability in the face of increasing political and economic inequalities and contestations. Subchapter seven shows how the development structure of MSDSP in the village has increased disputes over political and economic resources and how, ultimately, development programmes have become the subject of indigenous institutions. This particular case demonstrates the role of collective identities in adapting development structures and programmes.

A short overview of Shuroobod district: social and economic characteristics

Shuroobod district is a mountainous region, situated in the south-eastern part of the Kulob region (*mintaqa*) in Khatlon province. Before the relocation of the local population to cotton-growing districts in the 1960s, the three distinct areas of Sarichashma, Shuroobod and Dashtijum were classed as administrative units, i.e. village councils or jamoats under the auspices of the three districts of Moskovskiy, Leningrad and Dashtijum, respectively. The late 1980s' Perestroika in the Soviet Union legalised the ongoing return of relocated people to their home villages. In 1988, the then-Soviet government established Shuroobod district, which integrated the abovementioned areas.

The Shuroobod area, situated in the central part of the district, includes Devdor village, where I conducted my in-depth field research. The area is located to the east of Sarichashma area, to the west of Dashtijum area and to the north of Afghanistan at approximately 2000 metres above sea level in a mountainous region. Formerly, Shuroobod area was the southern jamoat of Leningrad (currently Mu'minobod) district. Despite scarce water resources, the area is more favoured for subsistence agriculture and cattle-breeding than other areas due to its abundant arable land. In a recently opened traditional bazaar, people only sell the surplus of their agricultural products to limited consumers. Rather, they prefer to transport agricultural products and livestock to Kulob markets during the dry seasons, while at the end of the harvest season, traders from the central cities of Kulob, Qurghonteppa and Dushanbe buy most of the apple harvest.

Shuroobod area contains two jamoats: Doghiston Jamoat and Shuroobod Jamoat. Shuroobod Jamoat consists of 23 small and large villages in its two sub-areas of Shuroobod and Devdor. The most populated settlements in Devdor sub-area are Zulmobod and Devdor villages, inhabited by about 177 and 96 households, respectively. Devdor village is adjacent to Zulmobod and Chorchashmai Tojik (four households) villages to the north and Khushkasangov (10 households), Ursikho (40 households), Tudani (60 households), Zardoluhak (20 households) and Zü (six households) villages to the south. The village is located about 20 kilometres away from the south-eastern part of the Dashtijum National Park and about 30 kilometres from the Tajik-Afghan border to the south.

Overview of Devdor village

There are 126 registered nuclear families inhabiting a total of 96 households in Devdor village. The village is divided up into three *guzars* (streets), namely mosque-guzar, where the village mosque is situated, School-*guzar,* where the village school is located, and *Guzari bolo* ('the upper *guzar*'), located on the upper steep side and to the east of two other *guzars*. According to older informants,[81] the two lower *guzars* – mosque-guzar in the south and School-*guzar* in the north – were separate villages of *Roghi* and *Khovalingi* descent groups before the first kolkhoz appeared in the 1920s and '30s. These distinct descent communities also had their own mosques and mahallas.

Kolkhoz veterans[82] recall that during the 1920s and '30s, two kolkhozes were established in two villages, which were then integrated into a single kolkhoz by the end of the 1940s. This collectivisation process institutionalised the centralised social and economic efforts of the Soviet government.

Consequently, two villages at opposite sides of the gully were unified under the same geographical administrative unit of Devdor village ('*qishloq*') and *uchastka* (a village-level economic entity of the kolkhoz). During the integration process, by the early 1960s three mosques of distinct descent groups were also eradicated. Since then, one of the veterans[83] asserts, the kolkhoz system has destroyed the inheritance patterns of residential units and land ownership along descent origins, while descent communities have started merging and sharing their residential units.

In 1964, the Soviet government organised the relocation of the majority of village families to the cotton plantations in the lowland (including Farkhor and Vose') districts of the Kulob region. During the early 1990s, after most of the villagers returned to their 'homeland', as they define their village, they were integrated into Devdor sub-area sovkhoz ('the sovkhoz', hereinafter). In the wake of the collapse of the socialist regime in 1991, and the consequent land reforms initiated by the central government of Tajikistan through 1997-2005, the sovkhoz was restructured into smaller economic entities, including private *dehqan* farms of extended families and collective *dehqan* farms. Due to the mountainous conditions, a subsistence economy is the main livelihood source of these farms, which is based on inherited patrimonial properties such as household and land resources, agricultural machines and other professions.

---

[81] Personal interviews (Notebook No 1-3, August 28, 2007: page 14; as well as Tape recording No 56-57; Notebook No 1-2, July 26, 2007: page 123).

[82] Personal interviews (Notebook No 1-3, August 28, 2007: page 14; as well as Tape recording No 56-57; Notebook No 1-2, July 26, 2007: page 123; Notebook No 1-2, June 27, 2007: page 36; Notebook No 1-2, June 28, 2007: page 44).

[83] Personal interview with Bomad Ghulomov (Notebook No 1-3, August 28, 2007: page 14; as well as Tape recording No 56-57).

The political and economic context of Devdor village

This subchapter introduces the political and economic context of Devdor village. Mainly a few powerful villagers, including kolkhozi elites, dominate political decision-making (3.1) and have privileged access to the village's economic resources (3.2). The other important point is that some villagers contest elites' privileged political positions and economic rights (3.3). Such a situation necessitates, in part, the collective identities that elites use to legitimise their privileged positions and rights, which is discussed in the following subchapters four, five and six.

Political domination of kolkhozi elites

In Devdor village, kolkhozi elites (especially Mardon Saydalov, Murodkhon Davlatkhonov, Bomad Ghulomov and their extended patrilineal families)[84] traditionally dominate key political and economic organisations such as the mahalla, village mosque and collective farm, as well as the jamoat and important departments of the district government. Quite apart from relevant laws on local self-governance (e.g. Law on Local Self-Governance 2007[1994]; Law on Local Self-Governance 2008), elites shape the central decision-making body of the village, the Mahalla's Council of elders.[85] The meetings of the Council are reduced to the heads of elite families, including the elite elders (Mardon Saydalov, the former sovkhoz chairman from the 1960s, and Murodkhon Davlatkhonov, the former brigadir and vakil of Devdor village). Other members are not able to participate most of the time due to their poor health (see also Table 4: Public organisations and personal networks in Devdor village). The current vakil (the son of the former sovkhoz chairman) explains the inclusion of these two men in the Council as respect for elders: "We keep it [include them in the Council of elders] as a sign of paying tribute to [these] respectable elders."[86]

Similarly, elites dominate the decision-making structure and thus possess privileged access to the public properties of the collective farm, despite the legal regulations de-jure recognising the equal rights of all employees. The current farm chairman replaced his predecessor (the vakil's junior brother), who was appointed as the head of the District Land Committee. Previously, the current

---

[84] I conditionally name some powerful men as '*kolkhozi* elites' or 'elites' who are identified by the villagers as *rais(h)o* ('chiefs').

[85] In Tajik: *Shuroi musafedon;* also Russian version *Soviet stareytshin* is used.

[86] Interview with vakil; Devdor village; Shuroobod district (Notebook No 1-2, July 26, 2007: page 122).

chairman of the farm was its chief agronomist, a key position in the management (use and distribution) of public properties, including land, livestock and agricultural machines. Moreover, kolkhozi elites struggle for total domination over remaining key assets and organisations in the village, including the Devdor Village Organisation (DVO) and the village school, which are led by their opponents.

Table 4: Public organisations and personal networks in Devdor village

#	Public organisations	Personal networks	Privileged actors
1	Jamoat	District government functionaries, influenced by elites' personal networks	Elites' allies
2	Mahalla	Jamoat functionaries, influenced by the personal networks of elites through district government authorities	Elites
3	Collective farm	Jamoat and district government functionaries, influenced by the personal networks of elites	Elites
4	Mosque	Mahalla, jamoat and district government functionaries, influenced by the personal networks of elites	Elites
5	School	District Education Board, influenced by the personal networks of challengers	Opponents
6	VO	MSDSP	Opponents

Source: My field research (May – September 2007)

Economic privileges of kolkhozi elites

The revised Law of the Republic of Tajikistan 'On *Dehqan* (*Fermeri*) Farms' (*Dehqan* Farms 2002) and its shareholding regulation in 2005 in Shuroobod district[87] legalised family inheritance rights to land and other properties. Kolkhozi elites established most of the 32 family farms and thereby privatised the most favourable land resources in Devdor village. As a deprived villager told me, "[t]hose who established *dehqan* farms earlier, they won because then

[87] The Government Decree 'On the Renewal *(Tajdid)* of *Dehqan* Farms in accordance with Shareholding Rights' (Expert interview with the chairman of the collective farm: Notebook No 1-2, July 17, 2007: pages 96-97).

there was enough land to privatise."[88] The entire privatisation process was dictated by kolkhozi elites and their allies in district, provincial and central state offices. Furthermore, the multilateral mediation (Tajik Government, USAID, UNDP and MSDSP) of the shareholding campaign in 2005 (*Tajdid*), for the fair distribution of land and other resources, did not favour especially poor families.[89] Adversely, this campaign actually favoured elites by legalising administrative rights and privileges 'inherited' since the Soviet sovkhoz. The campaign ensured their inherited rights to registered land plots, orchards, livestock, buildings, small enterprises, agricultural machinery and social and technical infrastructure and facilities. While monopolising state laws, they were able to secure most of the land and other resources of the former sovkhoz for at least 99-years as part of a family inheritance.

In June 2005 the multilateral delegation of the Tajik state and its international partners introduced the *Tajdid* campaign, i.e. the shareholding redistribution of the former sovkhoz's agricultural resources. Functionaries and potential shareholders agreed to create a set of equitable rules regarding the redistribution. It was decided to list shareholders in alphabetical order and then redistribute land resources in the lineal order of the land map provided by the District Land Committee. The sequential redistribution continued until the turn of the vakil, who refused to accept what he might get from the list. He claimed rights to a land plot near his house and justified this move by referring to his unpaid public position as vakil. Although mediated by mahalla authorities, the villagers made a concession in this respect. The next problem arose with another elite member, the vakil's brother-in-law, who wanted to inherit his grandfather's seven-hectare land plot. This was the last straw, as far as the common villagers were concerned, so collectively they left the meeting as a protest against the redistribution campaign. After several days of stalemate, state functionaries agreed with the people to arrange the redistribution by drawing lots (*qur'apartoi*), which involved writing down each land plot on separate pieces of paper and then giving these out to every individual. Once again, the elites' claim for privileges ended the campaign. Finally, state functionaries let the people choose and demarcate land plots for themselves. Many shareholders, however, could only choose what they had 'inherited' as 'support land plots' allocated during the Soviet sovkhoz, as the most favourable land plots had already been privatised by elite farmers.

---

[88] Personal interview (Notebook No 1-2, July 17, 2007: pages 97-98).

[89] According to shareholding principle, it was expected that every villager above 18 years old would appropriate 0.32 hectares of garden, 0.35 hectares of arable land and 1.2 hectares of pasture land. (Personal interview with the chairman of the collective farm: Notebook No 1-2, July 17, 2007: pages 96-97).

Similarly, for most villagers who did not favour personal relations with elites, procedures for registering a family farm were heavily nontransparent, expensive and time-consuming. Documents for a family farm should be formally registered and simultaneously negotiated through various state departments. Although the appealer was not engaged through formal procedures, his application depended on his personal ties with the functionaries of the key land reform organisations, including the District Land Committee, jamoat and collective farm – all dominated by village elites or related to their allies. Besides personal ties, which are vital in overcoming bureaucratic barriers, poor families lack other important means to establish private farms, namely a) not enough financial resources to arrange all bureaucratic documents, b) poor knowledge of legal, in part shareholding, regulations and procedures and c) not enough land resources and agricultural machinery.

Moreover, kolkhozi elites have privileged access to public assets and the economic resources of the collective farm.[90] Elites and their state allies maintain their privileged positions via the indigenous adaptation of formal structures. They make use of their privileged right to impose their decisions and thus to undermine the legal authority of other members of the collective farm. They effectively sold or privatised valuable public properties by manipulating their privileged or 'administrative'[91] rights, including the management right of distribution (Russian term '*oformlenie*'), the withdrawal right to collective utilisation and the right to write-off goods (Russian term '*spisanie*'). The functioning of remaining public properties (as listed above) and state and administrative tax systems is not accountable to the ordinary shareholders.[92] For those who require accountability, they have, for example, a different map adapted to informal taxation charges.

Within the confines of this system, kinship and patron-client negotiations between the chairman of the collective farm and the subject workers shape both formal and informal taxation institutions. In addition to state tax, which is

---

[90] These assets and resources include 600 hectares of arable land, 240 hectares of orchard, 700 hectares of pasture, about 400 cows and calves, and some technical facilities and infrastructure of the former sovkhoz. (Personal interview with the chairman of the collective farm: Notebook No 1-2, July 17, 2007: pages 96-97).

[91] The leaders of such public organisations make use of the legal rights of the members in management and alienation of public assets and goods. Verdery (2004) explains such privileged use of members' rights as "administrative rights."

[92] Personal observation from an informal talk between the chairman of the collective farm, the vakil of Devdor village and chairman of the VO and the chairman of the collective farm of the adjacent Tudani village (Notebook No 1-2, July 26, 2007: pages 124-126).

10-10.5 TJ Somoni per one hectare of arable land, subordinate members are charged an informal tariff of 50kg of grain per one hectare of arable land and more than 50 percent of the marketable (good quality) apple harvest from the orchards. These informal charges are registered (*'oformleni'*, i.e. formally recorded in official minutes and, if required by state authorities, reported) as financial means utilised to maintain the administrative expenditure of the collective farm. The shareholding contract is written and signed between the chairman of the farm and each member family's head 'for formal reporting' (Russian: *'dlya otchyotnosti'*) and statistical registration.[93] Thus, traditional tenure relations overshadow shareholding regulations, i.e. shareholder families are represented as tenant families and the chairman of the collective farm acts as their landlord. While taxes and dues are paid in different amounts and forms (by cash, by labour force and in-kind), their accountability depends upon and is reduced to the personal relationship between the chairman of the collective farm and the shareholder families. As the shareholders confirmed, the tariff for apple harvest depends on harvest quality and size, and especially on personal relations with elites.[94] The informal payments of tariffs, rental dues (*'haqqi ijora'*) and even state taxes have different political functions, including acknowledging the superiority and privileged property rights of elites.

Contested political and economic situations

To prevent and reduce conflict over the unequal redistribution of former sovkhoz public property, elites and their mediators employ various means. These means include collective norms and identities in addition to cooptation and threats from the police. Due to the weak material and military power of the state, however, elites only rarely co-opt or punish the opponents. During my field stay I witnessed a few cases whereby the mobilisers of mass disputes were imprisoned by the jamoat and district police departments but soon co-opted, crossed up and released. The head of the DVO was convicted for misleading the public fund of the organisation as a pretext, but in the end police officers released him and warned him that he should not 'provoke' the people.

Notably, elites' opponents do not struggle for the fair distribution of political and economic resources, as their claim for 'justice' might suggest. Also, they are

---

[93] Family female and junior members have no adequate rights.

[94] E.g. personal interviews (Notebook No 1-2, July 17, 2007: pages 97-98; Notebook No 1-2, June 28, 2007: pages 43-44; Notebook No 1-2, July 20, 2007: pages 74-75; Notebook No 1-2, June 28, 2007: page 45; Notebook No 1-2, June 30, 2007: pages 51-52).

not a 'community of action', but instead seek alliances for strategic purposes. Originally, most of them[95] held leading positions in the Soviet sovkhoz and other state organisations, but they were deprived of their positions in the aftermath of the political and economic crisis and reform of the sovkhoz. These 'friends' mostly gather in their own homes 'for a cup of tea' and discuss 'injustice' ('*nohaqqi*') caused by kolkhozi elites. However, as one host experienced: "I did not find anyone who could take ten straight steps with me."[96] Opponents easily change and forget their positions and concerns if they can negotiate and develop relations with more powerful and promising men, especially kolkhozi elites.

Rather, opponents' claims about 'the abundance of inequality' do not reflect their concern about the unfair or illegal distribution of land and other agricultural resources, as they may argue. They use the justice-seeking discourse of *haqiqat*[97] as a strategic manoeuver to communicate with kolkhozi elites in an attempt to negotiate their individual privileges or dues (*haq*). Their 'cup of tea' network is a strategic alliance used to influence elites rather than to reach and to address the needs of deprived people. To deny the denunciation that they are 'self-interested', opponents blame other deprived people for being loyal to – albeit exploited by – elites: "They never warm your back… [they] do not support you if you struggle for them, since they are elites' *odam* (indebted kinsmen and clients)."[98] Even the most passionate 'justice-seeker' propagates to his sons in his intimate family circle the experience of another 'justice-seeker', who "… struggled for a long time for the villagers but nobody supported him. He understood that people did not appreciate his efforts, so he established his own family farm. Now he is wealthy and reputable among the people and state officials."[99]

In such an environment of political and economic struggle and tension, actors use various means, including collective identities, to protect their own interests. Before I discuss this issue in line with different aspects and cases of local governance, I describe in the subchapter below the collective identities of local people.

---

95 Including Atokhoja Hamdamov, Zamon Gulov, and Mullo Ismatov.

96 Personal interview (Notebook No 1-2, June 30, 2007: page 53).

97 '*Haqiqat*' is literally translated as 'truth', 'right' as well as 'justice'.

98 Personal interview (Notebook No 1-2, July 15, 2007: page 90).

99 Personal interview (Notebook No 1-2, July 20, 2007: pages 112-113).

Constructing multilayered collective identities 'for acting and networking'

The current subchapter introduces the collective identities of the inhabitants of Devdor village, before I move on to discuss their political role in subchapters five, six and seven. The sections below briefly trace religious identity, kinship references, such as *avlod*, *qabila* and *qawmiyat*, village identity and *qawmdori*. It is worthwhile noting that *qawmdori* is a notion which involves all other references as merged religious, kinship and village affiliation in the cognitive representation of villagers. Figure 5 below (Multilayered identity of the villagers) illustrates the multilayered collective identities which both exclude and include affiliated people in different contexts. At the end of this subchapter I also provide a map based on *qawmdori* and its contested boundaries (Figure 6).

Figure 5: Multilayered identities of the villagers

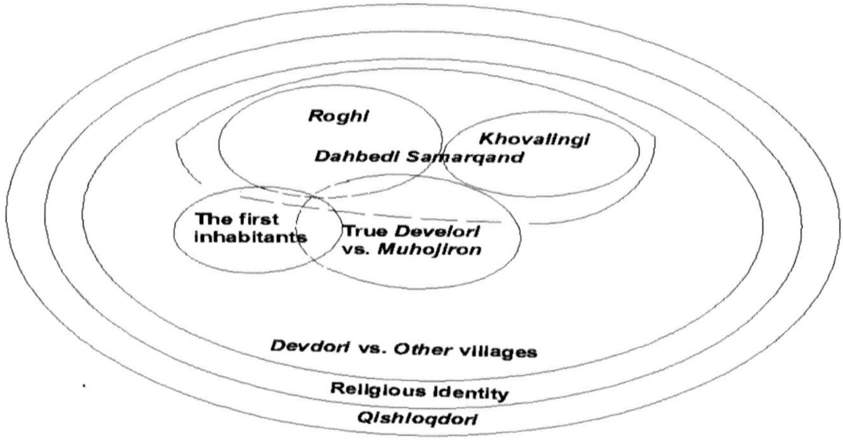

Religious identity of the villagers

A few sacred sites and religious notables in Shuroobod district symbolise villagers' integrated religious identity vis-à-vis *others*, such as guests from outside the district as well as outside Kulob region. Conversely, villagers categorise and value differently sacred sites located in the Devdor sub-area (e.g. scattered shahids and shrines in Zü village) or are subject to different spiritual saints and religious notables, even at the village level. In fact, villagers recognise and obey different religious assets and notables that represent their conflicting interests.

Opponents especially affiliate themselves with different sacred sites and spiritual notables and express these affiliations through distinctive stories, ritual practices and visits. Their separate visits to the most famous shrines – Hazrati-Imom-Askari shrine and the shrines of Zü village – the objects of pride for the Shuroobod people vis-à-vis others, reflect intra-communal divisions and contestations.[100] The histories of sacred shrines are either told exclusively by individual actors or are defined as 'shahid', whereby stories are not shared and thus remain unrelated and unattractive to some villagers.

The fragmented religious identity of the villagers, which reflects their conflicting interests in political and economic networking, therefore shapes Islam as the 'field' of contestation. More than four recognised and unrecognised village mullahs and religious notables refer to their inherited statuses, such as descent groups, religious ancestors and religious teachers, to make a claim for privileged authorities. For example, one of the claiming mullahs invests more than others in maintaining the village mosque in order to gain the patronage and recognition of kolkhozi elites and their mahalla mediators. At the same time, he represents the Islamic Renaissance Party in the village and thereby tries to gain the acknowledgment of young men by mobilising them through events the party organises in the district centre. The other claiming mullah is a school teacher, who always takes the Koran with him in search of recognition by his co-villagers.

Kinship affiliations: *avlod, qabila* and *qawmiyat*

Local idioms and practices surrounding *qawmiyat*, *qabila* and *avlod* refer to kinship affiliations. This reference, however, is not an end in itself but a search for networking opportunities, especially with elites. Many informants[101] assert kolkhozi elites' dominant *qawmiyat* or *qabila*, that is kinship and patron-client networks, among the villagers (also see Figure 6: The map of *qawmdori* and its contested boundaries). In such a context, the practice of *tarbiya* (the moral training of male juniors) teaches the morality of reputational respect.[102] Accordingly, people respect those who possess symbolic and material power.

[100] Personal observations on June 8 and July 29, 2007 (Notebook No 1-2, June 8, 2007: pages 3-4; Notebook No 1-2, July 29, 2007: pages 135-141).

[101] Personal interviews (e.g. Notebook No 1-2, June 26, 2007: page 33; Notebook No 1-2, July 13, 2007: pages 74-75).

[102] Respect is not purely a matter of religious or kinship norm, such as seniority. But rather, someone gains respect in accordance with his real possession of symbolic and material power. There are many elders and seniors whom juniors and women do not respect due to their powerless situation.

Due to such a practical form of morality, seniority is not the defining condition for hierarchical relations among the villagers. According to indigenous cultural idioms and practices, friendships with 'indebted' ('*qadrdon*') men exist for the sake of patron-client networking and thus reflect positive *tarbiya*. Men, regardless of their age, who have many (patron-client) 'ties' ('*odam*'), as the notion of an 'indebted [friend]' suggests, are seen as 'respectable' among their fellow villagers, evidenced by their moral goods such as 'the art to know who is who' (*odamshinosi*) and generosity. Notably, friendship without the purpose of networking, especially among juniors, is called a 'friend-game' ('*jurabozi*'), which indicates negative morality. While *tarbiya* and its ritual exercises (such as reputational respect and friendship) raise and enhance the networking skills of male juniors, the religious institution of *mahramiyat* constrains women within their patrimonial boundaries of inter-group marriage networks. Again, *mahramiyat* does not necessarily draw boundaries to shape the distinctive identity of women or patrimonial communities but rather commits them to 'respect' boundaries of kinship and patron-client networks.

Village identity

Different notions of village (geographical) affiliations play similar functions to kinship references. Apparently, geographical notions related to descent origin, the historical right to a 'homeland' or inter-village distinctions suggest multilayered boundaries among co-villagers or between Devdor and other adjacent villages. However, many cases show that these boundaries are not stable but rather are salient in certain contexts. Geographical boundaries do not reflect equivalent geographical divisions among villagers but rather express their political and economic contestations. Actors refer to the discourses and stories of descent origin, the historical right to a 'homeland' and inter-village differences to claim and protect contested political and economic rights and privileges.

Qawmdori as shared kinship and religious identity

Qawmdori is a notion whereby actors refer to the shared kinship and village identities of villagers. In some contexts they actualise the mental construct of *Devdori* vs. 'outsiders' to protect their position and reputation and to discredit opponents. While in reality, most Devdor villagers are related through kinship and descent lines, *qawmdori* or *qawmiyat* refers especially to kinship, patron-client and interdependent personal ties (shown as grey circles in Figure 6). Also, powerful actors (highlighted in grey spots) possess not only dominant kinship (black circles), patron-client (grey circles) and wider kinship and neighbourhood ties (blue circles) in the village but also personal relations with the state, religious and business networks outside the village. Here, the term *qawmiyat* suggests that some powerful actors hold superior positions due to their prevailing kinship ties in the village and their network of religious and state authorities as well as businessmen at different levels. Such a notion implies the self-acknowledgment of the powerless villagers of their limited ties and thus opportunities. The notion of *qawmdori*, in this sense, means an imposed and pressured collective commitment to 'peace' and concession in response to increasing political and economic inequality and exclusion.

Figure 6: The map of *qawmdori* and its contested boundaries

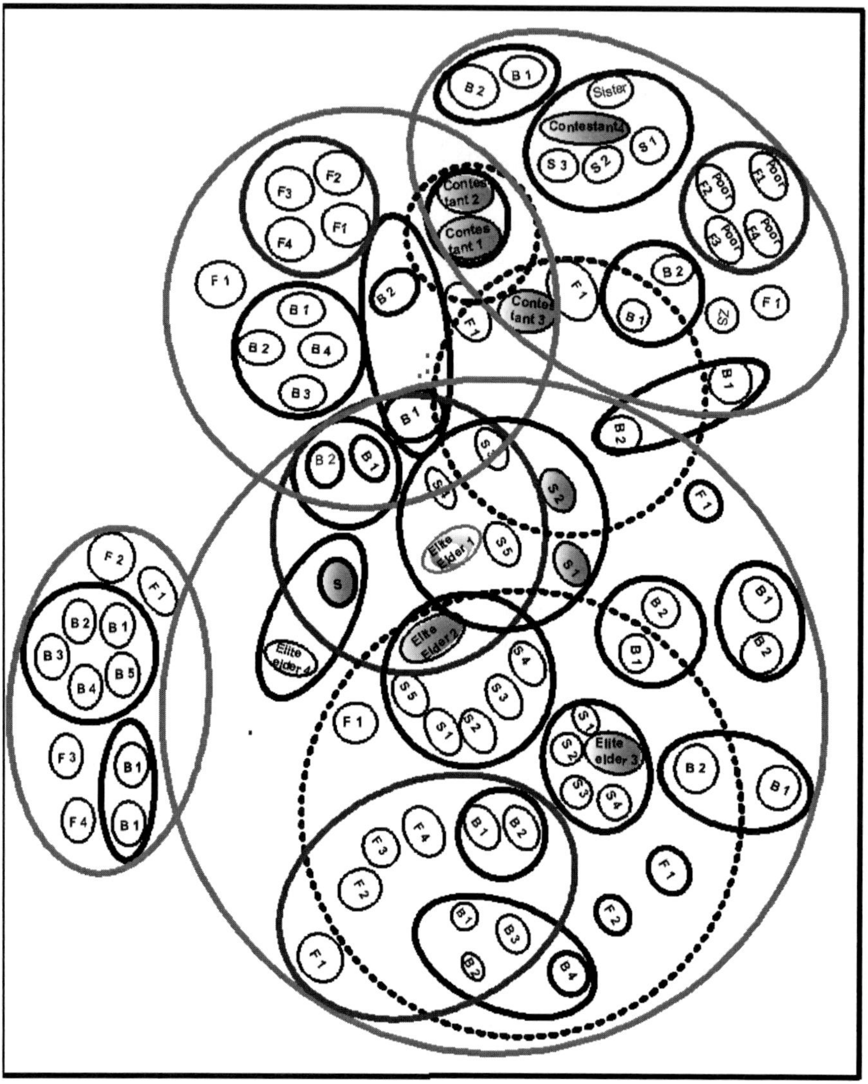

Legitimation of political and economic claims

This subchapter discusses how collective identities enforce key institutional practices in a subsistence economy, which are related to individuals' property claims. Kolkhozi elites particularly seek to legitimise their privileged access to the state and public assets and resources. Section one discusses the role of religious identity in sanctifying the privileged right of powerful men to village political structures. Section two analyses how the subject people refer to religious identity to seek favours from patrons, while section three shows how individual actors legitimise their economic claims and privileges by committing the subject people to a multilayered village identity.

Religious identity: bestowing power with sacredness

Powerful and wealthy villagers, especially kolkhozi elites, refer to religious identity to legitimise privileged but contested access to political positions and material resources. Such an effective reference underlines and expresses several of the shared normative and cognitive frames of local people. One of the fundamental frames is the myth surrounding the divine authority of powerful men to control 'dangerous' human nature and the material world. Otherwise, mundane interests would spoil even the hallowed souls of sacred 'teachers', including Odam (Adam) and Saint Bahovuddin.[103] Inheritance and 'personal ties' (*'odam'*)[104] are considered 'God-given' privileges and are thus acknowledged and praised by divine sources. The other related frame is the identification of elites especially with state agencies at different levels. This identification is reflected by the notion of *'davlat'*,[105] which refers to the exclusive connection of elites with the 'divine will' of the state authority. Thus, personal relations with state functionaries are the 'God-given' or divine right of elites.

Powerful men seek divinity in order to legitimise privileged access to key resources, including land and water – even though these may be assigned for common use and wellbeing.[106] Especially, elites claim their own religious superiority or commitment to Islam as the reason for their success in the material world. In order to manifest this divine superiority, they visit the village mosque 'for prayer' on a daily basis. Their close kinsmen and devoted clients admit on behalf of the poor villagers that "[w]e, the poor, are so busy and

---

[103] Personal interview with Atokhoja Hamdamov (Notebook No 1-2, July 20, 2007: pages 114-115)

[104] Kinship and patron-client ties with powerful men who are necessarily involved through state and business structures

[105] *'Davlat'* means material wealth, children, public position and professional skills as inherited attributes. The other direct meaning of *'davlat'* is 'state'.

[106] As defined by Constitution of Tajikistan in Article 13 (Constitution of Tajikistan 2003[1994]: 2) as well as by Water Code of Tajikistan (2001) in Article 5 on state ownership on water (http://www.base.spinform.ru/show_doc.fwx?regnom=2127)

greedy for worldly wealth that we even forget and miss performing our basic religious debt –prayer."[107]

Mahalla senior mediators (Mardon Saydalov and Murodkhon Davlatkhonov) visit the village mosque 'for prayer' daily and thus gain a reputation among co-villagers and validate their decision-making authority. They gather during evening prayer in the mosque and then transfer their already taken decisions to other villagers by visiting their households or by holding 'sacred' events such as religious feasts and initiation ceremonies. Due to their superior communal status, these elders are invited to most religious ceremonies and are trusted to visit all families on an individual basis. Without such status, as one informant explained, "You cannot enter [others'] houses."[108]

Besides senior mediators, ordinary people pay regular visits to the mosque, mainly for evening and night prayers during the one-month long Ramadan. Due to exhaustive fasting and the intensive work involved in maintaining their subsistence needs, however, they only take a routine part in acknowledging decisions already taken by the council of elders.

The central state established the institution of *imomat* (imam-khatib) to formalise the local representation of religious authority (Law on Religion 2009; Law on Religion 1994; Law on Religion 1990). So far, Devdor village has not been integrated into this formal representation of Islam,[109] so the elites have authorised the key mahalla mediator (Murodkhon Davlatkhonov) to lead and to maintain the mosque and other religious assets. He took over the mosque in 1994, after Mardon Saydalov, his colleague and friend since the Soviet sovkhoz, replaced him as vakil. To justify his authority, Murodkhon Davlatkhonov refers

---

[107] Personal interview (Notebook No 1-3, August 28, 2007: page 14; also tape recording No 56-57)

[108] Personal interview (Notebook No 1-2, July 13, 2007: pages 74-75)

[109] Central and local state elites and functionaries are concerned with the influence of different global Muslim brotherhoods and movements. Therefore, they have adjusted the whole Islamic representation structures through official committees and councils. *Imam-khatib* represents a primary residential-administrative unit (village and urban neighbourhood). *Imam-khatib* is subject to the district *sarkhatib* (chief *imam-khatib*), who runs the public mosque (*masjidi jome'*) at the district centre. *Imam-khatib* is appointed by the district *sarkhatib*, who in turn is appointed by the republican Council of Religious Scholars (*Shuroi ulamo*). Often, the *sarkhatib* has privileged personal connections to district state authorities. *Sarkhatibs* and *imam-khatibs* are trained and supervised by state Islamic institutions and academic programmes. It is remarkable to note that state elites seek the decision-making monopoly to appoint *sarkhatibs* and *imam-khatibs* by consulting with other religious notables at the local level, especially pilgrims, Sayyids and Sufi saints (eshons).

to or reinvents the pre-Soviet and post-Soviet histories of the mosque. He also contrasts the current village with its older self, which was not the same before the first kolkhoz was established in the 1920s. There were three mosques in two villages when, he assures, "[p]eople in this side [mosque-guzar] had two mosques and this one was ours. Our kinsmen prayed in this mosque, which was the public [inter-village] mosque as well."[110]

The key mahalla mediator also claims exclusive authority over the religious wellbeing of the village as a way of legitimising his privileged access to the mosque and other religious assets of the village. He recalls the recent history of the village-level *hashar* in 1991, which he initiated to re-build the local mosque: "There was mass reconstruction and the rebuilding of mosques in adjacent villages. Therefore, village honour ['*nangi qishloq*'] provoked me to collect money from the people, to carry bricks from the [Kulob] city and to rebuild the mosque. As you see, it is the biggest and most beautiful [mosque] around."[111]

Besides his narrative claims, the mahalla mediator constructs his material world to shape his exclusive religious image, again to legitimise his right to the mosque as a sacred decision-making setting. The village mosque, semi-encircled by his and his sons' private houses, is located in the central-southern edge of the mosque-guzar. Their household area consists of two parts. The first is a secluded part which is accessible through a man-sized wicket within the frame of a locked iron gate. When one is allowed to enter through the wicket, the guesthouse is first situated on the left-side front and the family houses come only next. The outer cycle embraces this secluded space, which is surrounded by family sheds leading the way to the mosque and the Devdor spring. Murodkhon Davlatkhonov, who lives with two married sons in the same household adjacent to another son's household, takes this 'intimate' path directly to the front gate of the mosque. A sacred place of shahids (martyrs) surrounds the mosque from the eastern side, thus demarcating the boundary running alongside the households and the mosque.

Sacred religious reputation bestows the mediation authority of this elite elder, Murodkhon Davlatkhonov, among his co-villagers as well as through his personal relations with notables and elites at various levels. He represents and protects the religious image and honour of villagers vis-à-vis *others*, such as guests and the inhabitants of adjacent villages. This superior status thus allows him to intervene in the private lives of many village families and to mobilise their resources in the names of image and honour.

---

110 Personal interview with Murodkhon Davlatkhonov (Notebook No 1-2, July 26, 2007: page 123).

111 Ibid.

In summer 2007, he arranged to register the mosque as a public (inter-village) mosque (*Masjidi jome'*). To meet the requirements for higher status, he had to build a prayer-bathroom for the mosque. As always, he managed to mobilise incomparable resources: the contributions of 38 households, including 630 TJ Somoni from 18 households, 200 TJ Somoni plus additional in-kind inputs from six households, free construction work (*hashar*) by 14 households in successive order and generous contributions from wealthy clients. Nonetheless, the remaining households were also expected to contribute to the project. The elite elder was even able to mobilise resources from his and elites' opponents, who claimed that the project was unaccountable, while the total cost might not exceed 500 TJ Somoni, including prices for purchasing construction materials and for hiring construction masters. Nonetheless, one of them told me that "If it is to be spent for the mosque, I give. It is his [the elite elder's] conscience and faith [*imon*] how he uses the money. I leave him with God. God witnesses what he is doing."[112] Here, '*imon*' literally means 'religious faith based on the fear of God'. Many informants also relate faith (*imon*) to shame or the fear of being different (*ayb*) from co-members and thus being reproached by *others*.

Religious commitment to patron-client relations

Not only do elites refer to religious sources to legitimise their political and economic privileges. But also Islamic moral norms, including generosity, commit elites to distribute patronage favours especially to loyal people. In return for these favours, ordinary people acknowledge the inherited and divine status of their patrons' material wealth, public positions and professions (*hunar*). In the local idiom, this status is defined as *davlat*, which means that the patrons have 'God-given' rights and hence the duty to share favours with subject people. Others, who seize such divine privilege through illicit means, forget about their religious duty.

Subject people do not believe blindly in this ontology but rather refer to religious identity to construct the duty of their patrons towards generosity or patronage favours. Due to such cliental demand and expectation, therefore, subject villagers not only admit but also applaud elites' privileged access to public goods of the Soviet sovkhoz. Thus, the call for the religious act of 'generosity' legitimises the privileged access of elites to public goods and natural resources. They gain 'God-given' prestige even though they dispense (the development concepts of) inequality and scarcity among their co-villagers.

---

112 Personal interview with Zamon Gulov (Notebook No 1-2, July 2, 2007: page 58).

In return for limited patronage favours, clients indebt themselves to their patrons and bestow upon themselves inferior status by sacrificing their voice and labour. They are indebted to their patrons because, as they assure, their patrons respect them, are aware of their health and family conditions and help them when they face difficulties. In Devdor village the most reputable patrons are kolkhozi elites, who are well-versed in the personal and family situations of their clients. The patrons' commitment to their clients is considered their religious duty, since "God endowed them *davlat* in order to see [care for] the poor," as a poor client told me.[113] A herdsman from the collective farm asserted his 'indebtedness' to the former chairman of the farm, who saved his life after a cow bit and severely injured him. He informed me that "I told the chairman that he was the very reason for me being alive" and thus felt "indebted forever." This incident happened in the winter of "the difficult 1990s," when the inter-village road between Devdor village and Shuroobod was packed with heavy snow. Nevertheless, the chairman of the farm cleared the road "at his own expense" and took the herdsman to hospital in his car.[114]

The religious demand for generosity, however, is not enough to commit elites and other powerful men to patronage favours. Generosity also cannot compensate for the unequal distribution of scarce resources while patrons utilise it along with other tools to indebt and subjugate less favoured people. Local wisdom says that "the well-off serves you on his *dastarkhan* [table] so that you enrich his *dastarkhan*." In return for the patrons' material support and bureaucratic or religious services, cliental villagers pay them in various forms, which are officially classed as bribes or corruption.

The cliental expectations of villagers thus legitimise the privileged access of elites to the public offices and goods of the former sovkhoz and state and international financial and material support schemes integrated through the mahalla and collective farm. Villagers perceive the state taxes and informal dues they pay to the vakil as part of their cliental obligation and loyalty, and therefore they seek his mediation services through bureaucratic offices of the state. Mahalla, jamoat and other district tax departments collect informal (illegal) dues in return for the mediation service they offer for local people, which is a well-practiced source of financial income for the elites. Subject people expect that their personal 'tribute' to the vakil and other elites is an 'investment' in smoothing the bureaucratic machine regarding dealings with state offices.

---

[113] Personal interview (Notebook No 1-2, July 13, 2007: pages 76-77).

[114] Personal interview (Notebook No 1-2, July 3, 2007: page 60).

Hence, villagers refer to religious identity to search for the patrons' bureaucratic mediation and economic favours. For this purpose, they tell stories about the generous ancestors of their patrons. A mullah, for example, uses this method to gain access to the water source of his wealthy neighbour. While clients may not always have the religious status to attract the generosity of their patrons, they refer to their Islamic identity to commit their patrons to *insof* (literally 'mercy').[115] *Insof* is a notion which demands patronage favours in return for cliental services and indebtedness. For example, a cliental subordinate, Zubayd Salimov, who serves his patron, Zamon Gulov, in his household and public position, claims that he has the 'right' (*haq*) to demand favours (*khayr*) from his patron. He explains *khayr* as follows: "When I go to the shop… [of his patron's son] in the city I take anything up to 100 TJ Somoni in value and then say 'I will not pay you'."[116] It is also in the interest of the patron's son, from time to time, to give *khayr* to his 'friend' "for the services he [has provided] for his father." The continuity of interactions between the client and his patron shows that cash is offered, not only to pay for the 'service' but also to pay in advance for the client's indebtedness to his patron.

Subject people judge that patrons are committed to the moral duty of *insof* in return for cliental devotions. As the herdsman, who has worked for the last forty years in the Soviet sovkhoz and its collective farm successor, confesses, *haq* ('cliental share'), which his patrons offer rather than a poor or delayed salary, is the main income for his family. The client prefers *haq* over salary if the latter does not maintain direct personal relations with patrons: "Salary is not an [stable] income and it is not yours. If the patron [*rais*] does not want to, he just does not pay it."[117] Rather, "having a *haq* from public goods [on a regular basis] is the right of anyone who takes care of it, and by having this right he is encouraged to serve."[118]

Thus, reference to Islamic identity highlights the moral norm of indebtedness (*qadrdoni*), which in turn enforces meager favours for clients. The clients themselves explain indebtedness as not only actual reciprocal exchanges with patrons but also the 'due' they must pay 'forever' for past and future patronage. Such moral commitment relieves tension and the discontent of marginalised villagers, which is why Zubayd Salimov, the client of two powerful men (Atokhoja Hamdamov and Zamon Gulov), has to ignore reproaches made by

---

115 '*Insof*' is an indigenous notion and concept about 'justice' which calls for powerful men to share reciprocal and patron-client favours with the people.

116 Personal interview with Zubayd Salimov (Notebook No 1-2, July 14, 2007: page 86).

117 Personal interview (Notebook No 1-2, July 5, 2007: page 67)

118 Personal interview (also tape recording No 29-31)

his friends and neighbours that he is doing "the work of others." One friend, a famous construction master, mocked him, saying that "[y]our home is in ruins but you are doing the work of others."[119] Although Zubayd Salimov readily admits that he is doing "useless works," he confesses that he has to be indebted to his patron (Daler Hamdamov) and his family. As he told me, "I have eaten their *bread and salt* … Each spring I ask him to lend me money to plough my land. If I need cash, he lends it to me."[120] Also, the patron appointed him as the DVO accountant and guard of the village school. Now he earns 66 TJ Somoni (about 17 USD at that time) from both positions monthly. He spends most of his time repairing and maintaining the school, arranging the accounts of the DVO and generally helping the patron's family. His intensive cliental services take precedence despite the fact that he has a lot of household work to do: "But because of loneliness and indigence I am busy with [these] useless works," he admits.[121]

Reference to multilayered kinship, village and religious identities

Here I discuss kinship, village and religious identities, which often have merged and intertwined meanings and uses. Villagers refer to the multilayered meanings of these identities as a way to legitimise their political and economic claims and privileges. I observed at least five references during my field research, which are as follows (see also Figure 5: Multilayered identity of villagers):

- 'The first inhabitants' vs. 'latecomers';
- 'Homeland' owners vs. *muhojiron* (resettled);
- *Devdori* village identity vs. geographical outsiders;
- Reference to descent origins and
- *Qawmdori* as the shared village and religious identity of villagers.

'The first inhabitants' vs. 'latecomers'

Some powerful men, especially elites, link their 'inheritance' of key resources and positions to their exclusive village identity defined as 'the first inhabitants of Devdor'. One such claimant, Bomad Ghulomov, refers to the establishment of the early kolkhoz in the 1930s when "Thirty traditionally wealthy households

---

[119] Personal interviews with Zubayd Salimov (Notebook No 1-2, July 1, 2007: page 55; Notebook No 1-2, July 24, 2007: page 119)

[120] Personal interview with Zubayd Salimov (Notebook No 1-2, July 24, 2007: page 119)

[121] Ibid.

fled to Afghanistan" in order to protect their wealth from collectivisation. Through this vague story he mentions the failure of his father to flee, instead maintaining his wealth despite the collectivisation due to his inherited right to the village vs. the 'latecomers'. Extended family members of elites claim their inherited right to key resources and positions in the mahalla and the collective farm. As already observed, a mahalla elder and mosque guard (Murodkhon Davlatkhonov) talks about his ancestors' right to the village mosque, in order to legitimise his privileged position in both the mahalla and mosque.

'Homeland' owners vs. 'resettled'

As in the case of 'the first inhabitants', mostly kolkhozi elites refer to the distinction of being 'homeland' owners vs. 'resettled' families (*muhojiron*). This claim underlines the 'inheritance' right to their 'homeland ('*vatan*', i.e. Devdor village). They refer to the '1960s resettlement', when in 1964 the Soviet government relocated most villagers in order to maintain cotton plantations in the lowland Farkhor and Vose' districts of Kulob region. Elites claim their distinctive identity as 'homeland' owners vis-à-vis relocated "families [*qabila*] [who] betrayed their homeland for their self-interest."[122]

This claim for superiority over the majority of villagers, however, is mainly stressed to confront contestations. Elites seek to protect their contested political and economic privileges as their 'family right'. The current vakil replaced his father in 2004 after he retired from his position as the deputy chairman of a central state company in Dushanbe. Their opponents challenged his appointment, made by the elite elders of the mahalla, and discredited this 'undemocratic' arrangement. In the General Council, where villagers were expected to elect a new vakil, Mardon Saydalov openly warned them that "the mahalla does not belong to anyone" but his family. Murodkhon Davlatkhonov, one of the most reputable elders in the village, moved to reject the election by declaring "I do not vote for anybody except for Mardon. For his entire life he was the chairman of the sovkhoz and the village's wellbeing is thanks to him. What did *others* do for the village?!"[123] This mediation legitimised the inherited rights of elite families by referring to their leadership positions in the Soviet sovkhoz which initiated the common goods in the village, including the road, bridge, school and orchard.

---

[122] Personal interview with Mardon Saydalov (Notebook No 1-2, June 27, 2007: page 36).

[123] Personal interview with Zubayd Salimov (Notebook No 1-2, June 30, 2007: page 50; also tape recording No 21-23).

Apparently, these boundary-making discourses and practices categorise all relocated villagers against the 1960s resettlement programme. Nonetheless, elites use them to intentionally and exceptionally stigmatise their most powerful opponents, especially Zamon Gulov, as they cannot defeat him by other means. In 1992, he moved from Vose' district to his 'grand-fatherland' ('*vatani boboi*') but caused a lot of trouble for the elites. He relies on his personal relations with the district governor, who is his compatriot and a former colleague in the professional-technical school of Vose' district.

Elites and their mahalla mediators enter into such boundary-making discourses and practices to protect their privileged status and rights in response to the contestation of six marginalised families in the 'poor's *guzar*' neighbourhood. The *guzar* is the lowest neighbourhood of the mosque-guzar. While elites have privatised the main water springs and some public water sources, more than half of the villagers have limited access to potable water and no access to irrigation water whatsoever. Residents of the 'poor's *guzar*' therefore transport potable water on the backs of donkeys from faraway and on a daily basis. As they assert, elites and the leaders of the mahalla and the collective farm prevent them from complaining about their marginalised situations to upper state departments.[124] These marginalised families feel that elites are able not only to punish them via bureaucratic and military means of the state but also to kick them out of the village due to their marginalised position in the kinship network. Here, reference to the distinctive identity of 'homeland' owners emphasises elites' inherited and privileged status in the kinship network of villagers.

Village identity vs. geographical outsiders

Another geographical and kinship-related reference is the so-called *Devdori* identity, namely the shared geographical boundary of villagers vis-à-vis some other villagers who are not originally from Devdor village. Along with cooptation and military means, powerful men manipulate *Devdori* identity to categorise and, if necessary, stigmatise their opponents. This immaterial tool is used to reject the claims of opponents[125] about the 'unfair' distribution of village resources. The majority of Mullo Ismatov's kinsmen inhabit his 'homeland' and only a few are scattered in adjacent villages, including Devdor

---

124 Personal interviews with the residents of the 'poor's *guzar*' (Notebook No 1-2, June 30, 2007: pages 51-52; Notebook No 1-2, July 13, 2007: pages 74-75; Notebook No 1-2, July 13, 2007: pages 76-77).

125 Including Atokhoja Hamdamov, Mullo Ismatov and Zubayd Salimov.

village. Rather, 'native' villagers categorise him as 'stranger' and mock his mistaken claim to equal status with them. The other protagonist, Atokhoja Hamdamov, was originally an inhabitant of the adjacent Tudani village before the Resettlement programme in the 1960s. In 1981, after he returned from the cotton-growing Farkhor district, he resettled in Devdor village. He took the important position of fuel distributor for the sovkhoz but was fired from the position and excluded from the circle of kolkhozi elites in 1997. Nevertheless, his son, Daler Hamdamov, would retain leadership of the village school and the DVO.

By referencing *Devdori* identity, elites discredit and stigmatise the 'inappropriate' claim of another non-*Devdori* villager, Zubayd Salimov. He recently complained formally to the provincial government about the 'intentional' barriers that district 'bureaucrats' (including the village *kolkhozi* elites) put up in opposition to his plan to establish a family farm. However, the elites managed to host and co-opt the government delegation commissioned to check out the complaint and even withdrew some of the appealer's shareholding land plot. This was 'punishment' in response to his act of challenging the elites. Moreover, the elites spread a rumour among the villagers and thereby discredited the appealer as a 'stranger' ('*begona*'), who "was struggling just for the interest of his *qabila* [here, patrilineal extended family] who live in Kulob."[126] This reference to *Devdori* identity, which invokes the cognitive construct about others or 'strangers', legitimises to a certain extent the punishment as a 'due response' to those who divulge 'village secrets'. Without such an attempt at legitimation, however, the mobilisation of external means, such as the government delegation, would spoil the elites' reputation instead.

At the same time, elites refer to *Devdori* identity to identify themselves with ordinary villagers and thereby attract their concerns about strangers, who are their personal opponents. They claim a moral commitment to the 'village honour' they share with 'their people', while their opponents do not. The stories and discourses shared by the majority tell that opponents 'betray' 'village honour' due to being non-*Devdori*. Most of the villagers believe that since Mullo Ismatov is not originally *Devdori*, he therefore provokes and discredits them by giving away 'village secrets'.[127] Even other 'friendly' opponents label him as a

[126] Personal interview with Zubayd Salimov (Notebook No 1-2, June 30, 2007: page 50; also tape recording No 21-23).

[127] My informants agree that there are inter-group conflicts which are 'secrets of the village' and they should not be known by any outsiders.

'plaintiff' (*'arizaboz'*), who "only strives for his personal profit and does not care about *qawmdori*."[128]

Reference to descent origins

Powerful men refer to another internal boundary, namely the descent origin of villagers, again to protect their privileged rights. Kolkhozi elites especially use – and actually create – the discourse of *Roghi* vs. *Khovalingi* descent groups to articulate their distinction and privilege as being the right of a 'true *Devdori*' and a 'homeland owner' [*vatandor*]. The 'true *Devdori*' identity of *Roghi* villagers is neither a 'geo-social boundary' nor a distinct reference to descent origin. Rather, it refers to the intra-village circle of elites and their loyal clients, who might not have originally established and built the village, as claimed sometimes by *Roghi* elites.

Elites again use the discourse about 'strangers' to disqualify and discredit the claims of their opponents and in return protect their own positions and privileges. They assure that strangers, including members of the *Khovalingi* descent group, do not care about 'village wellbeing' and 'village honour'. The claim that "the *Khovalingi* men came in order to capture their homeland [*vatan*]" refers to the fact that they lead the village school and DVO. In so doing, the claimants discredit the status of strangers, who "never care about *our* problems; rather, they divide villagers who are all kinsmen."[129] Principally, the claim about descent origin is used against the *Khovalingi* challenger, Zamon Gulov, as well as against his allies who come from different descent groups, but the elites assure that "[t]his *Khovalingi* misled them."[130] Thus, the memory of descent origin is not a story about descent groups and their necessary distinctions. The discourse instead serves as a raw resource to be reinvented and reinterpreted, in this case mainly by elites against their rivals.

Certainly, villagers recognise at least two descent groups – *Roghi* and *Khovalingi* – which refer to distinctive places of origin. The major patrilineal families belong to *Roghi* descent group whose ancestors are believed to have come from the Rogh region of Afghan Badakhshan. The *Roghi* villagers themselves refer to their rough linguistic expressions and scarce Dari[131] words and phrases as their own forms of distinction, while other families claim their ancestors came to the

---

[128] Personal interview with Atokhoja Hamdamov (Notebook No 1-2, June 28, 2007: pages 41-42).

[129] Personal interview with the vakil (Notebook No 1-2, July 26, 2007: pages 122-123).

[130] Ibid. (page 122).

[131] The Persian language is called 'Dari' in Afghanistan and 'Tajik' in Tajikistan.

Shuroobod area from Khovaling, currently a district situated to the north-west of Mu'minobod and Shuroobod districts.

Although the villagers know which extended families (*avlods*) belong to which descent groups, they have, as well as old men, blurred the memory of their past origin. Rather, they argue, particularly in the case of outsiders, for their common origin from 'Dahbedi Samarkand'[132] who resettled during unknown periods in two different regions – Rogh of Afghan Badakhshan and Khovaling (district) of contemporary Tajikistan. About one hundred years ago, they assert, their ancestors migrated and reunited in Devdor and other adjacent villages.

Qawmdori

Qawmdori is a notion that often refers to shared village, kinship and religious identity among villagers. This reference, first of all, actualises the belief that 'strangers' do not care about 'village honour'. Especially kolkhozi elites make use of this frame of mind to protect their reputation from the 'slander' of 'jealous' opponents. Villagers also agree with elites that opponents are self-interested strangers.

The reference to *qawmdori* further invokes suspicion of 'strangers' and their 'justice-seeking' activities. In part, villagers do not trust that elites' opponents struggle for justice by writing *ariza* (request or complaint letter) to state courts as well as to the provincial government and the presidential office. The fear of being prosecuted by elites and being labelled and reproached as 'strangers' thus stops opponents complaining about the unequal distribution of resources. In the *ariza* even the 'betrayers' of village honour and 'plaintiffs' do not break certain rules. Rather, they state their needs and refer to their legal rights. They especially conceal their cases from the public to avoid other people's skepticism.[133] Villagers and state officials reproach formal appeals to local and central state authorities, including the court. For example, a guard of the public birch garden was unable to privatise the garden until 2005, so he appealed to several district and central courts until he won the case through his cousin in the republican economic court. After a while, the district governor called him to his office and reproached him as a 'plaintiff': "I told him, that this was the first time I had seen his armchair and table [i.e. I am not claimant and do not visit

---

[132] Also in Shahritus district and in other regions of Tajikistan the members of different descent groups in the same villages claimed their common origin from 'Dahbedi Samarkand' (claimed as a settlement in Samarkand region) when the context required so.

[133] Personal interview (Notebook No 1-2, July 1, 2007: page 54).

state offices for such purposes]."[134] When he went to Dushanbe to express his gratitude to his cousin, the cousin advised him to be cautious, not to tell this story to anyone and not to confront the elites for the sake of others.

Also, cliental villagers refer to *qawmdori*, their shared 'village honour', to reproach and discredit those who contest the privileged rights of their patrons. For example, a client affirmed the 'need' of the village chairman, currently the head of the District Land Committee, to have privileged private access to the public water source, since "he always has guests in his house *from outside* who are also our [village's] guests."[135] According to the common perception, outsiders, including guests, are always *others* who potentially divulge 'village secrets'. Subject villagers expect that the 'village owners' ('*sohibo[n]i qishloq*') will protect 'village esteem' ('*obrui qishloq*') and that their houses should be adorned in a way that demonstrates the village's 'good image'. This argument was used to legitimise the contested distribution of a central government credit programme in favour of village owners. The bank-run programme was initiated to provide credit, for the agricultural activities of poor families, at a low interest rate of 0.7 percent; however, the elites misused the programme for their own private needs, including the reparation and renovation of their houses.[136]

In other contexts, *qawmdori* or its equivalent in such contexts – *qawmdori* – implicitly refer to the kinship and patron-client networks of kolkhozi elites. In the local idiom, such networks are defined as *qawmiyat.* The term *qawmiyat* suggests that kolkhozi elites especially hold superior positions due to their prevailing kinship ties in the village ('*qabila*') and alliance network with religious and state authorities at different levels ('*odam dar bolo*'). Such reference implies the villagers' self-acknowledgment of their inevitable limitations and subjugation, not only because of cliental expectation but also due to the fear that the elites will punish them by the means of bureaucratic barriers and other tools. One contestant believed that there were "always three to four *qawmiyat*" distinguished from other villagers by their wealth and superior positions. He asserted that the *qawmiyats* are 'village owners' and have a 'reaching hand', "since most of the people [villagers] are their *qabila*[137] and they have personal

---

[134] Personal interview (Notebook No 1-2, July 17, 2007: pages 99-100, 102).

[135] Personal interview (Notebook No 1-2, July 13, 2007: pages 74-75).

[136] Personal observation (Notebook No 1-2, July 17, 2007: page 102).

[137] The informant explains *qabila* as not only kinsmen but also *muttaham,* i.e. 'indebted' or clients.

ties at the upper-level [*odam dar bolo*]. Nobody will listen to me, because I have neither *qabila* nor *odam*."[138]

In fact, several cases highlight that kolkhozi elites's possession of both indigenous and external (such as state and development) power restricts and defeats their opponents. Along with bureaucratic tactics, cooptation, administrative tools and military threat, elites utilise indigenous means, including collective identities and the categorisation norms and practices of stigma and ostracism. The notion of *qawmdori*, in this sense, means an imposed and pressurised collective norm which commits the subject *qabila* to 'peace in the home of [their] daughters'. This threat reminds villagers of their kinship and bureaucratic dependence on the elites and leads them to a prudent and cautious (not even opportunistic) path of 'concession'. One striking example is the 2006 'uprising' of suffering villagers, who went to the district governor to deal with the unequal distribution of land resources. The governor promised to solve the problem but he did not raise the matter officially for a long time. Such a way of skipping appeals is a strategic manoeuvre used by government functionaries to allow local mediators to resolve a problem through indigenous means. As an informant asserted, "You write the complaint letter [*ariza*] and they do not respond to it until the second time you re-write and pass it personally on to the government official, if you have personal relations [*odam*]."[139] Subsequently, several men gathered and intended to go to the governor. However, mahalla elite elders convinced some of them not to go by reminding them that "it would not be good in *qawmdori*." The informants remember that their concession was not only due to some leaders who did not join the gathering the second time but also due to their fear of destroying their kinship ties in the village; the fear of '[violating] peace in the home of [their] daughters'.

Thus, *qawmdori* verifies the privileged role of elites both in the kinship network of villagers and in the political and military departments of the state. Due to such a role, elites' opponents therefore try to avoid direct confrontations. For example, in the school-*guzar* the former chairman of the collective farm and the current head of the District Land Committee, supplied water from an INGO-initiated public water source for his household. Next day, his neighbour, his implacable contestant, took an axe to cut off the water pipe taking water to the household of the elite. But his son, due to his fear of an 'uncertain future', prevented the direct retaliation of his father by vowing that he would leave the village. At the same time, a mahalla elite elder, who was responsible for dispute

---

[138] Personal interview with Atokhoja Hamdamov (Notebook No 1-2, July 20, 2007: page 111).
[139] Ibid. (page 40)

settlement among villagers, promised to resolve the dispute by talking with the elite's father. As the contestant stated, "For one month [the mahalla elite elder] promised to solve the problem, but then he kept silent. And he averted us."[140]

Such prudent and sometimes opportunistic concessions and mediation 'for the sake of *qawmdori*' favour kolkhozi elites who derived most benefits from the Public Water Project. In 2003, an INGO based in Qurghonteppa city, the provincial capital of Khatlon province, invested in this project, which was half-implemented during the late Soviet sovkhoz. The purpose was to supply each *guzar* with two distribution points of potable water and thus to distribute them equally to the inhabitants. Another priority was to allocate a distribution point in the school orchard for public access. Although the INGO and villagers elected the initiative group of the project from village engineers, veterinarians, medical practitioners and teachers to sustain the project in future, elites replaced them with their own selected members. The vakil appointed his brother-in-law as the project brigadir.

Initially the INGO planned to bring potable water from three springs (2 to 3 kilometres away from the village) and allocate three *guzars* per two distribution points (a total of six sources). In the smaller school-*guzar* one point was planned for households and the other for the school orchard. Ultimately, two water springs were supplied and distributed through five points in all *guzars*. The school-*guzar* had only one point for households situated next to the households of the vakil's family network. In the mosque-*guzar* one point was not allocated as it was initially planned but rather was set next to the project brigadir's household. Consequently, six households in the 'the poor's *guzar*' neighbourhood were deprived of pumped water.[141] In the upper-*guzar* both points were allocated next to the vakil's allied families, who also used this potable water for household irrigation.

The other case also shows how prudent concession was important in a powerful man seizing a collective water source. As a result, most of the 24 households of the upper-*guzar* were deprived of irrigation water during the dry season of 2007. Five years ago, neighbours organised a *hashar* and redirected a water source to irrigate their yards, but the source was seized by an elite member, a prosecutor in the capital city. He was building a villa in a two-

---

[140] Ibid. (page 43)

[141] In 'the poor's *guzar*', in the lower part of the mosque-*guzar*, as one of its inhabitants (Personal interview; Notebook No 1-2, July 13, 2007: page 74) affirms, six households have had no proper access to potable water and electricity since 1973. The public water source is used mainly by elite families. Only a few lower households can use the spring water flowing from the mosque to irrigate their household plots.

hectare garden in the former sovkhoz in the north-eastern part of the Upper-*guzar*. In the early spring he bought a pipe and redirected the water supply to his garden, without asking or talking with his neighbours. A young man cultivated a lot of vegetables next to the water stream, but he was not angry or envious even though he realised that without water his potatoes and cucumbers would dry up. When I talked with him, he was rather patient and even looked wise. He felt that 'the water owner' was a kind and generous man with whom his father was a relative and now was begging for water.

In this subchapter I have discussed the role that collective identities, such as Islam, intertwined village and kinship affiliations and *qawmdori*, play in legitimising political and economic claims and privileges. The following subchapter shows how collective identities stabilise the highly contested political and economic environment.

Persistence of the contested boundaries of *qawmdori*

The mahalla serves to sustain political and economic stability in Devdor village. As mentioned already, kolkhozi elites dominate key rural organisations, including the mahalla, and thereby shape decision-making practices. The organisation is an informal political structure which mediates to bring local and state (jamoat and district government) authorities together. It therefore serves to mobilise both local and state and material and immaterial resources to subjugate villagers to the 'peaceful' sustenance of existing political and economic relations.

One immaterial mean is reference to the re-invented notion of *qawmdori*, which shapes a shared collective identity of villagers based on their religious, kinship and village affiliations. In this case, mahalla mediators, who are at the same time elite elders, use logic opposite to what they usually refer to as collective identities. In the previous subchapter we observed that collective identities serve to legitimise the political and economic claims and privileges of powerful men at the expense of marginalising a significant amount of villagers. This subchapter shows how powerful mahalla leaders and mediators refer to *qawmdori* to reunite excluded villagers in order to stabilise political and economic relations. However, once again, *qawmdori* is less about the peaceful coexistence and prosperity of villagers and more about the 'peaceful' sustenance of the existing order of political and economic tensions and inequality.

The sections below discuss different activities of mahalla mediators for such 'peaceful' sustenance, including:

- Reciprocal practices;
- Social welfare;
- Common wellbeing and
- Dispute settlement.

Reciprocal practices of extended families and neighbours

Reciprocal practices (such as *hashar*, debt-giving, sharing of services and opportunities and care for old, sick and handicapped people) are regarded as the religious commitments of members of patrilineal extended families (*avlods*). Family members make relatively imbalanced reciprocal exchanges through ceremonies such as weddings, circumcisions (*khatna*) and funerals. They also share houses, land plots, seeds, agricultural machines and financial resources as part of a subsistence economy. During the sowing and harvest seasons, family members are mobilised for mutual support. Nuclear families lagging behind due to seasonal restrictions in their agricultural and household activities are supplied with a labour force made up from extended families' junior members. They are mobilised through *hashar*, an institutional practice of labour sharing organised to mobilise extended family members.

Both family seniors and mahalla mediators commit extended family members, including juniors and women, and sometimes neighbours to joint social life and mutual economic support. This is an effective way to use the reciprocal networks of a patrilineal extended family and neighbourhood for socio-political and economic 'stability' ('*tinji*') in the village. Mediators interpret the ritual performance of economic activities, household maintenance and ceremonies as the manifestation of a commitment to '*avlod* honour' ('*nangi avlod*') and a 'good neighbourhood' ('*hamsoyadori*'). Also, local state authorities agree that it is necessary to invoke these norms and emotions in order to use reciprocal practices for socio-economic stability. As a local state functionary suggested, "To invoke someone's honour (*ba nomus ovardan*) means to wake him up to see [to make him conscious of seeing] others…, that is, to see how other extended families and neighbourhoods succeed."[142]

As a measure of stabilisation, mahalla and religious notables spread stories about 'exemplary families'. The members of these exemplary families discharge their religious 'debts' (duties) before each other. The 'debts' of the family seniors include the initiation rites of circumcision (*khatna)* and marriage, and the

[142] Personal interview with the deputy chairman of Dashtijum Jamoat; Shuroobod district (Notebook No 1-2, June 13, 2007: pages 10-12).

transmission of the 'paternal profession' ('*kasbi padar*') and religious knowledge ('*ilm*') to junior members. In turn, male junior members especially are expected to manifest their 'honour' by devoting themselves to mutual support through ceremonies and economic activities (e.g. *hashar*). Their refusal to enter into mutual support diminishes their trustworthiness among family co-members as well as other co-villagers.

Many informants memorise stories that only the members of extended families can be trusted to keep for reciprocal exchange practices, including *hashar* and cash debt. They avoid asking *others* (including their neighbours) for reciprocal support, but rather regard it as a 'debt' and immediately return the exact value in case they become indebted. One of my informants felt that "once he borrows money from his neighbour, the bad word of the neighbour [telling 'others' about the debtor] easily damages his reputation." When he could not pay off the debt he borrowed from his neighbour to plough his land plot, the neighbour reproached him in front of 'friends and enemies'. He also set a higher interest rate and almost every day came to his home and demanded that he return what was owed.[143]

While distrust and distance divide neighbours, mahalla authorities refer to *qawmdori*, the shared village, kinship and religious identity of villagers, to strengthen the neighbourhood as a network of limited reciprocal practices. They do this by propagating the religious moral norms of 'Muslim debt' and a 'good neighbourhood'. 'Good neighbourhood' refers to mutual service, support and visits by neighbours during initiation ceremonies such as marriage, the religious feasts of Ramadan and Kurban and funerals. Such reciprocal support practiced as a balanced return is a norm enforced by religious sources. Especially, 'wall-to-wall' neighbours are obliged to the 'due of neighbour' which is set to cover food, financial and labour shortages during religious ceremonies.

Guzar neighbourhoods also have a few reciprocal practices, such as initiation ceremonies (*khatm*, *khudoi*, etc.), and practical mutual activities, such as sharing pasture land.[144] The solidarity networks of kinsmen, neighbours, friends and colleagues organise the initiation ceremonies. The role of mahalla mediators and local state elites is crucial in continuously regulating these practices and enforcing them by reference to the religious identity of villagers, which commits them to their *guzar* neighbourhoods. The practice is patterned as imbalanced reciprocity and enforced by the Islamic norm of *amonat* (deposit), which entails the institutional practice of a pledge (*garaw*), an equal and adequate

---

143 Personal interview (Notebook No 1-2, July 13, 2007: pages 74-75).

144 '*Navbati poda*': the turn of the *guzar* inhabitants to herd their livestock.

pledge, in the case of damage to private livestock. The practice mentions the high value of the personal involvement of neighbours, upon whom the burden of *amonat* is imposed only in this way: "One has his pasturing turn but he hires a different person. It is good that *others* earn money. But *others* [do not] care for the goods of the Muslims (*'moli mu'min'*)."[145] The hire is only permissible for trustworthy villagers, since it is feasible to withdraw the pledge from them as well.

Mahalla programmes of social welfare

Mahalla authorities, especially the vakil and the elite elder (Murodkhon Davlatkhonov), allocate and regulate support programmes, including the welfare programmes of the state, humanitarian aid from international agencies and the indigenous institutional practice of *sadaqa.* In addition to the stabilising effect of these means and resources, they serve to improve the reputation of kolkhozi elites, such as the vakil, and thus impose their authority upon the recipients – pensioners and disabled and poor people. As the vakil informed me, there are about 60 recipient families out of 96 village families, including: 1) five widowed women who head their households; 2) eight households who have less than five small animals and 3) 47 pensioners.[146] As external welfare schemes are insufficient, the recipient families appreciate 'the personal efforts of the vakil' in regularly providing pensions and humanitarian supplies of flour and oil.

The indigenous institution of *sadaqa* provides minimal survival support, such as food and clothes, for 'poor' (*bechora*)[147] families. Mahalla authorities refer to religious identity to commit villagers to such a practice. Also, related religious norms define the reason for, size and type of *sadaqa.* Food and sometimes clothes are provided for poor families if they are devoid of male adults or their male adults are handicapped and therefore cannot maintain their subsistence needs. Mahalla mediators, mainly the elite elder, arrange the practice through religious and group-related ceremonies, such as food-sharing during the religious feast of Kurban, family-related food-sharing (*khayru khudoi*), weddings and funerals. Additionally, they mobilise resources from villagers to organise

---

[145] Personal interview with Atokhoja Hamdamov (Notebook No 1-2, July 13, 2007: page 74).

[146] Personal interview (Notebook No 1-2, July 26, 2007: page 122).

[147] The poor are regarded as *bekasu bechora* (*'bekas'* – 'alone': without kin and *'bechora'* – 'without any chance' and 'poor'), i.e. families without male adults, especially widowed women and old families.

important initiation rituals for the poor, including marriages and funerals. So far, three families have needed and received such support from their co-villagers (see Table 5: Families receiving *sadaqa*).

Table 5: Families receiving *sadaqa*

#	Families who receive *sadaqa*	The types and purposes of *sadaqa*	How *sadaqa* is provided	Expected *sadaqa* in future	Networks that provide *sadaqa*
1	A widowed female-headed family	Occasional bread and food	Neighbours and family-related ceremonies	Villagers' duty to her survival and funeral (*'guru chub'*)	Neighbours and families who organise ceremonies
2	An old man-headed family	Financial and material support to marry his son off	Through the elders during religious feasts in the mosque	Not expected; his son is expected to generate income and to care for his old father	Almost every household in the village
3	Old couple with two daughters	Occasional bread and food	Family-related ceremonies	Funeral	Families who organise ceremonies

Source: My field research (May – September 2007)

Mahalla mediators highlight this shared *Devdori* identity to commit villagers to providing *sadaqa* for the poor as an attribute of their 'village honour' vis-à-vis others. As one of them told me, "[t]heir *tinji* [wellness, quietness] is the *tinji* [tranquility, stability] of the village. Their survival and funeral (*'guru chub'*)[148] are our duty. If we do not implement our duty, we are ashamed."[149] In order to facilitate the provision of *sadaqa*, mediators organise the related religious and customary ceremonies of food-sharing (i.e. *khayru khudoi*) through sacred religious sites and events. Without this mediation, which refers to *qawmdori*, villagers do not always provide *sadaqa* to unrelated poor in the village, since

[148] *'Guru chub'* literally means 'grave and wood'. Here, the phrase means support for survival and the funeral of the poor as a religious obligation of co-villagers.

[149] Personal interview with Atokhoja Hamdamov (Notebook No 1-2, June 28, 2007: page 42).

"this may cause harm to help those who do not beg for you." Rather, men and women go to the district centre or other cities to distribute *sadaqa* to beggars in markets, in order to "beg God for luck and the success of [their] families."

Resource mobilisation for 'village wellbeing'

Mahalla mediators, especially the elite elder, Murodkhon Davlatkhonov, organise practices of 'village wellbeing' such as a village-level *hashar*. These practices are ordered by the jamoat to 'prepare' and thus to demonstrate the 'desired look' of the village to 'guests', especially state visitors. Such an organised *hashar* commits individual households to repair and to adorn the physical appearance (e.g. to whiten walls) of their houses, their street (*guzar*) and visible land plots and gardens. To effectively mobilise the *hashar* (labour, in-kind and financial resources) of villagers, authorities articulate a superior 'exemplary' (*'ibratnok'*) village identity. As such, they invoke villagers' *taassub* ('fanaticism'; here, envious competition) vis-à-vis adjacent villages' inhabitants. The elite elder, the mediator of *hashar*, frequently refers to *qawmdori* and 'village honour' to interpret *hashar* as an important attribute of village identity.

Mahalla authorities call on the 'Islamic debt' of villagers to organise a regular *hashar* during religious feasts, in the early spring and late autumn, for the maintenance of the mosque, cemetery, inter-*guzar* and pasture bridges – all defined as religious assets of the village. In this manner, they also commit individual families to care for sacred sites, such as shahids, located next to their households and which are not maintained by the regular *hashar*.

The practices and 'projects' of 'common wellbeing' stabilise socio-economic and political situations in the village, while they also enhance *qawmdori* and the religious reputation of kolkhozi elites as well as increase their material and symbolic power. Also, these projects are especially important to identify and discredit those who do not obey the 'desired' order of *qawmdori*, i.e. those who contest the elites.

When the elite elder had collected per 32 TJ Somoni from each village household to construct the mosque's prayer-bathroom, collective identities were crucial in mobilising resources from villagers. One important measure involved visiting individual households and thereby committing them to 'village wellbeing' as their '*avlodi* honour' and 'religious debt'. Villagers contribute to the practices of 'village wellbeing', not so much due to their personal loyalty to mahalla authorities but rather due to their concern to protect their '*avlodi* honour'. Family honour and reputation are necessary to secure positions in the broader kinship, religious and patron-client networks of villagers. Even opponents, who assert that the collector misuses the contributed resources, do not dare disobey the campaign, as this would be interpreted as religious disobedience. One measure the vakil undertook against someone who did not contribute to the campaign was to highlight his 'alien' identity and thus impose psychological pressure upon him. By hinting at the indigenous perceptions regarding 'others' (who "do not inhabit the village with their extended families [and) do not join our deaths and dead'), the vakil threatened to "kick him out of the village."[150]

The 'on-site' measures of dispute settlement

Internal or 'on-site' means, including kinship, neighbourhood and religious commitments, are important in solving disputes and conflicts among village inhabitants. Mahalla mediators and local state elites use these internal tools of negotiation and coercion to 'stabilise' political and socio-economic relations. To achieve this goal, they manipulate the discourse about 'peace' or 'stability' ('*tinji*') and introduce 'on-site' measures to maintain it accordingly. Both jamoat and district state functionaries authorise their mahalla mediators to deal with and settle disputes via indigenous mechanisms, and they only inform them about unsettled issues. Personal access of the elite elder, Murodkhon Davlatkhonov, to individual households increases his mediation power over dispute settlement practices. Also, *guzar* representatives in the mahalla are obliged to 'observe and keep order' in their *guzars* and to inform mahalla leaders about any unresolved disputes.

State military intervention, undertaken by police officers of the jamoat and District Interior Department, is also used to pressurise local people into negotiating conflicts through indigenous means. This intervention also refers to the disputants' family (*avlodi*) and religious honours and identities.

Reference to family and religious honours and identities commits villagers to *qawmdori*, which interprets disputes as shame vis-à-vis others (*'ayb'* or '*sharmandagi*'). Villagers feel that others judge their disputes as disloyalty to their 'village honour' and 'Islamic debt'. Mahalla mediators, state elites and police officers then make use of this notion to resolve disputes. For example, at a wedding celebration a couple of 'disorderly' ('*betartib*') men slugged out their differences. Only after mahalla mediators and a jamoat police officer intervened and forcibly gathered them in the village mosque to teach them 'village honour' and 'Muslimness' did they reveal their open conflict.

---

[150] Personal interview with Zubayd Salimov (Notebook No 1-2, June 30, 2007: page 50; also tape recording No 21-23)

The mahalla integrates indigenous and external (state and international) means and resources to sustain political and economic stability in favour of elites. However, the following discussion on the Devdor Village Organisation (DVO) shows that kolkhozi elites do not have access to a significant amount of international resources, which endangers their *qawmdori* authority in the face of the increasing role of the current leaders of the DVO.

The case of the Devdor Village Organisation

This subchapter considers the role local people's collective identities play in organising a community-based development project in Devdor village – the so-called Devdor Village Organisation (DVO). Actors refer to collective identities to legitimise their privileged access to the decision-making practices and development resources of the new organisation. In the following sections I discuss how the introduction of the DVO led to competition between local actors (section one), the marginalisation of some families (section two) and the adaptation of development programmes to local institutions (section three).

Contested boundaries of the leadership of the DVO

On 21st May 2002, the MSDSP established the DVO – one of the first VOs in Shuroobod district – in Devdor village. The establishment of the DVO gave rise to the intensification of disputes between the elites and DVO leaders. Kolkhozi elites, who missed the opportunity to become DVO leaders, attempted to take over the organisation. They did not run DVO from the beginning not only due to the early preference of the donor organisation – the MSDSP – but mainly due to their own underestimation of this new organisation. Managers and MSDSP experts believed that village teachers were the "most educated, intelligent and committed" villagers regarding "community development" ideas.[151] Besides, the elites were not interested in leading the DVO. Like many other villagers, they believed that "The *foreign* organisation [DVO] is provisional and soon after [providing] two or three aid packages [humanitarian aid and development programmes] leaves the country."[152] The perception of the DVO as a provisional and 'alien' structure also played a decisive role. Consequently, elites hesitated to lead the DVO, which was not

---

[151] Personal interview with the manager of the construction section of the district office of the MSDSP in Shuroobod district (Notebook No 1-1, May 15, 2007: pages 154-155).
[152] Personal interviews with DVO leaders (Notebook No 1-2, July 4, 2007: page 66; Notebook No 1-2, July 13, 2007: page 79).

soundly endorsed by and represented in their patron-client network in state offices. The other important reason why the elites did not take over the new organisation was their internal conflict and further fragmentation. As discussed earlier, the privatisation and reform of public properties of the Soviet sovkhoz enriched only a few *kolkhozi* elites, current mahalla authorities, while others, current DVO leaders, gradually retreated back to their family farms.

To justify their confrontation with DVO leaders, kolkhozi elites refer to *qawmdori* (shared kinship, village and religious identities of villagers). In June 2007, 29 elite families did not accept DVO membership. They claimed that the teachers had no competency ('*uhdabaroi*'), i.e. experience and power in *qawmdori* to run the DVO. Elites accused the teachers of incompetence, which gave rise to the current discord and 'division' among villagers, who are all kinsmen. To legitimise their privileged leadership right, they discredit DVO leaders and disgrace the place, purpose and participants in related activities. The DVO office is named a 'slander-house', where "the head of the DVO and his friends gather and distinguish themselves from their kinsmen [villagers]."[153] This accusation is agreed upon by many villagers due to their belief that "no one works for public goods without any benefit." Hence, they treat the DVO as a family 'firm' ('*shirkat*') and reluctantly contribute to its development. The head's family prepared to accept the MSDSP guests in the office on July 24-25, 2007, while other members did not contribute to this event[154] (see Picture 5 below).

---

[153] Personal interview with the vakil (Notebook No 1-2, July 26, 2007: pages 122-123).
[154] Personal observation (Notebook No 1-2, July 24-25, 2007: pages 119-121).

Picture 5: Family preparations to receive MSDSP guests

To diminish the reputation of DVO leaders, elites also refer to the *Shia* origin of Aga Khan (the founder of the MSDSP).[155] This is a powerful argument for a community of Sunni Muslims who distrust and blame the 'adherents of an alien religion'. In return, not only do DVO leaders justify their competency in *qawmdori*, but they also protect their organisation and its development activities in response to increasing distrust and blame. To legitimise the presence of the DVO, its head constantly mentions agreements and cooperation between the MSDSP and local governments, including the jamoat and district government offices. He refers to the 'friendly ties' between Aga Khan and the President of Tajikistan and hangs their portraits in the DVO office to convince villagers that the organisation exists exclusively for improving their socio-economic conditions. Poor villagers expect and demand this function, which thus limits the agency of the new organisation.

Reference to and the perception of *qawmdori* reflects villagers' demands and expectations. They refer to *qawmdori*, their shared Islamic, kinship and village

[155] People usually call the MSDSP 'Aga Khan'.

identity, to adapt DVO programmes as patronage resources. They also agree with elites and use the discourse of 'stability' ('*tinji*') to integrate the DVO into the mahalla. They claim that otherwise, the DVO will cause discord and division among the kinsmen. They also explain the activities of the DVO as a 'chief-game' ('*raisbozi*' as well as '*kalonbozi*') and an 'organisation-game' ('*tashkilotbozi*'), i.e. the flippant and unsafe treatment of *qawmdori*. Villagers observe struggles between DVO leaders and their opponents not because of any principal difference in their 'goals and activities' but because of their 'localism' ('*mahalgaroi*') or 'self-interest', which divides villagers and makes them enemies. They believe that the integration of the DVO and its development programmes into either the mahalla or collective farm will resolve the disputes, as shown by VOs in adjacent villages.

Frequent reference to the endangered boundaries of *qawmdori* enforces the popular perception that only elites can secure 'peace' ('*tinji*') in the village. This reference is based upon and in turn intensifies the indigenous image of a '*rais*', a chief or leader with the proper credentials, who maintains the indigenous pillars of socio-political order and stability, especially peace ('*tinji*'), justice ('*insof*') and wealth ('*davlat*') (see Figure 7: The indigenous image of elites). The image, which is based upon the collective norms of *tinji*, *insof* and *davlat*, simultaneously legitimises the political and economic privileges of elites.

Figure 7: The indigenous image of elites

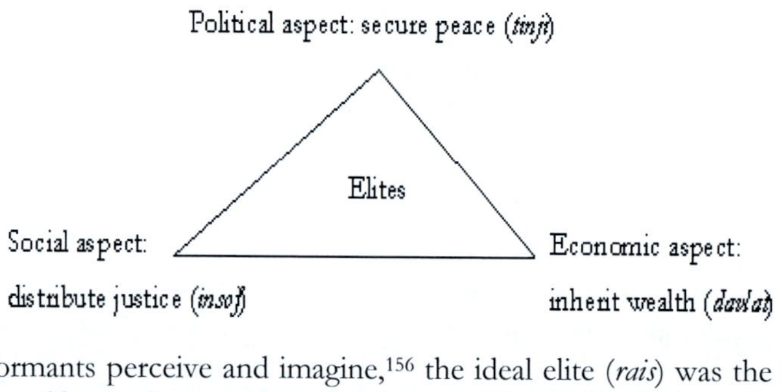

As my informants perceive and imagine,[156] the ideal elite (*rais*) was the head of the Soviet sovkhoz, who was powerful, just, wealthy and had personal relations with other powerful men and state elites. He could therefore dominate all

[156] Personal interviews with the DVO members (Notebook No 1-2, July 13, 2007: pages 76-77; Notebook No 1-2, June 28, 2007: page 46; also tape recording No 20; Notebook No 1-2, July 3, 2007: page 65).

political and economic structures of the subject villages. Today, such an exemplary *rais* is the head of Daraiob VO. In his earlier life he was the chief animal expert and the deputy chairman of the Soviet sovkhoz. Now he has substantial material wealth, including a private tractor to plough the land plots of poor co-villagers. He also effortlessly attracts external (state and development) resources for 'his people' due to his 'close ties' with the district government and the district branch of the MSDSP.

In 2004, kolkhozi elites and their mahalla mediators encouraged 16 members of the DVO to appoint the current vakil as the head of the DVO. At that time he had already substituted for his father, who ran the mahalla for more than ten years. Villagers, including the previous leaders of the DVO, did not resist this move until district representatives of the MSDSP disapproved due to its contradiction with the VO bylaw.[157] However, recent changes in the strategic orientation of the MSDSP mean it has to rely on kolkhozi elites, who now run VOs in many villages of Shuroobod district. Devdor village is no exception to this process. At least, elites and MSDSP staff meet in informal gatherings to strive for mutual trust against the current DVO leaders. The integration of the DVO into the elite-run mahalla was initiated by the MSDSP and Shuroobod government in order to follow the 'successful experience' of Mu'minobod district.

Furthermore, the alarming reference to the endangered boundaries of *qawmdori* belittles the public worth of the implemented projects of the DVO. Thereby, it discredits and disparages the implemented and ongoing activities of DVO leaders as 'begging', 'swindling' ('*qallobi*'; in this case, collecting resources from people against religious norms) and 'incompetence'. They interpret *qawmdori* and religious norms to justify this accusation. In such a way, mahalla authorities have devalued the implemented projects of the MSDSP, such as cobblestone pavements for internal roads and the construction of the inter-*guzar* bridge. The leaders of the DVO, who managed these projects, were blamed for misusing and stealing financial and material resources provided for the programmes. To convince the villagers, elites explain the 'self-interests' of DVO leaders as their disloyalty to 'village honour', and they refer to their non-*Devdori* origins to provoke villagers' distrust (the descent origins discussed above). Here, reference to '*Devdori*' vs. 'outsiders' legitimises the accusations of the DVO leaders in line with moral notions such as 'begging', 'swindling' and 'incompetence'. In the minds of the villagers, an 'outsider' characterises these notions, which in practice limit and undermine the authority of the 'outsider' DVO leaders.

---

[157] Personal interview with Daler Hamdamov (Notebook No 1-2, July 13, 2007: pages 78-79).

The limited and undermined authority of DVO leaders constrained their attempts to institutionalise MSDSP-initiated practices, such as the extraction of fees from grants, rent-outs as well as contributions from wealthy men.[158] In 2004, for instance, three members contributed only 10-15 TJ Somoni when they were personally asked by MSDSP representatives in a meeting of the DVO General Council.[159] The following typical case shows that members do not voluntarily contribute resources without knowing they will receive cliental expectations and favours in return. The MSDSP granted 3,000 USD to a member of the DVO in accordance with a contract that he pays the interest rate to the Village Development Fund[160] annually, at the end of the harvest season. As the head of the DVO told me, "Now we cannot explain to him the terms of the contract and every harvest season we have to ask him to pay the interest rate – as if we are begging him for money."[161]

As discussed before, the activities of 'village wellbeing' are an important source of both material and symbolic power for kolkhozi elites and their mahalla mediators.[162] Therefore, their alarmism makes sense, since the leaders of the

---

158 Personal interviews with the head and members of the DVO (Notebook No 1-2, June 30, 2007: page 53; also tape recording No 24; Notebook No 1-2, July 14, 2007: page 84; also tape recording No 33); also an observation of the dispute between the head and the member of the DVO (Notebook No 1-2, July 2, 2007: page 58).

159 The participation of members in the supreme decision-making body of the DVO General Council (*Majlisi umumi*) and in DVO programme activities must demonstrate "the fact that namely the members are the holders of the organisation" (Bylaw VO 2001: 11). At least 80 percent of the members are expected to organise the DVO General Council on a monthly basis as a central setting for decision-making practices at village level. Access to any, especially financial, activities and accounts of the DVO should be transparent to all members, not only to its leaders or some limited members.

160 The Village Development Fund of the DVO was established in 2002 in order to institutionalise the mobilisation of the villagers' financial means for development purposed. By July 2007, the total means were 5,826.23 TJ Somoni. The main sources were monthly membership fees (0.2 TJ Somoni per each member – totalling 1,041.90 TJ Somoni), interest rate (3 percent) from lending money from the fund and interest rate (0.3 percent) from MSDSP grants. The VO bylaw (Bylaw VO 2001) instructs that the fund may enforce the individual commitment and contribution of members to communal wellbeing, while "...poorer households may pay less and wealthier households more" (11-12).

161 Personal interview with the head of the DVO (Notebook No 1-2, June 30, 2007: page 53)

162 E.g. personal interviews with the elite elder, Murodkhon Davlatkhonov (Notebook No 1-2, July 26, 2007: page 123) and vakil (Notebook No 1-2, July 26, 2007: pages 122-123)

DVO are taking over their functions in the village and thereby endangering their *qawmdori* status and reputation among their fellow villagers.

Such concern explains why mahalla authorities did not participate in and contribute to the inter-*guzar* bridge construction project. And also it explains why they separately mobilised the labour and financial resources of villagers to *re-construct* the constructed bridge. In 2002, the DVO applied to the MSDSP to finance the technical infrastructure project for the inter-*guzar* bridge, which connects the mosque-guzar and school-*guzar*. The project was mainly financed by the MSDSP and implemented by the DVO in 2004. In all, 6,000 USD was assigned to build a 12x6-metre iron bridge on cemented stems standing 4 metres in height. However, as the then-head of the DVO recounted, only a few people contributed to the development project especially because mahalla authorities had no involvement in it.[163]

However, in the spring of 2005, mahalla authorities decided to build a separate cemented dam to the lower side of the constructed bridge "in order to prevent soil erosion under the bridge," – as the elite elder and mahalla mediator claimed.[164] For this purpose, the mediator was able to collect 30 TJ Somoni, both in cash and in-kind, from each household and to organise a *hashar* with the majority of villagers. In 2006, a heavy flood destroyed and washed away the cemented dam. Then, frequent spring rain eroded the easily absorbable soil under the bridge and consequently destroyed the lower stems of the bridge. Although primarily designated for any types of transportation, today only people can use the almost destroyed bridge. In the autumn of 2006, a mahalla mediator *re-stored* his *qawmdori* authority and collected wood (a donkey-burden, or about 2 cubic metres per household) to fill up the gully of the inter-*guzar* bridge and for another gully of the pasture bridge. In order to maintain the connection between the two *guzars*, before the sowing season in early spring, the mediator mobilised men for *hashar* to build a wooden-made bridge of about 10 to 15 metres which would usually last until the next spring when the heavy floodwaters would wash it away again.

The frequent reference of both the elites and DVO leaders to *qawmdori* first of all reflects their increasing contestation. This reference to *qawmdori*, which is less about direct confrontation but more about rumour, helps elites to bolster their endangered role in managing "common wellbeing" activities. As a result, Daler Hamdamov, the current head of the DVO, cannot convince his members to

163 Personal interview with the elders, Atokhoja Hamdamov and Zamon Gulov (Notebook No 1-2, July 14, 2007: page 84; also tape recording No 33)

164 Personal interview with the elite elder, Murodkhon Davlatkhonov (Notebook No 1-2, July 26, 2007: page 123)

collect 2,400 TJ Somoni to build an iron pendant bridge – the only way to avoid floods caused by heavy spring rains. The DVO leader feels that "[i]n order to be supported you must be powerful in all respects – be wealthy, have *odam* [personal ties with state functionaries] and *qabila* [prevailing kinship and patron-client relations with villagers]."[165]

Gradually, the current leaders of the DVO also lost their authority to operate programme activities and resources of the DVO. Therefore, they have to rely on the mediation of mahalla authorities, especially Murodkhon Davlatkhonov. Although mahalla authorities are not members of the DVO themselves, they influence decisions taken for resource mobilisation and distribution via the DVO. In 2004, the then-head of the DVO, Zamon Gulov, collected 2,730 TJ Somoni from 58 households for the construction of the village school. This school project was expected to be financed mainly (95 percent) by the district branch of the MSDSP and the district government.[166]

While the school project was not financed in the end, villagers demanded that their contributions be returned. Nevertheless, elite elders interceded to lend this contribution to wealthier traders, including one of their sons, who was a 'passive member' of the DVO, according to the classification list of DVO members. He used the fund during June 2005 to March 2007 and returned almost the same amount in the end. Again, in a meeting of the DVO General Council on March 2007, leaders and some members of the DVO suggested spending the fund on any 'well-being' purpose in the village: either for setting up an electricity transformer in a village *guzar* or restoring the flood-prone inter-*guzar* bridge. The majority prioritised the inter-*guzar* bridge. However, mahalla authorities forced the members to vote against the resolution of this council. As a sign of obedience, they again gave the funds to wealthy traders: 1,000 TJ Somoni to one trader and the other part, 1,793 TJ Somoni, to another, both elite members. Such privileged distribution of DVO funds is against MSDSP VO bylaw (Bylaw VO 2001), which instructs that DVO members should have privileged access to developmental programmes and services.[167]

---

[165] Personal interview with the head of the DVO (Notebook No 1-2, July 13, 2007: page 78).

[166] Among other measures used to strengthen the participatory voice of especially 'vulnerable groups' (poor families and women), the MSDSP contributes 90 percent of its financial and technical means, while villages are expected to cover the rest, including the labour force.

[167] Personal interview with the head of the DVO (Notebook No 1-2, July 13, 2007: pages 78-79).

Contested boundaries of membership

After discussing how elites compete with current DVO leaders to take over the DVO, this section focuses on how collective identities were used to marginalise or exclude certain people from the project. Villagers expect and demand that the DVO and MSDSP act as support organisations. They benefit from financial and material means of the DVO's Village Development Fund and the MSDSP for their household needs, especially subsistence agriculture, labour migration to Russia and traditional ceremonies: "Thanks to [them], one has not to bow before any neighbour, before any enemy [*nomard*] for debt," expressed a member.[168]

To legitimise their privileged and exclusive access to these means, DVO members therefore refer to their collective identities, including common village affiliation and the hierarchical norms of male vs. female and senior vs. junior family members. This is the indigenous adaptation of the DVO, which is in contravention of VO bylaw (Bylaw VO 2001), which instructs that any person, regardless of his or her gender, place of origin or residence can be enrolled and benefit as a member of the VO. However, again shared village ('*Devdori*') identity is a decisive argument in excluding geographical 'outsiders'. Situated half a kilometre away from Devdor village and consisting of about 10 households, Khushkasangov village has no VO and has never been involved in any MSDSP programme. To solve the issue, in 2005, the MSDSP led the inhabitants of Khushkasangov village to apply formally for membership of the DVO. The request was discussed in the DVO General Council but the *Devdori* people protested that "the violent *Khushkasangovi* men will seize all the programmes."[169] Although the leaders explained that the MSDSP matches its programmes with the number of VO members, they turned down their neighbours' request.

In the majority of other cases, however, the boundary of 'DVO membership' is not equivalent to the shared (socio-geographic) *Devdori* identity: DVO membership rather reflects the internal multilayered differentiations of villagers. They expect that their membership in DVO and loyalty to its leaders improves their chance to get favourable access to development programmes. From the very outset, they learned about minimal membership requirements, such as

---

168 Personal interview (Notebook No 1-2, July 2, 2007: page 56); also focus group with DVO members about their perceptions of the DVO, MSDSP and related programmes on July 2, 2007 (Notebook No 1-2, July 2, 2007: pages 58-59).

169 Personal interviews with the DVO accountant, Zubayd Salimov (Notebook No 1-2, June 30, 2007: page 50; also tape recording No 21-23) and the DVO head, Daler Hamdamov (Notebook No 1-2, July 3, 2007: page 61).

family representation and gender balance of membership, participation in the DVO General Council and payment of membership fees through participatory village mapping. They[170] remember the promise of the MSDSP VO policymaker, Khaleel Tetlay, that the DVO is a bridge between them and INGOs, including the MSDSP (Tetlay and Jonbekova 2005). To maximise their benefits from the programmes of the MSDSP and the DVO, members fit their behaviour and attitude to meet minimal membership requirements. Again, they adapt these requirements into the hierarchical norm "to respect and implement what the leaders [of the DVO] ask for."[171] Ordinary members expect their involvement in supporting programmes in return for their inferior status and personal loyalty to DVO leaders.

One of the central requirements of membership is participation in the DVO General Council on a monthly basis. However, the publicly attended meetings of the Council are organised only occasionally and usually during visits by MSDSP managers and local state functionaries. Members expect this occasional attendance, again as a requirement for their involvement in support programmes. As one of them told me, "If the representatives of the MSDSP see that we all participate in these meetings, they know that we respect them and therefore they support us."[172]

The most 'active' members of the DVO refer to their true allegiance to DVO leaders in order to claim for their privileged access to the development programmes. To ensure their privileged access, they also visit the DVO office daily, which is situated inside the shopping wagon of the head of the organisation. The regular opening hours of the office are around 6-9 pm, when the head of the DVO is free from teaching at the school and from his household commitments. He opens the wagon, where male adults gather and simultaneously negotiate their inclusion in the programmes of the DVO and the MSDSP while eating his wares. The regular gathering of these 'consumers' checks and thereby controls who visits the head and especially influences his direct interaction with *others*, including women. These *others* are also 'intriguers', who are expected to be excluded from the membership network. Active members encourage DVO leaders to exclude 'intriguers', who "just sit [in the

---

[170] The data are based on the focus group with the members of the DVO (Notebook No 1-2, July 13, 2007: page 79).

[171] Focus group with ('active') members of the DVO about their perceptions of the DVO, MSDSP and related development programmes on July 2, 2007 (Notebook No 1-2, July 2, 2007: pages 58-59).

[172] Personal interview (Notebook No 1-2, July 2, 2007: page 56).

office], collect information and then pass it on to our enemies."[173] Such a claim, which again refers to the common *Devdori* identity of villagers, has a clear political intention: the DVO leader and his 'consumers' reject 'intriguers' or non-client members' calling for 'accountability', that is, their inclusion in the programme opportunities of the DVO.

These 'consumers' also refer to local idioms of the female body and identity to mock and thus defame the 'relation' of the head with a few women who visit the office to negotiate their involvement in the programmes. They proclaim these women as '*klients*' (literally: 'clients'; here, 'prostitutes'), rather than as members of or stakeholders in the development programmes.[174] In other Tajikistani contexts, Idiev (2006) also observes that "a *klient* is perceived in relation to his or her ascriptive status (sex, age, belonging to a place and so on), rather than as a buyer, client, etc." (61). Many villagers, including women, share this normative judgment. The female informants in one focus group[175] sarcastically hinted at the female body that a '*klient*' has to offer to unrelated men, as they perceive such relations.

Thus, the head of the DVO demonstratively avoids any encounters with women, especially in his office, in the absence of his 'consumers' in order to avoid the scandal which once troubled him.

Reference to female identity as well as the kinship norm of juniority shapes the hierarchical representation of DVO members. Their status contradicts VO bylaw (Bylaw VO 2001), which instructs the individual representation of members through the DVO General Council and other development programmes. However, hierarchical representation is more convenient for DVO leaders, while the male seniors of member families "are accessible at any time and in any place."[176] Mostly male senior members, who delegate female and junior family members to the DVO, participate in decision-making activities and negotiate their involvement in the development programmes of the DVO. One typical case, for example, involved an elite elder, Murodkhon Davlatkhonov, who was not a DVO member himself but registered four of his sons and daughters-in-law as members in order to involve his extended family in the programmes. Similarly, fathers or senior brothers represent their juniors,

---

173 Personal interview with the DVO head (Notebook No 1-2, July 13, 2007: pages 78-79).

174 Personal interview (Notebook No 1-2, June 28, 2007: page 67 also the Tape recording No 20).

175 Focus group with women (Notebook No 1-2, July 12, 2007: page 112).

176 Personal interview with the head of the DVO (Notebook No 1-2, June 30, 2007: page 53; also tape recording No 24).

who are formally registered members but work outside the village, including in Russia. They replace their migrant sons or brothers and thus represent their families in the development programmes.

The limited inheritance rights of women and juniors to patrimonial properties (such as houses, land, livestock, agricultural machines and cash) also marginalise their membership role in the DVO. This condition excludes their personal involvement in development programmes, especially the Village Development Fund and microcredit programme, which require the pledging of household properties. The other, but no less important, condition for the marginalised membership status of women and juniors is their own acknowledgement of their status. Women claim for programmes which support their *hunar* or income-generating activities, which exclude them from their domestic domain and shape their traditionally required role and identity (including political and economic inferior roles without any inheritance rights). They promise more value to the Microcredit Programme for the Household Support of Women (the so-called 'Jam Pot Programme'), as they can "generate profit out of wasted apples, without the need to leave their houses." They mention a successful seamstress in the village, who is reputable among the villagers for helping her husband to generate additional income for the family.[177]

Especially, the discourse dominated by men about the limits and dependencies of the female body enforces the shared acknowledgment of the inferior status of women. In its turn, the shared acknowledgment of females' inferior status diminishes women's political decision-making roles in the DVO. Their participation in the decision-making process and in any discussion of village problems is interpreted by their male seniors as contempt and as 'disclosure' in the presence of (male) 'strangers'. This male-female distinction led the MSDSP to cut off the decision-making right of women and to limit their participation through the occasional and 'for-reporting-purposes' (inoperative) Women's Council of VOs (Bylaw VO 2001: 9). The DVO Women's Council, which was established in 2002, is expected to organise monthly meetings of female members to discuss 'their problems', which should automatically be approved by the DVO General Council for implementation. However, as the previous head of the Women's Council informed me, since 2002 the Council has met only twice but only 'for reporting purposes' on behalf of the MSDSP. This formalisation of the divided structures and problems of men and women expresses the repressed and inferior status of women.

---

[177] Focus group with women (Notebook No 1-2, July 12, 2007: page 112).

The public positions of women are complementary to the economic activities of 'their [*mahram*] men'. Similarly, female leadership through the DVO Women's Council is perceived and interpreted differently than male leadership. First of all, it expresses the perception about the hierarchical inferiority of women, even if they hold higher positions than men. The first female leader was a school teacher, who was selected by MSDSP managers in 2002. The members regarded her position as legitimate due to her husband's status, as he was the driver at the district branch of the MSDSP. If female leadership does not represent the family status of women, people regard it as illegitimate. In 2006, the present head of the Women's Council was appointed by the current DVO head after the previous female head moved to Kulob City, where her husband was employed by the regional office of the MSDSP. Her position is, however, regarded as illegitimate, and the 'friends' of the DVO head mock the 'cliental' tie between her and the DVO head. As a widowed family head, however, she must hold a number of different jobs and feed her small children without male support.

Development programmes as trust-building resources

After discussing how the DVO became a contested resource among villagers, let us now focus on the aim of the programme to build trust among villagers.

The election of the head of the organisation was dominated by expectations of villagers about a *rais* ('chief'), a wealthy and generous man. As many powerful men withdrew from the elections due to the reasons explained above, Zamon Gulov was the only choice. This wealthy teacher, a former kolkhozi elite and currently the close friend of the district governor, owned a Russian-made car for mountainous conditions and was thus expected to arrange the activities of the DVO. He retired from the leadership of the DVO in 2004, but preserved his position with his allies, including the current head, Daler Hamdamov, who is the deputy director of the village school as well.[178]

The DVO General Council, as the formal decision-making body, which should be based on participatory and democratic values (Bylaw VO 2001), does not function properly. The head of the Women's Council, the programme manager and the heads of expert committees are mainly direct clients of the previous or the current head of the organisation. The other direct client is the DVO accountant, Zubayd Salimov, who personally does not take part in the

[178] The Minutes Notebook of the DVO has registered the General Council's Decree No 1 from January 5, 2004.

distribution of financial or economic resources.[179] Villagers expect that development structures and actors serve their own personal networks. This *kolkhozi*-like, socio-cognitive construct stimulates the adaptation of the developmental structure into kinship and patron-client networks. Especially, the informal network of the DVO head and his allies is decisive in allocating the resources of the Village Development Fund, MSDSP grants and the money from the microcredit fund of the MSDSP.[180]

Ordinary members are not concerned about "why the leaders do not implement planned activities" but rather follow "what the *kalektiv* [literally "collective"] chooses in the first place."[181] As a rule, "the *kalektiv* chooses in the first place" what the leader decides in advance. This cognitive framework again reflects villagers' indebtedness in return for the patronage they expect from the *rais*. Despite VO bylaw (Bylaw VO 2001), therefore, the total body of the DVO General Council has no voice to elect DVO leaders annually. It is rather the leaders' kinship and patron-client networks which shape the decision-making body of the DVO.

Both the leaders and ordinary members of the DVO refer to kinship and religious identities to adapt and transform the political structure and programme resources of the DVO to their reciprocal and patron-client networks. Ordinary members also claim the development principles of membership and participation in DVO programmes against the kinship and religious norms of reciprocal relations.[182] Thus, some members insist on abolishing the 2 percent interest rate charged by the Village Development Fund while blaming such a market rule as 'usury' ('*sudkhuri*'). They believe that 'usury', or making a profit from the interest rate, is against the kinship and

---

179 Personal interview (Notebook No 1-2, July 24, 2007: page 120).

180 The Programme of the Agricultural Support for Households (2002-2004) and Microcredit Fund for Women (since 2003) aimed to improve the economic conditions of families and especially the economic and political situations of 'vulnerable groups', i.e. poor families and women. Since 2004, when the Agricultural Support Programme was terminated, the MSDSP and DVO have mainly provided grants and microcredit funds for the joint economic activities of individual households and for improvements to the social and technical infrastructure of Devdor village. These programmes are expected to shape the commitment of members of the DVO to mutual economic enterprises and to public goods and infrastructure in their village.

181 Personal interview with the client member (Notebook No 1-2, July 17, 2007: page 98).

182 Personal interviews with the client members (Notebook No 1-2, July 13, 2007: pages 76-77; Notebook No 1-2, July 2, 2007: page 58).

religious norm of reciprocal support ('*odamgari*') and against the religious norm (not necessarily the practice) of lending money interest-free ('*qarzi hasana*').

To a greater extent, the reciprocal and cliental expectations of ordinary members influence policymaking practices. In part, DVO leaders and MSDSP managers in Shuroobod district utilise the development programmes, including the Village Development Fund and MSDSP grants and credits, as material resources for trust-building with villagers. These programmes are granted in return for decisions taken on behalf of the DVO General Council and for the collection of membership fees and debts. To appeal to the DVO head to participate in the Women's Council, a female member responded that "If you supply water to my house [slightly mocking], then I participate [loudly laughing]."[183]

This giving-and-taking process, that is, giving grants and credits and taking decisions and voices, is again justified as a commitment to the norm of 'kinship concession' ('*ruikhotirbini*' or '*rui khotiri kheshutabori*'). Due to this norm the formally established supreme decision-making body – the DVO General Council, which does not exceed 30 percent of the total members – meets mainly during the winter months. Regular participants are mostly male adults of those households which are affiliated into the kinship and patron-client networks of the leaders. Some members have demanded to fulfill the formal instructions of the MSDSP about membership by excluding those who do not attend meetings and who do not pay their membership fees and microcredit debts regularly and properly.[184] However, the DVO head told me that "I only make *passif* (passive) member concessions, concessions for the sake of being kinsmen."[185] Here, the head claims kinship affiliation to legitimise his privileged decision-making role and in return his commitment to subject members. To report to the MSDSP, he formally registers the monthly meetings of the DVO General Council in a set of minutes (*protokol*).

Again, DVO leaders refer to *qawmdori*, which implies the shared kinship and religious identity of villagers, to legitimise their concession and facilitation of the payment procedures of membership fees and microcredit debts. Although at the outset the members were expected to contribute a monthly membership fee of 50 diram[186] per person, each of them paid 10 diram until January 2007,

---

[183] Personal observation; June 21, 2007.

[184] Minutes notebook of the DVO (Notebook No 1-2, June 24, 2007: page 20).

[185] Personal interview with the DVO head (Notebook No 1-2, June 23, 2007: page 19).

[186] 50 diram was 0.5 TJK Somoni, while 1 TJK Somoni was about 0.30 USD in 2002.

and since then 20 diram.[187] People agreed to the increase of the fee in the hope that the MSDSP would double its support programmes.[188] Also, the way in which leaders collect membership and other fees is justifiable as a kinship commitment to reciprocity: no forced pressure, no public announcement of debtors, no punishment and no court deal in return for solidarity and loyalty.

Since poor families especially are unable to pay monthly fees regularly, they are expected to pay them per annum. The duration of payment is loose and flexible and the harvest season is set as the end of the fee-collection year, when most villagers have enough financial income. The head and the accountant make up an open-deadline list of debtors and wait for the end of the harvest season or an even later period to return the rotating village development fund. For two poor men, who were unable to repay their debts for more than one year, the leaders did not take action in line with written contracted agreements. The accountant of the DVO is in charge of collecting fees and debts from families who are not able to pay their membership fees on time. Especially during the harvest season, the accountant visits these families frequently to collect the fees: "If I do not visit their houses almost every day… during the harvest, they are not able to pay, because they do not have opportunity to pay every day. If they have [money] and they know that I know they have, they cannot refuse to pay."[189]

Rather, the leaders and ordinary members of the DVO ignore the written agreements, contracts and other formally registered demands of the DVO General Council. As the DVO head told me, "The purpose of the MSDSP is to support; therefore, as the head of the DVO, I have one, but decisive, voice to object to those who demand to punish the debtors."[190] The concern of the leaders is not to disappoint debtors and their expectations about the DVO. Subordinate members must not enter into 'unsafe' involvement in the programmes of the MSDSP and the DVO as once they did. The last microcredit programme of the MSDSP in the agricultural field was terminated in 2003, during a drought season when crop production fell sharply. Many people were left in debt, since they were forced to return a considerable part of the donor's credit at their own expense. As a result, they lost trust in the

---

[187] Personal interview with the DVO accountant (Notebook No 1-2, June 30, 2007: page 50; also tape recording No 21-23).

[188] Focus group with ('active') members of the DVO about their perceptions of the DVO, MSDSP and related programmes; July 2, 2007 (Notebook No 1-2, July 2, 2007: pages 58-59).

[189] Personal interview with the DVO accountant (Notebook No 1-2, June 30, 2007: page 50; also tape recording No 21-23).

[190] Ibid.

MSDSP and in the DVO. As the head of the DVO told me, '[s]till the suffering people remind us that 'We are not safe with you'."[191]

Chapter conclusion

To summarise the role of collective identities, section one considers one of the central aspects of local governance which is related to property rights. Powerful actors use collective norms and identities to legitimise their own and to delegitimise others' political and economic rights and claims. These collective identities reflect *contested boundaries* among the opponents. Section two elaborates on this issue by using the example of *qawmdori*. Section three summarises the case of the development organisation (the DVO), which again increases conflicts among powerful actors.

Legitimation of political and economic claims

This aspect of local governance considered the role of collective identities, including Islam, intertwined village and kinship affiliations and *qawmdori*, in the legitimation of political and economic claims. In Devdor village, kolkhozi elites manipulate these local identities to dominate key political and economic organisations at the local level. These organisations include the mahalla, mosque, collective farm, jamoat and District Land Committee. Thus, elites enjoy a privileged position to distribute and privatise public properties of the former sovkhoz and the current collective farm, including land, livestock and agricultural machinery. They adapt the formal economic rules of public management, withdrawal and alienation rights, to the patron-client practices of '*oformlenie*' (individual management right to distribute public goods) and '*spisanie*' (individual withdrawal and alienation rights to write-off goods), respectively. Furthermore, elites have legalised their administrative privileges over public goods by family inheritance since the initiation of land reform in 1997.

The study shows that a number of powerful actors contest the privileged access of kolkhozi elites to important positions and resources, and in some cases they have also mobilised villagers against them. To prevent and reduce such contestations and mass mobilisations, as well as to legitimise their privileges, elites and their state allies use various means such as cooptation, bureaucratic and military threat and commitment to collective norms and identities. Due to scarce materials and military resources, however, elites only rarely co-opt or

---

[191] Ibid.

punish their opponents. Hence, they refer especially to Islam to enhance their reputation and thereby to legitimise their access to political and economic resources.

Multilayered religious boundaries reflect political and economic differentiations and struggles and therefore shape Islam as the 'field' of contestation among powerful men. By highlighting and interpreting Islam from different perspectives, opponents seek to legitimise their privileged rights. For this purpose, religious references underline certain shared social and cognitive norms and frames of local people. They include the discourse of '*tinji*' ('peace'), norms expressed in notions such as '*odam*' (the principle of personal relations), '*davlat*' ('God-given inherited right') and '*insof*' ('mercy'; the principle of reciprocal and patron-client justice). The discourse of 'peace' refers to the myth about the divine authority of powerful men to control human nature and the material world. It suggests that the political and economic domination of elites is necessary to ensure the stability of socio-political life. The divine authority of the elites also legitimises their 'God-given' status of having privileged personal relations ('*odam*') with other powerful men, especially state and religious notables. Due to such personal relations they maintain *qawmdori* or peace, integrity and justice among their village kin. These privileged personal relations are also regarded as '*davlat*', i.e. the 'God-given' or inherited privileged right to political and economic resources. The notion of '*davlat*' also suggests religious superiority, which mostly legitimises elites' success in the material world. Their daily visit to the mosque 'for prayer', as well as their privileged role in religious ceremonies, thus bestows sacredness to their economic wealth and political decision-making authority.

Besides the legitimation of the privileged rights of powerful men, reference to Islamic identity also commits people to patron-client relations. Ordinary people seek to commit their patrons by interpreting generosity as the central religious norm. The norm of generosity, from one side, legitimises the privileged right (*davlat*) of powerful men to material and administrative resources within the village. Conversely, the villagers' norm is their claim for patronage favours from these resources. The term *rais* (elite) refers not only to patrons' privileged rights but also to their commitment to patronage, namely bureaucratic benevolence and economic generosity. The reference to Islamic identity highlights and praises the moral norm of *insof* as the religious commitment of the patrons to benevolence and generosity in return for their clients' loyalty and service.

Due to limited patronage favours, therefore, any reference to village and kinship identities seeks to legitimise or delegitimise the privileged rights of kolkhozi elites and other powerful men. The following references and their political roles were discussed throughout the chapter:

(1) 'First inhabitants' vs. 'latecomers', which especially legitimise elites' inheritance claims over strategic resources, such as land plots, public positions and resources of the former sovkhoz, and religious assets.

(2) 'Homeland owners' vs. 'resettled' families, which is a claim of privileged inheritance and the right to reside in the village. As with the first reference, elites and their opponents seek to legitimise their domination over political assets and economic resources in Devdor village. Elites enforce their contested authority over the mahalla as their 'family right'. Apparently, this boundary-making practice categorises elites from all other villagers while actually stigmatising the most powerful opponents.

(3) The other reference which elites use to maintain their reputation in the face of their opponents is 'village identity' vs. 'outsiders'. This merged village and kinship reference highlights opponents as 'outsiders', those who are not originally from Devdor village. This allusion relies on the socio-cognitive framework surrounding 'outsiders', whereby elites attract the attention of subject villagers and turn them against these strangers. Consequently, elites discredit their opponents as 'the betrayers of village honour' and thus legitimise their counteractions.

(4) Reference to the *Roghi* and *Khovalingi* descent groups again enforces the socio-cognitive frame of 'outsiders'. Elites refer to these 'outsiders' to accuse them of dividing village kinsmen, thereby protecting their privileged rights and discrediting their opponents and especially their leadership of some rural organisations (including the village school and the DVO). Notably, memories of descent origin do not include stories about descent groups and their necessary distinctions but rather revolve around struggles between elites and their opponents.

(5) *Qawmdori* is a notion that political actors use to refer to the shared religious, kinship and village identities of villagers. As in the cases of other boundary-making practices, powerful actors, especially kolkhozi elites, refer to *qawmdori* to protect their administrative positions and economic privileges vis-à-vis their opponents. This reference articulates the general level of distrust in these 'outsiders', who do not care about *qawmdori*, about the 'peace' and 'honour' of village kinsmen. In such a context, *qawmdori* reproaches any means of contestation, including formal appeals (*ariza*) to state and court authorities. The reference to *qawmdori* also reflects the cognitive construct of villagers about kolkhozi elites as the protectors of 'village esteem'. Their material wealth and

administrative positions are legitimate as long as they demonstrate a good village image to guests and strangers.

The other notion related to *qawmdori* is *qawmiyat*, which suggests the superior position of powerful elites due to their prevailing kinship ties in the village (*qabila*) and their alliance network with state and religious authorities inside and outside the village (*odam*). This reference reminds the subject villagers about their inevitable limitations and defeat, especially due to their kinship and bureaucratic dependencies upon kolkhozi elites. Elites also limit and defeat their opponents by utilising the *qawmdori* practices of stigma and ostracism, along with bureaucratic tactics, cooptation, administrative punishment and military threat. *Qawmdori*, which especially generates fear surrounding the rupturing of kinship ties, commits villagers to concessions 'for the sake of their kinsmen' and for the sake of 'peace in the [their] daughters' home'. This fear consequently commits the villagers to withdraw from collective uprisings against the unequal distribution of political and economic resources.

Persistence of the contested boundaries of *qawmdori*

Kolkhozi elites dominate the mahalla in Devdor village, which mobilises indigenous and external (state and international) economic and political resources to stabilise the contested political and economic order at village level. For this purpose, mahalla mediators, including the vakil, elite elders and neighbourhood 'assistants', use indigenous ('on-site') means to commit villagers to *qawmdori* or their shared religious and kinship affiliation. State authorities also integrate such means as 'organisational measures', 'explanation works' or police intervention, again to empower the mediation role of the mahalla.

As the central 'on-site' means of stability, mediators refer to kinship and religious identities in order to commit villagers to their reciprocal practices and networks of extended families and neighbourhoods. These practices include joint economic activities, compensation in the form of food, financial and labour shortages and old-age care. For the same purpose, mahalla leaders allocate and regulate support programmes, including state welfare programmes, humanitarian aid from international organisations and the religious practice of *sadaqa* (minimal support of the poor with food and clothes). These means and resources stabilise socio-economic situations, in part, by indebting recipient families to the elites. To mobilise *sadaqa*, mahalla mediators refer to the shared identity of *qawmdori*, which actualises the norms of 'Muslim debt' and 'village honour'.

Mediators highlight 'village honour' to commit villagers to practices of 'common wellbeing' such as village-level *hashar* and the renovation of village assets and infrastructure (such as roads, bridges, the cemetery, mosque and sacred sites). To organise effective practices, these mediators highlight the superior image of Devdor village and thereby invoke 'village honour' vis-à-vis 'outsiders'. These practices improve the religious reputation and status of the elites, since most of the 'objects of common wellbeing' are religious assets of the village. They additionally gain actual political and material power by mobilising internal resources, legitimising their access to resources of 'common wellbeing' and reducing their 'community' of users. They also use these practices and resources to categorise and disempower their opponents, i.e. those who do not obey or contribute to their desired 'order' of 'common wellbeing'.

Mahalla mediators also use the 'on-site' means of dispute settlement in order to maintain socio-political and economic stability in the highly contested environment. These means rely on the superior role of elders in resolving disputes and conflicts in their families and neighbourhoods. To enforce their role, both mahalla mediators and local state functionaries highlight 'stability' ('*tinji*') which commits villagers to *qawmdori*, that is, village honour and integrity. The mediators discredit and thereby prevent court appeals and deals which, they assure, disrupt 'village esteem' and 'divulge village secrets' to 'outsiders'. Likewise, local state administrative and police intervention bodies (such as jamoat, jamoat police and the district interior department) employ and endorse these indigenous means of dispute settlement.

Adaptation of the external development structure: the case of the DVO

Kolkhozi elites, who missed the opportunity to dominate the DVO leadership, use the notion of the shared identity of villagers, including *qawmdori*, *Devdori* and Sunni Muslim, to contest and categorise the DVO and its leaders as 'outsiders' and as 'the missioners of Shia ['the alien religion']'. As such, they justify their non-membership and delegitimise the presence of the DVO without their own leadership. They contest the authority of DVO leaders by disgracing the place and purpose of, and participants in, their gatherings. The DVO office is labelled a 'slander-house', which gathers those who do not care about village honour and integrity or division among kin.

These references and accusations find the wide acclamation of ordinary villagers, since they are based on and in turn intensify the indigenous mental constructs and images about *rais*, 'teachers' and 'outsiders'. DVO leaders, who are judged as 'teachers' and sometimes as 'outsiders', are regarded as incompetent in the affairs of *qawmdori*, since they do not protect 'village honour' and integrity. This shared claim undermines the authority of DVO leaders and limits the agency of the new organisation. Villagers instead expect to integrate the DVO into an internal structure of either a mahalla or collective farm, under the authority of kolkhozi elites. This expectation of the subject people is also due to their perception about elites, because they believe that only elites can secure 'peace' ('*tinji*') and distribute 'justice' ('*insof*') in the village. Consequently, villagers acknowledge elites' action to undermine the leadership role of non-elites and thus to belittle the public value of projects implemented by the DVO leaders. This is the main reason why the MSDSP has changed its strategy and thus allowed elites to run VOs in many villages of Shuroobod district.

Reference to collective norms and identities also adapts the programmes of the DVO into reciprocal and patron-client patterns. As already mentioned, the activities of 'village wellbeing' are important sources of both material and symbolic power for the kolkhozi elites. Hence, they impede and compete with DVO leaders to take over such activities and consequently to diminish their reputation and power in *qawmdori*. The reference to *qawmdori* thus reduces the authority of the DVO leaders to collect internal resources for 'common wellbeing'.

To claim for their decision-making right, DVO leaders refer to kinship commitment, that is, 'kinship concession' (*rui khotiri kheshutabori*). This is used to commit villagers to the development schemes of resource mobilisation, such as grants, microcredit programmes, village development funds, membership fees, grant fees, rent-out tariffs, microcredit interest rates and contributions from wealthy men. However, DVO leaders rely on mahalla mediators to mobilise and redistribute – and thus adapt – these development resources.

Furthermore, individual villagers refer to religious and village identities to adapt the development programmes of the DVO into kinship and patron-client networks. Therefore, they turned down the inquiry of an adjacent village for membership in their organisation. The claimants distinguish them as 'active' members vis-à-vis 'passive' ones. They shape this boundary by attending daily gatherings in the shopping wagon of the DVO head, consuming his products and negotiating their privileged access to any available programmes. Their regular gathering, consumption and negotiation check and control who visits the head and especially influence his personal interaction with *others*, including 'intriguers' and women. 'Active' members highlight local idioms of female identity and the body, again to discredit and thereby exclude women from direct interaction with the DVO head.

Likewise, the inferior hierarchical status of women and juniors adapts the representation structure of the DVO, which in turn constrains their direct involvement in the development programmes. The limited inheritance right of women to patrimonial properties (such as household, land, livestock and agricultural machines and farms) also marginalises their membership role in development programmes. Their economic involvement through the development programmes is adapted into their domestic seclusion and traditional desired role and identity. The shared acknowledgment of limits and dependencies of women has led the MSDSP to cut off the decision-making entity of the Women's Group from the male community. Such an adaptation of the development structure reduces female participation mainly through an occasional and 'for-reporting-purposes' (inoperative) Women's Group.

THE INTEGRATED BOUNDARIES OF SOCIAL ORDER: The case of Sayyod village in the cotton-growing area

This chapter discusses the case of Sayyod village in the cotton-growing Shahritus district of Qabodiyon oasis. Like many cotton-growing communities in Qabodiyon oasis, Sayyod village is large in size and heterogeneous in the ethnic composition of its population. The cotton sector is an important political and economic factor which shapes distinctive local governance processes in this case. State and local elites enforce the integrated political structure of the Mahalla Committee of Sayyod village (hereinafter 'the mahalla') in order to sustain cotton-growing 'communities' or cotton farms. This integrative policy is the central distinction of local governance in the cotton-growing villages from that of the mountainous communities. Thus, the central discussion in the current chapter is to understand the role of collective identities in promoting this integrative policy.

The following subchapters one and two concisely describe the socio-economic characteristics of Qabodiyon oasis as a whole and Sayyod village in particular. Subchapter three discusses villagers' collective identities, including ethnicity, kinship and Islam. The following subchapters analyse the role of these collective identities in shaping local governance institutions. The analysis covers local governance aspects elaborated in the theoretical framework chapter, including the legitimation of political and economic rights (subchapter four), the political structure of power relations (subchapter five) and the mobilisation of means and resources for socio-political stability (subchapter six). The case study about the political cotton economy deserves separate discussion (subchapter seven), while state elites and local notables adapt any other aspects of local governance in order to sustain the cotton-growing 'communities' of the village.

Overview of Qabodiyon oasis

Qabodiyon oasis embraces the Qabodiyon, Shahritus and Nosiri Khusrav (formerly Beshkent) districts. The oasis is situated to the southern edge of the Kofarnihon valley, expanding up towards the basin of the Kofarnihon, Vakhsh and Panj tributaries of the Amudarya River. Prior to the Soviet Union, the oasis was administered by Qabodiyon *Begigari* (the second-level, top-down administrative division) under the Bukhara Emirate.

Today, Shahritus district, where I conducted the main part of my field research in Qabodiyon oasis, is located in the middle of the oasis – to the west of Qabodiyon district cut along Kofarnihon River and to the east of Nosiri Khusrav – a Tajik-Uzbek border district. From the south, all three districts are adjacent to the Amudarya River, which continues demarcating the Tajik-Afghan border.

All three districts in the oasis have some common characteristics in terms of ecological and economic conditions as well as ethnic compositions. The abundance of water resources, especially in the densely populated Shahritus and Qabodiyon districts, favours cotton monoculture. Since most arable land is allocated to the cotton plantations of a few powerful men, the majority of people therefore search for other opportunities to make an income, including labour migration to Russia. Qabodiyon oasis is ethnically heterogeneous, like many places in Qurghonteppa region. The *mahalli* ('native') people, as they define themselves, have inhabited the oasis since pre-Soviet times and are internally categorised as Tajiks, Arabs and Sayyids[192] or Shaykhs.[193] Before or during the Soviet Union, the Arab population of Hisor valley and Uzbeks of the Durman and Qunghurot tribes from other parts of Tajikistan as well as from Uzbekistan resettled the oasis. Eventually, they were identified as '*mahalli*' as a result of the increase of their kinship ties with the *mahalli* people. Since the 1950s, the Soviet government had relocated '*kuhistoni*' ('mountainous') Tajiks, mostly from the mountainous Rasht and Hisor valleys. They had either constructed separate neighbourhoods in the *mahalli* settlements or established distinct villages. Apart from others, however, the *kuhistoni* people have less developed kinship, social and economic relations with the *mahalli* and Uzbek populations in the oasis.

Overview of Sayyod village

The *mahalli* people consider Sayyod village among one of the oldest settlements, including Ayvoj, Chashmajon and Beshkappa villages, and Qabodiyon town, in

192 Sayyids: The plural form for '*Sayyid*' which refers to the descent origin of people who claim they are direct descendants of the Islamic prophet Muhammad through his grandsons, Hasan ibn Ali and Husayn ibn Ali, who were the sons of his daughter Fatima Zahra and his cousin Ali ibn Abu Talib. Today, especially since Soviet Union rule, Sayyids are no longer a distinctive descent group, but they still claim such status and have started compiling a *shajaranoma* (genealogical book) to legitimise their privileged access to political and economic resources.

193 Traditional owners or claimants (due to their loss of ownership) of sacred sites.

Qabodiyon oasis. The village is situated about 7 km south of Shahritus town, the administrative centre of Shahritus district. It is 30 km from the southern Ayvoj village, which is located about 6 km from the Tajik-Afghan border marked by the Amudarya River. From the eastern part of Sayyod village, the Kofarnihon River flows down to the Amudarya River, which divides Shahritus and Qabodiyon districts. The Chirik and Kurot villages of Qabodiyon district are situated on the eastward bank of the river. On the westward bank, Sayyod village is embraced by three other villages: to the north is Yangiobod village, totally populated by Durman Uzbeks, to the west lies Lolazor (formerly Budyon), a village inhabited mainly by Arabs, and to the south is Qizilaskar, a village of *kuhistoni* Tajiks.

Today, Sayyod village is one of the most densely populated and ethnically diverse settlements in Shahritus district. According to the account of Sayyod Jamoat, it has more than 450 households, or about 730 registered nuclear families of 3,928 inhabitants.[194] The village represents almost every ethnic group in the Qabodiyon oasis, including *mahalli* villagers of different origins (such as *mahalli* Tajiks, Arabs, Sayyids, resettled Arabs and Uzbeks) and resettled *kuhistoni* Tajiks.

The main sources of economic income are subsistence agriculture, cotton growing and, to a great extent, labour migration to Russia. More than the often stated 500 villagers, mostly young men, work in Russia and thereby cover most of their economic and social needs and shortages. Others, especially junior and older family members, maintain a family subsistence economy as well as cotton farms.

Collective identities in Sayyod village

This subchapter describes collective identities and the multifaceted and overlapping references of village inhabitants to locality, kinship, Islam and ethnicity. In the following, section one discusses the shared identities of *mahalli* ethnic and descent groups (including native Tajiks, different Uzbek tribes, Arabs and Sayyids) found in and around the Qabodiyon oasis. Section two shows the distinct boundaries between these groups and *kuhistoni* Tajiks who

---

[194] However, this official Sayyod Jamoat data (personal interview with the deputy chairman of the Jamoat: Notebook No 1-4, November 10 2007: page 55) is outdated. One of my key informants, Chupon Aliev (personal interview: Notebook No 1-6, January 19, 2008: page 21), registered his extra land plot as a household plot (*tamarqa*) for his son in 2005. His household plot was registered under No 741. This means that the Jamoat registered 741 nuclear families in the same period.

inhabit the village as well as some adjacent villages. Section three talks about the village identity of *mahalli* villagers, which is highlighted vis-à-vis not only *kuhistoni* Tajiks but also other *mahalli* peoples of the oasis. The last sections, four and five, also reveal other sub-village references, including references to descent groups, 'great families' and neighbourhood-based Islamic affiliations.

Common *mahalli* references to locality, kinship and Islam

Due to the heterogeneous composition of Sayyod village, its history is carefully constructed by a number of important men. On a broader scale, their stories and narratives seek to protect the common origins of all *mahalli* ethnic (Tajik, Uzbek, Arab and Sayyid) and descent (*Sayyodi*, *Khojamashhadi*, *Rabotaki* and *Samarkandi*) groups in the village. Obviously, ethnic dimension is not relevant to constructing shared *mahalli* village[195] identity. Rather, kinship and religious affiliations and commonalities determine collective boundaries between *mahalli* villagers and *others* in the Qabodiyon oasis who are *kuhistoni* Tajiks. On this scope, *mahalli* villagers identify with other *mahalli* communities in the oasis, with whom they have institutionalised kinship and religious ties. Hence, the reference to '*mahalli*' does not necessarily imply its linguistic meaning, that is, 'native', but rather actualises such ties. On the second scope, *mahalli* reference is also distinctive from some Uzbek communities in the oasis with whom they have had less institutionalised (including kinship) ties in the past. These communities consist of homogenous tribes who entered and resettled in the oasis at the turn of the 20th century and abandoned their nomadic lifestyle from the second half of that century.

Mahalli villagers refer to kinship as an important source of their shared *mahalli* identity with each other and with other *mahalli* villages in the Qabodiyon oasis. According to village elders, "It is not acceptable to say that *mahalli* [villagers] are strangers [to each other]";[196] rather, they "have had kinship relations with each other *from the very beginning*."[197] They have kinship ties mainly with other *mahalli* people in the oasis. When people talk about the oasis, first of all, they perceive villages and peoples who are 'related' to them by kinship ties: "You can call the Qabodiyon [oasis] Sayyod,"[198] said an informant, thus referring to those people in the oasis who have institutionalised kinship ties with *mahalli* villagers (for details, see Table 6: Kinship network of *mahalli* villagers). Today, only Arabs in

---

[195] *Mahalli* villager – 'native' population of Sayyod village.
[196] Personal interview with an elder (Notebook No 1-5, December 10, 2007: page 56).
[197] Personal interview with an elder (Notebook No 1-6, January 19, 2008: page 21).
[198] Personal interview with an elder (Notebook No 1-6, January 28, 2008: page 116).

Sayyod village are not fully regarded as *mahalli*, although recent interpenetration due to increasing kinship ties absorbs this perception.

Table 6: Kinship network of *mahalli* villagers

#	Place (village, town, district, city, country)	Ethnic and descent group affiliation	Frequency of kinship ties
1	Sayyod village (Shahritus district) Dushanbe city Uzbekistan	*Mahalli* Tajiks, *Shaykhs*, Uzbeks and Arabs	244
2	Shahritus town, Leninobod, Qahramon, Chuyanchi and Poligon villages (Shahritus district) Qabodiyon town (Qabodiyon district) Kamsamol village (Nosiri Khusrav district)	*Mahalli* Tajiks and Uzbeks	193
3	Qumshokh and Sverdlov villages (Shahritus district) Varashilov village (Nosiri Khusrav district) Kurot village (Qabodiyon district)	*Mahalli* Uzbeks, Tajiks and *Shaykhs*	100
4	Ayvoj and Budyon villages (Shahritus district) Arabkhona and Qizilkedman villages (Nosiri Khusrav district) Arabkhona village (Qabodiyon district)	Arabs	31
5	Khushodi, Parishkamon, Chinor, Traktir and Gidra villages, Iskra kolkhoz (Shahtitus district) Okhunboboev village (Qabodiyon village)	Uzbeks	25
6	Sayyod, Qizilaskar villages (Shahritus district) Pakhtakor, Laklakuya and Jarqurghon villages, Vatan Sovkhoz (Qabodiyon district) Qurghonteppa city Gharm and Varzob districts Russia, Belarus, Afghanistan	Others (*Kuhistoni* Tajiks, Turkmen, outside Qabodiyon oasis, Russians, Afghans)	14

Source: Personal survey (October 2007 – March 2008)

As Table 6 illustrates, despite some distinct patterns among different *mahalli* ethnic and descent groups, they have dense kinship ties with the *mahalli* communities of the Qabodiyon oasis. Even *Rabotaki* Uzbeks, who have a less dense kinship network in the oasis, now prefer "*mahalli* pup [non-*Rabotaki* people] over their relatives" who live in Uzbekistan.[199] In the same way, Arabs and Shaykhs of Khoja-Mashhad shrine, who claim their bilineage Sayyid descent origin, acknowledge that their 'pure blood' and 'white bones' ('*oqsuyak*') have been destroyed. Village elders remember that these distinct kinship patterns vanished in the 1950s' resettlement of people from other regions to the cotton plantations and the kolkhoz-initiated household planning (*tamarqa*) initiative during the 1960s and '70s.[200]

They also remember that, in the past, 'bone' or descent origin was a principal criterion for kinship relation. Today, however, the once distinct kinship networks of *elkheshi* (extended family) or *qawm* (descent group) of the *mahalli* people[201] are not invariant social categories. Rather, reciprocal and patron-client relations are more important in developing inter-group kinship networks. As villagers express this situation, "If a stranger has comings-and-goings with you, he is your kinsman; if the kinsman interrupts these comings-and-goings with you, he is your stranger." The costly institutional transactions of marriage alliance with other groups, such as *mahr*[202] and dowry[203], could not prevent widening kinship ties among different *mahalli* groups. Thus, the central principle of the kinship network is not only the ritual acknowledgment of *mahalli* 'religious' boundaries but also the pledge of reciprocal networks. As the former principal mullah of the village told me, "Today, girls and boys meet each other on the street, which is their *proof letter* [*hujjat*] for marriage."[204]

---

199 Personal interview with a *Rabotaki* elder (Notebook No 1-6, January 23, 2008: page 53).

200 E.g. personal interview with an elder from Qumshokh village (Notebook No 1-6, January 20 2008: page 26; also tape recording No DS 300256-8).

201 Terms such as '*qawmu qarimdosh*' or '*urugh*' are also used for distinct kinship networks.

202 *Mahr* is the religiously established due of a bride's parents for her upbringing; a symbolic cost of the alienation of a daughter.

203 A dowry is the cost of the bride's wedding, which is paid by her groom's family. In Sayyod village, the cost of a dowry, which is provided together with *mahr*, includes 1 *kip* of cotton (40-50 kg), four blankets, eight pillows, two sheep, 30 kg rice, 15 kg oil and 30 kg sweets and fruits (personal interview with Shoniyoz Eshniyozov – the deputy head of Sayyod Mahalla: Notebook No 1-6, January 28, 2008: pages 117-8).

204 Personal interview with Sufikhuja Begakov (Notebook No 1-5, December 8, 2007: page 26).

Despite all these, however, still there are very few exceptions under which *mahalli* villagers have established kinship ties with *others*, i.e. *kuhistoni* Tajiks (see Table 7: Exceptional marriages).

Table 7: Exceptional marriages of *mahalli* people with non-*mahalli* people

#	Exceptional marriages	What happened afterwards?
1	Husband from Qurghonteppa city and wife from the *mahalli* villagers	Husband married a second wife and 'disappeared' and left his first wife (the *mahalli* villager) with two children in her parents' home.
2	Wife from *kuhistoni* Tajiks and husband from Qirghiz-Arab villagers	No relations with their kinsmen on both sides
3	Wife from *kuhistoni* Tajiks and husband from the *mahalli* villagers	No relations with their kinsmen on both sides; the husband frequently 'disappears' to Uzbekistan
4	Husband from *kuhistoni* Tajiks and wife from the *mahalli* villagers	Their son was 3 months old when they divorced and the husband married a *kuhistoni* woman
5	Wife from *kuhistoni* Kyrgyz-Tajik villagers and husband from the *mahalli* villagers	There are relations between the families, besides kinship ties
6	Husband from *kuhistoni* Tajiks and wife from the *mahalli* villagers	There are relations between the families, besides kinship ties
7	Husband from *mahalli* Turkmans and wife from the *mahalli* villagers	There are relations between the families, besides kinship ties; there is attempt to persist with these kinship ties
8	Second husband from the *mahalli* villagers and second wife from *kuhistoni* Tajiks	There are rare cases of kinship activity between the two families; there is an attempt to build on these ties

Source: Personal survey (October 2007 – March 2008)

Ethnicity: *mahalli* vs. *kuhistoni*

Today, *kuhistoni* Tajiks remain the only *total other* to *mahalli* men. As older *mahalli* informants recall, the Qabodiyon oasis was inhabited by *mahalli* ('native')[205]

[205] They use the following synonymous terms '*mahalli*', '*muqimi*' or '*tahjoi*'. They also interchangeably use the Russian term '*mestnyy*'.

people before the 1950s, when the Soviet government transferred *kuhistoni* Tajiks to supply the cotton-growing plantations with labour. The relocated *kuhistoni* families of the Tajik and Kyrgyz origins from the Jirgatol district[206] of the Rasht valley constituted a neighbourhood in Sayyod village. *Mahalli* people categorise them through notions such as '*kuhistoni*' ('mountainous'), '*furori*' ('refugee') or '*bevatan*' ('homeland-less').[207] They also categorise the relocated people as 'Kyrgyz-Tajik' ('*Qirghiz-Tojik*'), although two ethnic (Kyrgyz and Tajik) groups have occasional kinship ties.

During the civil war, when many *kuhistoni* families fled to Afghanistan and the Rasht valley, the Kyrgyz government repatriated all Kyrgyz families. The remaining families of Tajik origin joined them and lived in Kyrgyzstan through 1993-2000. While the Kyrgyz government only naturalised Kyrgyz families, in 2000 the UN refugee mission returned and mediated the reintegration of *kuhistoni* Tajiks into Sayyod village. As a result of such replacement, many families lost their primary houses and household plots, while today the *kuhistoni* Tajik community is scattered across different neighbourhoods, mostly on the south-northern edge of the village.

The *mahalli* people and *kuhistoni* Tajiks did not develop stable kinship and religious networks. *Kuhistoni* Tajiks distinguish themselves from *mahalli* people by reference to the latter's Uzbek-dominated Tajik dialect and especially to their 'infidel' practices. They do not accept *mahalli* religious assets and authorities of worship (including *mahalli* saints and shrines) but rather demonstratively practice distinctive Islam and regularly visit their 'homeland' in the Rasht valley for worship rituals. Instead, local religious notables and sacred sites, such as the authority of Qabodiyon Eshon, the shrines of Chiluchor-Chashma[208] and Seven *khojas* (including Khoja-Mashhad shrine in Sayyod village[209]) in the Qabodiyon

[206] A Tajik-Kyrgyz border district inhabited by Tajik and Kyrgyz populations.

[207] Personal interview with Mahkam Boyakov (Notebook No 1-4, October 3, 2007: pages 22-24).

[208] The most hallowed religious good in the oasis is the Chiluchor-Chashma shrine, located in Nosiri Khusrav district. It historically belongs to the Shaykh descent group of Qumshokh village. Today, it is a symbol of religious pride for all *mahalli* people while there are contestations among the current owner and other claimants. In part, they reinterpret stories of the holy place as well as reinvent their descent groups to justify it both as a symbolic good of their *mahalli* identity and their privileged right.

[209] The Khoja-Mashhad shrine is one of the most valuable historical monuments of Tajikistan which, therefore, goes under the direct auspices of several state organisations, including the Ministry of Culture of Tajikistan, district government, Sayyod Jamoat and Sayyod Mahalla Committee. At the same time, recently Iran and USA have separately provided significant financial support for the restoration of its elegant cupolas.

oasis, symbolise the parochial boundaries of *mahalli* people which divide them from *kuhistoni* Tajiks.

Mahalli village dignity

In some contexts, *mahalli* villagers refer to their 'culturedness' ('*madaniyatnoki*'), which especially implies their religious superiority, to distinguish them from *kuhistoni* Tajiks and resettled Uzbeks. To argue about their 'culturedness', 'educated' informants struggle against the 'bad memories' of their elders, who do not remember that "there were two Islamic high schools [*madrasa*] before the Soviets."[210] Again, they have to counterattack *kuhistoni* Tajiks who claim *mahalli* men are religiously 'uneducated and imperfect'. Rather, 'educated' *mahalli* men tell the story that in the past, Sayyod was the religious educational centre of Qabodiyon *Begigari*. To prove this point, they claim that the Khoja-Mashhad shrine, currently situated inside the village cemetery, was built during the dissemination of Islam in Central Asia in the eighth and ninth centuries. The Khoja-Mashhad shrine, they argue, was then the "Islamic education centre where one of the most famous Islamic scholars, Nosiri Khusravi Qabodiyoni,[211] was trained."[212] In addition, *mahalli* men respond to the accusation about a 'lack of their own mullahs' during Soviet rule by the fact that their 'great men' were victims of the 1930s' GULAG.[213] Only a few of them, including the *mahalli* saint and their co-villager, Eshon-i Miyontura, escaped the cleansing and permanently left for Afghanistan "thanks to their spiritual miracle power." My informants affirmed that the current saint of *mahalli* men – Qabodiyon Eshon – is not only the intermediary disciple of Eshon-i Miyontura (through his father,

---

210 Personal interview with Mahmad Yusupov (Notebook No 1-4, October 2, 2007: page 19).

211 Nosiri Khusravi Qabodiyoni (1004-1088) was a *doi* (missioner) of an Islamic sect, and as a part of his mission he was sent to the regions of Khorasan and Badakhshan.

212 Personal interview with a teacher (Notebook No 1-4, October 20, 2007: pages 37-40).

213 GULAG (Russian: 'Glavnoe upravlenie ispravitel'no-trudovykh lagerey i koloniy') – Chief Administration of Corrective Labour Camps and Colonies of NKVD. It was officially created on April 25, 1930, and dissolved on January 13, 1960. This agency administered the main Soviet forced camp system. Approximately 14 million people passed through the GULAG labour camps from 1929 to 1953, and a total of 1,053,829 people died in these camps during 1934-1953 (http://en.wikipedia.org/wiki/gulag).

Eshon-i Abdulazizkhon) but also is related to his descent group, i.e. to Sayyids.[214]

Additionally, the nationalist invention of pre-Islamic history in Sayyod village by some ideological scholars of *mahalli* origin[215] inspires educated villagers to deepen the roots of the authentic ascendancy of *mahalli* villagers over *others*. 'Educated' storytellers integrate the nationalistic inventions of these scholars into the indigenous historical reading of *mahalli* boundaries.[216] They assure that Sayyod was (in the unknown past) the centre of a kingdom of 40,000 households. At that time, its borders demonstrated its absolute spatial extension: from the north up to the current Shahritus town, from the south down to the current Ayvoj village, from the east cut by the Kofarnihon River and with the blurred western horizon lost into the desert and mountain range. The frequent acknowledgment of absolute extension declares two basic claims of *mahalli* villagers: first, *others*, especially *kuhistoni* Tajiks, unfairly entered their territory, and second, but mostly importantly, the claim reflects the kinship relations of *mahalli* villagers with other *mahalli* groups, as illustrated in the Kinship Networks Table 6, above.

Descent groups and 'great families' of the *mahalli* people

With all the honourable stories and references, however, the shared *mahalli* identity of villagers is expressive and meaningful vis-à-vis their total *others*, i.e. *kuhistoni* Tajiks. Otherwise, individual actors divide *mahalli* villagers into mainly five *qawms* or descent groups, including (1) *Sayyodi* Tajiks, (2) *Khojamashhadi* Tajiks, (3) *Samarkandi* Tajiks, (4) *Rabotaki* (or *Uzbekistoni*) Uzbeks and (5) Arabs. Although kolkhoz-led household planning (*planirovka*) through the 1960s-70s destroyed the *qawm*-dominated residential units (*avuls*), the largest neighbourhoods or *mahallas*[217] still symbolise three of these groups – *Sayyodi*, *Khojamashhadi* and *Rabotaki*. The central part of the village is called Sayyod-

[214] Personal interview with Mahkam Boyakov (Notebook No 1-4, October 3, 2007: pages 22-24).

[215] E.g. the late Aliqul Devonaqulov from the Academy of Sciences of Tajikistan.

[216] E.g. personal interview with Mahkam Boyakov (Notebook No 1-4, October 3, 2007: pages 22-24).

[217] Here, it is necessary to distinguish between mahalla (or mahalla committee) as a political structure of a village and *mahalla* as the largest neighbourhood unit in the case of Sayyod village. In Sayyod village *mahalla* refers to three *mahalli* descent groups and one *kuhistoni* group which traditionally inhabited separate large *kuchas* (streets). But especially after kolkhoz-led household planning (*tamarqa planirovka*) in the 1970s, their distinct borders were merged and shared by families from different descent groups.

mahalla, its northern part is referred to as Khoja-Mashhad-*mahalla* or Khoja-Mashhad Street and the southern part is named Rabotak-*mahalla* or the 'street of *Rabotak-mahalla* people'.

Members of the *Sayyodi* descent group claim that their forebears were the first residents and, therefore, the founders of the village. The *Khojamashahdi* men believe that they came from Mashhad of Iran during the early dissemination of Islam and established the Khoja-Mashhad Islamic Centre in order to convert 'fire-prayer Aborigines' to Islam. Only then, they argue, was Sayyod village built. A few *Samarkandi* families can trace their origins back to their grandfather, who was a mullah and fled from Samarkand city to escape the Bolshevik intrusion in the 1920s. A *Samarkandi* senior calls his *qawm* a 'bridge' between all *qawms* in the village who came from 'Dahbed of Samarkand' but forgot about their primary origin.[218] As many older informants assert, more than 70 households of the *Rabotaki* descent group came from Sherobod of Uzbekistan during 1932-33.[219] A few informants do not agree with this dominant view and claim that *Rabotaki* men are not originally Uzbeks but Arabs from the Surkhondaryo region of Uzbekistan who resettled in Sayyod village about one and half centuries ago. There are a few other extended families in the southern and south-western parts of the village who are commonly called 'Arabs'. They also define as Arabs those whose grandfathers came from Hisor district at the turn of the 20th century. Until recently their kinship ties have been limited to the native Arab communities of the Qabodiyon oasis.

The claims of some villagers about their descent origins also retell and consequently confuse the history of the village and the meaning of its name ('Sayyod'), which all refer to the inheritance privileges of some descent groups to the village and its assets. However, such inheritance claims are not shared by all villagers, who mention contradictory stories about the Khoja-Mashhad shrine and sometimes asked me to clarify its history, which is often told differently: some say it was constructed overnight while others claim that their ancestors built it as an Islamic centre.

During the frequent interaction with my informants from different groups, I found out that the contradictory stories surrounding the Khoja-Mashhad shrine and the village have resulted in conflicts between powerful *Sayyodi* and *Khojamashhadi* men. These contestations avoid open skirmishes between the respective descent groups and attempt instead to coin inheritance stories.

---

218 Personal interview with Mahkam Boyakov (Notebook No 1-4, October 3, 2007: pages 22-24).

219 Personal interviews Qamar Jumaev (Notebook No 1-4, October 20, 2007: page 41) and Farmon Hamzaev (Notebook No 1-4, October 3, 2007: page 22).

Claimants assert their individual inherited right to the village by reference to such rights of their descent groups. Two central sources of reference are, therefore, the story of how the Khoja-Mashhad shrine was constructed and the name of 'Sayyod', both of which hint at the origin of each group. *Khojamashhadi* men refer to the title of their descent group (i.e. '*Khojamashhadi*') to claim that when they came to this place there was no such village as Sayyod. They created the Khoja-Mashhad Islamic centre, founded the settlement and only later did *Sayyodi* hunters abandon their 'vagrancy' and settle in the village. They insist that this history should have been written in their genealogical book (*shajaranoma*), which is kept by the offspring of their saint, Eshon-i Sayyid Akramkhon, who fled to Afghanistan in the 1920s.[220]

In turn, *Sayyodi* descent group members[221] refer to the meaning of the village's name. They reject those who translate it as '*sayohatjoy*' ('the place for resort') but assert its direct meaning as 'hunter'.[222] Consequently, they tell the story about their 'great fore-fathers', or four hunters, who first inhabited the Qabodiyon oasis, including Sayyod village.

The following passage from the contentious conversation between *Sayyodi* and *Khojamashhadi* men illustrates the abovementioned disputes:[223]

> *Sayyodi* member: At the outset, four hunters (*mergan*) came and inhabited Sayyod – our [*Sayyodi*] grand-grandfathers, including my father. All of them were brothers. They came and built Sayyod… I don't know from where and when they came. Our grandfathers said that 'You are the natives of Sayyod'.
>
> *Khojamashhadi* member: [appealing to me:] He [*Sayyodi* member] says their grandfathers came as hunters… Nobody knows when; it was in the early times.
>
> *Sayyodi* member: I know that you are a *Khojamashhadi* native. But now the Khoja-Mashhad [shrine] is not in your hands. The peoples of *Khoja-Mashhadi* and *Sayyodi* (descent groups) are the same; we have exchanges [kinship relations]. We [all] respect the greatness of Khoja-Mashhad [the shrine].
>
> *Khojamashhadi* member: It should be found out if there is *shajara* [*shajaranoma*]…
>
> *Sayyodi* member: … If your father is not there but your grandfather is in the *shajara*… But it is difficult to find it… The book is not available, how can one find it?

---

220 Personal interview with Shoniyoz Eshniyozov (Notebook No 1-6, January 28, 2008: pages 117-8).
221 Personal interview (Notebook No 1-4, October 3, 2007: page 22).
222 Indeed, the Arabic word '*sayyod*' means 'hunter'.
223 Personal interview (Notebook No 1-6, January 31, 2008: pages 141-142).

> *Khojamashhadi* member: ...One can find the book... Its history should be transferred by our [*Khojamashhadi*] *pir* [saint]. Our *pir* is Sayyid Akramkhon...
>
> *Sayyodi* member: ... The book exists, [but] it was sent to England... You do not know your saint's son, am I right?
>
> *Khojamashhadi* member: In Afghanistan... [men from there] came [and they told] that his sons live there...
>
> *Sayyodi* member: [Tired from the debate and now turning the talk to apparent peace:] My grandmother [a *Khojamashhadi*] told that 'Your home will be blessed...' [Referring to *Khojamashhadi* man] Your grandfather's books are here... This story happened and we do not know much of it.

Multifaceted Islamic identity of the *mahalli* people

Individual actors search for their political and economic rights by relating (*mahalli*) Islamic sacred figures and assets to their own *qawms* (descent groups). In this way, they use their *qawm*-related or neighbourhood mosques (*choykhona* – literally 'tea-house') to enforce the religious solidarity of their co-members. *Qawm* co-members pray in their *choykhonas* in spite of the religious moral good of public (*jamoa*) prayer. Besides the officially registered mosque of *Rabotak-mahalla*, there are three *choykhonas* and some other *qawm*-related mosques of the *mahalli* (*Khojamashhadi* and *Sayyodi*) and *kuhistoni* people.

Inheritance contestations over (and through reference to) religious notables and assets mostly engages powerful men from the *Sayyodi* and *Khojamashhadi* descent groups. *Sayyodi* men refer to their exclusive relation to and bestowal from the *mahalli* saint – Eshon-i Miyontura. They refer to the fact that the Eshon-i-Miyontura shrine, formerly their saint's house, is currently situated in Sayyod-*mahalla*. In return, the *Khojamashhadi* men refer to the Seven-Khojas' (sacred souls) shrines, which suggest their religious superiority as Sayyids in the oasis. The seven shrines of the Seven-Khojas are located in different places in the oasis which, they assure, were built by their descendants – seven notables ('*khojas*'). They claim their superior religious status by reference to their mission to convert the population of the entire oasis to Islam. Therefore, they extend beyond 'the recent history of the hunters' and date back to the eighth and ninth centuries.

Notably, the date of origin (8th-9th centuries) and the place of origin (Mashhad of Iran) are perhaps attributable to the archeological inscription on the front gate of the Khoja-Mashhad shrine and the name of the shrine itself. I say nothing against the claim of the *Khojamashhadi* men for their descent group, but just note that story-telling and invention do not require exact details. Rather, the requirement is to leave the details of the stories open in order to use them as a flexible resource to protect one's claims.

The other reference of *Khojamashhadi* men for religious superiority is their claim to absolute or bilineal (patrilineal and matrilineal) *Sayyidi* origin. Accordingly, their ancestors stemmed from the Islamic prophet Muhammad via his cousin and son-in-law, Ali Ibn Abu Talib. To assert their superior descent origin, they refer to their 'proper performance' of religious practices. Their *Sayyidi* origin also rejects the spiritual privilege of the *Sayyodi* descent group. The *Khojamashhadi* claim they belong to the first and at least to the second castes of 'white-bone' ('*ustukhonsafed*') Shaykhs. The term 'white-bone' suggests that they are either absolutely, that is, from both paternal and maternal lines, or principally, that is, from a paternal line, Sayyids. Within the caste system, they assure, the status of '*miyontura*' is at best a 'secondary' Sayyid, a descendent from the matrilineal line, as the term '*miyon*' literally means 'middle' or 'secondary'. Some even deny, or at least reinterpret, the spiritual power of Eshon-i Miyontura. His name ('Miyon-Tura'), they claim, reveals that he was neither from a pure nor from a 'half' or secondary Sayyid caste, but rather he was a 'trusted servant' of Sayyids.[224] Claimants to the titles of Sayyid and Shaykh thus insist that Eshon-i Miyontura was a resettled Uzbek religious notable in Sayyod village, 'fed by *Khojamashhadi* grandmothers', who was Sayyid Akramkhon's disciple and consequently gained his personal trust and spiritual intercession. According to these claimants, Sayyid Akramkhon, who fled to Afghanistan during the 1920s, was the central and sacred religious authority (saint) of the oasis.

To elevate the superior position of Sayyid Akramkhon over Eshon-i Miyontura, the claimants also interpret the meaning of the term '*eshon*'. They purport that the term does not refer to any exceptional descent origin or past spiritual adventure. Rather, '*eshon*' is a Tajik-Persian pronoun, synonymous with '*onho*' ('they'), literally signifying the third-person plural. Indeed, the word '*eshon*' means 'they'. It is especially used when someone wants to both address and respect the third-person singular. As a claimant argued, "'*Eshon*' is a respectful appeal to a singular person who sits and listens to the wisdom of *avliyo* [great spiritual men empowered directly by the will of God to execute miracles]... Sayyids are *avliyo*."[225]

In return, *Sayyodi* claimants do not emphasise the religious mission of the *Khojamashhadi* descent group in early Islam or the related function of the Khoja-

---

224 Personal interview with Chupon Aliev (Notebook No 1-4, November 23, 2007: pages 116-117; also tape recording No DS 300227).
225 Ibid.

Mashhad shrine. They support the dominant story, which does not imply any inheritance relation of the shrine to the *Khojamashhadi* descent group but rather asserts it as a common sacred site for all *mahalli* people. According to this story, the 'mathematically excellent architecture' of two cupolas of the shrine is not a human deed but rather a miracle of the inhuman force which 'built it overnight'. Also, villagers talk about their childhood memory that the shrine was 'nothing' but a place where people went out to celebrate their mundane and even 'irreligious' feasts, including *nawruz* (the start of the sowing season) and especially *fotihatuy* (a pre-marriage celebration). The latter had no relevance to religious practices and even contradicted it, since unmarried and newly married women celebrated their marriage ties. Villagers remember that "only recently, after the 1960s [their, *Sayyodi*] *pir*, Eshon-i Abdulazizkhon [the father of Qabodiyon Eshon], had forbidden women to enter and celebrate in the territory of the shrine." To legitimise his right, the current owner of the shrine, who is *Sayyodi* by descent origin, claims that the village cemetery was then not a part of the shrine. This story rejects the claim that the Khoja-Mashhad shrine was primarily a sacred site where especially women were not allowed to enter and to celebrate their weddings.

Individual claimants to especially *Khojamashhadi* origin refer to the history of the village cemetery. All villagers of different descent origins agree that the current cemetery, situated behind the Khoja-Mashhad shrine, belonged to the *Khojamashhadi* descent group while *Sayyodi* and other groups had different cemeteries. Only after the 1950s, when *kuhistoni* Tajiks resettled in the village and when extensive cotton plantations were developed, did state functionaries assign the *Khojamashhadi* cemetery as a shared cemetery for all descent groups. However, again, this evident history is attractive to *Khojamashhadi* men for its relevance to the stories of their descent group and its inheritance rights. They refer to the buried corpses in two cupolas of the shrine and claim that they belonged to their ancestors who came from Mashhad, disseminated Islam and were buried in the building of their Islamic centre. Again, this story is not shared by other powerful men from other descent groups, who refer to the archeological finding of corpses inside the jugs as a pre-Islamic ('fire-praying') burial ritual.[226]

This subchapter has discussed politically the most relevant collective identities in Sayyod village, including locality and kinship affiliations, multifaceted Islam and ethnicity. In the first place, we have observed the shared boundaries of locality, kinship and Islam among all *mahalli* ('native') ethnic and descent groups

---

226 Personal interview with Mahkam Boyakov (Notebook No 1-4, October 3, 2007: page 22-24).

(i.e. *mahalli* Tajiks, Uzbek tribes, Arabs and Sayyids) in the Qabodiyon oasis. These groups have shaped their kinship and religious networks so that they do not include *others*, i.e. *kuhistoni* Tajiks. In Sayyod village, however, *kuhistoni* Tajiks, geographically scattered across different neighbourhoods, have not developed kinship and religious exchanges with the *mahalli* people.

Furthermore, we have observed multilayered internal boundaries within the shared kinship and religious identity of the *mahalli* peoples. In certain contexts they distinguish themselves from Uzbek tribes and Arabs with whom they have only recently started developing institutionalised kinship ties. This boundary reflects *mahalli* village dignity, which praises Sayyod village as an important religious centre in the Qabodiyon oasis. 'Educated' villagers refer to the Khoja-Mashhad shrine as the first religious school at the beginning of the dissemination of Islam in the oasis. References to past and present religious nobles and saints, as well as to the nationalistic invention of the pre-Islamic history of the village, also serve the same purpose.

Beyond the shared *mahalli* village dignity of *mahalli* villagers, individual actors also divide villagers into mainly five *qawms* (descent groups), namely (1) *Sayyodi* Tajiks, (2) *Khojamashhadi* Tajiks, (3) *Samarkandi* Tajiks, (4) *Rabotaki* Uzbeks and (5) Arabs. The large neighbourhoods or *mahallas* in the village are based mainly on three of these *qawms*, i.e. *Sayyodi*, *Khojamashhadi* and *Rabotaki*. The claims of individual actors about their descent groups, which in part tell different histories of the village and its important sacred assets (e.g. Khoja-Mashhad shrine) and nobles (like saints), originate from their own political and economic struggles.

The following subchapters provide empirical cases about the role of the observed collective identities in shaping the mainstream aspects of local governance in Sayyod village. Subchapter four discusses the role of multifaceted *mahalli* identities in legitimising or delegitimising the political and economic claims and rights of individual actors. Subchapter five considers how these identities serve to shape the inclusive representation structure of the mahalla. Subchapter six examines how mahalla authorities use collective identities to integrate means and resources for socio-political stability at the local level. Finally, subchapter seven discusses the political case of the cotton industry, which is the central concern of the state and local elites for socio-political stability.

Legitimation of political and economic claims and rights

In Sayyod village, there is no substantial contestation over the unequal distribution of the positions and resources of the former kolkhoz, due not only to forced measures that local and state elites undertake but also due to patron-client relations and expectations that shape interdependency between privileged and underprivileged villagers. In most cases, however, socio-cognitive constructs have a significant enough impact to generate the perceptions and commitments of subject villagers for a differentiated and unequal, but inherited and sacred, order of property rights. The following three sections discuss the post-Soviet transformation and rearrangement of property rights predominantly affected by indigenous socio-cognitive constructs, including *mahalli* collective identities.

Political and economic domination of elites

Before discussing the role of socio-cognitive constructs, especially collective identities, the current section describes the political and economic situations in Sayyod village. Post-Soviet privatisation and the consequent redistribution of public goods mostly favoured kolkhozi elites and their *mahalli* clients. As mentioned already, the term '*kolkhozi* elites', or '*kuhistoni kolkhozi* elites', refers to those who dominate inter-village state and non-state economic and political entities, such as the jamoat and collective farms. Their *mahalli* clients are powerful men from among *mahalli* men in Sayyod village who run village-level political and economic organisations, such as mahallas, mosques, cotton brigadas and *dehqan* farms (hereinafter, cotton farms), and who own the majority of the most profitable economic resources and enterprises (see also Table 8: Personal networks of the *mahalli* clients of kolkhozi and cotton elites).

The privileged access of kolkhozi elites to the bureaucratic and military means of the state helped them to privatise and benefit from public goods and positions. Today, they own the most favourable land resources, gardens, agricultural machinery and small economic enterprises of the former kolkhoz. Also, their administrative positions are important in rejecting the request letters (formal *ariza*) of many villagers to private ownership. Instead, they legalise their own privileged access by 'administrative' means such as *oformlenie* (management) and *spisanie* (alienation or write-off). They utilise these means to manipulate the formal rights of the subject population and thereby privatise the remaining public goods. According to the statutory write-off regulation (*spisanie*), a strategic public good or property can be sold or alienated from public use only if the General Meeting or the meeting of all members of the collective farm decides so. However, administrators do not call a meeting for such a task but instead decide themselves based on their personal ties with villagers.

Table 8: Personal networks of the *mahalli* clients of kolkhozi and cotton elites

Name	Family and *qawm*-related status	*Kolkhozi*, state and other privileged membership
Shoniyoz Eshniyozov	Extended family elder; one of the most reputable *Khojamashhadi* elders	Head of a brigada in a railway company; one son is a state officer in the province
Polvon Kholmatov	Extended family elder; the most reputable *Khojamashhadi* elder	Agronomist, Communist Party leader and deputy director of kolkhoz; one brother is a successful farmer
Haji Ismoil Eshgulov	Extended family elder; the most reputable *Sayyodi* elder and religious notable	His brother was the head of the mahalla
Turdiqul Hamzaev	Extended family elder; a reputable *Sayyodi* elder	Head of the Livestock Farm of Kolkhoz; his brother was formerly the director of the village school
Nazar Numonov	Extended family elder; one of the most reputable *Sayyodi* elders	He and his brothers and sons are most reputable construction masters in the village; his father was the construction teacher of the school
Mahkam Boyakov	Extended family elder; one of the most reputable *Samarkandi* and *Sayyodi* elders	School sports teacher; he and his father were famous wrestlers; grandfather was the principal village mullah and had close ties with Eshon-i Miyontura
Haji Bobo Quliev	Extended family elder; most reputable *Rabotaki* elder and religious notable	His father was the head of the Soviet kolkhoz in the 1960s; he and his three brothers were elites of the Soviet kolkhoz; personal relation with Cotton Hero; currently he and one of his brothers have two family brigadas; he is himself *haji*
Qamar Jumaev	Extended family elder; one of the most reputable *Rabotaki* elders	Brigadir of one of the main brigadas (*Rabotak-mahalla*) of the village since the Soviet kolkhoz
Abdullo Munimov	Extended family elder; the religious leader of the *Sayyodi* and *Samarkandi* people	*Imam-khatib* and religious leader of the mahalla; related to and authorised by Qabodiyon Eshon

Source: Personal field research (October 2007 – March 2008)

There is no significant contestation over the unequal distribution of political positions and economic favours in Sayyod village. Only a few villagers mentioned the misuse of public properties by elites and their *mahalli* clients, the current administrators of the collective farm. This is, first of all, due to the access of elites and their clients to the bureaucratic and military means of local state. I observed only rare but 'behind the door' ('*az pusht*' or 'from the back') complaints about proprietorship rights to both collective and private land resources, despite the fact that most of the villagers told me that their support (especially so-called '*presidenti*'[227]) land plots had been appropriated by the farmers and then fully or partially given to other villagers. A woman expressed that, like other appealers, she had no chance to obtain the land plot by legal means.[228] As a suffering farmer told me, "If you say something, they will tighten their grip on you. They can do everything to ensure you cannot live in the village anymore."[229] The expert analysis of a local advocacy NGO, "Arbitrazh", in Shahritus district also noted the small amount of disputes over property rights appealed through arbitrary and state courts.[230]

Similarly, in the case of 10-*sotikha* (1/10 of each hectare of a cotton field) land plots, I witnessed frequent cases when farmers prohibited the access rights of ordinary workers who did not work in the cotton fields. 10-*sotikha* has been practiced since Soviet times as a technical measure for leaving idle certain parts of cotton fields by sowing less intensive crops, including wheat and maize. Since 1996-1997, state authorities have modified '10-*sotikha*' as a measure for wheat production and food security and also as an in-kind payment of salaries for subject workers on cotton farms. In practice, 10-*sotikha* is the seasonal

---

[227] 75,000 hectares of arable, so-called '*presidenti*', land plots were distributed twice, on the bases of the Decrees of the President of Tajikistan No 342 in 1995 and No 874 in 1997 for wheat production and the food security of individual households (Government 2011: 39). It was formally titled a 'support' ('*yorirason*') land resource for families who did not have more than 15 *sotikh* (0.15 hectares) of household yards (*tamarqa*) for agricultural activities. The allocation of three *sotikh* per individual member was set for Sayyod inhabitants. However, the increasing erosion of land resources and shifts in demographic structures, such as the increase of inhabitants and households and internal and external migrations, were not taken into account (Personal interview: Notebook No 1-5, December 7, 2007: page 19).

[228] Personal interview (Notebook No 1-4, November 24, 2007: pages 119-120).

[229] Personal interview with Samad Ghayurov (Notebook No 1-7, March 10, 2008: page 113).

[230] Personal interview with a representative of the NGO "Arbitrazh" (Notebook No 1-7, March 13, 2008: pages 121-122).

(nonreusable) usage right based on an informal contract between farmers and their workers in return for their full-time work on cotton farms. Workers, who for different reasons (sickness, pregnancy, etc.) cannot work properly, therefore do not receive this plot of land. While exempted from taxes, 10-*sotikha* land plots are registered as salaries and in-kind support for workers. However, due to the hugely physical demands required to work these land plots, which are distributed from uncultivated and eroded cotton fields as well as from the irrigation infrastructure (including technical land resources of dams, canals and irrigation drains and ditches), many women cannot use them.[231]

The workers themselves do not regard both *presidenti* and 10-*sotikha* land plots as their own private properties but rather as patronage favours for their work on the cotton farms. Privileged access to such land plots is also judged as being due to the 'benevolence' of the President of Tajikistan and kolkhozi elites, again for their full devotion to the cotton sector. Besides, the cliental expectation is important, in that villagers do not take special account of their right to a salary. For example, tractor drivers prefer their low-paid jobs mainly because of their significant additional income derived from 'serving' villagers, e.g. by sowing private land plots. Also, the preference of family male seniors legitimises payment for cotton work in such a material form. An informant told me that since many workers on the cotton farms are juniors and women, salary payment would spoil them because they would no longer obey their seniors and would spend the money on harmful things.[232]

These administrative and bureaucratic means, patron-client exchanges and expectations and the indigenous status of juniors and women are not always effective in helping to enforce the current political and economic order. The following discussion shows how local people's collective identities legitimise the privileged rights of some powerful men.

Search for legitimation of political and economic claims and rights

Reference to collective identities as a discursive practice accompanies and legitimises unequal and contested privatisation and de-collectivisation processes in the post-Soviet period. The important role of collective identities is to highlight the socio-cognitive constructs of villagers which shape the core pillars of the current political and economic order in the village. In the subsections

231 Personal interview with Samad Ghayurov (Notebook No 1-7, March 10, 2008: pages 112-114).

232 Personal interview with Chupon Aliev (Notebook No 1-7, March 1, 2008: pages 83-84).

below, I discuss separately collective identities, including (1) kinship (*elkheshi* and *qawm*) affiliations, (2) Islam and (3) descent origin.

Kinship (elkheshi and qawm) affiliations

To gain privileged access to public assets, claimants create a circle of symbolic legitimacy by ascribing these assets to 'their own people' (see also Figure 3: The circle of symbolic legitimacy in the theoretical chapter). They refer mainly to their *elkheshi* and *qawm* groups as the privileged (sacred or hereditary) owners of the assets for which they claim. The Bibi-Mayramjon shrine, located at the southern edge of the Rabotak-*mahalla*, is the 'honour' asset of 70 *Rabotaki* households. The *Rabotaki* brigadir, Qamar Jumaev, mobilised his co-members and restored the site in 1974. Again, recently, he mobilised the *hashar* of his co-members and renovated the sacred healing site for wider suppliants (spiritual visitors). The site endows sacred values on his co-members while providing for the brigadir's religious reputation and private access to the material benefits of the shrine.

By reference to *qawm* identity, another claimant, Chupon Aliev, attempts to attract the concern of his *qawm* (*Khojamashhadi*) co-members to the 'fate of their *choykhona*'. The building of their *choykhona* or *qawm* mosque is registered as a silkworm-house at the collective farm. Invoking *qawm* concern is thus one way that the claimant struggles with *other* more powerful claimants to privatising the silkworm-house situated next to his household.[233]

Cotton farmers especially refer to *elkheshi* and *qawm* identities to mobilise related workers on their farms, of which I give a detailed account in the subchapter on the cotton economy. Also, any reference to these identities legitimises the privileged and sometimes exclusive rights of the farmers to land and other important resources of the cotton enterprises. Reference is sought to commit subject co-members to 'concessiveness' (*ruikhotirbini*), i.e. to acknowledge the privileged rights of their farmers. Referencing *elkheshi* and *qawm* identities thus seeks to enforce the common perception that contestation is against and corrupts kinship norms and ties.[234]

A brigadir justified his family's exclusive right to 10-*sotikha* resources on 'his *qawm*'s farm', since, he assures, "[his] family sacrificed their time and labour on

---

[233] During my recent field visit in March 2012, the silkworm-house was privatised in favour of his cousin, the chief agronomist of the District Agricultural Department.
[234] E.g. personal interviews with farm workers (Notebook No 1-5, December 26, 2007: page 140; Notebook No 1-5, December 28, 2007: pages 146-147).

behalf of their *qawm*." He assured me that the cotton farm is the property of his *qawm* co-members but nobody wants to work for it. He therefore "ha[s] to use 10-*sotikha* [the land plots of his subordinate workers] in order to cover cotton-related expenses."[235] The farmers widely claim such judgment to legitimise their privileges. In the extract below, I provide a conversation between the farmer and one of my key informants, which reflects how they perceive and use land resources:

> Chupon Aliev: Many [of your subordinate workers] say they have no 10-*sotikha*.
>
> Brigadir: They do not work. How can I give it to them!? They hoe and fluff up the soil, but it is not work.
>
> Chupon Aliev [now supporting the farmer]: They eradicate weeds incompletely.
>
> Brigadir: They send their children for hoeing. All the same, even if you go to their doorsteps, they do not work. They say: 'It is your job'. My family and I are always working for them… They have 10-20-*sotikh* of the *presidenti* land plots, but they do not use them; they waste them. You give them 10-*sotikha*, but they are haughty or lazy. They want you to serve them, to lament them at their doorsteps.[236]

Islam

Ordinary villagers have frequently contested the sacred status and hereditary privileges of elites and their *mahalli* clients. Therefore, the mediating elders of the village refer to Islamic identity and discredit the 'infidel' behaviour and claims of any opponents. They recount, at public gatherings and religious ceremonies, the moral distortion of opponents who "do not respect the chiefs [*kalono*] and who… insult them for their own low salaries. [They are] infidels."[237]

As already discussed, a claim for inheritance is one of the most effective strategies in legitimising political and economic rights and privileges. Powerful men invent stories about how they or their descendants are related to selected properties. These stories portray their descent and spiritual connection or bestowal and professional privilege over sacred sites, land, gardens, economic enterprises and technical infrastructure in the village.

---

235 Personal interview with the brigadir – Rauf Fattoev (Notebook No 1-6, January 26, 2008: page 89).

236 Ibid.

237 Personal interview with Mahkam Boyakov (Notebook No 1-4, October 4, 2007: pages 26-29).

To ensure their privileges, powerful men of Sayyod village, mostly *mahalli* clients of kolkhozi elites, claim their inheritance rights, for example, to the former kolkhoz's public properties. For example, four of them claim that they personally, or their fathers or grandfathers, grew the gardens and thus privatised them as *dehqan* farms.

In most cases, actors legitimise their inherited or acquired rights to positions and resources by reference to socio-cognitive constructs and myths. The frequent reference to Islamic identity is necessary to highlight and approve these constructs and myths. The actors refer to their connections with holy saints and sacred experiences (such as dreams and 'Muslim sickness'). For example, the myth of the intercession ('*nazar*') of Khujai Khizr (a supernatural saint) legitimises inherited or acquired wealth and power and suggests that each Muslim meets the saint three times during his life. If he is a proper Muslim, then he will be granted wealth and power.

Moreover, powerful men make use of the cognitive frames of villagers to bestow exclusive religious status to their own persons and properties. One important shared construct is the accompaniment of the saints, which implies sacred and thereby protected property boundaries. Thus, adults teach their children that some gardens belonging to powerful men are harmful to trespass upon, since supernatural beings protect them. Qamar Jumaev seeks his privileged right to the formerly four-hectare garden of his brigada as the boundary of his (*Rabotaki*) *qawm*-related Bibi-Mayramjon shrine. His claim that he grew the garden during his work as a brigadir during the Soviet kolkhoz is not enough to legitimise his private ownership. Therefore, he seeks to incarnate the spiritual site and its boundary to his person by reference to his exclusive religious commitment to the wellbeing of the shrine.

Dreams also serve as a divine source to legitimise privileged positions and resources. The principal mullah of the village remembers that he was "not on the due way of God until he dreamt of his *great* grandfather, who ordered him to start prayer."[238] He did not see the grandfather alive and had only heard from his father that he was the principal mullah of the village before he was sent in the 1930s to GULAG. Although the principal mullah does not have intensive training, his dream legitimises his inheritance of religious knowledge and leadership.

---

238 Personal interview with the principal village mullah (Notebook No 1-6, January 22, 2008: pages 41-42; also tape recording No DS 300259).

Search for the sacred status of the descent group

Although today there are no clear-cut kinship or *qawm* boundaries among the *mahalli* people of Sayyod village, claimants refer to their distinct descent origins to legitimise their inheritance rights. For example, the *Khojamashhadi* Shaykhs claim they possess authentic knowledge of religious science, which ascends them to the status of *avliyo*.[239] 'Others', who do not inherit but only acquire secondary religious knowledge, must obey them. Thus, they have privileged rights to possess sacred sites and collect *nazr*[240] from suppliants.[241] To approve the sacred status of their *qawm* and its inheritance rights, they want "to restore relationships with their kinsmen in Afghanistan" in order to revive their genealogical book (*shajaranoma*). As such, they claim that the current '*mutavvali*' (guide) or '*shaykh*', who belongs to the *Sayyodi qawm*, has no inheritance right to the Khoja-Mashhad shrine or 'blessing rights' ('*haqqi duodehi*') from suppliants. As claimants told me on behalf of their *qawm*, "[p]rincipally, we are *shekhs* [Shaykhs] of the Khoja-Mashhad [shrine], but *others* eat [own it]."[242] In return, the current *mutavalli*, *Sayyodi* himself by descent origin, rejects his opponents' notions by indicating that "The possession is God's will that prescribes the blessing right."[243] He is employed as a guard by the Ministry of Culture of Tajikistan. He inherited the position not only from his father, who guarded the shrine through 1962-1996, but also because he was the college friend of the head of the relevant ministry's department in Dushanbe.

The Khoja-Mashhad shrine is the most frequently visited spiritual site, after the Chiluchor-Chashma shrine, in the entire oasis, which generates religious reputation and substantial economic income for its *mutavalli*. This is the central reason for any form of contestation. Women and men from different *mahalli* villages visit the shrine for healing and pilgrimage purposes and "to ask for help and protection if they are sick, have problems, are childless, their young men are in labour migration, etc."[244] They devote *sadaqa* in different forms – cash, food and animal sacrifices – which are collected mainly by the *mutavvali*'s family. According to my estimations, the shrine can bring in about 500 TJ Somoni

---

239 Great spiritual men empowered directly by God's will to execute miracles.

240 Personal favour for a religious service provided at sacred sites.

241 Personal interview with Chupon Aliev (Notebook No 1-4, November 27, 2007: pages 140-142).

242 Personal interviews (Notebook No 1-6, January 22, 2008: page 44; Notebook No 1-4, November 28, 2007: pages 150-152).

243 Personal interview with Mahmad Yusupov (Notebook No 1-4, October 24, 2007: pages 44-46).

244 Personal interview with Mahmad Yusupov (Notebook No 1-4, October 2, 2007: page 19; also Notebook No 1-4, October 1-4, October 24, 2007: pages 44-46).

weekly for the guard, while he also uses a 20-*sotikh* (0.2 hectares) land plot in the shrine's yard.[245]

Similarly, several Shaykhs, who inhabit different villages of the oasis (including Qumshokh and Sayyod), attempt to restore their genealogical books (*shajaranoma*), which refer to their exclusive inheritance right to the Chiluchor-Chashma shrine. They declare that their certifying books were destroyed or damaged by the 'infidel' (*kofir*) Soviet state. The current holder of the shrine does not reject the status of other claimants as Sayyids but rather claims that there are four castes of Sayyids or Shaykhs and he belongs to the first pure caste. His ancestors, who were sent to this place to disseminate Islam, derive from the 'root' of the Islamic prophet.

Again, for the purpose of privileged access to both religious and mundane resources and positions, powerful men refer to their sacred *qawm* bestowed with Islamic sources and saints. Two powerful men of *Sayyodi* and *Samarkandi* descent origins claim privileged personal relations between Eshon-i Miyontura and their fathers. The claim seeks to legitimise their ownership of the Eshon-i Miyontura shrine, including its healing site and the central mosque of Sayyod village. The shrine, once a household of Eshon-i Miyontura, is situated in the neighbourhood of the *Sayyodi* extended family of Abdullo Munimov, whose members are its *jorubkash* (guard and cleaner). The senior sister of the extended family inherited her right from her grandmother, who is claimed to be the 'reception mother' ('*peshduromad ocha*') of Eshon-i Miyontura's wife. According to local traditions, a female member of the bridegroom's *elkheshi* group will be adopted as the bride's reception mother, who then replaces the bride's natural mother and introduces her to the bridegroom's relatives. This status is equal to that of the natural mother and endures for a lifetime.[246]

The claim also legitimises the right of the junior son, *imam-khatib*, Abdullo Munimov, as the shaykh of the shrine and its village mosque. The male *mutavalli* of the Eshon-i Miyontura shrine is the son of *Samarkandi* Mahkam Boyakov, who also claims a personal relationship between Eshon-i Miyontura and his father, who was the principal mullah of the village.[247] The spiritual connection also legitimises the privileged right of Munimov's family to a cotton-collecting tent due to its location just behind the shrine. A farmer privatised this public

---

[245] Personal observations on October 2, 2007 (Notebook No 1-4, October 2, 2007: page 19) and October 24, 2007 (Notebook No 1-4, October 1-4, October 24, 2007: pages 44-46).

[246] Personal interview (Notebook No 1-5, December 28, 2007: pages 147-148).

[247] Personal interview with Mahkam Boyakov (Notebook No 1-4, October 3, 2007: pages 22-24).

good via his privileged access to bureaucratic services and then sold it to the *imam-khatib*. In order to prevent possible conflicts, kinsmen have spread a rumour that "Not everyone can [own] this place, if he has no *pusht* ['back', i.e. ancestral or spiritual right]'. This rumour interprets the tent as a part of the sacred site (the shrine) which was 'trampled' over by the Soviet kolkhoz.

Men also seek the spiritual bestowal of their *qawms* by saints and souls in order to claim their own rights to sacred sites and professions. For example, there are about seven 'inside'- or household-related shrines – *Shahids* and *Charoghjoys* – which are maintained by their 'possessors'. Three of them are visited by people, mostly kinsmen, neighbours and friends, in order to 'ask for help and healing'. Most of the suppliants are women who pray for pregnancy and the health and success of their children. The 'possessors' claim the spiritual power of their ancestors, which thus legitimises their rights to such sacred sites. To claim the healing power of the most frequently visited *Charoghjoy*, its female owner and healer refers to her deceased father-in-law, enamored by a *pari* (an angel which bestows physical and spiritual power to his subject), in regard to his exceptional skill in hunting any form of prey, such as deer.[248] The claim of spiritual ancestry and connection is legitimate due to the common belief that *shahids* ('martyrs') and the *pari* of *Charoghjoys* and shrine souls actually have spiritual power that not only protects them but also empowers the 'possessors' and their boundaries: "A *shahid* who cannot protect itself [referring both to the *shahid* itself, the possessor and the natural surrounding] is not a real *shahid*," my key informant recounted.[249] The possessors of these sacred sites claim that they or their ancestors met with the sacred martyrs, angels and souls. Especially the pure and sinless ancestors ('*pusht*', which literally means 'back') are necessary references to claim such privileges.

In this way, the possessors refer to their spiritual experiences and intercessions (*shafoat*) to assert their distinctive descent and religious identities. They frequently mention their experience of hallucination to claim that the souls and saints accompany, intercede and spiritually empower them. Such mystification of spiritual experiences and encounters has a direct link with the practical intentions of the possessors. The possessor and healer of Ghoib-shahid (or Ghoibona-shahid – 'martyr by correspondence') linked the shrine to his healing powers inherited from his grandmother to justify his claim. He claims that he has inherited healing powers to cure any diseases, including scorpion stings,

---

[248] Personal interview (Notebook No 1-4, November 29, 2007: pages 154-155, also tape recording No DS 300231-232).

[249] Personal interview with Chupon Aliev (Notebook No 1-6, January 29, 2008: page 124).

snake bites and bee stings: "If you have bad intentions [when you enter the home], you will be hopelessly sick. If you are intending to cause harm to the household, you are not allowed to enter: either you encounter a family member or you hallucinate a black dog. Only *avlods* [kinsmen and well-intended suppliants] can enter here."[250] He reifies his mystical claim by referring to the fact that the household gate does not fully cover the entrance to his shrine.

Picture 6: Entrance to the sacred household

His claim is used to distance rather than to isolate himself from others. He instead prefers more compliance from others so that they believe in and visit the Ghoib-shahid shrine in a proper manner. If people visit 'with good intentions and faith', their desires will be accomplished. The signs of good intentions and faith are frequent and obedient visits, which necessarily include sacrifices and *sadaqa* for the sake of the *shahid.*

[250] Personal interview (Notebook No 1-6, January 29, 2008: pages 122-123).

Although so far limited to kinsmen, neighbours and friends, *Charoghjoys*, like other shrines and healing activities, are also becoming the business enterprises of individual actors, who refer to their inherited professions and seek people's acknowledgement by organising *khatm*. A professional healer trained during his labour migration to Russia could not legitimise his knowledge and profession until he had organised *khatm*, where he expressed his 'experience' to the villagers. The visitors acknowledged his claim that "I inherited the healing profession from my grandmother…"[251]

Similarly, powerful men refer to their descent origins to claim for the inheritance of religiously and economically important professions and thus maintain a certain pattern of labour division. The claim is based on an indigenous mental construct, i.e. exclusive trust in the masterly skills of craftsmen – people do not trust others who do not inherit such skills. In Sayyod village, most of the masterly and prestigious professions, such as bee-keeping, gardening, construction, circumcision and other religious services are 'paternal professions' ('*padarkasbi*') or inherited from ancestors. The family members of Numonov master construction and bee-keeping skills, Naimov has a gardening farm and a carving enterprise, Munimov is a religiously 'pure' family and Quliev inherits and thus knows the 'delicacies' of sheep-raising.

The most successful construction brigada in Sayyod village belongs to the junior brothers and sons of Usto Nazar Numonov, who himself is a deputy head of the mahalla. They learned the profession from their grandfather (the father of brothers), who was a construction teacher at the village school. The other four construction brigadas and many single workers use construction work only as an additional source of income. They mainly work in Sayyod village and rarely in Shahritus town. In contrast to the prestigious and profitable activity of Usto Nazar, these are categorised as *mardikor* ('black worker') or *raznarabochiy* ('unprofessional worker'). The latter, especially single workers, are underpaid or not paid appropriately.

[251] Personal observation (Notebook No 1-4, November 16, 2007: pages 65-66).

Table 9: Frequency of livelihood sources among different categories of people

Categories of income generation	Main income from one source	Main income from two sources	Main income from three sources	Main income from four sources
Wage labourers		3	7	
Individual land tenants			2	
Labour migrants (in Russia)		2	12	
Kolkhoz workers (workers in cotton farm)			3	
Wage and rent labourer (workers at the cotton plant, construction workers, including unskilled, non-inherited masters and rent labourers) and household workers			21	5
Qualified specialists, including technicians, inherited construction masters and inherited bee-keepers		5	1	

Source: Personal survey (October 2007 – March 2008)

In this subchapter we have observed that the multiple kinship and religious references of *mahalli* villagers enforce and actualise the socio-cognitive constructs of the unequal distribution of strategic assets and resources. Kolkhozi elites dominate key political and economic positions and resources at the inter-village level (including the jamoat and collective farm). They and their *mahalli* clients (powerful villagers) have privatised important economic goods and enterprises of the former kolkhoz and possess privileged rights to the remaining public goods. Reference to *mahalli* identities serves to legitimise the unequal and thus contested privatisation and distribution of resources. Privileged men protect their contested positions and assets by interpreting them as the goods of 'their peoples'. For this purpose, they highlight *elkheshi* (extended family) and *qawm* (descent) identities in order to generate the commitment of 'their people' to these goods.

Powerful men also seek sacred status and inherited privileges over the contested goods. They and their mahalla mediators refer to multifaceted Islamic identity and thereby legitimise their own rights and discredit the 'infidel' behaviour of their opponents. These possessors invent stories about, for example, how they or their descendants are related to selected properties. These stories or symbolic goods of legitimacy validate their descent and spiritual connections or the bestowal of professional privilege over sacred sites, land plots, gardens, economic enterprises and some technical infrastructure in the village. The frequent references to Islamic identity are necessary to prove such a search for legitimacy. Also, reference to an Islamic identity seeks sacred status for individual possessors and their descent groups. Hence, proclaiming the religious sacredness of descent origin is a frequently used strategy to legitimise political and economic rights.

The inclusive representation structure of the mahalla

As the preceding discussion suggests, villagers refer to Islamic and kinship (extended family and descent group) affiliations to achieve their own political and economic goals. Besides such personal use, local and state authorities reconstruct and reinterpret collective identities to shape cotton-growing political and economic structures. The current subchapter discusses the role of collective identities in shaping the political body of the mahalla as an inclusive representation structure. The following sections discuss how the mahalla represents almost all kinship and neighbourhood networks (section one) and how *mahalli* Islamic identity is sought to bestow sacredness on the mediation function of the mahalla (section two).

The inclusive representation of the *mahalli* people

In Sayyod village, ethnic affiliation has a decisive role in shaping the political structure of the mahalla. Although the mahalla officially involves *kuhistoni* Tajiks as well, their powerful men shape their own distinctive and isolated but formally unrecognised political structure. They separately organise ceremonies, mobilise collective actions and resolve internal disputes. These activities maintain social cohesion within their ethnic community, cotton-growing neighbourhoods, and simultaneously distinguish them from the *mahalli* people. *Kuhistoni* Tajiks also separately organise their own religious practices and ceremonies and do not share the sacred notions and categories of locality, kinship and Islam with their *mahalli* co-villagers. This distinction is categorical, especially when *kuhistoni* men do not interpret the same meanings about religious assets as the *mahalli* men do. Also, they do not join the annual *hashar* of the *mahalli* men to clean the village cemetery on the eve of Ramadan but instead clean the space allocated for their own ancestors in the same cemetery.

Sometimes, five *mahalli* descent groups (*qawms*) organise different and isolated activities. Nevertheless, they are represented in the same mahalla, which is the mediation structure of local and state elites at village level. The mahalla represents most of the political, economic and religious entities of the *mahalli* people in Sayyod village. These entities include two village secondary schools, six *dehqan* farms, four larger brigadas and six 'family' (small) brigadas on the collective farm, the Eshon-i Miyontura (village) mosque, the Khoja-Mashhad shrine, three *kusha-* or *qawm*-related mosques (*choykhonas*) and descent or extended family neighbourhoods. Moreover, the mahalla represents employees of the jamoat and collective farm, who are all original *mahalli* village inhabitants.

Local and central state functionaries insist on the principle of the inclusive representation of the mahalla in order to shape effective neighbourhood 'communities'. Here, they refer to *mahalli* identities, including Islam, *elkheshi* (extended family), *qawm* (descent group) and neighbourhood affiliations to enforce the representation authority of mahalla mediators (leaders, elders and religious notables). Such reference is effective since the mediators represent their extended families and other neighbourhood households. Besides powerful men and *oqsaqols*, *kucha*[252] mullahs represent *kucha* neighbourhoods. To enforce the authority of *kucha* mullahs, mediators therefore highlight the Islamic identity of *kucha* residents and shape it around *kucha* or *qawm* mosques (*choykhonas*). Reference to *qawm* identity is another important source in shaping *kucha* identity. For this purpose, the mahalla gives the names of powerful men or their predecessors to their *kucha* neighbourhoods.

The mahalla consists of officially recognised leaders, family and neighbourhood elders (*oqsaqols*), religious notables and other powerful men. They are hierarchically positioned in the categories of 1) leaders, or 'biggers', 2) elders (*oqsaqols*) and 3) 'assistants' of the leaders.[253] It is not by accident that most mahalla members possess the political and economic resources of the former kolkhoz.

To continue and justify the principle of inclusive representation, both mahalla mediators and local state functionaries highlight distinctive or shared *mahalli* identities. Especially, the shared identity of five *mahalli qawms* is reflected in

---

[252] *Kucha* (literally: 'street') is a residential unit mapped along the main streets of the village.

[253] The Committee members are the head of the mahalla, Ravshan Eshgulov, three of his deputies – Shoniyoz Eshniyozov, Mahkam Boyakov, Nazar Numonov – and other Committee members, including *Haji* Ismoil Eshgulov, Polvon Kholmatov, *Haji* Bobo Quliev, Haji Ataboy Qiyomov, two principal brigadirs of the collective farm – Qamar Jumaev and Salom Qiyomov – the *imam-khatib* – Abdullo Munimov – and the veteran of the jamoat – Ghayurova Marifat.

their commitment to the 'bearers of [village] honour' ('*nangbardor*'). Among these 'bearers of honour' are veterans of the Soviet kolkhoz or state elites.[254] Mahkam Boyakov is one of these, who was a wrestler (*polvon*) in the past and thus "elevated village honour for many years."[255] These 'bearers of honour' are trusted by villagers to recount the 'glorious' history of Sayyod village. They, especially Mahkam Boyakov and Shoniyoz Eshniyozov, dominate historical and religious discourses about the common identity of the *mahalli* people in the oasis. Also, elite elders and Islamic pilgrims (hajis) are counted as reputable and privileged mahalla leaders.[256]

Many of these 'bearers of honour' are traditionally powerful men who at the same time represent their extended families (*elkheshi*) and descent groups (*qawms*) in the mahalla. They represent 23 extended families which at the same time embed all *mahalli* descent groups and *kucha* neighbourhoods. The mediation power of these men is linked directly to their spiritual and inherited reputation as well as to their material wealth. Often, they are the wealthiest men among their co-members and at the same time own most of the political and economic resources and enterprises (including cotton farms) of their extended families (see also Table 10: Extended families and descent groups in Sayyod village). In cases when some powerful men cannot mediate and represent 'their people' in the mahalla, elders or *oqsaqols* replace them.

254 Including Polvon Kholmatov, *Haji* Bobo Quliev, Qamar Jumaev and Salom Qiyomov.

255 Personal interview (Notebook No 1-4, November 14, 2007: page 62).

256 Including Rasul Nazirov (the only living veteran of World War II), Ochil Teshaev (veteran teacher) and Mullo Obloqul (the principal mullah).

Table 10: Extended families and descent groups in Sayyod village

<table>
<tr><th>Qawms</th><th>Khojamashhadi</th><th>Sayyodi</th><th>Samarkandi</th><th>Rabotaki</th><th>Arab</th></tr>
<tr><td rowspan="8">Elkheshi families</td><td>Eshniyozov</td><td>Eshgulov</td><td></td><td>Quliev</td><td>Yuldoshev</td></tr>
<tr><td>Kholmatov</td><td colspan="2">Boyakov</td><td colspan="2">Mamadyorov</td></tr>
<tr><td>Qiyomov</td><td colspan="3">Hamzaev</td><td>Norboev</td></tr>
<tr><td>Ahmadov</td><td colspan="2">Munimov</td><td>Alamov</td><td></td></tr>
<tr><td colspan="2">Numonov</td><td></td><td>Duldiev</td><td></td></tr>
<tr><td colspan="2">Ahadov</td><td></td><td>Jumaev</td><td></td></tr>
<tr><td colspan="2">Saidaliev</td><td></td><td></td><td></td></tr>
<tr><td></td><td>Naimov</td><td></td><td></td><td></td></tr>
</table>

Source: Personal survey (October 2007 – March 2008)

For example, Alamov Panji is the *oqsaqol*[257] of one of the five *kucha* neighbourhoods of *Rabotak-mahalla* and at the same time performs the function of *muezzin* (prayer-watchman) for the *qawm* mosque. He is not wealthy but represents his powerful patrilineal group (Alamovho) in the *Rabotak* descent network and in the mahalla based on the principle that he has inherited his status from his father. His status is also enforced due to the fact that three of his five sons are married to the daughters of other powerful men in his *elkheshi* and *qawm* networks – *Haji* Bobo Quliev, Khudoi Mamadyorov and Qamar Jumaev.[258] The mentioned powerful kinsmen represent and run four other *kucha* neighbourhoods and cotton farms attributable to the *Rabotaki* people.

This kinship system gradually transformed the representation structure of the mahalla especially in 2006, when it was shaped along the mentioned 23 *elkheshi*, *qawm*, *kucha* and *mahalla* sub-groups. Their self-evident leaders were automatically selected as mahalla members. For example, the current deputy head of the mahalla, Polvon Kholmatov, told me that he was 'elected' by his *elkheshi* co-members despite his absence from the meeting. As he explained,

---

[257] In this case, the status of "*oqsaqol*" is given to mahalla members who represent and lead *kucha* neighbourhoods. These *oqsaqols* are usually reputable elders or powerful men in their neighbourhoods.

[258] Personal interview with Panji Alamov (Notebook No 1-7, March 15, 2008: pages 125-126).

"Because I was outside the village I could not participate in the meeting, but I was [s]elected[259] as a mahalla member anyway."[260]

The position of mahalla head, however, is less dependent upon *elkheshi*, *qawm* and other affiliations. In the same meeting, Ravshan Eshgulov, the current mahalla head, was appointed. The elders who elected him to the position judged his capacities according to his inherited privilege, patron-client network, oratory skills and material wealth. In the village, his extended family (Eshgulov) is one of the most powerful and reputable networks. During the 1990s, his father was mahalla head, and today his uncle is a key mahalla member. Also, his sister is a district government employee who helps him to access district government offices easily. The most reputable elder explained his capacity: "He is a young man and has close personal ties with different people in the village and outside. Besides, he has good [oratory] skills to relay our requests to the jamoat and district [government]."[261] The other necessary privilege the head enjoys is his private bus, which he uses to serve elders during important ceremonies, especially funerals, inside and outside the village.

Religious identity: bestowing *mahaldori* authority with sacredness

Religious ceremonies serve to heighten the *mahaldori* or mediation reputation and authority of more than 23 mahalla leaders and mediators. These ceremonies include family-related wedding and funeral rituals as well as neighbourhood- or village-level feasts.[262] Village elders utilise these ceremonies

---

[259] There are several synonyms for both 'to select' and 'to elect' in Tajik language, but people mainly use '*ta'in kardan*' ('to appoint') instead.

[260] Personal interview with Polvon Kholmatov (Notebook No 1-5, December 28, 2007: pages 149-151).

[261] Personal interview with Rasul Nazirov (Notebook No 1-7, March 9, 2008: page 108-109).

[262] As the mahalla head, Ravshan Eshgulov (Notebook No 1-7, February 13, 2008: pages 47-48), told me about 35-40 'village elders' (who are not always old enough and not all old men have such status) are obliged to participate in important ceremonies. Among them, 15 men are *Sayyodi* and *Samarkandi,* 10 of them are *Khojamashhadi* and 10-15 are *Rabotaki* and *Arab.* In the initiation ceremonies of outsiders, i.e. non-*mahalli* inhabitants of Sayyod village, such as *kuhistoni* Tajiks and *budyoni* Arabs, these so-called 'important village elders' represent the villagers. The regulation of initiation ceremonies at funerals and weddings is also the commitment of the mahalla head and his deputies and 'assistants' (including Shoniyoz Eshniyozov, Nazar Numonov, Polvon Kholmatov, *Haji* Ismoil Eshgulov, Mahkam Boyakov, *Haji* Bobo Quliev, *Haji* Ataboy Qiyomov,

to generate the religious commitment of villagers to their mediation authority. Especially the principal mullah, *imam-khatib* and *kucha* mullahs interpret both Islam and the state as intertwined agencies of local social order. As the principal mullah told me himself, "[w]e explain, there are decrees of the state [he does not exclusively mean formal decrees but rather refers to the divine will of the king or president], orders of the king, which are necessary ['*hukmi poshchoh vojib*']. We are slaves of the law, slaves of the Koran. If the state issues a law, we must obey it. The law of the state and the law of Sharia are the same."[263]

Besides Islamic identity highlighted through ceremonies, the other powerful legitimation source is the shared Islamic identity of *mahalli* villagers. This inclusive religious affiliation among the *mahalli* people of the Qabodiyon oasis is reflected in subordination to Qabodiyon Eshon. Eshon 'recommended', that is, appointed, Abdullo Munimov as the *mahalli imam-khatib*, the youngest leading member of the mahalla. Eshon also authorised the *imam-khatib* to represent the 'religious honour' of the *mahalli* people and the Eshon-i Miyontura shrine, which includes the central village mosque and a sacred healing site. Recently, mahalla leaders and mediators have elevated the shrine's mosque to the status of 'the central mosque of Sayyod village' in order to make use of the authority of their current saint – Qabodiyon Eshon. Mahalla leaders and religious notables, personally the head of the mahalla and Qabodiyon Eshon, called villagers to mobilise their resources to reconstruct the Eshon-i Miyontura mosque. For this purpose, they interpreted the central village mosque as the central attribute of their religiosity: "It is to the shame of villagers [vis-à-vis *others*] that so far such a big village has no common mosque," expressed an elder during *hashar*. The *choykhonas* serve as *qawm*-related mosques (of *Sayyodi*, *Khojamashhadi*, and *Rabotaki qawms*). The elders therefore agreed to change the formerly *Sayyodi* central *choykhona* into the central mosque of the village. The *choykhona*, formerly a cultural centre (*klub*) and a kindergarten of the kolkhoz, is situated next to the Eshon-i Miyontura shrine.

The family and *qawm* representatives of the mahalla referred to *mahalli* Islamic identity to commit the subject people to organising the *hashar* and providing financial resources for the construction of the Eshon-i Miyontura mosque. *Rabotaki* men did not join the *hasher*, claiming that they had their own *qawm* mosque. To prepare the village mosque for the religious feast of Kurban in a few weeks' time, the mediators mobilised almost all working-age villagers,

---

Rasul Nazirov, Mullo Obloqul – the village principal mullah – and Abdullo Munimov – the village *imam-khatib*).

[263] Personal interview with Mullo Obloqul (Notebook No 1-6, January 22, 2008: pages 41-42).

including four construction masters, and collected 10 TJ Somoni from each household in the *Sayyodi*, *Samarkandi* and *Khojamashhadi qawms*.[264]

This subchapter has traced the role of *mahalli* identities in shaping the inclusive representation function of the mahalla. This mediation structure of local and state elites organises ceremonies, mobilises collective action and resolves internal disputes as means of enforcing the solidarity networks of cotton-growers. The following subchapter discusses the mahalla as a mediation authority in integrating means and resources for socio-political stability in the village context.

Integration of means and resources for socio-political stability

Mahalla mediators and local state functionaries in the jamoat, district government and police service integrate means and resources for socio-political 'stability' in Sayyod village. These means and resources are necessary to protect the political and economic privileges of powerful men and especially to maintain the cotton farms. They include reciprocal networks, support (indigenous, state and development) schemes and programmes, practices of 'common wellbeing' and 'on-site' and 'delegation' mechanisms of dispute settlement. Mahalla mediators and their state allies use them to resolve tensions within and among kinship (*elkheshi* and *qawm*) networks and sub-village (*kucha* and *mahalla*) neighbourhoods. The stability of these networks and neighbourhoods, which are often based on cotton farms, is one of the central functions of the mahalla.

The following sections discuss the role collective identities play in shaping and enforcing reciprocal practices and networks (section one), modified reciprocal practices and networks (section two), practices of 'common wellbeing' (section three) and indigenous means of dispute settlement (section four).

Stabilisation of political and economic situations by reciprocal exchanges

In Sayyod village, the reciprocal practices of extended (*elkheshi*) families are a significant source of balance for political and economic stability. These practices mitigate tensions due to increasing economic inequalities between privileged and marginalised families. Mahalla mediators, including family elders

---

264 Personal observation (Notebook No 1-5; December 14-17, 2007; pages 108-110; also tape recording No DS 300242-244).

and religious notables, refer to the *elkheshi*, *qawm* and Islamic identities of family members to commit them to reciprocal practices. Such a commitment is especially generated through the prayer communities of the *qawm* networks around their mosques (*choykhona*). Without such references, reciprocal practices would be reduced to a few religious ceremonies and to periods of extreme economic hardship. Rather, villagers are reluctant to share their household space, to provide joint economic activities or to distribute material wealth. A two-year conflict between two brothers from the *Khojamashhadi qawm* over the inheritance of their parents' household was only resolved after the *qawm* community of prayers in the mosque and in a religious ceremony of *khatm* intervened and committed them to the religious duty of 'proper brotherhood' to share the household space.

Mahalla mediators refer to *elkheshi* identity and honour to praise household support, reciprocal insurance and privileged public services for co-members. They mediate to organise a family *hashar* (i.e. sharing the labour, financial and material resources of *elkheshi* members) to mitigate the intensive economic activities of individual families. The mediators interpret the institutional practice of *hashar* as an attribute of *elkheshi* honour. The moral commitment to *elkheshi* honour is interpreted as 'proper brotherhood' and expressed through the maintenance of shared patrimonial properties and joint economic activities. This moral debt commits wealthier brothers to share their excessive properties and resources to cover shortages of land, manpower and financial means. Also, wealthier *elkheshi* co-members provide shelter, cover food shortages and share economic benefits with poorer co-members, including widowed and divorced women and disabled men. This measure is essential to both economically support and politically control poor co-members. In addition, co-members are mutually committed to lend money for house-building, organising marriage ceremonies and travelling to Russia for labour migration. In this way, reciprocal exchanges of labour and cash indebt poor families to their powerful kinsmen and consequently stabilise the economic and political situation in the village (also see Table 11: Indigenous support networks).

Table 11: Indigenous support networks

#	Indigenous support networks	Types of support	Terms	Frequency
1	*Elkheshi* co-members	Food, everyday household supplies, cash debts for different purposes (subsistence agriculture, labour migration, ceremonies, additional income sources)	Without interest rates and without fixed payment dates	12
2	Shop-keepers from the same *kucha*	Food and everyday household supplies	Without interest rates and with flexible repayment dates	7
3	Friends in the village	Cash debt for emergency needs like food shortages	Without interest rates and without fixed repayment dates	3
4	Office and work managers and friends	Cash debt for emergency needs like food shortages and medical treatment	Without interest rates and with flexible repayment dates	3
5	Neighbours	Cash debt for emergency needs for everyday food shortages	With a low interest rate and a fixed repayment date	2

Source: Personal survey of poor families (October 2007 – March 2008)

The institution of reciprocal care or insurance additionally stabilises political and economic conditions and enforces the hierarchical norms and interactions of close kinsmen. Senior and junior members of *elkheshi* families (such as fathers and sons) are mutually committed to care about each other. Such a commitment also extends to patrilineal junior males (*bulabacha*) during economic hardship and important ceremonies. Again, mahalla mediators highlight the *elkheshi* identity and honour of co-members to regenerate the mutual commitment of both seniors and juniors. Junior *elkheshi* males, especially the youngest sons (*kenja*), are committed to take care of their old parents as well as sick and handicapped co-members.

Due to family commitment, almost all patrimonial goods, professions and enterprises have been transferred through inheritance, unless they have been managed by state or *kolkhozi* elites. Family commitment also legitimises the distribution practices of public goods. Especially, family elders and other mahalla mediators highlight *elkheshi* identity, which in turn legitimises a good deal of economic privileges, including access to the land resources of farmers as a sign of 'family integrity' ('*oilai ahl*'). They are also committed to transferring public properties to their *elkheshi* co-members. This reciprocal commitment legitimises the privileged access of co-members to public positions and goods based on the practices of reciprocal return ('*muroso*') and reciprocal bargaining ('*muomila*'). Thus, elites exclusively offer their co-members public resources, such as pastureland, hay and field tents on the collective farm to breed livestock.

Reference to *elkheshi* identity interprets the mundane practices of birthday parties, *suhbat* (literally: 'talk') and *gashtak* ('round visit') as the sacred attributes of *elkheshi* integrity and wealth. They serve to enforce support practices, to resolve internal disputes and to mobilise a labour force for joint economic activities. The 'talk' of Saidaliev's *elkheshi* network is an example of such community celebration and mobilisation for mutual support. *Elkheshi* elders initiated the practice when individual families experienced economic hardship in the aftermath of the civil war in the 1990s. Its participants are 12 'heads' (*sardor*), that is, the fathers and mothers or husbands and wives of related nuclear families. Once a month they gather as a family, celebrate by throwing a party, and then discuss and consult on ceremonies and shortages, resolve disputes and provide practical support and mediation. As one female organiser told me, "The *elkheshi* [co-members] have been dispersed and they have quarrelled among each other a lot. My husband and I decided to gather the kinsmen and organise this talk. Now the quarrels have ceased and we support each other with food and other material goods… We do not beg [for dishes, carpets, cash and food] from strangers to organise our ceremonies. The disputes we resolve ourselves, before strangers know about them."[265]

Moreover, reciprocal practices among *elkheshi* family members improve the reputation of those who redistribute these resources to poor families. Powerful men and elders thus acquire the status of seniority and represent their co-members at the mahalla. As Table 12 (Families receiving reciprocal support) illustrates, in Sayyod village a significant proportion of families receive reciprocal resources. Political relevance is thus the essence of these reciprocal practices.

---

[265] Personal interview (Notebook No 1-6, January 29, 2008: page 128)

Table 12: Families receiving reciprocal support

Recipient families	Supporter	Type and frequency of support	Reported recipients
Close relatives of patrilineal line	Mutual	Permanent shared food, regular financial aid, minor money during ceremonies and funerals, travel for labour migration, regular shared remittance, monthly food and financial support of students Labour aid during *hasher*, shared land resources, permanent agricultural advisory service, support with agricultural machines permanent care for children	79
Close relatives of any line	Mutual	Occasional food and financial aid, minor financial aid during sickness, care of sick relatives labour aid during *hashar* – construction of minor and unprofessional buildings, shared means (land, donkey, cow, etc.)	45
Poor families	Non-wealthy relatives of patrilineal line	Occasional food and minor financial aid	22
Poor and disabled relatives	Wealthy relatives of any lines	Regular food and financial aid	8
Old people	Relatives of any line	Regular labour aid and physical care	5
Farmers	Relatives of any line	Seasonal labour aid	5
Widowed women	Relatives of any lines	Food support during ceremonies	1
Colleagues	Mutual	Occasional financial aid	1

Source: Personal survey of recipient families (October 2007 – March 2008)

However, there is no absolute authority of any senior member of the *elkheshi* group, hence the comparative adjective *'kalontaro'* (i.e. 'biggers'). Rather, the enforcement of seniority depends on constant justification via reference to *elkheshi*, *qawm* and Islamic identities. For this purpose, mahalla mediators frequently refer to the norm of '*elkheshi* integrity' or '*elkheshi* honour' manifested in hierarchical regards and reciprocal practices. In part, the process of family and public moral training (*tarbiya*), myths about the distinct natures of seniors and juniors and regular ceremonies serve to normalise and ritualise such regards and practices. Junior family members are 'God-given good' ('*ne'mati khudodod*') only if the strict pursuit of *tarbiya* avoids their distortion by 'strangers' or by their own 'evil nature'. The 'youth' in their 'nature', many informants asserted, are creatures who do not know anything but 'pleasure and bliss'. If their seniors do not control them, they 'spoil the world'.[266]

The reciprocal networks of *elkheshi* families maintain not only hierarchical regards and mutual support but also cotton-growing 'communities', that is, farms. Mahalla and state authorities therefore refer mainly to *elkheshi* identity to enforce these networks. Despite Soviet kolkhoz-initiated household planning (*planirovka*) through the 1960s-1970s based upon *tamarqa*,[267] today many villagers inhabit their *elkheshi* households and neighbourhoods. Since *elkheshi* families consisted of multiple (e.g. more than five) patrilineal nuclear families, most of them got their *tamarqa* in their inherited lands. As a result, the mahallas (*qawm*-related large neighbourhoods) of Sayyod, Khoja-Mashhad and Rabotak shape most of their sub-residential (*kucha*) neighbourhoods along with *elkheshi* families and often their cotton farms.[268]

This condition is also favoured due to the significant proportion of nuclear families of the same patrilineal line who share the same households. My informants recalled the pre-kolkhoz *avul* neighbourhoods where the same *elkheshi* families lived in shared households. As Table 13 below (Frequency of household compositions) shows, today most of the surveyed households consist of more than one nuclear family (101 shared households vs. 52 unshared households out of the surveyed households). The shared households also have shared livelihood sources and activities such as remittance, manpower, agricultural resources and therefore cotton farms.

---

[266] Personal interviews with Mahkam Boyakov (Notebook No 1-4, October 3, 2007: pages 22-24) and Chupon Aliev (Notebook No 1-7, March 8, 2008: page 107).

[267] *Tamarqa* is household-based land distribution and neighbourhood structuring.

[268] E.g. the *elkheshi* families of Polvon Kholmatov (*Khojamashhadi*), Ravshan Eshgulov, Nazar Numonov, Abdullo Munimov, Vosit Yuldoshev, Tura Juraev and Samad Ghayurov (*Sayyodi*) (the survey conducted during January 1 – February 2, 2008).

Table 13: Shared households of nuclear families

Household composition	1 nuclear family	2 nuclear families	3 nuclear families	4 nuclear families	5 nuclear families
Number of nuclear families[269]	52	73 (mostly parents with junior (*kenja*) sons)	29	1	1

Source: Personal survey (October 2007 – March 2008)

Mahalla-mediated modification of reciprocal networks

Without mahalla mediation, reciprocal practices are mainly reduced to *elkheshi* networks. Only some forms, such as generosity and *sadaqa*, are paid as patronage favours to loyal men or distributed to beggars. Some villagers even stigmatise such practices as begging 'behind the door' or 'on the doorstep' of wealthy men. As a 77-year-old woman told me, "I feel ashamed to ask for support, but I cannot conceal my *secret*: I have five sons and four of them disappeared to Russia and the other one is poor himself. If I complain, people will say that she is dishonouring her own sons."[270] Another poor woman has a trading stall in the front of her household to feed her mentally disabled son. Her school-age daughter earns a miserable income from the business to avoid the 'bad words' of their neighbours and mahalla authorities, who would otherwise discredit them as 'beggars'.[271]

To balance political and economic situations, however, mahalla authorities and especially religious notables (such as *imam-khatib* and *kucha* mullahs) mediate to modify the practice of *sadaqa* to support poor families. Also, jamoat and other state functionaries authorise the mahalla to institutionalise *sadaqa* for social and political stability in the village. Mostly *elkheshi*, *qawm* and some village-level networks and ceremonies (including funerals, weddings, religious and seasonal feasts) serve as sources for supporting the poor. Here, the role of the shared Islamic identity of *mahalli* people is central to committing them to *sadaqa*, which is the reciprocal neighbourhood support of 'the poor' ('*bechora*'). According to religious practices, these poor are orphans, handicapped men, widowed women

[269] A nuclear family is a primary social unit consisting of parents and their offspring.
[270] Personal interview (Notebook No 1-6, January 28, 2008: page 112).
[271] Personal interview (Notebook No 1-6, February 2, 2008: page 155-156).

without the support of male adults, old men and women without *elkheshi* networks.[272]

Through mahalla mediation in regular ceremonies, neighbours provide minimal food, clothes and sometimes shelter to some widowed women. For example, a woman (born 1941), originally from Sayyod village, returned to her home village after her husband died in Ayvoj village. She had no sons and two married daughters, who could not take care of her. Her cousin sold her house in Ayvoj and in return bought a house for her in Sayyod village. Today, she lives with her grandchild and is supported mostly by her neighbours, who provide her with food to cover the extreme shortage while other livelihood sources are insufficient, including a monthly pension (20 TJ Somoni) and a 0.06 hectare *tamarqa*.[273]

For mahalla mediators who intervene to redistribute reciprocal favours to the poor, the main concern is not only the poor's survival needs but also their political control. For example, a brigadir from the collective farm gave his handicapped worker about one hectare of land to cater for his subsistence needs in order to help prevent his 'struggle' with local and state authorities over 'unequal' rights.[274] But there are many poor families in the village who are not politically considered as 'dangerous' ('*notinj*') and are thus neglected. For instance, two homeless and chronically sick widows, who also have small children, do not receive any support.

Organisation of the practices of 'common wellbeing'

Local and state authorities mobilise villagers' resources to maintain the material and technical 'wellbeing' of public assets, especially religious sites and cotton-related infrastructure. This function is not easily fulfilled without frequent reference to *mahalli elkheshi*, *qawm* and Islamic identities, which commit villagers to certain practices.

Mahalli Islamic identity is more salient and expressive when villagers mobilise their resources for the wellbeing of religious assets, such as cemeteries, shrines

---

[272] Personal interview with the village *imam-khatib,* Abdullo Munimov (Notebook No 1-4, November 13, 2007: pages 61-62; also tape recording No DS 300212 from February 7, 2008) and Halim Norboev (Notebook No 1-4, November 14, 2007: page 62).

[273] Personal interview (Notebook No 1-4, November 19, 2007: page 86).

[274] During my recent field visit in spring 2012, the land plot had been taken back by the farmer, while the son of the handicapped man was now at the age to generate income for his family.

and mosques. *Hashar* for cemetery cleaning is a sacred practice for *mahalli* villagers. Traditionally, before the religious feast of Ramadan, and before men visit the cemetery to pray for their ancestors, the cemetery should be cleaned of weed and other waste. Mahalla mediators fix in advance the appropriate weekend day of *hashar.* The decision is then announced through village-level and family-organised ceremonies, especially through *iftor* (food-share during the one-month Ramadan fast). Because of this religious commitment and sacred meaning of cemetery cleaning, the cemetery *hashar* is a celebration of the solidarity of the *mahalli* male community. Age and group concerns suddenly disappear and everyone strives to contribute his own labour (see Picture 7: Collective *hashar* on the eve of Ramadan Holiday).

Picture 7: Collective *hashar* on the eve of Ramadan Holiday

In addition, mahalla mediators and local state functionaries organise the village-level *hashar.* In so doing, subject people repair the village mosque at the Eshon-i Miyontura shrine, occasionally clean the main inter-village irrigation canal, maintain the village school, electricity and irrigation infrastructure and support the cotton harvest. For this purpose, again they highlight the *mahalli* Islamic, *qawm* and *elkheshi* identities of villagers. In the case of the cotton harvest, which I discuss in the subchapter on the cotton economy, the most respected elder, Rasul Nazirov, and the religious saint of all *mahalli* men in the Qabodiyon oasis, Qabodiyon Eshon, are among the key 'initiators'. They personally go out to the cotton field and harvest the cotton in order to motivate and commit collective mobilisation. Their personal 'initiation' of 'collective *hashar*' through reference to *mahalli* Islamic identity awakes villagers' 'honour' and thereby compensates for the low economic cost and favour of such practices.

One of the most successful district governors in Tajikistan, as the president of Tajikistan himself assessed,[275] is the governor of Shahritus district. His 'success' depends on his mobilisation of local resources through close collaboration with mahalla mediators. His initiated programme of improvements to the infrastructure of village schools in 2007 has been adopted as an exemplary model in the country. Besides the resources of local governments, NGOs and other public and private enterprises, his local mediators can easily mobilise the labour, financial and material resources of villagers.

I observed this practice in the process of constructing a new building for village school No 11 in Sayyod village. For the purpose of collective mobilisation, mediators, including religious notables (Qabodiyon Eshon, *Haji* Bobo Quliev, *Haji* Ismoil Eshgulov, *imam-khatib* and *kucha* mullahs) and *elkheshi* elders constantly referred to villagers' *mahalli* village and Islamic identities. According to the school director, mahalla authorities managed to mobilise labour, financial and material resources, including about 14,000 TJ Somoni (20 TJ Somoni from each family).[276] In addition, the JRC of Sayyod Jamoat contributed 200 roofing slates, machinery from the District Water Department (UNKOS) were used for technical works and the district Department of Population Occupation and Social Protection provided cement – all under the personal auspices of the district governor. Teachers and pupils from village schools No 21 and No 7 worked permanently and gratis in the construction of the new building. Teachers from the jamoat's villages also made a contribution by fulfilling the quota of constructing a 10x2-metre wall for each village, while engineering and

---

[275] First Channel of the Public TV of Tajikistan; January 6, 2008; 20:00-22:00 Dushanbe time.

[276] Personal observation and interview with the director of school No 11 (Notebook No 1-6, January 21, 2008: pages 35-37), Nazar Numonov (Notebook No 1-6, January 21, 2008: pages 30-31), Rasul Nazirov (Notebook No 1-7, March 9, 2008: pages 108-109) and *Haji* Bobo Quliev (Notebook No 1-7, March 11, 2008: pages 119-120).

professional construction works were done by village construction masters who were paid half of their normal fees and exempted from some state taxes. Many families also contributed labour at no charge.

Without local state elites and their mediators, however, the village-level *hashar* and other practices of common wellbeing are mainly limited to the reconstruction or cleaning of some religious assets. However, ditches, which are constructed to hold and carry away the increasing amount of underground water from the cotton fields into the river, are not cleaned more than once every ten years or so; instead, they are used as open landfill sites for garbage. Today, increasing levels of underground water, for example in Sayyod village, negatively affect livelihood conditions, aggravating the health of the local population and eroding soil and buildings. The uncleaned drains also hamper the smooth and efficient flow of irrigation water, which in turn gives rise to water shortages in upstream fields. Water scarcity in inter-village canals and the inefficient loss of water in upstream villages (including Sayyod) cause water shortages in downstream villages, such as Qizilaskar and Leninyuli.

Mahalla mediators refer to villagers' *elkheshi* and *qawm* identities to constantly organise the practices of common wellbeing. For this purpose, *elkheshi*-, *qawm*- or *kucha*-related ceremonies serve to organise sub-residential 'communities' for such an undertaking. Mahalla mediators (*elkheshi*, *qawm* and *kucha* seniors and mullahs) announce, scrutinise and monitor the practices of common wellbeing, including the wellbeing of sub-residential or neighbourhood mosques, shrines, roads, bridges and electricity and irrigation infrastructure. They interpret these practices as attributes of integrity and thus the honourable duty of related kinship networks and neighbourhoods. Among the mediators, Shoniyoz Eshniyozov, one of the most respected elders of *Khojamashhadi qawm*, is the member of the mahalla responsible for announcing and scrutinising the practices of 'his people'. He participates in ceremonies of *Khojamashhadi* families and commits subject families to the wellbeing of their neighbourhoods. Such commitment is generated by reference to Islamic, *elkheshi* and *qawm* identities. A teacher was deeply aggrieved when he was wrongly announced as part of an 'indebted family' – that he did not contribute to the reconstruction of the village mosque at the Eshon-i Miyontura shrine. As he told me, "It is offensive when you sit among people, on the *dastarkhon* [table] of people, and you are the only person announced."[277]

For the same purpose, mediators generate the commitment of subject people to their *oqsaqols* and 'servants' in three large, *qawm*-related neighbourhoods of

---

[277] Personal observation (Notebook No 1-7, February 16, 2008: page 52).

Sayyod, Khojamashhad and Rabotak. These *oqsaqols* and servants are mahalla members responsible for the mobilisation of resources within their neighbourhoods. Each of these *qawm*-dominated neighbourhoods is mediated by its own 'servant', who due to his knowledge of the '*kharakter*' (individual dispositions) of 'his people' can more easily mobilise financial and labour resources. As one 'servant' told me, he knows the '*kharakter*' of his *side* [i.e. his *qawm* co-members] and how to invoke their honour: "Because they know [trust] that I do not cheat or badger them if they have no money, and more importantly they know [trust] I do not talk about their financial woes to *others*."[278] Such categorisation of mahallas (*qawm* neighbourhoods) vis-à-vis each other is often used to mobilise subject people's resources for maintaining especially the neighbourhood, cotton-related and religious assets and infrastructure.

Religious and seasonal ceremonies also serve to enforce the solidarity of neighbourhoods for the wellbeing of cotton-related infrastructure and related activities. One such solidarity ceremony is *oshi kucha* (food-sharing between separate *kucha* residents), organised annually on the eve of the sowing season. The practice is sought to generate residents' solidarity for the seasonal *hashar* and to maintain the cotton infrastructure as well as for work on the cotton farms. Food-sharing in each of the six *kucha* neighbourhoods is organised and celebrated by the member families of *kucha* three times over three weeks spanning the early sowing season. Traditionally a ritual of *'sadaqa – raddi balo'*, of urging the sky and angels to bring 'a gracious year', the meaning of food-sharing has been modified to serve the purposes of kolkhozi elites and cotton farmers.

Similarly, mahalla and jamoat representatives attempt to highlight *kucha* affiliation and thereby consolidate and mobilise subject neighbourhoods through *hashar*. As part of their '*kucha* wellbeing', participants in *hashar* clean cotton irrigation infrastructure in their neighbourhoods. Some *kuchas* also shape their own cotton farms.

Often, women implement practices related to the wellbeing of their neighbourhood assets, including roads, irrigation canals and drainage systems located alongside their households. To commit them to this practice, their *oqsaqols* articulate neighbourhood assets as the attributes of their 'family honour'. Here, respectable women of the village, including Nasiba Nurmatova and Bibikalon Eshgulova, who are among the leading female members of the mahalla, mobilise their fellow females by referring to their kinship and neighbourhood identities: "They maintain their *kucha*, clean their roads, whiten

---

[278] Personal interview with Chupon Aliev (Notebook No 1-7, March 8, 2008: page 107).

their walls, while seeing [women from] other *kuchas* do the same."[279] Female mediators scrutinise and announce the 'works of women', and they even dishonour those women who do not implement their 'duties of honour'. These transgressors are announced to neighbours and co-villagers as 'dirty housekeepers' and 'disloyal to their husbands'.[280]

Like mundane assets, not all sacred assets are maintained by the village-level practices of 'common wellbeing'. Possessed by powerful men, these assets are regarded as sacred properties of their *qawm* or *elkheshi* co-members and thus they are maintained jointly. These sacred assets include the Bibi-Mayramjon, Eshon-i Miyontura and Khoja-Mashhad shrines, some sacred healing sites and *qawm*-related mosques (*choykhonas*). To maintain the wellbeing of these assets, mahalla mediators refer to subject people's family and *qawm* identities.

The family of *Haji* Bobo Quliev initiated a plan to build the Rabotak-*mahalla* mosque in 2002. By referring to the *qawm* identity of *Rabotaki* men, they collected 30 TJ Somoni from 70 *Rabotaki* households and constructed the mosque through the *hashar* of *Rabotaki* men.[281] Individual families and especially their 'exemplary' labour migrants dedicate resources (labour, cash, carpets and dishes) to maintain the wellbeing of their sacred property. Recently, *Rabotaki* men did not join the village-level *hashar* to repair the Eshon-i Miyontura village mosque, claiming that they had their own registered mosque.

The *Rabotaki* cotton-growing brigada, led by Qamar Jumaev, built in 1974 the Bibi-Mayramjon shrine, a sacred healing site located on the southern edge of the village, near Rabotak-*mahalla*. Today, the brigadir himself is the *mutavalli* or the shrine's cleaner and receiver of suppliants. Being a powerful and respected man of *Rabotaki qawm*, he has recently mobilised his *qawm*'s financial and labour resources to renovate the shrine for a wider group of suppliants. At the same time, the shrine demarcates and thus legitimises the adjacent 4-hectare land and garden of the brigadir as his sacred property.[282]

---

279 Personal interview with Nasiba Nurmatova (Notebook No 1-4, November 11, 2007: pages 58-59).
280 Ibid.
281 Personal interview with Panji Alamov (Notebook No 1-7, March 15, 2008: pages 125-126).
282 Ibid; personal interview with Qamar Jumaev (Notebook No 1-4, November 19, 2007: page 79; also DS 300222).

Picture 8: Land and garden demarcated and sanctified by shrine

Mahalla mediators mobilise financial resources of the labour migrants for the 'wellbeing' of especially the central religious and spiritual assets of the village. They interpret these assets, including Khoja-Mashhad shrine and Eshon-i Miyontura shrine as *mahalli* village and religious honour of villagers. Among the labour migrants, two 'bearers of [village] honour'[283] act as the 'initiators' ('*tashabbuskor*') of resource mobilisation. However, in recent years, labour migrants have rarely dedicated financial means to the wellbeing of these assets. Both labour migrants and other villagers do not trust the way in which mahalla authorities redistribute mobilised resources. As these labour migrants explain,[284] they collected financial means for the wellbeing of the Khoja-Mashhad shrine, which is the central attribute of their *mahalli* religious pride, on several

[283] One 'initiator' in the past was the school teacher. The other 'initiator' is a journalist currently working in Moscow with the Russian interior service. He supports migrants if they have any problems with registration, work or the militia (police).

[284] Personal observation of a discussion between three labour migrants in the home of one of the most reputable migrants – Nimatov Barot (Notebook No 1-4, November 21, 2007: pages 82-83).

occasions: "We collected money to buy carpets, dishes and necessary stuff in order to receive guests from Dushanbe and other places in an appropriate manner. Today, it is shameful if a guest comes. There is nothing. We do not know where the *shekh* [*mutavvali*] squandered the money."[285]

Today, migrants' resources for 'common wellbeing' are mobilised and managed mostly by their *qawm*-related *oqsaqols* and *qawm*-related and sometimes village-level owners of sacred sites (including mosques and shrines). For example, the financial resources of *Rabotaki* migrants have often been mobilised by their *qawm* elders and strictly for their *mahalla* mosque. They have already contributed about 100 carpets and significant dishes for *qawm*-related and religious ceremonies which take place in their mosque.[286]

Recently, only during the religious feasts of Ramadan and Kurban, labour migrants have sent small amounts of financial resources to the mahalla to support recognised poor families. In most cases, they include a *sadaqa* amount in regular cash transfers to their families and ask their women "to beg for their blessing [*duo*]" at the Khoja-Mashhad and Chiluchor-Chashma shrines. Hence, 'family honour' and *qawm* affiliation become crucial in sustaining the practice of *sadaqa* among labour migrants. Competition to highlight the fame and dignity of labour migrants' families and *qawms*, vis-à-vis each other, thus commits them to dedicate *sadaqa*. Among other families and *qawms*, the women of Rabotak-*mahalla* organised two collective *sadaqas* (on January 24 and on February 2, 2008) during their husbands' 'work season' and brought big platters of food, sweets and cash to the Khoja-Mashhad shrine. They also collectively sacrificed a goat for the saints and souls.

Stabilisation of the threatened pillars of social order

The stability of family and neighbourhood networks, ensuring proper forms of marriage and divorce, control over the 'new generation' and the security of private property are central aspects of local governance. Elites and their mahalla mediators dedicate material and immaterial resources to these aspects, first of all to stabilise cotton-growing 'communities'. This is the very reason why the mahalla, jamoat, district interior department and civic court coordinate the practices of dispute settlement. They use coercive measures and violent means

---

285 Personal interview with Nimatov Barot (Notebook No 1-4, November 21, 2007: pages 82-83). You can also compare financial and economic incomes from the Khoja-Mashhad shrine, as described earlier.

286 Personal interview with Panji Alamov (Notebook No 1-7, March 15, 2008: page 126).

of the state only when indigenous or 'on-site' means, including collective identities, are not effective in achieving stability.

The important 'on-site' means of dispute settlement is mediation organised by mahalla authorities, such as family elders, religious notables and school teachers. They, in part, highlight *mahalli* village, *mahalli* Islamic, *qawm* and *elkheshi* identities to commit villagers to negotiating disputes and conceding to one another. I observed three main types of dispute settlement which are predominantly affected by the collective identities. These types are: (1) 'on-site' practices, (2) 'delegation' practices and (3) public discourses and stigma.

Mahalla mediators and local state functionaries of the jamoat, police station and public court foster internal or 'on-site' ('*dar darun*', '*dar joyash*') tools of dispute prevention and settlement. *Oqsaqols* and *kucha* mullahs are the recognised 'assistants' of mahalla leaders in such matters. They use immaterial means, including *elkheshi* and *qawm* identities, to resolve disputes and conflicts among their *elkheshi* and *qawm* co-members. Especially, the duty of the *kucha* heads is "to gather all *kucha oqsaqols*, work together and solve the problems on-site."[287] For example, the gathering of *Rabotaki oqsaqols* and powerful men[288] prevents and resolves disputes between related families and neighbourhoods. Besides *oqsaqols*, *kucha* mullahs and *kucha* heads, local state functionaries, school teachers and *mahalli* religious notables, including Qabodiyon Eshon, are involved in 'on-site' mediation.

Teachers at two village schools also cooperate with mahalla mediators and thus use the village schools to apply institutional pressure to the 'new generation'. The main concern is training them to be obedient to the hierarchy and at the same time to prevent unacceptable behaviour. In this case, teachers whom pupils fear are more reputable among parents and mahalla authorities.[289]

The head of the mahalla is responsible for informing state authorities of any dispute which cannot be prevented by 'on-site' means.[290] Mahalla, jamoat and police officers mediate to resolve these disputes. They take over the jurisdiction (legal) authority of courts to levy informal fines and punishments against those who set their livestock to pasture on private lands and steal private goods. These informal fines and punishments do not necessarily refer to legal norms

---

[287] Personal interview with Panji Alamov (Notebook No 1-7, March 15, 2008: page 126).
[288] Including Panji Alamov, *Haji* Bobo Quliev, Khudoi Mamadyorov and Qamar Jumaev.
[289] Personal observation (Notebook No 1-4, October 20, 2007: pages 37-40).
[290] Personal interview with the head of the mahalla, Ravshan Eshgulov (Notebook No 1-7, February 13, 2008: pages 47-48).

but do depend on the personal authority of state functionaries. The sizes of fines and the levels of punishment depend directly on the positions of the state functionaries and their personal relations with the two sides (accusers and defendants).

The mediation role of *oqsaqols* is more effective when they are trusted by their *elkheshi* co-members. The latter share family or neighbourhood 'secrets' because the *oqsaqols* "do not spread them about to friends and enemies," an *oqsaqol* told me.[291] In fact, *oqsaqols* interpret disputes and discord among *elkheshi* or *qawm* co-members as 'secrets'. The divulging of 'secrets' distorts the reputations of both individual disputants and their *elkheshi* or *qawm* groups. Such interpretation of these disputes thus effects the internal mechanisms of dispute settlement. For this purpose, they use regular ceremonies with their co-members to highlight their *elkheshi* and *qawm* identities, as well as the religious norm of a 'good neighbourhood'. In these ceremonies they directly or, if the issue is too sensitive, indirectly mention any disputes and discord to provoke collective concern.

For example, for a couple of years, two brothers had been in dispute over the household they inherited from their parents. The junior brother was forced to move to his father-in-law's house, where he and his young family stayed for more than a year. To return the son-in-law's family to his father's household, the father-in-law actualised the matter at a *qawm*-related religious feast (both belonging to the same *Khojamashhadi qawm*). Consequently, this 'secret' was shared with other *qawm* co-members who reproached the senior brother for neglecting the dispute between his junior siblings. To meet the norm of 'brotherhood' dignity, the senior brother immediately returned his junior brother to the parents' house.

Thus, ceremonies serve not only their primary purpose but also acts as conduits for the direct discussion, moral exhortation and ritual solution of disputes and conflicts. In such cases, *kucha* mullahs initiate the discussion from a religious morality viewpoint in order to commit the visitors to mutual forgiveness as a sacred attribute of their *elkheshi*, *qawm*, and *mahalli* Islamic identities. As a *kucha* mullah told me, "We gather in ceremonies to reconcile people who are upset with each other. For example, our two neighbours quarrelled over a three-centimetre yard wall and did not talk to each other for a year. When the mother of one of them died, the Islamic duty of his neighbours was to go and support him. We demand them to fulfil this duty."[292] The call to Islamic commitment

---

[291] Ibid.

[292] Personal interview (Notebook No 1-4, November 16, 2007: page 69).

thus requires that men forget about personal disputes and help each other through ceremonies. In the other case, two brothers could not forgive each other due to certain family conflicts, but when one of them intended to go to Hajj, the mullah conciliated between them as a requirement for the acceptance of the pilgrimage by God and by religious notables.

Furthermore, religious authorities highlight Islamic identity to shape communal solidarity against the theft of private property especially. For this purpose, *kucha* mullahs sanction thievery through the ritual practice of *kurkhat*, which urges God to curse the thief in the eyes of people and thus calls for their communal solidarity. The practice is sanctioned mainly against those who are of equal status, who thus may 'endanger' the solidarity of *elkheshi*, *qawm* or *kucha* co-members. In most informed cases, *kurkhat* has brought positive results because of the 'communal' solidarity or common spell expressed via the 'curse' of God summoned by the mullahs.

Since 'on-site' means and measures are not always effective, *oqsaqols* are obliged to report any unresolved disputes within their neighbourhoods to mahalla and local state (first of all, jamoat) authorities, following which the authorities send a 'delegation' to resolve disputes. Members of the 'delegation' are deliberately chosen from among those who hold the relevant status to resolve disputes by 'peaceful' means, especially by reference to *mahalli* collective identities. Besides *oqsaqols* and *kucha* mullahs, the 'delegation' includes the head or any of three deputy heads of the mahalla (Shoniyoz Eshniyozov and Mahkam Boyakov), three hajis (*Haji* Bobo Quliev, *Haji* Ismoil Eshgulov and *Haji* Ataboy Qiyomov), *imam-khatib* (Abdullo Munimov), two female elders (Nasiba Nurmatova, who is the head of the mahalla's Council of Women, and Munzima Saraeva) and a representative of the jamoat.[293] The delegation highlights *elkheshi*, *qawm*, *mahalli* village and *mahalli* Islamic identities, which commit the disputants to the norms of 'family integrity' ['*oilai ahl*'] and a 'good neighbourhood'.[294]

Among the key 'delegation' authorities, an *imam-khatib* serves to settle disputes through regular religious ceremonies such as funerals, holidays and other institutional practices and village gatherings. He is the personal representative of Qabodiyon Eshon and therefore holds the necessary privileged status to highlight the *mahalli* Islamic identity of villagers. Jamoat and district state functionaries and the district *sarkhatib* also authorise the *imam-khatib* to ensure stability by enforcing religious practices. In part, he ensures strict rules are

[293] Personal interview with Shoniyoz Eshniyozov (Notebook No 1-4, October 5, 2007: pages 30-31).

[294] E.g. personal interview with *Haji* Bobo Quliev (Notebook No 1-7, March 11, 2008: page 119).

enforced against young couples divorcing, which is regarded as a substantial destabilising factor. He employs the religious institutions of betrothal (*nikoh*) and divorce (*taloq*) to prevent such divorces by extending decision-making exercises over family relations to mahalla authorities. According to the general rules of Islamic Shariah, only husband has right to issue *taloq*; wife has no such right. However, in practice as the *imam-khatib* himself expressed, "*Taloq*[295] is not a simple measure to bring up whenever you wish. You must have serious excuses and you must inform us about these excuses before you issue *taloq*. 'Three times *taloq*' means that you must think it over for three months."[296]

The other important 'delegation' tool is fulfilled by civil and police functionaries of the jamoat, district interior department and state courts, who intervene and support the functioning of mahalla mediation by preventing and discrediting court deals and especially by committing disputants to their *elkheshi*, *qawm* and neighbourhood *oqsaqols* and mullahs. One dispute between two kinsmen and neighbours illustrates such mediatory intervention. Some years ago, Chupon Aliev's father grew an apricot tree which his son later gifted to his uncle and neighbour, Ochil Teshaev. Due to the shortage of wood in the severe 2007 winter, Chupon Aliev's son cut down a lot of trees, including the aforementioned apricot tree, which gave rise to an open dispute between the sons. The uncle appealed to the mahalla to intervene in the dispute. The mahalla head came and settled the dispute in favour of Chupon Aliev, most likely due to his service to the mahalla as an assistant, as I witnessed the case. The appealer was not satisfied with the decision of the mahalla, though, and again sent his son to the jamoat police officer. This time, the mahalla head and a police officer came and took Chupon Aliev and his cousin (while 83-year-old Ochil Teshaev could not go personally) to the district interior department in Shahritus town. In the end, the disputants gave in to the persuasion of the authorities under police threat – and especially due to the stress on their *elkheshi* commitment.

A fragment of the persuasive talk was as follows:

> Police officer (asking the cousin): As I found out, you are neighbours… And you are relatives as well! Did Chupon [Aliev] do any helpful things for you in the past?
>
> Cousin: Yes.

---

295 The religious institution of *taloq* (divorce) is exclusively issued by a husband but necessarily negotiated with *elkheshi* elders, mahalla leaders, an authorised mullah and jamoat representatives.

296 Personal interview with Abdullo Munimov (Tape recording No DS 300212 from February 7, 2008).

> Police officer: What namely? Did he respond to your requests?
>
> Cousin: Yes. He helps us if we slaughter any sheep… He herds for us if anyone from our families is not available…
>
> Police officer: So, you are relatives and have a lot of debts in between. Should you require a tree from him at the expense of distorting your relations? Do you forget what goods Chupon Aliev did for you?
>
> Cousin: I have no claim anymore…

However, 'bringing to honour' ('*ba nang ovardan*') through 'on-site' and 'delegation' means is not always effective, especially when the devastating situations of the poor give rise to discontent and disputes. Mahalla authorities seek to generate social pressure over disputants who, they assure, threaten the villagers' positive *mahalli* image and identity, both characterised as 'peaceful' ('*tinj*') and 'loyal' ('*ahl*'). The authorities categorise and thereby neglect and discredit individuals and whole families who do not inform them about problems and disputes but rather directly appeal to courts and upper (rather than jamoat)-level state institutions. Also, in the perceptions of both local people and state officials, there are no state structures independent of each other (such as the executive branch from court). Rather, they are considered as vertically dependent upon each other, while the court is subject to the executive branch of the state.

The complaints of women and junior men against powerful men and elders are particularly neglected or discredited, and subject people have to tolerate and make concessions to privileged men who exploit their rights. Some state and kolkhoz veterans (Ochil Teshaev and *Haji* Bobo Quliev) make use of their status to graze their sheep on the *presidenti* land plots of other villagers. They and other privileged men draw favours from their personal ties with local state elites. As many villagers informed me, their frequent complaints to the jamoat are not dealt properly, for example, in regard to the livestock of *Rabotaki* people that trample over private land and spoil crops. Rather, the jamoat protects the wellbeing of the cotton fields and the infrastructure of kolkhozi elites and their *mahalli* clients.

Mahalla mediators and local state authorities stigmatise the court appeals of women and junior men in particular. They brand them as 'provocateurs' ('*ighvogar*') and 'dangerous' ('*notinj*'), people who therefore spoil the positive image of the *mahalli* people. Mediators also label them as being 'indifferent' to 'village honour', people who thus quarrel with their neighbours and give the wrong impression to *others* about the image and identity of *mahalli* villagers. Especially mahalla mediators suppress, neglect and even discredit women through family and neighbourhood disputes. A woman told me that her neighbour intentionally leaves his cows to trample over the wired fence of her household yard and to graze on her grains: "My husband is in [labour migration in] Russia… [He] must be here to talk with the man. It is not the job of a woman to enter into a direct dispute with a man, and also I cannot ask his parents… The mahalla and jamoat did not listen to me."[297]

The other case also shows that both mahalla and jamoat authorities intervene to prevent and neutralise court appeals. As another suffering woman told me, "The neighbour's shed fell down onto the trees in my yard. It has been several months, and nobody has come to check it. The trees have dried up and the water stream has changed to run alongside the house wall. I went to the mahalla head, to the [deputy] head of the jamoat… and appealed to the court [through them]. They did not come but threatened me because I am widowed."[298]

In extreme cases, indigenous practices also serve to stigmatise or punish individuals for pre-marital sexual relations and the theft of private property. For this purpose, mahalla authorities employ both 'public' punishment ('*dar bayni jam'iyat*') and the state court. For instance, when a man found out that his neighbour had stolen two sacks of almonds from his household yard, he immediately informed the head of the mahalla. The latter in turn called mahalla authorities and other male adults from the village and revealed the name of the thief and his deed. Obviously, women and children also gather at such public shows out of curiosity.

The role of local state and court structures is significant in preventing similar cases by publicising, punishing and stigmatising perpetrators of wrongdoing as destabilising factors in kinship and religious ties. For example, a man attempted to steal his cousin's cow and two sheep, but the owner's dog stopped him from following through with his plan. *Qawm* elders, together with other mahalla mediators, discussed the issue during mosque prayers and decided to inform the jamoat authorities about the thief. Under the authority of the jamoat, the case was passed to the district court, which sentenced the thief to two years in jail. The court decision, which exceeded the penal code's norms, "was necessary in order to frighten others [*ba digaron pand shavad*]"[299] who might wish to harm private properties and kinship ties. For the same purpose, the district court excessively sentenced a young girl for pre-marital sexual relations.

---

[297] Personal interview (Notebook No 1-4, November 26, 2007: pages 137-138).

[298] Personal interview (Notebook No 1-5, December 9, 2007: page 39).

[299] Personal interview with Chupon Aliev (Notebook No 1-7, February 22, 2008: page 67).

Mahallas and their state allies mediate in and integrate political means and economic resources to sustain socio-political 'stability' in the cotton-growing village. The above sections have discussed the role of collective identities in the provision and adaptation of reciprocal practices and networks, practices of 'common wellbeing' and indigenous mechanisms of dispute settlement. Such a principal function of the mahalla has two important purposes: (1) to protect the political and economic privileges of elites and their direct clients and (2) to organise the effective running of the cotton farms of *elkheshi*, *qawm* and *kucha* 'communities'.

The reciprocal exchanges that individual extended (*elkheshi*) families practice are a significant way of balancing political and economic situations. These practices prevent and dissolve contestations in the face of increasing economic inequalities between elites and marginalised families. Thus, mahalla mediators, including family elders and religious notables, highlight *elkheshi*, *qawm* and Islamic identities to commit family members to these customs. Reference to '*elkheshi* honour' praises the institutional practices of household support via everyday exchanges and *hashar*, reciprocal insurance and privileged public services for family members. Moreover, referring to *elkheshi* and Islamic identities commits *elkheshi* family members to their elders and wealthy men. These men represent their extended families in the political body of the mahalla and in many cases possess religious and economic goods and enterprises in their related neighbourhoods. These mahalla mediators refer to the *mahalli* kinship and Islamic identities of the subject villagers to adapt and modify reciprocal practices and thus to improve their political and economic power. Mediators enforce and adapt those practices which provide minimal support for marginalised families, maintain the objective of 'common wellbeing', especially related to the cotton industry and its infrastructure, and resolve family and neighbourhood disputes. These practices in turn enforce the solidarity networks of cotton-growers or cotton farms, which I discuss below in subchapter seven.

The Political Cotton Economy in Sayyod Village

This subchapter discusses the role of collective identities in shaping institutional arrangements in the cotton sector. Central, regional and local government authorities, as well as their mahalla mediators, devote their material and symbolic resources to maintain this sector. State elites and mahalla mediators jointly integrate the cotton-growing 'communities' and refer to *mahalli* kinship and Islamic identities to enforce rules accordingly. They exert all possible efforts to generate the integrative effects of local people's collective affiliations – and thus prevent internal conflicts and disintegrations on the cotton farms –

shaped around solidarity (*elkheshi*, *qawm* and ethnic) networks. This case study is thus a comprehensive example of collective identities as *integrated* boundaries of social order.

The following sections discuss how ethnicity is decisive in shaping the personal networks of kolkhozi elites, who dominate local political and economic structures in the cotton sector, and how multilayered *mahalli* identities are used both to select leading members and to mobilise subject workers on the cotton farms.

The role of ethnicity in organising cotton political economy

Today, central state elites and their investment (so-called '*fyucherist*' or futures) companies monopolise the cotton sector in Tajikistan. In this case study, I define these monopolisers as 'cotton elites'. As the International Crisis Group states, "'…[p]articularly in southern Tajikistan, these local futures companies have carved entire regions into spheres of control, where they enjoy unchallenged monopoly on credit, inputs and purchasing. One controls the market in Qubodiyon, Shahritus, Nosiri Khusrav, Qumsangir, Kolkhozobod, Jilikul, and Panj (over 60,000 hectares), while a second, based in Qurghonteppa, enjoys a monopoly in Bokhtar, Sarband, Vakhsh, and Vose'.[300] Often, these companies have powerful political connections" (2005: 8).

Cotton elites dominate key cotton enterprises in three districts of the Qabodiyon oasis (including collection points, cotton plants and MTC or the station of agricultural machines of Qabodiyon, Shahritus and Nosiri Khusrav districts). They use these structural conditions to prevent other investors and customers from investing in the raw cotton domestic and international markets. Also, local representatives of the cotton elites are district governors who bind cotton farms to an investment futures company in the Qabodiyon oasis, namely TASS.[301] As a result, cotton elites have the absolute right to fix crop types and harvest sizes for irrigated land resources.[302]

---

300 The World Bank (2004): Tajikistan: Welfare Implications of Cotton Farmland Privatisation: A Poverty and Social Impact Analysis (June, 24 2004): page 41.

301 This is the shortened version of the title of the futures company.

302 Personal interviews with private farmers Samad Ghayurov (Notebook No 1-7, March 10, 2008: pages 112-114), Valijon Isomatov (Notebook No 1-6, January 18, 2008: pages 14-15) and with a representative of the NGO Arbitrazh (Notebook No 1-7, March 13, 2008: pages 121-122).

The representatives of cotton elites, their direct clients in the Sayyod Jamoat, are *kuhistoni kolkhozi* elites (see also Figure 8: The cotton and *kolkhozi* elites). The latter dominate local political and economic structures, including the Sayyod Jamoat, the Sayyod collective farm and the JRC. Kolkhozi elites have privatised most public properties which are not directly related to the cotton sector, including land plots, gardens, livestock, agricultural machinery and social and technical infrastructure. They also have privileged access and rights (management and alienation) to the remaining public (including cotton-related) properties, such as land plots, gardens, public buildings and economic enterprises.

The ethno-national discourse is induced to generate the direct commitment of kolkhozi elites to effectively organise the cotton political economy at jamoat level. Their commitment to the cotton elites is interpreted as their loyalty to ethno-national values, while in part, raw cotton is considered as a 'strategic resource of the nation'. As the position is officially expressed, "[c]otton is not only an important crop for our Republic; it is entwined with our history and with the lives and future of our people" (Government of Tajikistan 2007: 4). However, neither the cotton elites nor kolkhozi elites openly emphasise or highlight ethnicity, since the cotton economy relies heavily on *mahalli* solidarity networks in Sayyod village.

Nevertheless, especially after several military rebellions led by the Uzbek Colonel Mahmud Khudoyberdiev in the winter of 1996, in the summer of 1997 and in autumn 1998, state (cotton) elites transformed their networking strategies. Earlier, central state (*kulobi*) elites mostly favoured their *mahalli* (including Uzbek) allies during the civil war. However, the *mahalli* people widely supported the rebellious Uzbek colonel, who had previously led pro-government military forces in the Qurghonteppa region during the civil war. After central state elites defeated the colonel, they shifted key offices at district and the inter-village levels to the control of ethnic Tajiks. Thus, the former *kuhistoni kolkhozi* elites of the Soviet kolkhoz recovered their status, which they distorted due to their opposition to the *kulobi* and *mahalli* people during the civil war. Today, they have taken over most of the administrative positions at jamoat level and over some key district and provincial governmental departments. They merge around the family network of the former chairman of kolkhoz, the 'Hero of Socialist Work of USSR', the 'Cotton Hero', who is himself a *kuhistoni* Tajik from Qizilaskar village. His son, who was immediately appointed as the chairman of the Sayyod collective farm, left this job in 2006 to represent the districts of the Qabodiyon oasis in the Lower Chamber of the National Parliament. His kinsman replaced him as chairman of the farm.

Figure 8: Personal networks of the cotton and *kolkhozi* elites

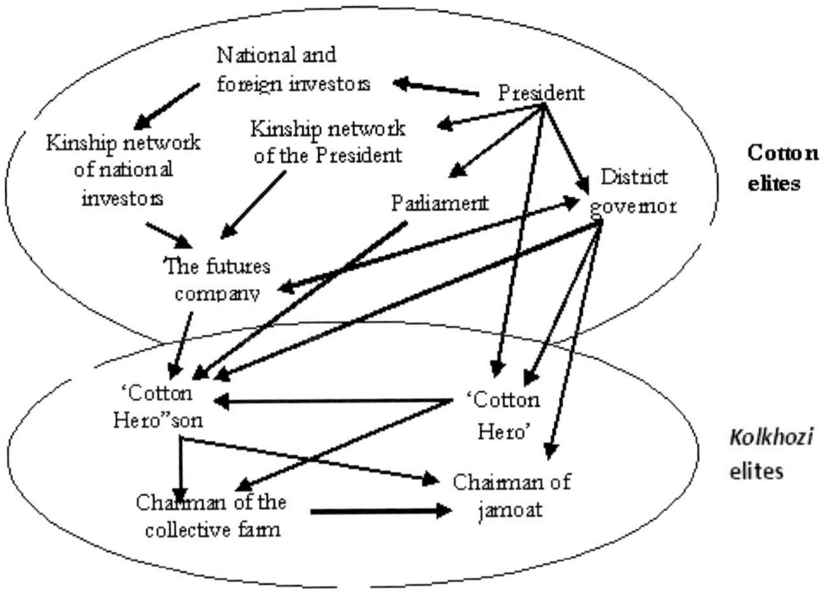

Gradually, ethnic affiliation (*kuhistoni* vs. *mahalli*) has evolved into discrimination in critical situations. The *mahalli* people believe that kolkhozi elites "have personal ties with the central state" which secure their privileged rights. They describe kolkhozi elites' provision of privileged favours for their *qawm* (ethnic) co-members as 'nationalism' ('*millatchigi*') or 'concessionism' ('*ruikhotirbini*'). Such ethnic favouritism, the *mahalli* men told me, had been practiced since the Soviet kolkhoz.[303]

Today, kolkhozi elites diminish the demands of Sayyod village for irrigation water by controlling the central inter-village canal. They practice such control in favour of their kinsmen and ethnic co-members in downstream Qizilaskar and Leninyuli villages due to water scarcity during the irrigation season for the cotton fields.

The disobedience of the *mahalli* people to the cotton economy is less tolerated than even the collective withdrawal of the *kuhistoni* people. Kolkhozi elites are

[303] E.g. personal interview (Notebook No 1-4, November 17, 2007: page 68).

entitled to implement the orders of the district governor, who in turn fixes the harvest 'plans' (quotas) for raw cotton and cocoon. In theory, therefore, if a cotton farm or even a village does not implement its plan, other farms and villages are committed to implement it accordingly. In 2006, Tojikobod village, a village of *kuhistoni* Tajiks in a different jamoat, withdrew from silkworm-breeding. In the end, the *mahalli* people of Sayyod village, among others, were obliged to implement the doubled plan (e.g. one box weighing 20 kg instead of set 9-10 kg). The decision was not directly or formally taken by any state organisation, but the *mahalli* farmers committed themselves to their *kuhistoni* patrons in Sayyod Jamoat, who perhaps undertook this inter-jamoat measure to support their ethnic co-members. For example, the brigadir of *Khojamashhadi qawm* of Sayyod village had the fixed plan of 225 kg from 5 boxes of silkworm seeds and about 100 kg of *uhdadori* (cliental obligation to kolkhozi elites). This time he got an additional four boxes from the withdrawn people and thus harvested about 500 kg from nine boxes[304] (for a broader view, see Table 14).

[304] Salom Qiyomov (Notebook No 1-7, March 8, 2008: page 102).

Table 14: Basic, additional and obligatory plans

Cotton farmers	Total fields (hectare)	Cotton fields (hectare)	Fixed state plan (1 ton per 1 hectare)	Total harvest (plus additional and obligatory) (ton)
Salom Qiyomov	22	20	2.3	62
Munzima Saraeva	6.4	6	2.5	17.6
Mutriba Saidalieva	12.5	11.5	2.2	34
Rauf Fattoev	11.5	10	2.3	28
Nurullo Kholmatov	13	11	2.5	43
Naim Ahadov	15	13	2.6	36
Samad Juraqulov	13.5	11	3.2	42
Samad Ghayurov	14	12	2.2	36.6
Nuriddin Ahmadov	18	16	3.5	45
Sunnat Tabarov	13	10	2.2	25
Sharifbek Zaripov	47	42	2.5	93.5
Tuhfa Eshgulova	5.2	4.5	2.4	16
Zamira Shonazarova	3	2.7	2.3	14
Halim Norboev	2.5	2.2	2.5	8
Juraboy Toshev	9	8	2.3	30
Bobo Qiliev	10	8	2.3	26
Namoz Quliev	4	2.5	2.3	8.1
Cotton farmers	Total fields (hectare)	Silkworm seed (box)	Fixed state plan (kg per box)	Total harvest (plus additional and obligatory) (kg)
Salom Qiyomov	22	5	45	500
Munzima Saraeva	6.4	1	45	57
Mutriba Saidalieva	12.5	1.5	75	101
Naim Ahadov	15	1.5	56	75
Samad Ghayurov	14	1.5	60	90
Nuriddin Ahmadov	18	2	45	167
Sunnat Tabarov	13	1	45	55
Sharifbek Zaripov	47	6	45	370
Zamira Shonazarova	3	1	50	60
Halim Norboev	2.5	1	55	65
Juraboy Toshev	9	1	55	72
Bobo Qiliev	10	1	60	80

Source: Personal survey (October 2007 – March 2008)

Mahalli identities of the cotton-growing 'communities'

The cotton economy cannot be reduced to the ethnic preferences of cotton and *kolkhozi* elites while it relies heavily on the wider mobilisation of the *mahalli* people. It is therefore a deliberate task, a well-practiced strategy of the cotton elites, to select *mahalli* clients. They should be wealthy and respectable *mahalli* men in order to successfully organise their cotton farms (private *dehqan* farms, *qawm* and family brigadas at the collective farm) and mobilise their workers. First of all, these clients are *mahalli* veterans, i.e. former colleagues of *kuhistoni kolkhozi* elites in the Soviet kolkhoz. Most of the 'successful' farmers inherited their leading positions following the Soviet kolkhoz (see Table 15: Personal networks of elites and clients). Two current farmers were brigadirs,[305] one a tractor driver,[306] five kolkhoz administrators[307] and some others formerly or currently district government officers, including a physician. Among them, two former kolkhoz administrators[308] enjoy the personal protection of the 'Cotton Hero' and thus run privileged 'family brigadas' on the collective farm. Obviously, personal indebtedness would be less decisive if the farmers were less capable of mobilising 'their people' for the benefit of the cotton economy. Thus, 'unsuccessful' farmers, including some kolkhoz veterans, have been replaced by other powerful men and women.

---

[305] Salom Qiyomov and Qamar Jumaev.

[306] Nurullo Kholmatov.

[307] Samad Ghayurov, *Haji* Bobo Quliev, Namoz Quliev, Shoista Muzaffarova and Munzima Saraeva.

[308] Kolkhoz technical manager *Haji* Bobo Quliev and his brother, the kolkhoz accountant.

Table 15: Personal networks of elites and clients

Patron	Personal relation	Client farmer
Cotton Hero	Haqdod Mirzoev – kinsman	Collective farm of Sayyod Jamoat
District interior officer	Fayzullo Ahadov – uncle	The head of *dehqan* farm Naim Ahadov
Chairman of the jamoat (due to the position of Polvon Kholmatov in the mahalla)	Polvon Kholmatov – brother	The head of *dehqan* farm Nurullo Kholmatov
District governor	Tojiddin Ahmadov – father	The head of *dehqan* farm Nuriddin Ahmadov
District physician	Uncle	The head of *dehqan* farm Samad Ghayurov
District physician	Uncle	Valijon Isomatov – successful labour migrant
Cotton Hero	Ethnic co-member	Abdusamad Norov
Cotton Hero	Ethnic co-member	Shoista Muzaffarova
District governor	Mother	Tuhfa Eshgulova – secretary of district government
Cotton Hero	Indebted to his father	*Haji* Bobo Quliev
Cotton Hero	Indebted to his father	Namoz Quliev

Source: My field research (October 2007 – March 2008)

Since the Soviet period, kolkhozi elites have sought effective tools to mobilise the kinship, descent and neighbourhood networks of cotton-growers. Among these, the *zveno* (Russian: 'lower unit') or work-team was introduced during the 1950s to enforce and use these networks for the cotton industry. For this purpose, two large brigadas of *mahalli* people in Sayyod village[309] were divided into smaller and lower units of so-called 'family *zveno*' ('*zvenoi oilavi*') and 'neighbourhood *zveno*' ('*zvenoi hamsoyagi*'). The teams mobilised *elkheshi*, *qawm* or *kucha* co-members, while the *zveno* leaders were respected men or women. These leaders were called 'timekeepers' ('*tabelchi*'), who formally submitted to

309 According to my informant, Qamar Jumaev (Notebook No 1-7, March 9, 2008: pages 107-108), during Soviet Union rule there were two brigadas made up of *mahalli* villagers – the brigada of Qamar Jumaev (165 hectares) and the brigada of Salom Qiyomov (180 hectares).

the brigadirs. In fact, the brigadirs, who were called 'organisers' ('*tashkilotchi*'), influenced the subject workers less than the timekeepers did.[310]

Today, in a similar way, both inclusive (*mahalli*) and sub-village (*mahalla*, *qawm* and *elkheshi*) identities are sought to mobilise cotton workers. A more inclusive *mahalli* or *Shahritusi* identity and honour is necessary to generate the commitment of the *mahalli* people to their praised and honoured name as 'exemplary cotton-growers'. The distinguishing feature of the *mahalli* people of Shahritus district as 'the pioneers of cotton growing and plan implementation in the Republic' is highlighted to generate their commitment to the competitive campaign of the cotton harvest. This reference is effective in sustaining cotton-growing and harvest activities.

Villagers remember that in early 2000, the representatives of central, district and jamoat governments visited the village, gathered them in a mahalla general council and called upon their 'big men' (*kalono*) to organise their 'family' and '*qawm*' farms. Since then, two large *mahalli* brigadas of the former kolkhoz in Sayyod village have been split up into 11 smaller ('family') brigadas on the current collective farm and eight private farms. In order to overcome a 'crisis' or lack of manpower, the farms were organised on the basis of *elkheshi* and *qawm* groups. These 'big men' were encouraged or even forced to run cotton farms to highlight the *elkheshi* and *qawm* identities of their subject workers and thereby to mobilise them for this intensive but low-paid monoculture.

Farmers refer to *elkheshi*, *qawm* and ethnic identities to mobilise villagers for cotton growing and harvesting. Reference to collective identities is necessary to interpret the cotton farm as *elkheshi*, *qawm* or ethnic commitment. Without especially related *elkheshi* or *qawm* workers, it is therefore impossible to run farms and to maintain the cotton sector. Rauf Fattoev, for example, cannot change his brigada into a private farm due to the lack of subject workers. As he told me, "[w]e have no *odam* [kinsmen]. Without brothers and cousins, it is impossible to work during the cotton [season]."[311]

This is the very reason why powerful men (and here, elites support them too) usually resist against *elkheshi* co-members establishing their own private farms. Chupon Aliev consulted with Polvon Kholmatov, his *elkheshi* 'big man', whose brother owns an *elkheshi* farm, to establish a private farm. Polvon Kholmatov strongly opposed him and referred to their *elkheshi* identity whereby "two of your sons are not married and you establish a *dehqan* farm – what do people

---

310 Personal interview with Vosit Yuldoshev (Notebook No 1-7, March 10, 2008: pages 114-115)

311 Personal interview with Rauf Fattoev (Notebook No 1-6, January 26, 2008: page 89)

say? They say that the sons of Chupon are not married but he receives land [*dehqan* farm], as if they are saying it about me. I will be dishonoured in the gatherings because of you."[312]

Often, 'successful' farmers employ the discourses of unity and integrity, which praise 'their people' for being more 'loyal' ('*ahl*') and 'solid' ('*tifoq*') than others. For example, one of the most successful and experienced brigadirs, Salom Qiyomov, talks about the good qualities of *Khojamashhadi* people, who make up the bulk of his workforce. To make the claim meaningful, *brigadirs* and farmers use the services of their mediators, their 'desirable' and 'active' workers. These are usually elders and respectable men of related workers who propagate the cotton farms and plans as honourable symbols of 'their people'. They invent stories about how farms have been created and how they belong to their *qawms*. The farmers spread stories about the relation of the farms to their *elkheshi* families or *qawm* networks. As Table 16 (Invented stories and discourses about the cotton farms) illustrates, any reference to 'their elders', who 'led the farmers to establish the *dehqan* farms of their people' and who 'promised their people would help them', seeks the solidarity of cotton farms.

312 Personal interview with Chupon Aliev (Notebook No 1-4, November 11, 2007: pages 57-58).

Table 16: Invented stories and discourses about the cotton farms

Status of farms	Farmers	Affiliations of the subject workers	Invented stories and discourses about farms
Brigada	Mutriba Saidalieva	Extended family of Jumaev	- 'For the sake of *Rabotaki*' - 'For the sake of kinsmen'
Brigada	Salom Qiyomov	Extended family of Qiyomov and other *Khojamashhadi qawm* members	- 'The members are all related to the root of *Khojamashhadi Shaykhs*' - 'We are working for the sake of *elkheshi* dignity'
Private farm	Nurullo Kholmatov	Extended family of Kholmatov and Eshniyozov	- 'For the sake of [*Khojamashhadi*] *qawm*' - 'Our elders asked and promised to mobilise the workers' - 'The [subordinate] members guided to take [establish the farm]'
Private farm	Nuriddin Ahmadov	Extended family of Ahmadov	- 'The brothers and cousins are working as our grandfather told his last will'
Private farm	Shoista Muzaffarova	Extended families of Muzaffarov and other *kuhistoni* people	- 'The farm is *avlodi*' - 'We try to have it only with kinsmen'

Source: Field research (October 2007 – March 2008)

If the cotton farms (brigadas or private farms) are larger and require more workers than there are members of the same extended families, then mostly *qawm* (descent or ethnic) co-members are mobilised. Such farms include the brigadas of Salom Qiyomov and Rauf Fattoev and the private farm of Abdusamad Norov, who mobilise *Khojamashhadi* people and *kuhistoni* Tajiks, respectively. These farmers highlight *elkheshi*, *qawm* and ethnic identities in order to mobilise people, while cotton farms and plans are interpreted as their *qawm* or ethnic attributes. The workers also perceive the cotton enterprises and the set plans of the cotton harvest as material attributes of their *qawm* or ethnic identity and honour and therefore display a great deal of commitment to such attributes. To reinforce common belonging and commitment, most of the farmers name their farms after the honoured men of their *elkheshi* families. Only the seedling farm has a practical title, 'Payvand' (here, 'grafting trees'), which seeks clients in the markets beyond Sayyod village and therefore does not need immaterial references for the wider mobilisation of workers (see Table 17: Symbolic names).

Table 17: Symbolic names: titular relation of cotton farms to their farmers and workers

Farmer	Relation of the title to the farmer and workers
Nurullo Kholmatov	Named after farmer's paternal grandfather
Naim Ahadov	Named after farmer's father
Samad Juraqulov	Named after farmer's father
Samad Ghayurov	Named after farmer's cousin, a colonel who died during the 1990s' civil war
Nuriddin Ahmadov	Named after farmer's paternal grandfather
Abdusamad Norov	Named after farmer's father
Shoista Muzaffarova	Named after farmer's kinsmen and *qawm* co-member; formerly *kolkhozi* elite
Tuhfa Eshgulova	Named after farmer's son
Haqdod Mirzoev	Named after farmer's *qawm* co-member
Sharifbek Zaripov	Named after *mahalli* sacred site – Khoja-Mashhad shrine
Samariddin Naimov	No relation but rather practical title – 'Payvand'

Source: Field research (October 2007 – March 2008)

Only a few people work for so-defined 'strangers', because either they have no *elkheshi* farmers or their *elkheshi* farms are overemployed. The largest private farm in the village, titled the 'Khoja-Mashhad *dehqan* farm', employs workers of different *elkheshi* and *qawm* origins. The farmer, who comes from the provincial capital, established the farm in 2003 and named it after the Khoja-Mashhad shrine, as a sign of appreciation of the most important religious attribute of the *mahalli* people. It is a way to invoke villagers' sympathy towards his farm and thereby mobilise them for cotton production on about 70 hectares of cotton fields. As one informant told me, "We have been left and thrown *in between* ['*dar mobayn*']: from one brigada to the other one. The brigadirs work with their kinsmen; therefore, they do not want us. This year, I do not know where to go, maybe to Khoja-Mashhad farm."[313]

By claiming the cotton farms as their *elkheshi* or *qawm* properties, farmers as well as 'active' workers praise reciprocal exchanges among workers. Employment on

313 Personal interview (Notebook No 1-4, November 22, 2007: page 106; also tape recording No DS 300225).

the cotton farms is interpreted and treated as an *elkheshi* commitment to reciprocal support, which discredits the demand for immediate payment (e.g. in the form of a salary) as being against the norms of 'kinship relations' ('*kheshutabori*') and 'the manner of being human' ('*odamgari*'). Such imposed commitment also adapts and transforms contract negotiations between farmers and their *elkheshi* technicians to reciprocal return (*muroso*). On the basis of *muroso*, close kinsmen, who have (state, collective or private) trucks and sowing tractors, serve the farmers.

Reference to *elkheshi* and *qawm* identities also shapes reciprocal expectations and commitment to the hard and underpaid work involved in silkworm-breeding.[314] Some farmers, who have smaller cotton fields, breed silkworms themselves or act together with their *elkheshi* co-members. Others, who have larger cotton fields, ask for help from their workers, who are usually their *elkheshi* or *qawm* co-members. As an experienced silkworm-breeder, Chupon Aliev, told me that in the season of 2007, he was committed to breeding 10 boxes of silkworm seeds, an amount which is normally distributed among five families: "In the beginning, I only took [the silkworm plan] from [the farm of] my cousin… Then, Salom Qiyomov came and told that we are from the same [*Khojamashhadi*] *qawm* and promised to pay 40 TJ Somoni and a sack [about 50 kg] of fertiliser. He knew that last year my cousin gave me fertiliser as well. [Another farmer] asked my wife to take her [plan] as well. I went to the silkworm-breeding store (*pillakhona*) for silkworm seeds and saw the agronomist, my cousin, there. He asked me to take his [farm's plan] also… I could not reject him for the sake of our kinship relation ['*ba khotiri kheshutabori*']. He would say, 'See, you took from all *others* but you have no *odamgari*'. Moreover, he lent me 300 USD for my son's travel to Russia. If I had not taken it [his farm's plan], he would say, 'See, I gave him a loan when he was in a hole but now he does not support me'. A week

---

[314] The contract with the District silkworm-breeding office is in advance written and signed between the office and collective or private *dehqan* farms. However, the individual silkworm-breeders do not know about the contract and they are only paid after they grow, harvest and carry the raw cocoon to the office themselves. The economic income is limited, including cash which is 1 TJ Somoni per 1 kg of harvested and accepted raw cocoon and the firewood from mulberry branches used to feed silkworms. The work proceeding and negotiation are personally and informally dealt between the farmers and their subject workers. But the provision of mulberry leaves, the food of silkworm for two months of intensive breeding, is the sole burden and care of the workers. Although the individual brigadas and farms have mulberry orchards in the edges of their cotton fields, however, they are not always sufficient to fill the feeding season. Therefore, the silkworm-breeders must personally ask other farmers in their village or beyond in order to cope with food shortage they face to feed silkworms.

later, *Haji* Bobo Quliev came and asked me to take his box of seeds which nobody else would take… They come to your doorstep, if you are at home, and you cannot refuse. This time, my wife and I will leave the village during the distribution of silkworms."[315]

Reference to *elkheshi* or *qawm* identities also mutually commits farmers and their male workers to the institutionalised practices of reciprocal bargaining or '*muomila*' (literally: 'demeanour'). Water suppliers to the cotton fields (*obmon*)[316] mostly trust and work for their *elkheshi* and sometimes *qawm*-related farmers. Also, the farmers prefer to hire adult men from their *elkheshi* or *qawm* groups, who due to their old age or other family conditions cannot travel outside the village to earn a decent income, such as labour migration to Russia. Only a few farmers have different and unrelated water suppliers, because either they have no *elkheshi* co-members to take on the job or the irrigation conditions are exhaustive. But in such a case, they lose these water suppliers every season because there is no immaterial incentive to encourage them to otherwise stay (see Table 18: Personal relations between water suppliers and farmers).

Table 18: Personal relations between water suppliers and farmers

Cotton farmer	Relations of water supplier to the farmer
Munzima Saraeva	Husband and son (two water suppliers)
Halim Norboev	Son
Tuhfa Eshgulova	Brother-in-law
Namoz Quliev	Junior brother
Mutriba Saidalieva	Uncle
Nuriddin Ahmadov	Cousin
Qamar Jumaev	*Qawm* co-member
Salom Qiyomov	*Qawm* co-member

Source: My personal survey (October 2007 – March 2008)

Again, *elkheshi* and *qawm* identities serve to negotiate informal contracts between the farmers and their water suppliers. There is no formal contract between them, but rather they bargain over cooperation according to their patron-client expectations (e.g. seasonal financial or in-kind payment, reward

---

315 Personal interview with Chupon Aliev (Tape recording No DS 300266).

316 Water supply to cotton fields is a male job which requires hard and intensive physical work to irrigate the fields for four months. The first two months are especially intensive, as the water suppliers are often standing in the water.

and registration of a salary for a retirement fund). *Muomila* bargaining, first of all, ensures both 'service' and payment for the 'service' or the work of the water supplier through reciprocal practices. The 'service' is in the form of a minimal economic income and a commitment to serve the *elkheshi* or *qawm* farmers. As such, the actual payment for more than 5 hectares does not exceed 400 TJ Somoni over the four months of irrigation, despite a formal contract which fixes the price of irrigating a field at 50 TJ Somoni per hectare. Usually, cash payments are provided mainly at the start of the irrigation season, while at the end of the season they decrease or are even terminated. Rather, contracts are written in advance by the farmers themselves and only signed by their water suppliers. The agreement, which is called a '*muomila*' as well as a '*dogovor*' (Russian: 'contract'), is based on personal and day-to-day relations between the two protagonists. As a water supplier told me, "In order to get money you must run after them [farmers]."[317] Additionally, water suppliers work for households or on the private fields of their farmers based on reciprocal trust (*muomila*). Patron farmers pay their water suppliers in different forms, including cash, cotton stalks, fertiliser and food, when they are available. If not available, the water suppliers agree that the farmers must register salaries and social welfare packages on the payroll (*vedomost*) so that they count towards their retirement fund.

Immaterial compensation of the female work in cotton field

Besides the farmers, their technicians and water suppliers, the majority of the workers of cotton farms are women and rarely male juniors. As my survey of 18 cotton farms shows, out of 379 cotton workers, 335 of them were women, including four brigadirs and 331 ordinary workers, as compared to 44 male workers (14 farmers and brigadirs and 30 ordinary workers). The material incomes of the female workers include firewood from the cotton stalks (*ghuzapoya*), small land plots (10-*sotikha* and *presidenti*), a salary or *mehnat*, which often does not exceed 100 TJ Somoni per annum, and irregular (seasonal) patronage favours (agricultural goods) from the farmers. As Table 19 (Economic incentives of the female workers in the cotton sector) shows, salaries and retirement funds are of minor importance to female workers, while a 10-*sotikha* land plot is an important incentive only for some (96 surveyed) female workers to work on the cotton farms. At the same time, 57 female workers informed me that they didn't have a 10-*sotikha* because it is a less stimulating material benefit. For the majority (217 surveyed workers), cotton

[317] Personal interview (Notebook No 1-6, January 22, 2008: page 40)

stalks or firewood were the most attractive material incentives, which they received only if they worked full-time on the farms.[318]

Table 19: Economic incentives of female workers in the cotton sector

Economic incentives	The number of female workers who informed me of their incentives
Cotton stalk	217
10-*sotikha*	96
Salary	3
'For *vedomost'* (Retirement fund)	2

Source: Personal survey (October 2007 – March 2008)

As Table 19 shows, material benefits from cotton farms are miserable and insufficient in mobilising female workers. Therefore, farmers use immaterial incentives, among them *elkheshi* and *qawm* identities, which also highlight 'family honour' and the gender status of women.

The employment of female workers on cotton farms is interpreted as their *elkheshi*, *qawm* and family commitment. Farmers and their mediators highlight *elkheshi* and *qawm* identities to interpret their *brigadas* or private farms as reciprocal networks of female workers. In part, they initiate the celebration of special holidays which seek to enforce the *elkheshi* or *qawm* 'communities' of the female workers. These holidays include 'Women's Day', on 8th March, and *Nawruzi*, in the second half of March when the cotton-growing season begins. Moreover, these celebrations improve the reputation of the farmers among their female workers as generous patrons.[319]

---

[318] Cotton stalks are the main fuel of households due to the scarcity of naturally occurring wood and a shortage of electricity during winter-time. Only a few people who have privileged access and rights to private and collective gardens do not need this fuel source. A few others, who do not work on the cotton farms, collect scarce wood and biomass from the countryside. Sometimes, villagers buy wood at a cost of about 5 to 10 TJ Somoni per day, depending on the season.

[319] Personal interview with Samad Ghayurov (Notebook No 1-7, March 10, 2008: page 113).

Family seniors, farmers and *mahaldori* men refer to 'family honour' to mobilise their juniors for work on the cotton farms. They interpret this work as the direct status of junior women especially (daughters and daughters-in-law) in their families. The junior women themselves also acknowledge that such work is an extension of their family status as 'housekeeper' ('*khonashin*') and 'black guard of the house' ('*khonanda qara*'). Cotton work is considered both their seasonal subsistence activity and especially part of their extended household work. Hence, their intensive work on the cotton farms improves their reputation. People expect that junior women will express their relations and devotion to their seniors via this minimal subsistence activity. 'Family honour' and 'family integrity' commit junior female 'aides' ('*yordamchi*') to hierarchical patterns of patrimonial labour division, in order to replace their formally registered family female seniors (see also Table 20: Family status of cotton farm aides).

Table 20: Family status of cotton farms aides

Family status of aides	Number of subordinate female workers
School-age daughters (*dukhtari khona*)	98
School-age sons	41
Mothers	11
Daughters-in-law (*kelin*)	8
Fathers	5

Source: Personal survey (October 2007 – March 2008)

If they do not take on this role, the aides are discredited as 'bad housekeepers' and as being disloyal to their husbands. One farmer, for example, stigmatised an unmarried woman who gave up working on his farm and opened a shopping stall in the small bazaar in the village: "You see, this family is selling two or three chewing gums on the street the whole year, both in winter and in summer, both she [mother] and her daughter. You encounter different people on the street. A drunk comes and says, 'You are selling chewing gum, so it means you are selling yourself as well'."[320]

Women who are engaged in economically profitable and independent activities (including petty trade and labour migration to Russia), without any serious excuse, are stigmatised and alienated as 'licentious' and 'dirty'. They may have

[320] Personal interview with Rauf Fattoev (Notebook No 1-6, January 26, 2008: page 89)

excuses if their men accompany them, if they have no men of working age, if their children are small or disabled or if their land plots are not large enough to sustain them accordingly. In such a case, women are categorised as 'poor' ('*bechora*'). However, most women have no such 'serious' excuses and their duty is to maintain their households, in part, and work on the cotton farms.

Thus, the manipulation of female reputation is a key tool in mobilising young girls by and under the auspices of female farmers or male farmers' female time-keepers (*tabelchi*), who have the respectful titles 'female brigadir', if they are farmers themselves, and '*bibi*' (literally 'grandmother'), if they serve as time-keepers for male farmers. Female farmers and time-keepers actually supervise the female workers. They not only impart the economic needs of the poor workers to the male farmers but they also serve as mediators for junior female workers. Their recommendation of the moral qualities of female workers immediately shapes the latters' images in the village and thereby improves their chances of entering into a proper marriage.[321] The 'luck' ('*bakht*') or successful family life of a woman depends on her good reputation regarding her 'honest' work on the cotton farms, since men prefer to have such brides.

The *elkheshi* and *qawm* identities, and in part 'family honour', of female workers compensates for their intensive but low-paid job. The small salary[322] is in return for reciprocal support and patronage favour and inclusion in cotton-growing 'communities'. As veteran cotton workers remember, since the Soviet kolkhoz, salary payment has been practiced as a reciprocal exchange in the form of *mehnat* [literally: 'labour'], which is in-kind or financial payment for the set material amount and size of the work.[323] *Mehnat* includes incentive cash or an in-kind reward ('*havasmandi*') and emotional encouragement ('*dilbardori*'). Farmers refer to *elkheshi* or *qawm* identities to interpret their provision of *mehnat* as the reciprocal support and patronage favours of their *elkheshi* or *qawm* co-

---

[321] Personal interview with Nasiba Nurmatova (Notebook No 1-4, November 11, 2007: page 58; also tape recording No DS 00195-196).

[322] According to the formal contract, the futures company TASS must pay cotton farms monthly 50 TJ Somoni per hectare of their cotton fields for salary payment. In reality, as informed by the majority of the farmers, money is only paid three times per annum and less than 50 TJ Somoni per hectare. In 2007, the family brigada of Halim Norboev, who has 2.5 hectares of cotton fields, received the total sum of 400 TJ Somoni for eight workers. However, women get a lower salary than men do. Their salary is paid only hoe and weed the cotton fields from February to July, mainly three times ranging from 5 to about 35 TJ Somoni. The highest salary for women does not exceed 100 TJ Somoni over the entire season.

[323] Personal interviews (Notebook No 1-4, October 23, 2007: page 43; also tape recording No 30-31 FB; Notebook No 1-7, March 8, 2008: pages 103-105).

members, rather than as their legal obligation to their workers. This, in turn, commits the workers to the related cotton farms. *Mehnat* "indebts [*muttaham*] them to their brigadirs," an experienced informant told me.[324]

Compared with salary, *mehnat* necessitates the frequency of personal relations between the farmers and their workers. *Mehnat* is not measured in relation to the size and quality of the work but rather depends on the worker's family status and personal relations. It is paid strictly on the basis of the patrimonial hierarchy of men vs. women and seniors vs. juniors. In part, female workers are paid a lower *mehnat* than male workers. Senior female workers on cotton farms are paid more, regardless of the size and quality of their work. Junior female workers are either paid less or work without *mehnat* (*bemehnat*), although they constitute the majority of the cotton-growers (see Table 21: Family status of female workers on cotton farms). They are often called 'aides' (*'yordamchi'*), who work on behalf and for the sake of their female seniors. In this case, reference to 'family honour' legitimises the underpaid *mehnat* for these 'aides'.

Table 21: Family status of female workers on cotton farms

Family status of female workers	Number of the subordinate female workers
School-age daughters (*dukhtari khona*)	81
Daughters-in-law (*kelin*)	62
Middle-age women	61
Young women	23
Old-age women	22
Female pensioners	2

Source: Personal survey (October 2007 – March 2008)

The commitment to 'family honour' is institutionalised additionally through the indigenous and imposed practices of *agat* (an Uzbek word for 'the bed of a cotton field') and *norma* (a Russian word for 'quota') for cotton growing and harvesting. Farmers impose the institutional practice of *agat* to assign physical units of cotton fields to individual families to work on through the entire season of cotton growing, harvesting and after-harvesting. The practice is actualised by invoking the 'family honour' of especially female workers, expressed in their collectively agreed commitment to *agat*. The 'shame' of any

[324] Personal interview with Mahkam Boyakov (Tape recording No DS 300309).

family, if it lags behind other families in implementing *agat*, thus commits female juniors to help their co-workers to 'make [them] level to people'.[325]

Likewise, jamoat and district state functionaries impose a *norma* (quota) of raw cotton to be collected by subject institutions such as schools, government departments, bazaars and families. While the state's coercive measure is not effective enough to mobilise individual families, farmers and mahalla mediators interpret their commitment to *norma* as an important attribute of their 'family honour'.

Immaterial incentives for the cotton harvest

Like most irrigated land resources, the plan (the fixed size) of raw harvested cotton is also a monopoly for cotton elites. The district governor is personally in charge of 'state-fixed' ('*nishondodi davlati*') and 'obligatory' ('*uhdadori*') plans relating to the cotton harvest. In 2007, the newly appointed district governor exerted all efforts to implement a state-fixed plan, before 9 October, as a gift to mark the birthday of the Tajik president. Although he was unable to reach his target, the intention itself was approved by his patron. At the turn of the new year, at the annual meeting, the president praised his efforts and announced a 'Republican seminar' for other district governors to come to Shahritus district in the spring of 2008 and to learn how to replicate his 'achievements'.[326] After Shahritus district implemented the 'fixed' plan on 23 October 2007, its governor committed to the president to harvest the 'obligatory' plan of 3 thousand tonnes to 'support other lagging districts'.

Two days later, I observed the harvesting campaign in the cotton fields of Sayyod village. I saw no-one, although abundant blossoming cotton sepals whitened the extensive fields. I was curious to see how the harvesting machinery used for the 'fixed' and 'obligatory' plans was fuelled and re-fuelled and how the cotton pickers were mobilised during the harvest season between August and December.

The cotton harvest is an intensive activity throughout the entire cotton production season and requires enormous labour resources. As always, the district governor had issued an order which committed individual households, cotton farms, schools, state organisations and urban enterprises to the cotton harvest. Individual families and village schools play a major role in harvesting

---

325 Personal interview (Notebook No 1-5, December 13, 2007: pages 98-99).

326 First Channel of the Public TV of Tajikistan; January 6, 2008; 20:00-22:00 Dushanbe time.

raw cotton, while external cotton pickers (such as urban state employees and traders) play only a minor role.

However, the economic benefits from the cotton harvest are not an incentive for the cotton pickers. The futures company TASS formally contracts collective and private cotton farms to 0.12-0.15 TJ Somoni per 1 kg of harvested raw cotton,[327] while the cotton pickers are paid 0.08-0.10 TJ Somoni instead. This smaller payment is due to either the futures company or the farmers, who misuse financial resources designated for harvesting. The situation also differs from farm to farm, while most of them do not pay regular cash. Again, junior workers are paid less than senior workers, which is a way in which farmers accumulate financial means for their own needs. Cotton pickers are properly paid, mainly in the early parts of the season, in order to encourage them to continue for the rest of the intensive harvest campaign. It is widely reported that they are not paid for especially the last few weeks of work.

Therefore, it is impossible to implement even a 'fixed' harvest plan without the mobilisation of junior family members, especially school-age daughters and daughters-in-law (see also Tables 20 and 21 on family status). Collective identities serve as immaterial incentives to generate their commitment to the cotton harvest. *Hashar* and *norma* (quota) are among key institutional practices aligned with the cotton harvest which cotton mediators interpret as the pickers' commitment to their *mahalli* and religious identities. *Hashar*, for example, symbolises honourable and sacred practices attributed to *mahalli* and Islamic identities. For this purpose, the religious saint of the *mahalli* men, Qabodiyon Eshon, and other men of 'village honour', such as hajis, veterans, mullahs and elders, personally initiate the harvest campaign.

The invocation of 'family honour' effects the competitive institution of *norma* (quota). In this regard, mostly junior family members of school age implement their family and school *normas*. As my key informant told me, "School children, rather than kolkhozi workers, implement the plan."[328] Sometimes, forced mobilisation by the state and school authorities, and mainly the invocation of 'family honour', commit them to the cotton harvest, which is one of the very rare sources available to gain cash for buying school uniforms, which is treated with the highest regard by the school children, because the smartness of their uniform protects their 'family honour' and symbolises the wellbeing and wealth of their families.

---

[327] Personal interview with Qamar Jumaev (Notebook No 1-7, March 9, 2008: pages 107-108).

[328] Personal interview with Chupon Aliev (Notebook No 1-5, December 7, 2007: page 20).

In this section, we have observed that cotton elites and their local mediators devote material and symbolic resources to maintaining the cotton economy. Cotton elites favour ethnic Tajik *kolkhozi* elites, who thus dominate key resources and organisations within the cotton sector, including jamoats and collective farms. To commit them sufficiently, reference to ethnic identity generates their loyalty to the cotton elites and to raw cotton as a 'strategic resource of the nation'.

At village level, we have also observed that neither the cotton elites nor kolkhozi elites openly emphasise or highlight the ethnic superiority of Tajiks. Rather, the cotton economy depends heavily on the mobilisation of local people. It is therefore a deliberate task, a well-practiced strategy of central and local governments, to identify their *mahalli* clients, i.e. farmers and their mediators. These farmers and mediators have privileged status among the local people to mobilise the latter by reference to their family, *elkheshi*, *qawm* and Islamic identities. The cotton-growing activities and harvesting campaign are thus dominantly practiced as family and religious commitments by female workers to their farmers.

Chapter conclusion

This concluding subchapter summarises the mainstream aspects of local governance in the cotton-growing Sayyod village. Section one below shows the institutional practices surrounding property rights similar to those in the case of Devdor village. However, the main difference we observe is not so much contested property rights but rather the sacred (such as inherited) boundaries of related institutions. Section two also describes the mahalla as a political structure which is not elite-dominated, as in the subsistence-based community, but is rather more representative of most villagers. As the last section three summarises, the representative political structure of the mahalla is necessary in order to stabilise and mobilise cotton-growing 'communities' or family and *qawm* farms.

Legitimation of political and economic rights

Kolkhozi elites at jamoat level and their *mahalli* clients in Sayyod village have 'administrative' or privileged access to public goods and to their subject workers' private rights. Recently, they have privatised their privileged access to the former kolkhoz's public goods, including the most favourable land resources, gardens, agricultural machinery and economic enterprises. They enjoy bureaucratic and military means of the state to insist on their privileged access to the rights and shares of local people, including monthly salaries and support land plots (*presidenti* and 10-*sotikha*). Also, subject people do not contest elites' privileged access to their rights and shares but rather consider them as patronage favours in return for their work on the cotton farms.

The bureaucratic and military means of the state and patron-client relations, however, do not prevent contestation over the unequal distribution of agricultural positions and resources. Thus, reference to collective identities serves to legitimise the privileged and inheritance claims of elites and to discredit the contestations of underprivileged people. Mediators mobilise the significant proportion of cotton workers from women and juniors. To discredit any demands for a proper salary, they interpret the individual cash income of women and juniors as means which will spoil their family loyalty. As for male workers, they legitimise their miserable and partly in-kind payment of a salary as being due to their reciprocal commitment to their family or *qawm* farms. They preach to the workers that "concession is for the sake of kinship relation" and claim that contesting a miserable salary and unequal rights is against and corrupts kinship ties and norms. Public and religious ceremonies also serve to discredit any form of contestation as 'infidel' behaviour and thus shape the sacred status of elites.

Reference to family and *qawm* identities also legitimises the privileged rights or sacred status of elites in relation to public goods (such as cotton farms) by establishing a symbolic relationship between the goods and the highlighted groups. To cement their sacred relations with the goods, some of them tell stories about their spiritual intercession or exclusive relationship with holy saints and souls, while others refer to their superior descent origins (such as *shaykhs* or *sayyids*) and restore their genealogical books (*shajaranoma*) to legitimise their inherited rights to sacred sites and any related financial and material resources. These economically important resources include *nazr* (personal favours for religious services provided by religious notables) and *sadaqa* (devotions and sacrifices for the sacred sites). Powerful men also refer to their ancestral and spiritual privileges (so-called '*pusht*'; literally 'back') to claim their right to sacred sites, positions, professions, land and other properties. They organise the initiation ceremony of *khatm* to make this claim to their exclusive descent and religious status.

Mahalla as a mediation structure for socio-political stability

Besides *kuhistoni* Tajiks, the mahalla integrates and represents all *mahalli* families, neighbourhoods and farms of Sayyod village, including five *qawms* (descent groups), 23 *elkheshi* (extended) families and 16 *dehqan* farms. Powerful men, elders, *oqsaqols* and religious authorities, who represent their descent groups, extended families and cotton farms, are the leading members and mediators of the mahalla. They settle disputes, mobilise the labour, financial and material resources of villagers and adapt state and development programmes and institutions. These integrative functions sustain political and economic stability and especially shape cotton 'communities' in the village.

Mahalla mediators refer to the multilayered *mahalli* (such as *mahalli* village, *mahalli* Islamic, descent, neighbourhood and family) identities of villagers to enforce the mahalla's integrative and mediatory functions. *Mahalli* identities enforce the representation authority of the farmers and mediators of cotton farms, including elders, veterans, *oqsaqols* and religious authorities (*eshon*, *imam-khatib*, hajis and village and *kucha* mullahs). The regular religious ceremonies and settings (mosques and shrines) serve to highlight *mahalli* identities and thereby commit villagers to the cotton farms.

Stabilisation and mobilisation of cotton-growing 'communities'

Mediators mobilise means and resources to sustain the 'stability' and effectiveness of cotton-growing 'communities' or the farms of *mahalli* people. These means and resources include mediation ('on-site' and 'delegation') institutions of dispute settlement and reciprocal and modified practices of resource mobilisation for the 'common wellbeing' and for cotton farms.

The sustenance of the cotton-growing (descent group, extended family and *kucha*) networks in the village depends on the peaceful co-existence of their members. To achieve this end, mahalla mediators and state elites use internal ('on-site') mechanisms of dispute settlement within the 'communities' of cotton-growers (such as family or descent group farms). Family elders and religious notables organise the 'on-site' tools of dispute settlement and refer to *elkheshi* and *qawm* identities to commit disputants to peace and to discredit other non-traditional means (especially court deals). They also use regular religious ceremonies to commit disputants to peace and mutual support as normative attributes of their family, *mahalli* village and *mahalli* Islamic identities.

The 'delegation' also seeks to resolve tensions among the cotton-growing networks by invoking their *mahalli*, religious and family honour, if mahalla mediators fail to find a solution. The 'delegation' includes both mahalla mediators and local state and court representatives, other religious notables (including *imam-khatib* and Qabodiyon Eshon) and school teachers. If such mediation is not effective in harmonising the cotton-growing networks, state and police authorities intervene to suppress any trouble, again via reference to kinship and religious identities. These 'delegation' authorities extend decision-making exercises over family and neighbourhood relations to the mahalla. In part, they discredit court deals and other formal means of dispute settlement. For this purpose, they organise 'public' and state courts to punish, and principally to stigmatise, those who threaten the core pillars of stability, especially the privileged rights of elites and the cotton networks. The 'delegation' thus mobilises communal solidarity against the theft of private property and pre-marital relations committed by the 'new generation', which would otherwise endanger family and neighbourhood networks.

Mahalla leaders and mediators arrange reciprocal practices, again to sustain socio-political and economic stability. These institutional practices are often reduced to individual extended families and include shared households, joint economic activities, shared patrimonial properties and resources, *hashar*, privileged public services, mutual support during ceremonies, old-age insurance and the support of widowed and disabled family members. Family elders and religious notables refer to kinship and Islamic identities to commit family members to such practices. Some important practices, such as *hashar*, food sharing, public services, labour migration and support of the poor are interpreted as the honourable attributes of a descent group or extended family co-members. Furthermore, supporting the poor is regarded as the Islamic commitment of wealthy co-members. Those who ignore this form of family support are discredited and ostracised by family elders and mahalla mediators. Also, mahalla mediators redistribute internal resources to support poor villagers who are not embedded in the reciprocal networks of extended families. For this purpose, they articulate *mahalli* village and Islamic identities to modify *sadaqa* and to identify its recipients, who include widowed women without any male adults, poor women without *elkheshi* networks, orphans and handicapped men. The mediators provide *sadaqa* through neighbourhoods and regular ceremonies (such as funerals, weddings, religious and seasonal feasts).

Besides reciprocal networks, the practices of 'common wellbeing' also serve to sustain socio-political and economic stability in the village. Mahalla mediators refer to *mahalli* village, *mahalli* Islamic, *qawm* and *elkheshi* identities to mobilise villagers' labour, financial and material resources. The 'collective *hashar*', for example, maintains the 'wellbeing' of religious assets (cemetery, shrines and village and neighbourhood mosques), cotton-related infrastructure (the main inter-village canal, irrigation infrastructure, drainage systems, roads and bridges) and the cotton harvest. Regular religious ceremonies and prayer communities in *choykhonas* are settings where *hashar* is announced, organised and monitored. Family elders, village veterans and religious notables personally 'initiate' *hashar* as a sacred and honourable action, which thus commits and mobilises the resources of neighbours, villagers and labour migrants. The objects of 'common wellbeing' are interpreted as the attributes of their neighbourhood, *mahalli* village and *mahalli* Islamic identities. While women maintain most of the objects of 'common wellbeing', female mahalla mediators commit themselves by interpreting these objects as 'family honour'.

Cotton and *kolkhozi* elites show favour to their *mahalli* clients and allow them to run their 'family' and '*qawm*' farms, including 11 brigadas on the collective farm and eight private farms. These clients enjoy a privileged status to mobilise their co-villagers to work intensively in low-paid cotton farm jobs. They commit 'their people' by referring to their *elkheshi* and *qawm* identities. The stories of how these farms were established and how they came to be named are tailored to indicate how they belong to the subject workers. For this reason, most of the farmers name their farms after important men of 'their people'. Cotton farms and harvest plans are interpreted as honourable attributes of workers' *elkheshi*, *qawm* and *mahalli* identities.

Subordinate work in the cotton farms is interpreted and dealt with as *elkheshi* or *qawm* commitment to the farms. Demands for immediate and fixed payment (e.g. in the form of a salary) are discredited as being against the norm of 'kinship relations'. Such commitment adapts formal (contract) negotiations between the farmers and their *elkheshi* male workers (tractor drivers and silkworm-breeders) into *muroso* (the institution of reciprocal return). The institutional practice of '*muomila*' ('demeanour') or reciprocal bargaining underpins the work of water suppliers and also shapes informal contracts on the basis of reciprocal and cliental exchanges (such as seasonal financial or in-kind payment, reward and registration of salary for retirement funds, underpayment of salary in different forms, including cash, cotton stalk, fertiliser and food).

The lower incomes of the majority of workers, who are also predominantly women, are practiced as (seasonal) reciprocal and patron-client returns and rewards. Since the economic income of women is miserable, farmers interpret their work in the cotton sector as 'family honour' and what constitutes female status. Female work is thus judged as the positive moral quality of especially junior women. The hierarchical patterns of patrimonial labour division are important in mobilising and exploiting mainly junior female family members, who replace their family seniors although their work is underpaid or not paid at all. The underpaid salaries of women are treated as reciprocal exchange and patronage favours in the institutional form of *mehnat*. This form is often in-kind and rarely paid for by cash for the set material amount and size of the work on the cotton farms. Contrary to salary, *mehnat* payment is based on the personal relations of the farmers and their workers; in part, payment is affected by the inferior status of women and juniors. 'Aides' (junior female workers) are either paid less or work without any salary (*bemehnat*), although the latter applies to the majority of workers on the cotton farms. Reference to *elkheshi* and *qawm* identities commits workers to the practice of *mehnat* as the reciprocal and patronage support of workers by their *elkheshi* or *qawm* farmers. While junior women constitute the majority of the cotton workers, it is necessary to generate their commitment by interpreting their work as part of their family (household-keeping) status.

Farmers and mahalla mediators refer to 'family honour' and *qawm* identity to sustain the institutions of *agat*, *hashar* and *norma* for the effective organisation of cotton-growing and harvesting. These institutions set quotas for individual families for which they grow and harvest raw cotton. As mentioned already, *agat* is a physical unit of cotton field per individual family. *Norma* is a cotton harvest quota for families, schools and state departments. *Hashar* is the mobilisation of labour for cotton harvesting. Mediators interpret the practices of *agat* and *norma* as the commitment of individual families to their 'family honour' and to their *mahalli* village and Islamic identities. *Hashar*, which is initiated by mahalla mediators (including religious notables, family elders and state veterans), is practiced as a sacred attribute of *mahalli* village and Islamic identities.

COMPARATIVE AND GENERAL CONCLUSIONS

This chapter is divided into two subchapters which draw comparative and general conclusions. In subchapter one, I compare the role collective identities play in enforcing local governance institutions in two different contexts. Subchapter two generalises the interplay between the collective identities of local people and the core institutional aspects of local governance in the region of southern Khatlon. Furthermore, the second subchapter highlights the relevance of my study to other regions of post-Soviet Tajikistan and other Central Asian countries.

Comparative conclusions

This study has traced local governance processes in the diverse southern Khatlon region. The comprehensive analysis of these processes in two villages in the region revealed three mainstream aspects of local governance, namely: (1) the political adaptation of mediation and development structures, (2) the legitimation of political and economic rights and claims and (3) the stabilisation of socio-political and economic relations. In the following sections I discuss the comparative value of each of these aspects.

Political adaptation of mediatory and development structures

The village studies in this thesis suggest that political structures in subsistence-based and cotton-growing communities are established differently in order to perform different functions. In the cotton-growing community of Sayyod village, the mahalla is an inclusive – albeit hierarchical – representation structure which serves to enforce rule over cotton farms. Therefore, socio-political and economic stabilisation is the central function of the mahalla in the cotton industry. This function is also important due to scarce land resources, the heterogeneous composition of ethnic groups and the large size of the population in this context. Collective identities serve as integrative means which thus enforce indigenous (family, descent and neighbourhood) networks and represent them in the mahalla.

In the subsistence-based community of Devdor village we see quite the opposite picture: elites dominate the mahalla and other important rural organisations. They refer to *qawmdori*, which is both a shared and fragmented concept on village, kinship and religious identities, to legitimise their dominance and to confront the rights and claims of others. Reference to the endangered boundaries of *qawmdori* highlights their indigenous image as the only persons allowed to secure 'peace' ('*tinji*'), possess 'wealth' ('*davlat*') and distribute 'justice' ('*insof*') in the village.

In such a context of struggle between legitimation and contestation in this subsistence-based community, the other main aspect of local governance is related to the adaptation of development programmes and structures of the international community. DVO leaders rely on the mediation of mahalla authorities to operate development activities and resources, including development grants, microcredit programmes and membership fees. Also, the DVO has been integrated and adapted into the patron-client and male-dominated network of 'active' members. This network is important in shaping the hierarchical representation and participation of members in the distribution of development programmes. In particular, the network constrains the representation and participation of female and junior members. To shape and enforce this network, 'active' members categorise women and especially their opponents through the norms and discourses of exclusion and by referring to collective identity to discredit and thus reject the claims of opponents as far as 'accountability' is concerned, that is, in order to secure their privileged inclusion in development programmes.

Legitimation of political and economic rights and claims

Actors make use of their 'administrative' rights, personal ties, inheritance rights and practices of 'common wellbeing' to legitimise their political and economic privileges. The 'administrative' rights of kolkhozi elites are relevant to many places in the region. Elites have benefited from these informal practices since Soviet Union rule and thereby legitimise their privileged access to public positions and resources. This privileged access is enforced by kinship and patron-client relations with state elites. At the same time, subject people accept and praise such personal relations as a necessary condition for political and economic privileges.

However, especially in these subsistence economies, some people contest the privileged rights of kolkhozi elites. To prevent and reduce contestations, elites use cooptation and the bureaucratic and military means of the state. While these means are not often sufficient and effective, mahalla mediators refer to *qawmdori*, i.e. the shared concept of village and Islamic identities, to commit subject people to concessions. For this purpose, they refer frequently to the indigenous normative concepts of 'justice' ('*insof*') and 'peace' ('*tinji*'). *Qawmdori* also serves to legitimise the privileged rights of elites as their 'God-given' or inherited rights due to their religious superiority, as the indigenous concept of '*davlat*' (literally 'wealth' and 'state') suggests. These norms also demonstrate the divine authority of powerful men to control 'dangerous' and unpredictable human nature as well as the material world.

In the cotton economy, underpreviliged people occasionally contest the privileged rights of powerful men who are the *mahalli* clients of kolkhozi elites. This distinction occurs because most of the land and other agricultural resources are assigned to the cotton sector. In this case, collective identities and norms perform integrative functions, as cotton elites and mediators use them to integrate and enforce cotton-growing networks or farms. Kinship (*elkheshi* and *qawm*) and village identities are sought to shape these networks and commit subject workers, especially women and juniors, to intensive but underpaid work. Any form of contestation is interpreted as 'infidel' behaviour, which is against kinship and religious relations and norms. The way that the cotton farms are interpreted as the symbolic goods of *elkheshi* or *qawm* identities legitimises the privileged rights of the farmers.

Inheritance is another effective claim and practice, so actors legitimise their rights in both subsistence and cotton economies. The main distinction, however, is the role and function of the collective identities the actors refer to for this purpose: in Devdor village, they reflect contested boundaries, while in Sayyod village, they shape the actors' sacred boundaries of inheritance claims and rights. In the cotton economy, actors reinvent the histories of their ancestors, descent groups, villages, personal lives and deeds. Through the increasing prevalence of religious ceremonies, such as *khatm*, they seek public acknowledgment of their inherited sacred properties, both material and symbolic. In the subsistence communities of Shuroobod district, many families have inherited the right to land and other agricultural resources. However, we have observed increasing contestations due to the unequal distribution of these resources and due to the lack of state interest in – and thus a monopoly of – economic production.

In the subsistence economy, the principles of kinship networking and support (defined as '*qabila*') and personal (kinship and patron-client) favours given by state elites and religious notables (captured by the concept of '*odam*') legitimise the privileged – although contested – rights of elites. In this light, the discourse of *qawmiyat* reminds villagers about their inevitable limitations and defeat because of their kinship and bureaucratic dependency on the elites. Subject people accept the privileged rights of elites, first of all, due to their fear that otherwise they would spoil any personal relations forged through kinship networks and state bureaucratic offices. While such objective and psychological dependencies are not always effective, elites claim their inheritance rights and refer to their right to 'their homeland' as a privilege to take over strategic political organisations and economic resources of the village. They refer to the descent origins of their opponents to reproach their claims, formal appeals (*ariza*) to state and court authorities as a betrayal of 'village secrets' and to 'peace among the kin'.

In the cotton economy, inherited claims and rights are less contested, while they reflect the sacred relations of properties to their possessors. To proclaim and legitimise these relations, possessors refer to their superior descent and Islamic (such as Shaykh or Sayyid) origins and to their exclusive connection with the holy saints. For this purpose, they talk about sacred experiences, including dreams and spiritual intercessions with holy souls and saints. They also restore their genealogical books (*shajaranoma*) and organise religious initiation ceremonies (*khatm*). Consequently, they claim ancestral and spiritual privileges for sacred sites and related resources, as well as over mundane positions, professions and agricultural properties.

In both the subsistence-based and cotton-growing communities, the practices of 'common wellbeing' serve to increase and legitimise the symbolic and actual power of elites. The indigenous and modified practices of 'collective *hashar*' and *khayriya* increase their religious reputation. Primarily, these practices are devoted to the 'wellbeing' of sacred and certain public assets, such as cemeteries, mosques, shrines, schools, roads and bridges. Mahalla mediators commit subject people to these practices by reference to *qawmdori*, that is, shared village, kinship and religious identities. They also use these practices to categorise and disempower elites' opponents, i.e. those who do not obey rules or contribute to the 'common wellbeing' of the village.

Stabilisation of socio-political and economic relations

Two general types of institutional practices have been observed which stabilise political and economic relations and structures, namely the institutions of a) resource redistribution and b) dispute settlement.

The institutions of resource redistributions are reciprocal practices, modified reciprocal practices (such as *sadaqa*) and adapted external (state and development) schemes. Mahalla and state authorities enforce the reciprocal practices of family and neighbourhood networks to stabilise contested hierarchical structures and unequal rights. The reciprocal practices of family networks include shared households, joint economic activities, shared patrimonial properties and resources, patrimonial inheritance, mutual support during economic hardship, family *hashar*, privileged public services, parental commitment to children, old-age care (insurance) for parents, the support of widowed and disabled family members and the redistribution of remittances.

Again, in both the subsistence-based and cotton-growing communities, these practices are not stable and self-evident per se. Rather, family elders, mahalla mediators and state functionaries refer to 'family honour', kinship and Islamic identities to commit especially male juniors to such practices. In the case of Sayyod village, for example, reference to family (*elkheshi*) identity highlights the moral norms of 'family integrity' and 'good brotherhood'. Islamic identity shapes the prayer communities of reciprocal networks around *choykhonas*. *Hashar*, everyday mutual support, public services, mutual support during labour migration and especially support of poor co-members are the honourable attributes of the kinship and Islamic identities of extended families and neighbours. These identities also commit family members to hierarchical norms and relations among each other and ostracise those who do not obey them. Family elders and mahalla mediators organise and use reinitiation ceremonies (such as *khatm*) to enforce solidarity among family members.

Besides indigenous reciprocal practices and networks, local and state authorities modify reciprocal practices, extend support networks and adapt external (state and development) schemes and resources to stabilise socio-political and economic relations and structures. They modify the religious institutions of *sadaqa*, *khayriya*, *zakot* and *ushr* to provide support for poor families who are not involved in family or neighbourhood networks. Regular religious and other important ceremonies, such as funerals, weddings, religious and seasonal feasts, serve to highlight collective identities and norms for this purpose. These modified practices are used especially to prevent poor families' struggling with privileged families and making complaints through state and court structures.

Mahalla and state authorities also redistribute external (state and development) support schemes to enforce existing political and economic structures and relations. These schemes include the state 'welfare' schemes of pensions, poverty allowances, *lgot* (exemption from some taxes) and the aid and development programmes of international agencies. These practices are devoted to indebting the recipient families of these schemes to the elites.

Again, in both the subsistence and cotton economies, 'on-site' or indigenous means of dispute settlement are important in stabilising contested socio-political and economic relations. These means include collective norms and the honour of 'stability' or 'peace' ('*tinji*'), the mediatory role of family elders and mahalla authorities, exclusion from family and religious networks and services, religious institutions of betrothal and divorce and the practices of correction and surveillance by the mosque and school. These norms and practices enforce the hierarchical patterns of political relations between elites and subject people, between seniors and juniors and between men and women. While these means of hierarchical differentiation are not stable as such, mahalla mediators refer to kinship and Islamic identities to enforce them.

In the cotton economy, the main concern is preventing and resolving disputes which might endanger the integrity of cotton farms based on kinship and neighbourhood networks. Hence, reference to kinship and other collective identities seeks to commit subject people to 'on-site' means of reconciliation. These identities commit disputants to 'peace' in their kinship and neighbourhood networks and discredit non-traditional means, such as court deals. If 'on-site' means do not resolve these disputes, mahalla mediators and local state authorities use the 'delegation' mechanism, which involves gathering together family elders, mahalla mediators and local state functionaries who visit the disputants to urge them to reconcile their differences and offer forgiveness 'for the sake of kinship relations'. To safeguard the solidarity of cotton working teams, the delegation minimises the use of other means, including state court and military intervention. Only occasionally will the delegation organise 'public' and state courts to punish and stigmatise cases which endanger the core pillars of stability, especially those which damage elites' properties and undermine family and neighbourhood relations.

In the subsistence economy, the 'on-site' measures of dispute settlement, especially overwhelming references to collective norms and identities, are used less to enforce indigenous networks but are more concerned with the highly differentiated and contested political and economic rights of villagers. To enforce these internal mechanisms, elites and mahalla mediators manipulate the discourse of 'peace' and discredit court deals. Unlike the cotton economy, here the 'on-site' means of dispute settlement are not effective enough. Rather, elites and their state allies use a variety of other mechanisms, including cooptation, bureaucratic and military procedures, threats and punishments to reduce disputes.

General conclusions: The interplay between collective identities and local governance institutions

This study has defined local governance as the institutional arrangements of power relations at the primary level of human interactions. The process involves different actors who represent family and religious networks and state and international agencies. They interact through historically and culturally embedded institutions or externalised socio-cognitive constructs. The theoretical framework in this study has sought to determine the interplay between local governance institutions and the collective identities of local people. Among other socio-cognitive constructs, particular collective identities (such as Islam and kinship) serve to perpetuate these institutions.

To understand the role of collective identities as cognitive boundaries of individuals, I reflected on their perceptions, habitus, collective norms and indigenous discourses required to employ the classical methods of anthropological research, including participant observation and semi-structured interviews in an informal environment. Moreover, I compared my data and cases to other studies in Central Asia on the role of concepts such as 'sotsium' or 'etnos' (Idiev 2006; Nourzhanov 2005; Olimova 2000), 'regionalism' (Tadjbakhsh 2008; Roy 1997, 2000), 'clan identity' (Collins 2002, 2003; De Martino 2004; Abdullaev 2004; Freizer 2004) and 'communal identity' (Sievers 2002; Freizer 2004; Abdullaev 2004; Radnitz 2005). According to these concepts, certain institutions and networks reflect distinctive boundaries of certain ethnic or other local groups.

In contrast, my research follows another avenue, as I argue that different groups share similar, overlapping or shared institutional orders and networks of political and economic organisation. Not in favour of the mentioned concepts, different actors shape personal (such as kinship and patron-client) networks regardless of their affiliations in ethnic or local communities and in state or indigenous structures. These patron-client networks are not limited to separate clans or kinship groups but rather integrate various actors of different origins through local, religious, state and development structures at various levels. A primary administrative unit, for example a village community, is not an encapsulated and isolated world set apart from other 'communities' or 'the state'. Rather, my framework defines 'community' and 'the state' as embedded in the personal network of different actors, including state elites, development brokers, religious notables and family elders.

The cases often show that political actors invest heavily in material and immaterial resources, such as political and economic incentives, military pressure and collective norms and identities, in order to sustain contested power structures. Individual actors frequently refer to collective identities to preserve their domination through post-Soviet and post-civil war shifts and transformations, including the stabilisation of political structures, the privatisation and shareholding of socialist properties and the integration of international development programmes. Contestations over the distribution of positions and resources and demands for the stability of political and economic relations characterise local-level politics. In this context, collective identities serve to achieve certain political and economic goals, or the principal aspects of local governance, which I classify and generalise as follows:

1) Commitment of people to the patron-client institutions of power relations,
2) Legitimation of elite-dominated and inherited property rights and
3) Stabilisation of contested socio-political situations.

Patron-client institutions of power relations

Local and state elites, religious notables and development brokers shape patron-client networks which integrate and adapt district government departments, jamoats, *dehqan* farms, mahalla committees and development organisations. Such crosscutting networks of different actors and institutions also reflect the cognitive patterns of local people, who perceive state and development offices and resources as the private and at the same time patronage means of elites. Similar 'syncratic' networks and the "'polycephaly' of local political arenas" and actors have also been observed by some scholars in the case of other regions of Tajikistan (Idiev 2006; Matveeva 2009) and other developing countries (e.g. in African Benin by Bierschenk and de Sardan 2003).

Elites and their local mediators, including family elders and religious notables, refer to collective identities and norms to enforce such political structures. In part, they adapt the political functions and institutions of state, religious and development organisations and programmes, while mosques serve as settings in which to ritualise participatory (PRA) exercises and thereby transform these intensively integrated development structures into 'community' of male worshipers. Reference to kinship and Islam seeks to justify the exclusive competency of elites in managing political structures and reflects the belief system of local people that elites have exclusive competency to maintain 'peace' (*tinji*) and to distribute 'justice' (*insof*). Hence, reference to *qawmdori* invokes the concerns of elites and subject people about the incompetent leadership of others, which in turn gives rise to injustice and disputes. Due to such concerns, representatives of district government and the MSDSP office in Shuroobod district pursue the 'experience of Mu'minobod' in integrating development structures and programmes into the patron-client networks of elites in order to prevent the problems of 'two-fold power' and 'three-fold power' or the struggle of powerful actors to dominate political structures.

In successful cases, elites also refer to Islam to categorise integrated international development actors and structures as 'foreigners'. Such categorisation hints at their non-Muslim and religiously stigmatised ('Shia',

'Ismaili' or 'infidel') identities. As such, elites limit the scope of development action: 'foreigners' or international organisations and their local development structures and programmes are acceptable, but only if the elites or their clients represent them or mediate their activities. The unrelated local representatives of international agencies are propagated as 'betrayers' and 'servants of the foreigners'. Thus, elites increasingly represent development structures such as the Jamoat Resource Centre (JRC), the Local Development Committee (the LDC) and the Village Organisation (VO) in Mu'minobod, Shuroobod and Shahritus districts. They also shape the prioritised aspects of development activities and thereby define and limit the social and political capacities of these structures. Stevens (2005) observes a similar situation in Uzbekistan, where development agencies are welcomed principally due to their economic resources and non-political activities. Similar to other countries and contexts (e.g. Bierschenk et al. 2002), therefore, development aid mainly empowers development brokers and their local clients and thus feeds and endures repressive power structures (Williams 2004).

Elite-dominated and inherited property rights

Studies and reports (e.g. Nissen 2004; International Crisis Group 2005) assert the unequal distribution of land and other strategic resources in the agricultural sector, notwithstanding the scarcity of these resources (Government of Tajikistan 2002a; Government of Tajikistan 2002b) and the shareholding norms of the state (Dehqan Farm 2002; Duncan 2000). The 'administrative' or privileged access of elites to important natural and public resources, as observed in other post-socialist countries (Verdery 2004), is relevant to many places in the study region, including the villages where I conducted in-depth studies. They are informal practices or institutions which legitimise the privileged access of elites to public positions and resources. Their personal relations with family elders, religious notables, state functionaries and development brokers maintain and enforce their privileged access.

To prevent and reduce increasing contestations over privileges, elites and their local and state mediators use patronage favours and bureaucratic or military means, and especially refer to collective norms and identities to reward, co-opt and punish opponents. They refer to Islam to enhance their reputation, to seek 'God-given' rights and thereby to legitimise their privileged access. Any reference to Islamic identity and *qawmdori* serves to commit local people to the patron-client norms of the unequal distribution of opportunities and resources, such as 'personal ties' ('*odami*'), 'generosity' or cliental favour ('*odamgari*') and 'God-given' or inherited rights ('*davlat*'). These norms and their sacred sources justify the divine authority of elites to control 'dangerous' human nature and the material world. Reference to *qawmdori* or the shared kinship, village and religious identity of villagers reflects local people's desire for the stability of patron-client relations with elites in order to benefit from bureaucratic services and patronage favours. Furthermore, reference to *qawmdori* interprets contestation over the privileged rights of elites as the rupturing of kinship ties and the distortion of Islamic and village honour, which many people avoid.

The claims and practices of inheritance legitimise privileged access to certain positions, professions and properties. In both the subsistence and cotton economies, elites and other privileged people restore their genealogical books (*shajaranoma*), celebrate the initiation ceremony of *khatm* and fulfill or pretend to fulfill appropriate Islamic practices, such as five-time prayers and pilgrimages (Hajj and visiting local shrines). They also refer to their superior descent (e.g. Sayyid and Shaykh) origins and personal or family ties with and blessing from saints and souls. Although even old men cannot remember historical events that have occurred during their lifetime, claimants reinvent the stories and histories of their villages and descent origins. In the same villages, I witnessed various and contradictory stories and histories relating to individuals, descent groups and villages. These stories and histories do not necessarily draw distinctive boundaries between ethnic or social groups, as some scholars argue (e.g. Idiev 2006); rather, they use these strategies to claim for and thereby to legitimise their ancestral and spiritual privileges over both sacred and mundane positions, professions and properties.

Stabilisation of contested socio-political situations

In rural settlements of southern Khatlon, the mahalla mediates to stabilise contested political and economic relations. Elites and their mediators (such as religious notables and family elders or *oqsaqols*) lead this rural organisation. State laws on *Tanzim* (2007), Local Self-Governance (2008) and the Freedom of Conscience and Religious Associations (1994, 2009) seek to formalise the mahalla as a mediatory structure of religious, state and other actors. Sievers (2002) also observes the similar representation and mediation role of a mahalla in Uzbekistan, especially in the case of the *oqsaqol*, who "… is an older male in the *mahalla* selected by consensus from his generational cohort" (Sievers 2002: 100). Thus, we observe the increasing role of mediation structures and mediators, especially the mahalla, across post-Soviet Central Asia.

We also observe the increasing number of religious practices and ceremonies (such as public prayer, funerals, weddings and other feasts) which serve to enforce and sanctify the mediation role of mahalla leaders. Idiev (2006) and Sievers (2002) also stress such a role of religious ceremonies achieved through the mahalla in Tajikistan and Uzbekistan. Mosques reproduce and spread socially important information and experiences of the mediators. The way in which the people fear that saints and mullahs can call upon souls and exclude disloyal men from religious communities, ceremonies and services subjugates them to the will of the latter. Steinberger (2003), Sagdeev (2000) and Malashenko (2000) also underline such a legitimation role of Islam throughout Central Asian countries. At all levels of political life former communist elites go to Hajj, swear on the Koran and pursue a just religious life in order to rehabilitate their religious image and reputation.

At the local level, the mahalla is a central institution employed to maintain socio-political stability due to the increasing uncertainties of social life and to contestations over the unequal distribution of resources. In the study region, mahalla mediators often use two general types of institutional practices to stabilise political and economic relations, namely a) the reciprocal practices of resource redistribution and b) 'on-site' means of dispute settlement.

The mobilisation and redistribution of local and external (including state and development) resources serve to stabilise socio-political and economic relations. The provision of these resources maintains the core pillars of stability in the local context, including the reciprocal practices of individual families, the inclusion of 'unsafe' poor people in support networks and the 'wellbeing' of religious and other important assets. Sievers (2002) observes and defines some of these functions used by families and the mahalla in Uzbekistan as 'insurance mechanisms'.

To ensure stability in the face of increasing political and economic inequality, elites and their mediators sustain the reciprocal practices of extended families, which include joint agricultural work, support during ceremonies and economic hardship, old-age care, the inheritance of goods and professions and the everyday exchange of food. Reference to 'family honour' and Islamic identity commits family members to reciprocal exchanges. In part, religious ceremonies (such as *khatm*) strengthen the family commitments of labour migrants and check their trustfulness and religious fidelity by mobilising financial resources for the wellbeing of family, *qawm* and religious circles.

Mahalla mediators also 'take care' of poor people who, due to their desperate situation, may endanger the socio-political order. Mediators use religious circles (mosques and *choykhonas*) and ceremonies (funerals and feasts) to involve the poor in the reciprocal networks of neighbourhoods and farms. Among them, religious notables refer to *qawmdori* or the shared village, kinship and Islamic identities of village inhabitants, to modify religious practices such as *sadaqa*, *khayr*, *ushr* and *zakot*. The adopted Law on *Tanzim* (2007) integrates state and religious authorities in order to modify these indigenous support networks and practices.

Practices of 'common wellbeing', which serve to improve the political and economic power of elites, are primarily devoted to the 'wellbeing' of sacred and public assets, such as cemeteries, mosques, shrines, schools, irrigation infrastructure, roads and bridges. In fact, 'common wellbeing' is a discourse which actually serves to improve the mediation role and religious reputation of elites and their local clients. For this purpose, mahalla mediators modify the reciprocal practices of the collective mobilisation of labour and other forms of collective resources (*hashar*) and individual donations (*khayriya*). In addition, mediators refer to the kinship and religious identities of local people to commit them to these modified practices.

In the face of increasing contestation over the distribution of political and economic resources, elites use 'on-site' measures of dispute settlement. This function historically shaped mahallas throughout Central Asia and still persists in Tajikistan and Uzbekistan (Idiev 2006; Sievers 2002). Elites and their mahalla mediators refer to kinship, village and religious ties and honour to commit disputants to peace and hierarchical and differentiated relations, while mediators interpret disputes as 'village secrets' that should not be divulged to 'strangers'. Such reference to village and kinship identities discredits and thus excludes court deals as the distorted behaviour of disputants. Consequently, as the NGO 'Arbitrazh' registers in Shahritus and other districts of the Qabodiyon oasis as well as in some other regions of the country, only minor parts of court appeals deal with disputes over property rights in the agricultural sector (Arbitrazh 2007). In the cases of Tajikistan and Uzbekistan, Collins (2003) and Sievers (2002) explain court avoidance due to the 'community solidarity' or 'clan identity' of the subject people. However, thorough analysis shows the reason both in mistrust of courts and other state structures (Falkingham 2000; Noori 2006) and especially in reciprocal and patron-client patterns of dispute settlement.

Such indigenous means of dispute settlement have been observed in other parts of the country (Idiev 2006; Heathershaw 2007; Matveeva 2009) and around the world. Scholars have observed such means as 'internal *mahalla* exile' in Uzbekistan (Sievers 2002) and 'stalemate' in Indonesian communities (Barron et al. 2004). Idiev (2006) mentions the role of the mahalla in the central region of Tajikistan, which enforces hierarchical family relations to commit family members to peace and integrity. This scholar, however, talks mainly about the 'unconflictive structure of relations between people'. Rather, the often used discourse of '*tinji*' (stability) reminds local people about threats and dangers, such as the disruption of kinship and cliental ties, civil war, epidemic diseases and natural disasters, if they do not obey the current conditions.

This thesis has discussed the role collective identities and related norms, patterns and discourses play in shaping the institutional order in several important aspects of local governance. The cases from local-level political and economic relations cast doubt on the prevailing understanding that local people take institutional principles, practices and orders for granted. Due to the increasing unequal distribution of political positions and economic resources, they have to refer frequently to their collective identities to rearrange institutional orders in the aspects of (1) power structures, (2) property rights and (3) socio-political stability. Hence, collective identities are not stable and invariant but are instead individually and contextually constructed to constantly justify and modify certain institutions or institutional orders. The research highlights that the link between identities and institutions is a result of the socio-cognitive world of the people, which includes norms, values and behavioural patterns and discourses. While collective identities express the cognitive sphere of this world, institutions represent the externalised materialisation of this internal sphere. To commit people to certain institutions or an institutional order, relevant cognitive and institutional dimensions are interpreted as immediate attributes of their collective (religious, kinship, ethnic and so on) identities. Attempting to initiate institutional reform or change, which, for example, development agencies demand or expect, means dealing with the socio-cognitive frames and constructs of local people, a fact rarely realised but often desperately ignored.

BIBLIOGRAPHY

Abdullaev, Kamoludin (2004): Current Local Government Policy Situation in Tajikistan, in: Luigi De Martino (ed.): Tajikistan at a Crossroad: The Politics of Decentralization. Geneva: CIMERA Situation Report 4: 8-16

Agrawal, Arun and Elionor Ostrom (2001): Collective Action, Property Rights, and Decentralization in Resource Use in India and Nepal, in: Politics and Society 29 (4): 485-514

Akbarzadeh, Shahram (1996): Why Did Nationalism Fail in Tajikistan? In: Europa-Asia Studies 48 (7): 1105-1129

Akerman, Ella (2002): Power and Wealth in Central Asian Politics: Clan Structures versus Democratization, in: Conflict Studies Research Center. <http://www.csrs.ac.uk> (accessed February 3, 2003)

Akiner, Shirin (2001): Tajikistan: Disintegration of Reconciliation? (Central Asian and Caucasian Prospects). London: The Royal Institute of International Affairs

Appadurai, Arjun (2003): Sovereignty without Territoriality: Notes for a Postnational Geography, in: Setha M. Low and Denise Lawrence-Zuniga (eds.): The Anthropology of Space and Place. Oxford: Blackwell Publishing: 337-349

Arabov, Oumar (2004): A Note on Sufism in Tajikistan: What Does It Look Like, in: Central Asian Survey 23 (3-4): 345-347

Arbitrazh (2007): Nakhustkonfronsi millii hakamoni Tojikiston [The First National Conference of the Arbitration Judges of Tajikistan]. Dushanbe: The Public Fund of the Development of the Arbitration Courts and Advocacy Centers of "Arbitrazh" (in Tajik)

Ashmore, Richard D., Kay Deaux, and Tracy McLaughlin-Volpe (2004): An Organizing Framework for Collective Identity: Articulation and Significance of Multidimensionality, in: Psychological Bulletin 130 (1): 80-114

Atkin, Muriel (1997): Tajikistan: Reform, Reaction, and Civil War, in: Ian Bremmer and Ray Taras (eds.): New States, New Politics: Building the Post-Soviet Nations. New York: Cambridge University Press: 600-627

Atkin, Muriel (1999): The Survival of Islam in Soviet Tajikistan, in: Middle East Journal 43 (4): 604-618

Babajanian, Babken V. (2006): The Social Exclusion Framework and Poverty Reduction Strategy in Tajikistan, in: Central Asian Survey 25 (4): 403-418

Bachman, Reinhard (1998): Trust – Conceptual Aspect of a Complex Phenomenon, in: Christel Lane and Reinhard Bachman (eds.): Trust Within and Between Organizations. Oxford: Oxford University Press: 298-322

Banfield, Edward C. (1958): The Moral Basis of Backward Society. New York: Free Press of Glencoe

Barnard, Alan and Jonathan Spencer (2006): Encyclopedia of Social and Cultural Anthropology. London: Routledge

Barron, Patrick, Claire Q. Smith and Michael Woolcock (2004): Understanding Local Level Conflict in Developing Countries. Theory, Evidence and Implications from Indonesia. World Bank: Social Development Papers, Conflict Prevention and Reconstruction, Paper No 19

Barth, Fredrik (1969a): Introduction, in: Fredrik Barth (ed.): Ethnic Groups and Boundaries. The Social Organization of Culture Difference. Oslo: Oslo Universitetsforlaget: 1-39

Barth, Fredrik (1969b): Pathan Identity and Its Maintenance, in: Fredrik Barth (ed.): Ethnic Groups and Boundaries. The Social Organization of Culture Difference. Oslo: Oslo Universitetsforlaget: 117-134

Bartol'd, Vasiliy Vladimirovich (1965). K istorii orosheniya Turkestana [About the History of Irrigation of Turkestan], in: Sochineniya, Volume 3: 95-121 (in Russian)

Berger, Peter L. and Thomas Luckmann (1984 [1967]): The Social Construction of Reality. A Treatise in the Sociology of Knowledge. London: The Penguin Press, Reissued in Pelican Books

Bierschenk, Thomas and Jean-Pierre Olivier de Sardan (2003): Powers in the Village: Rural Benin between Democratisation and Decentralisation, in: Africa 73 (2): 145-173

Bierschenk, Thomas, Jean-Pierre Chauveau and Jean-Pierre Olivier de Sardan (2002): Local Development Brokers in Afrika. The Rise of a New Social Category. Johannes Gutenberg Universität, Institut für Ethnologie und Afrikastudien, Department of Anthropology and African Studies: Working Paper No 13

Bourdieu, Pierre (1984): Distinction: A Social Critique of the Judgement of Taste. London: Routledge

Bourdieu, Pierre (1989): Social Space and Symbolic Power, in: Sociological Theory 7 (1): 14-25

Bretton Woods Project (2002): Building with Science or Encouraging Debate? Part II World Bank Analysis Determines PRSP Policies <http://www.brettonwoodsproject.org/art.shtml?x=15847> (accessed December 14, 2006)

Brubaker, Rogers and Frederick Cooper (2000): Beyond "Identity," in: Theory and Society 29 (1): 1-47

Burde, Dana (2004): Weak State, Strong Community? Promoting Community Participation in Post-Conflict Countries, in: Current Issues in Comparative Education 6 (2): 73-87

Bylaw VO (2001): Ustav Kishlachnoy Organizatsii MSDSP (Programma pomotshi razvitiya obtshestv gornykh regionov) [Bylaw of the Village Organisation of the MSDSP (Mountainous Societies Development Support Programme)]. Khorog: the MSDSP (in Russian)

Chambers, Robert (1994): The Origins and Practice of Participatory Rural Appraisal, in: World Development 22 (7): 953-969

Chambers, Robert (2007): Poverty Research: Methodologies, Mindsets and Multidimensionality. University of Sussex Brighton, Institute of Development Studies: Working Paper No 293

Christophe, Barbara (2003): Bringing Culture Back into a Concept of Rationality: State-Society Relations and Conflict in Post-Socialist Transcaucasia, in: Jan Koehler and Christoph Zürcher (eds.): Potentials of Disorder. Manchester and New York: Manchester University Press: 193-207

Cohen, Anthony P. (1985): The Symbolic Construction of Community. New York: Tavistock Publications

Cohen, Anthony P. (1994): Self Consciousness. An Alternative Anthropology of Identity. New York: Routledge

Coleman, James S. (1988): Social Capital in the Creation of Human Capital, in: The American Journal of Sociology 94 (Supplement): 95-120

Collins, Kathleen (2002): Clans, Pacts, and Politics in Central Asia, in: Journal of Democracy 13 (3): 137-152

Collins, Kathleen (2003): The Political Role of Clans in Central Asia, in: Comparative Politics 35 (2): 171-190. < http://www.jstor.org/stable/4150150> (accessed December 15, 2009)

Conrad, Burkhard (2006): Informal Politics, in: Hamburg Review of Social Sciences 1 (3): 256-272

Constitution of Tajikistan (2003[1994]): Konstitutsiyai (Sarqonuni) Jumhurii Tojikiston [The Constitution of the Republic of Tajikistan]. Dushanbe (in Tajik)

Coser, Lewis A. (1956): The Functions of Social Conflict. New York: The Free Press

Dadmehr, Nasrin (2003): Tajikistan: Regionalism and Weakness, in: Robert I. Rotberg (ed.): State Failure and State Weakness in a Time of Terror. Washington: Brookings Institute Press: 245-264

Davis, Marilynne, Jonathan Dunn, Khursheda Nazirova (2003): Assessment of Intergovernmental Relations and Local Governance in the Republic of Tajikistan. Dushanbe: Urban Institute Report for USAID

Dehqan Farms (2002): Law of the Republic of Tajikistan 'On *Dehqan* (*Fermeri*) Farms'. Dushanbe: OSCE (No 48, published 2005)

De Martino, Luigi (2004): Tajikistan at a Crossroad: Contradictory Forces at the Heart of the Tajik Political System, in: Luigi De Martino (ed.): Tajikistan at a Crossroad: The Politics of Decentralization. Geneva: CIMERA Situation Report 4: 152-159

Denzau, Arthur T. and Douglass C. North (1993): Shared Mental Models: Ideologies and Institutions. http://129.3.20.41/eps/eh/papers/9309/9309003.pdf (accessed June 19, 2008)

DiMaggio, Paul J. (1998): The New Institutionalisms: Avenues of Collaboration, in: Journal of Institutional and Theoretical Economics 154 (4): 696-705

Donish, Ahmad (1967): Traktat Akhmada Donisha "Istoriya mangitskoy dinastii" [Treatise of Ahmad Donish "The History of Manghit Dynasty"]. Dushanbe: Donish (in Russian)

Douglas, Mary (1976): Purity and Danger: An Analysis of Concepts of Pollution and Taboo. London and Henley: Routledge and Kegan Paul

Dudoignon, Stephane A. (2004): From Ambivalence to Ambiguity? Some Paradigms of Policy Making in Tajikistan, in: Luigi De Martino (ed.): Tajikistan at a Crossroad: The Politics of Decentralization. Geneva: CIMERA Situation Report 4: 120-151

Duncan, Jennifer (2000): Agricultural Land Reform and Farm Reorganization in Tajikistan. Rural Development Institute Reports on Foreign Aid and Development: Report No 106. http://www.landesa.org/wp-content/uploads/2011/01/RDI_106.pdf (accessed October 26, 2011)

Edgar, Adrienne L. (2002): Review of Oliver Roy, The New Central Asia: The Creation of Nations and Paul Georg Geiss, Nationenwerdung in Mittelasien, in: Kritika: Explorations in Russian and Eurasian History 3 (1): 182-190

Eidheim, Harald (1969): When Ethnic Identity Is a Social Stigma, in: Fredrik Barth (ed.): Ethnic Groups and Boundaries. The Social Organization of Culture Difference. Oslo: Oslo Universitetsforlaget: 39-57

Evans-Pitchard, Edward E. (1940): The Nuer: A Description of the Modes of Livelihood and Political Institutions of a Nilotic People. Oxford: Clarendon

Falkingham, Jane (2000): Women and Gender Relations in Tajikistan. Manilla: Asian Development Bank Country Briefing Paper

Foucault, Michel (1991): Governmentality, in: Graham Burchell, Collin Gordon and Peter Miller (eds.): The Foucault Effect: Studies in Governmentality. Hemel Hempstead: Harvester Weatsheaf: 87-104

Francois, Monika and Inder Sud (2006): Promoting Stability and Development in Fragile and Failed States, in: Development Policy Review 24 (2): 141-160

Freizer, Sabine (2004): Tajikistan Local Self-Governance: A Potential Bridge between Government and Civil Society? In: Luigi De Martino (ed.): Tajikistan at a Crossroad: The Politics of Decentralization. Geneva: CIMERA Situation Report 4: 17-25

Gambetta, Diego (1988): Can We Trust? In: Diego Gambetta (ed.): Trust: Making and Breaking Cooperative Relations. Oxford: Blackwell: 213-237. http//www.sociology.ox.ac.uk/papers/gambette213-237.pdf (accessed August 7, 2006)

Geertz, Clifford (1972): Deep Play: Notes on the Balinese Cockfight, in: Daedalus: Myth, Symbol, and Culture 101 (1): 1-37. <http//www.jstor.org/stable20024056> (accessed August 12, 2009)

George, Alexander L. and Andrew Bennett (2005): Case Studies and Theory Development in the Social Sciences. Cambridge: MIT Press

Giddens, Anthony (1984): The Constitution of Society. Outline of the Theory of Structuration. Cambridge: Polity Press

Giddens, Anthony (1990): The Consequences of Modernity. Cambridge: Polity Press

Government of Tajikistan (2002a): Poverty Reduction Strategy Paper. Resolution No 666 of the Parliament (Majlisi Namoyandagon of Majlisi Oli) of the Republic of Tajikistan about Approval of Poverty Reduction Strategy Paper. Dushanbe (June 2002). <planipolis.iiep.unesco.org/.../Tajikistan/PRSP/Tajikistan%20PRSP%202002.pdf> (accessed January 13, 2010)

Government of Tajikistan (2002b): Postanovlenie Pravitel'stva Respubliki Tadzhikistan "O reorganizatsii sel'skokhozyaystvennykh predpriyatiy i organizatsiy na period 2002-2005 godu. Postanovlenie № 385 [Resolution of the Government of the Republic of Tajikistan "On Reorganization of the Agricultural Enterprises and Organization for the Period of 2002-2005. Resolution No 385"] (October 1, 2002) (in Russian)

Government of Tajikistan (2005): Poverty Reduction Strategy Paper: Second Progress Report of the Government of the Republic of Tajikistan. Dushanbe. <http://siteresources.worldbank.org/INTPRS1/Resources/Tajikistan_APR2-PRSP(June-2005).pdf> (accessed July 9, 2006)

Government of Tajikistan (2007): The Cotton Sector of Tajikistan. New Opportunities for the International Cotton Trade. At: http://siteresources.worldbank.org/INTTAJIKISTAN/Resources/MB_300407_E.pdf (accessed February 22, 2012), 58 pages

Government of Tajikistan (2011): Hukumati Jumhurii Tojikiston, Barnomai islohoti kishovarzii Jumhurii Tojikiston. Hujjati jam'basti [Government of the Republic of Tajikistan, Program of the Agricultural Reform of the Republic of Tajikistan. Concluding Document]. Dushanbe (April 15, 2001) (in Tajik)

Gretsky, Sergei (1995): Civil War in Tajikistan: Causes, Developments and Prospects for Peace, in: Roald Z. Sagdeev and Susan Eisenhower (eds.): Central Asia: Conflict, Resolution, and Change. Washington: The Center for Political and Strategic Studies. <http://www.cpss.org/casiabk/chap16.txt> (accessed August 24, 2002)

Gumilev, Lev N. (1967): O termine "Etnos," v: Doklady geograficheskogo obtshestva SSSR [On the Term of "Etnos," in: The Reports of the Geographical Society of USSR]. Issue 3: 3-17 (in Russian)

Hardin, Garrett (1968): The Tragedy of Commons, in: Science 162 (3859): 1243-1248

Hardin, Russell (1995): One for All. The Logic of Group Conflict. Princeton: Princeton University Press

Harriss, John (2002): On Trust, and Trust in Indian Business: Ethnographic Explorations. London: London School of Economics and Political Science, Working Paper Series of Development Studies Institute: Paper No 02-35

Heathershaw, John D. (2005): The Paradox of Peacebuilding: Peril, Promise, and Small Arms in Tajikistan, in: Central Asian Survey 24 (1): 21-38

Heathershaw, John D. (2007): Peace as Complex Legitimacy: Politics, Space and Discourse in Tajikistan's Peacebuilding Process, 2000-2005 (PhD Thesis). London: University of London, School of Economics and Political Science

Heathershaw, John D. and Edmund Herzig (2011): Introduction: The Sources of Statehood in Tajikistan, in: Central Asian Survey 30 (1): 5-19

Hogg, Michael A., Deborah J. Terry and Katherine M. White (1995): A Tale of Two Theories: A Critical Comparison of Identity Theory with Social Identity Theory, in: Social Psychology Quarterly 58 (4): 255-269

Hogg, Michael A., Dominic Abrams, Sabine Otten and Steve Hinkle (2004): The Social Identity Perspective. Intergroup Relations, Self-Conception, and Small Groups, in: Small Group Research 35 (3): 246-276

Idiev, Khayriddin U. (2003): Transformiruyutsheesya tadzhikskoe obtshestvo [Tajik Society in Transition]. Dushanbe: Irfon (in Russian)

Idiev, Khayriddin U. (2006): Traditsii i novatsii v kontekste izmeneniya obtshestvennoy zhizni sovremennogo Tadzhikistana [Traditions and Innovations in the Context of Social Change in the Contemporary Tajikistan]. Dushanbe: Irfon (in Russian)

International Crisis Group (2005): The Curse of Cotton: Central Asia's Destructive Monoculture, in: Crisis Group Asia Report 93 (February 28, 2005)

International Organization for Migration (2011): Message from the Chief of Mission. http://www.iom.tj/ (accessed August 22, 2011)

Jenkins, Richard (2005): Social Identity. London and New York: Routledge

Juetting, Johannes (2003): Institutions and Development: A Critical Review. OECD Development Centre Research Programme on Social Institutions and Dialogue: Working Paper No 210. <http://www.oecd.org/document/3/0,3746,en_2649_201185_1837187_1_1_1_1,00.html> (accessed May 21, 2011)

Knight, Jack (1992): Institutions and Social Conflict. Cambridge: Cambridge University Press

Koehler, Jan and Christoph Zürcher (2003): Institutions and the Organization of Stability and Violence, in: Jan Koehler and Christoph Zürcher (eds.): Potentials of Disorder: Explaining Violence in the Caucasus and in the Balkan. Manchester and New York: Manchester University Press: 243-265

Kulchik, Yuriy, Andrey Fadin and Victor Sergeev (1996): Central Asia after the Empire. Chicago and London: Pluto Press

Kuper, Hilda (2003): The Language of Sites in the Politics of Space, in: Setha M. Low and Denise Lawrence-Zuniga (eds.): The Anthropology of Space and Place, Oxford: Blackwell Publishing: 247-263

Law on Local Self-Governance (2007[1994]): Qonuni Jumhurii Tojikiston "Dar borai maqomoti khudidorai shahrak va deha," № 1094 [Law of the Republic of Tajikistan "On the Self-Governance Authorities of Towns and Villages," No 1094]. Dushanbe: Bokhtar. (in Tajik)

Law on Local Self-Governance (2008): Zakon Respubliki Tadzhikistan "Ob organakh obtshestvennoy samodeytel'nosti," № 347 [Law of the Republic of Tajikistan "On Local Self-Governance Authorities," No 347]. Dushanbe (in Russian)

Law on Religion (1990): Qonuni Jumhurii Tojikiston "Dar borai ozodii vijdon va tashkilothoi dini." Vedomosthoi Soveti Olii RSS Tojikiston, № 24, moddai 419, № 194 [Law of the Republic of Tajikistan "On the Freedom of Conscience and Religious Associations." Minutes of the Supreme Soviet of Tajik SSR, No 24, Article 419, No 194]. Dushanbe (in Tajik)

Law on Religion (1994): Qarori Shuroi Olii Jumhurii Tojikiston "Oidi tartibi ba amal jori namudani Qonuni Jumhurii Tojikiston "Dar khususi darovardani taghyiru ilovaho ba Qonuni Jumhurii Tojikiston "Dar borai ozodii vijdon va tashkilothoi dini." Akhbori Shuroi Olii Jumhurii Tojikiston: № 23-24, moddai 453, 1994, № 1097 [Decree of the Supreme Soviet of the Republic of Tajikistan "On Realization of the Law of the Republic of Tajikistan "On

Changes and Amendments to the Law of the Republic of Tajikistan "On the Freedom of Conscience and Religious Associations"." News of the Supreme Soviet of the Republic of Tajikistan, Issues 23-24, Article 453, 1994, No 1097]. Dushanbe (in Tajik)

Law on Religion (2009): Qarori Majlisi Namoyandagoni Majlisi Olii Jumhurii Tojikiston "Oid ba qabul namudani Qonuni Jumhurii Tojikiston "Dar borai ozodii vijdon va ittihodiyahoi dini." Akhbori Majlisi Olii Jumhurii Tojikiston, № 3, moddai 1400 [Decree of the Lower Chamber of the Supreme Majlis of the Republic of Tajikistan "On the Adoption of the Law of the Republic of Tajikistan "On the Freedom of Conscience and Religious Associations"." News of the Supreme Majlis of the Republic of Tajikistan, No 3, Article 1400]. Dushanbe (in Tajik)

Law on *Tanzim* (2007): Qonuni Jumhurii Tojikiston "Dar borai tanzimi an'ana va jashnu marosimho dar Jumhurii Tojikiston" [Law of the Republic of Tajikistan "On Re-ordering Traditions, Celebrations and Customs in the Republic of Tajikistan"], Jumhuriyat: 68 (21275) (June 9, 2007): 1-3 (in Tajik)

Logofet', Dmitriy N. (1909): Strana bezpraviya. Bukharskoe khanstvo i ego sovremennoe sostoyanie [The Country without Law. Bukhara Khanate and Its Current Situation]. Saint-Petersburg (in Russian)

Logofet', Dmitriy N. (1911): Bukharskoe khanstvo pod russkim protektoratorov (t. 2) [Bukhara Khanate under Russian Protection]. Saint-Petersburg: B. Berezovskiy (in Russian)

Lommitz, Larisa A. (1988): Informal Exchange Networks in Formal Systems: A Theoretical Model, in: American Anthropologist (New Series) 90 (1): 42-55

Low, Setha M. and Denise Lawrence-Zuniga (2003): Locating Culture, in: Setha M. Low and Denise Lawrence-Zuniga (eds.): The Anthropology of Space and Place. Oxford: Blackwell Publishing: 1-47

Low, Setha M. (2003): The Edge and the Center: Gated Communities and the Discourse of Urban Fear, in: Setha M. Low and Denise Lawrence-Zuniga (eds.): The Anthropology of Space and Place. Blackwell Publishing: 387-407

Luhmann, Thomas (1988): Familiarity, Confidence and Trust: Problems, and Alternatives, in: Diego Gambetta (ed.): Trust: Making and Breaking Cooperative Relations. Oxford: Blackwell

Luong, Pauline J. (2000): Sources of Institutional Continuity: The Soviet Legacy in Central Asia. Paper for Annual Meeting of the American Political Science Association (August 31 – September 2, 2000). Washington D.C. http://www.yale.edu/macmillan/ocvprogram/licep/2/luong/luong.pdf (accessed August 7, 2006)

Luong, Pauline J. (2002): Institutional Change and Political Continuity in Post-Soviet Central Asia: Power, Perceptions and Pacts. Cambridge: Cambridge University Press

Lutz, Georg and Wolf Linder (2004): Traditional Structures and Local Governance for Local Development. Berne: University of Berne, Institute of Political Science

Malashenko, Aleksei (2000): The Islamic Factor in Relations between Russia and Central Asia, in: Roald Sagdeev and Susan Eisenhower (eds.): Islam and Central Asia. An Enduring Legacy or an Evolving Threat? Washington: Center for Political and Strategic Studies: 155-169

Malinowski, Bronislaw (1944): A Scientific Theory of Culture and Other Essays. Chapel Hill: The University of North Carolina Press

Martin, Terry (2001): The Affirmative Action Empire: Nations and Nationalism in the Soviet Union, 1923-1939. Ithaca and London: Cornell University Press

Matveeva, Anna (2009): External Democracy Promotion in Post-Conflict Zones: Evidence from Case Studies. Tajikistan. Berlin: Freie Universität Berlin <http://www.polsoz.fu-berlin.de/polwiss/forschung/international/frieden/ib/projekte/democracypromotion/index.html> (accessed December 21, 2009)

Mehta, Lyla (1997): Social Difference and Water Resources Management: Insights from Kutch, India, in: Institute for Development Studies Bulletin 28 (4): 79-90

Mehta, Lyla, Melissa Leach, Peter Newell, Ian Scoones, K. Sivaramakrishnan and Sally-Anne Way (1999): Exploring Understandings of Institutions and Uncertainty: New Directions in Natural Resource Management. Brighton: University of Sussex: Institute for Development Studies Discussion Paper No 372. http://www.eldis.org/vfile/upload/1/document/0708/DOC7794.pdf (accessed November 12, 2008)

Mielke, Katja and Conrad Schetter (2007): Where Is the Village? Local Perceptions and Development Approaches in Kunduz Province, in: Asien 104: 71-87

Mielke, Katja, Conrad Schetter and Andreas Wilde (2011): Dimensions of Social Order: Empirical Fact, Analytical Framework and Boundary Concept. Bonn: ZEF Working Paper Series 78 (April 2011)

Mirzaev, K. M. (1954): Amlyakovaya forma feodal'noy zemel'noy sobstvennosti v Bukharskom Khanstve [The Amlak Form of Feudal Land Ownership in Bukhara Khanate]. Tashkent: Academy of Sciences of UzSSR (in Russian)

Misztal, Barbara A. (1996): Trust in Modern Societies. Cambridge: Polity Press

Monroe, Kristen (2003): How Identity and Perspective Constrain Moral Choice, in: International Political Science Review 24 (4): 405-425 <http://www.jstor.org/stable/1601630> (accessed November 11, 2009)

MSDSP (2002): MSDSP Strategy 2002-2006. Khorog: the MSDSP

Nadzhafova, Inna Aleksandrovna (1967): Perevod, predislovie i primechanie I. A. Nadzhafovoy, v: Akhmad Donish (1967): Traktat Akhmada Donisha "Istoriya mangitskoy dinastii" [Translation, Foreword and Notes of I. A. Nadzhafova, in: Ahmad Donish (1967): Treatise of Ahmad Donish "The History of Manghit Dynasty"]. Dushanbe: Donish (in Russian)

Nissen, Soren W. (2004): Tajikistan's Land Reform Programme: Sowing the Seeds of a Brighter Future, in: OSCE Magazine (July 2004) 1 (3): 4-12. http://www.ppl.nl/ebooks/files/3343_en.pdf (accessed November 15, 2008)

Niyazi, Aziz (1998): Tajikistan I: The Regional Dimension of Conflict, in: Michael Waller, Bruno Coppieters and Alexei Malashenko (eds.): Conflicting Loyalties and the State in Post-Soviet Russia and Eurasia. London: Frank Cass: 145-170

Noori, Neema (2006): Expanding State Authority, Cutting Back Local Services: Decentralization and Its Contradictions in Uzbekistan, in: Central Asian Survey (December) 25 (4): 533-549

North, Douglass C. (1990): Institutions, Institutional Change and Economic Performance. New York: Cambridge University Press

Nourzhanov, Kirill (2001): The Politics of History in Tajikistan: Reinventing the Samanids, in: Harvard Asia Quarterly,

<http://www.fas.Harvard.edu/~asiactr/haq/200101/0101a003.htm> (accessed September 30, 2002)

Nourzhanov, Kirill (2005): Saviours of the Nation or Robber Barons? Warlord Politics in Tajikistan, in: Central Asian Survey 24 (2): 109-130

Nugent, David (2004): Governing States, in: Joan Vincent and David Nugent (eds.): A Companion to the Anthropology of Politics. Oxford: Blackwell

Nygaard, David, Davlatyor Jumakhonov and Kris Hendrickx (2005): Seizing Opportunities to Promote Development and Improve Food Security in the Mountainous Regions of Central Asia, in: International Workshop on "Strategies for Development and Food Security in Mountainous Areas of Central Asia." Dushanbe: Aga Khan Foundation, INWENT and GTZ (June 6-10, 2005). www.akdn.org/publications/2005_akf_mountains_paper1_english.pdf (accessed July 2, 2006)

Olimova, Saodat (2004): Regionalism and Its Perception by Major Political and Social Powers of Tajikistan, in: Luigi De Martino (ed.): Tajikistan at a Crossroad: The Politics of Decentralization. Geneva: CIMERA Situation Report 4: 86-119

Orrnert, Anna (2006): Missing Pieces: An Overview of the Institutional Puzzle, in: Public Administration and Development 26 (5): 449-455 (Published online in Wiley InterScience www.interscience.wiley.com) (accessed November 22, 2006)

Ostrom, Elionor (2000): Private and Common Property Rights, in: Boudewijn Bouckaert and Gerrit De Geest (eds.): Encyclopaedia of Law and Economics, Vol. II Civil Law and Economics. Cheltenham: Edward Elgar: 332-379

Passaro, Joanne (1997): "You Can't Take the Subway to the Field!": "Village" Epistemologies in the Global Village, in: Akhil Gupta and James Ferguson (eds.): Anthropological Locations. Boundaries and Grounds of a Field Science. Berkeley, Los Angeles and London: University of California Press: 147-162

Pinzani, Alessandro (2003): The Contrabassist and the CEO: Moral Judgment and Collective Identity, in: Florianopolis 2 (2): 120-136

Polletta, Francesca and James M. Jasper (2001): Collective Identity and Social Movements, in: Annual Review of Sociology 27: 283-305.

http://www.jamesmjasper.org/files/collective_identity_2001.pdf (accessed November 28, 2006)

Powell, Walter W. and Pavel J. DiMaggio (1991): The New Institutionalism in Organisational Analysis. Chicago: University of Chicago Press

Putnam, Robert D (1993): Making Democracy Work. Civic Traditions in Modern Italy. Princeton, New Jersey: Princeton University Press (with Robert Leonardi and Raffaella Y. Nanetti)

Radnitz, Scott (2005): Networks, Localism and Mobilization in Aksy, Kyrgyzstan, in: Central Asian Survey 24 (4): 405-424

Rasanayagam, Johan (2002): Spheres of Communal Participation: Placing the State within Local Modes of Interaction in Rural Uzbekistan, in: Central Asia Survey 21 (1): 55-70

Roth, Guenther (1968): Personal Rulership, Patrimonialism, and Empire-building in the New States, in: World Politics. Princeton: Center of International Studies: 194-206

Roy, Oliver (1997): Is the Conflict in Tajikistan a Model for Conflicts Throughout Central Asia? In: Mohammad-Reza Djalili, Frederic Grare and Shirin Akiner (eds.): Tajikistan: The Trials of Independence. New York: St. Martin's Press

Roy, Oliver (1999): Kolkhoz and Civil Society in Central Asia's Independent States, in: Ruffin M. Holt and Daniel C. Waugh (ed.): Civil Society in Central Asia. Seattle: University of Washington Press

Roy, Oliver (2000): The New Central Asia: The Creation of Nations. London: I.B. Tauris

Sagdeev, Roald (2000): Central Asia and Islam: An Overview, in: Roald Sagdeev and Susan Eisenhower (eds.): Islam and Central Asia. An Enduring Legacy or an Evolving Threat? Washington: Center for Political and Strategic Studies: 7-26

Sayyod JRC (2004): Review of the Program of Community Development for the Period of 2004-2009. Shahritus District: Development Committee of 'Khoja Mashhad' of Jamoat of Sayyod

Scott, James S. (1976): The Moral Economy of the Peasant. Rebellion and Subsistence in Southeast Asia. New Heaven and London: Yale University Press

Seligman, Adam B. (1997): The Problem of Trust. Princeton: Princeton University Press

Sen, Amartya (1985): Goals, Commitment, and Identity, in: Journal of Law, Economics, & Organization 1 (2): 341-355. <http://www.jstor.org/stable/765061> (accessed June 13, 2009)

Shozimov, Pulat D. (2003): Tadzhikskaya identichnost' i gosudarstvennoe stroitel'stvo v Tadzhikistane [Tajik Identity and State Building in Tajikistan]. Dushanbe: Irfon (in Russian)

Sievers, Eric W. (2002): Uzbekistan's *Mahalla*: From Soviet to Absolutist Residential Community Associations, in: The Journal of International and Comparative Law at Chicago-Kent 2: 91-158

Smith, Graham, Vivien Law, Andrew Wilson, Annette Bohr, Edward Allworth (1998): Nation-building in the Post-Soviet Borderlands. The Politics of National Identities. Cambridge and New York: Cambridge University Press

Snow, David (2001): Collective Identity and Expressive Forms, in: eScholarship Repository of University of California. <http://repositories.cdlib.org/csd/01-07> (accessed January 7, 2007)

Sökefeld, Martin (1999): Debating Self, Identity, and Culture in Anthropology, in: Current Anthropology 40 (4): 417-447

Somers, Margaret R. (1992): Narrativity, Narrative Identity, and Social Action: Rethinking English Working-Class Formation, in: Social Science History 16: 591-630

Steinberger, Petra (2003): 'Fundamentalism' in Central Asia. Reasons, Reality and Prospects, in: Tom Everett-Heath (ed.): Central Asia. Aspects of Transition. London and New York: Routledge Curzon: 219-243

Stevens, Daniel (2005): NGO – *Mahalla* Partnerships: Exploring the Potential for State-Society Synergy in Uzbekistan, in: Central Asian Survey 24 (3): 281-296

Stryker, Sheldon (2008), From Mead to a Structural Symbolic Interactionism and Beyond, in: Annual Review of Sociology 34: 15–31

Tadjbakhsh, Shahrbanou (2008): International Peacemaking in Tajikistan and Afghanistan Compared: Lessons Learned and Unlearned, in: Les Etudes du CERU. Program for Peace and Human Security, No 143. http://www.ceri-sciencespo.com/publica/etude/etude143.pdf (accessed February 22, 2009)

Tajfel, Henri (1974): Social Identity and Intergroup Behaviour, in: Social Science Information 13 (2): 65-93

Tetlay, Khaleel and Marhabo Jonbekova (2005): Development of Social Organisation in Tajikistan: the MSDSP's Approach in Mountainous Areas, in: International Workshop on "Strategies for Development and Food Security in Mountainous Areas of Central Asia." Dushanbe: Aga Khan Foundation, INWENT and GTZ (June 6-10, 2005). www.akdn.org/publications/2005_akf_mountains_paper1_english.pdf (accessed August 17, 2006)

Tilly, Charles (1993): National Self-Determination as a Problem for All of Us, in: Reconstructing Nations and States. Daedalus 122 (3): 29-36. <http://www.jstor.org/stable/20027180> (accessed July 28, 2009)

Tilly, Charles (1995): To Explain Political Processes, in: The American Journal of Sociology 100 (6): 1594-1610. <http://www.jstor.org/stable/2782682> (accessed July 13, 2009)

Tilly, Charles (1998): Contentious Conversation, in: Social Research 65 (Fall 1998): 491-511

Tilly, Charles (1998): Durable Inequality. Berkeley: University of California Press

UNDP (2003a): National Human Development Report 2003. Dushanbe: UNDP

UNDP (2003b): Progress toward the Millennium Development Goals in Tajikistan. http://www.untj.org/files/reports/MDGReportEng.pdf (accessed June 26, 2006)

USAID (2004): Land Reform and Farm Reorganisation in Tajikistan. USAID Tajikistan: Associates in Rural Development: Policy Issues Paper

Verdery, Katherine (2004): Property and Politics in and after Socialism, in: Joan Vincent and David Nugent (eds.): A Companion to the Anthropology of Politics. Oxford: Blackwell

Water Code of Tajikistan (2001): <http://www.base.spinform.ru/show_doc.fwx?regnom=2127> (accessed November 12, 2009)

World Bank (2000): Republic of Tajikistan. Poverty Assessment. World Bank: Human Development Sector Unit: Report No 20285-TJ (June 29, 2000)

World Bank (2004): Making Services Work for Poor People. World Development Report 2004. Washington: World Bank

Williams, Glyn (2004): Evaluating Participatory Development: Tyranny, Power and (Re)Politicisation, in: Third World Quarterly 25 (3): 557-578

APPENDIX (FIELD RESEARCH METHODS)

Occasional field visits, expert interviews and secondary data collection are not sufficient to understand interactive influences between collective identities (including kinship ties and Islam) and institutionalised local governance or politics. The subject is related to socio-cognitive constructs (collective perceptions, collective norms and indigenous discourses) and the political structures of local people. Thus, the classical methods of anthropology, especially participant observation, semi-structured interviews in informal environments as well as life histories, network mapping and statistical data deriving from, complementing and crosschecking these methods, were necessary tools in my field research.

In the following parts I discuss the challenges I personally encountered during my field stay, and then I discuss the research methods I applied, including participant observation, semi-structured interviews and quantitative methods.

Challenges of scientific research in a suspicious field

Conducting intensive field research in the post-Soviet environment of Tajikistan is not an easy or previously well-established job, first of all due to the institution of the security service which collected, and perhaps still collects, personal and family data about the local population. The methodology of data collection that the security servants employed is to a greater extent similar to anthropological methods of field research, such as participant observation and semi-structured interviews in informal, everyday settings. Often, data collectors are inhabitants of the communities they are 'responsible for' and where they usually hold suitable and privileged positions. This practice attempts to institutionalise state control and, if necessary, the punishment of local people. Consequently, besides some forms of folklore, the collection of data invokes the suspicion and distrust of collectors by local people.

The other major methodological challenge involved in field research is related to scientific enterprise, which has rarely used anthropological inquiry. This also constrains the researcher's opportunity to legitimise his or her presence and activity before the academic and state structures which issue the official permission to engage in field research.

Personally, I faced such difficulties when I conducted my field research in several villages in the southern borderland districts of Khatlon province.

One example, which introduces the methodological challenges perhaps most expressively, can be drawn from my personal experience during the field research. After a short interview with development agency experts in the capital city, I initiated field entrance into Shahritus district in March 2007. I chose an old acquaintance as my research assistant, who guided me around some villages in Shahritus and Qabodiyon districts for a couple of weeks. A teacher of mathematics by training, he had recently retired from an international aid and development agency due to the completion of its mission. The expectation of local people from the development workers was therefore helped greatly toward easy and legitimate access to the local community.

The introductory phase was soon over and I continued to visit separate villages alone more frequently. The practical hindrances also took me by surprise. People who already knew me and had previously offered their hospitality now ignored my presence or even avoided encounters with me. Due to the beliefs of local people, any 'stranger' who is wandering around and 'collecting words for nothing' is not a 'trustworthy person', as he may be 'collecting words' for the security office on politically suspicious men or he may invoke the suspicion of local government officials about his work. The anthropological research is not a part of the Soviet-born mentality of 'suspicion' and the researcher remains a 'stranger' to it.

Following a month of field visits, one encounter would jeopardise the legitimacy of my stay and research in Shahritus district. In one village I interviewed a brigadir (a team leader) in his home. Later, his son came in, sat in the corner and listened to us talking for a couple of minutes. Suddenly, he turned red with anger and interrupted our conversation. He alleged that I was interrogating his 'uneducated' father and trying to 'dig out the garbage'. I zealously attempted to explain my work, but only in vain. He then started asking for my permission documents. For the first time, I understood I was ill-suited to such 'interrogations'. That day I returned to Shahritus town, where I was staying in the home of my previous assistant. He had already been informed of the incident, since the village was just a few kilometres away he had friends living there as well. He told me he had already met the head of the mahalla of that village, who wanted me to ask the provincial government for a permission letter. He also mentioned that the young man with whom I had had the incident was on a security service 'black list' due to his involvement in a banned religious movement. His personal fear was the main reason why he vehemently opposed my presence and reported me to the government functionaries. At this point, I felt my fieldwork faced serious danger. My host also wanted me to inform the government about my research.

The next day, I went to Qurghonteppa City, where I gained unexpectedly easy access to the chairman of the ideological department of the provincial government, once I had passed the guard less officially. After talking with me, the chairman was of the firm belief that I would make 'a very helpful scientific contribution' to the history and culture of the region. This also seemed obvious due to my university affiliation in Germany, which is more than a mere 'friend' of Tajikistan.

Participant observation

Trust-building with my key informants was not only a process of personal relations but also depended on how I was accepted and initiated into local communities, in the first place, through their political structures and cultural events. It was necessary that local authorities knew and endorsed my unusual stay and intention in the villages. To choose case studies sites, I visited and stayed in several villages in the Shahritus and Shuroobod districts for up to one week, while in the two selected villages I conducted field research for about ten months. Besides the official letters of permission from the provincial and district governments, the selection stage did not require any particularly special arrangements.

The next stage of the case studies, however, exceeded the expectations of the local authorities and hospitable populations. I managed to develop connections and relations with governmental officers more easily than with local notables and the subject populations.

In the case of cotton-growing Sayyod village, several first-hand encounters challenged and questioned especially my anthropological stay or participant observation.

Local notables always told me about tales of 'stability' and 'progress' in their village. The challenge was how to look beyond these established discourses while not conflicting with the expectations of the story-tellers.

In addition, it was impossible to start developing direct relations with the subject villagers without the mediation and informal approval of their direct authorities. Therefore, from the outset I followed the advice of the village leaders to stay in the home of one of them who at the same time was employed with the jamoat and whose brother was a district deputy governor. I stayed in his place only for a couple of weeks, since among other things he was an extremely busy jamoat employee. Only in the evenings did he guide me to the places of his extended family. Although this process was important in terms of entrance and trust-building, the effect remained limited. To cut off this 'family relation' without any serious reason could also raise questions about my own status in the community; so far, I was a stranger who had earned the expectation of the authorities 'to write a paper on the history and culture of the village' so limited interaction with them deemed to be sufficient. The 'family relation' with the host was arranged in accordance with local traditions of hospitality. To give my subject up to these traditions would constrain my understanding of inter-family, inter-group relations – of the true, comprehensive picture of local political and social processes. The challenge was how to get out of the hospitality whirlpool, but the only way was to strictly obey local traditions of initiation.

Gradually, I gained friendly relations with reputable men and told them about my 'inappropriate' stay in the house of my host, who had a young wife and they lived alone. Respect of and obedience to local Islamic norms were almost the shared keys to any doors. Local authorities started trusting and initiating my studies, sometimes even against the implicit disagreement of local state officers. The next stage made my stay in the village enjoyable, as I was attending ceremonies and visiting sacred sites and individual families. In the middle part of my research, it was also possible to tell the local people about my true intention to learn about interactions between their collective identities and power structures. I felt it necessity to impart this information when I needed to approach individual informants and ask them a series of semi-structured questions.

My initiation into the community of 'native' (*mahalli*) families in Sayyod village also had a negative side effect. The ethnically distinct category of *kuhistoni* Tajiks of the village considered me the 'guest' of their war enemies and distrusted my 'journalistic' visit to their community. Only after establishing relations with their ethnic co-members in government and non-government offices did some of them believe in my neutrality. However, doubts surrounding this neutrality remained a challenge throughout the entire process of the field research.

This doubt regarding neutrality was also my central problem in the mountainous Devdor village. For the entire period, I stayed in the house of the head of the village organisation (VO), which helped me to develop friendships with a number of villagers who were involved in the network of this development organisation. Since every family was not embedded in the network, a significant part of the village still remained dark, unintelligible and intangible to me. Many villagers also received me as a guest of the related families of the head of the VO and therefore expected my exit, as the 'three-day-guest' norm required.

Soon, I started visiting the village mosque and sacred sites in the region. I became acquainted with the *mutavalli* (guard) of the mosque and several shrines, who at the same time was a key mahalla leader. Later contacts with other mahalla authorities were not successful, though, due to their long conflict with the VO leaders, but my attempts nevertheless generated a positive impression about my neutrality in regard to any family. Disputes and conflicts over important village resources were on the rise, so every time the shadow of doubt on my neutrality arose, I was met with inaccessible boundaries. Even government and non-government (including international) functionaries and managers in the jamoat and district centres invited me to their offices or to informal gatherings, where they suggested that I avoid certain people.

In general, I gained a good reputation and felt comfortable in my surroundings, not only due to my formal enrolment with the umbrella international agency of the VO, i.e. the MSDSP, but also due to my initiation into the Devdor community thanks to my diligence, awareness and respect as well as visits to local sacred sites. The grandfather of the host family, *mutavalli* and some mullahs, who were involved in mundane disputes between themselves, enjoyed teaching me about their shared religious and historical knowledge and traditions.

Semi-structured interviews and focus group

Besides the notes I made in my diary about my personal impressions and encounters, I tried to identify potential informants from the outset. My informants had different social backgrounds, experiences and affiliations, and they came from different segments of the population, such as ordinary rural inhabitants, elites and religious notables who participated in local political and economic processes (see Table 22: The list of key informants and focus groups). Participant observation, case study and network analysis were employed to learn about how collective affiliations were expressed in local politics. The central question was how and why they refer to collective identities when claiming their political and economic rights, i.e. how their collective experiences and affiliations are fluid and context-responsive. I observed how multilayered expressions of locality, kinship and religion sustained and modified the particular institutions of local governance or the basic principles of political and social order in local communities.

Another strategy for my observations was to crosscheck my hypothesis and central question, to reformulate sub-questions and to build them into the body of a semi-structured interview. However, I didn't need to exert any particularly special effort to shape a comprehensive and guiding list of questions or a structured framework for a questionnaire. The central question inquired about the interactive influence of local politics and the socio-cognitive constructs of local people, including their collective identities. Therefore, I resisted posing direct questions and rarely organised interviews in formal settings, as earlier attempts had failed. I tried to fit my questions into the context of everyday events and occasions, which also helped to introduce and involve my studies into the communities. For example, I paid visits or sometimes resources to shrines, mosques and other common public entities in order to understand my informants' commitment towards such goods. In addition, I stayed throughout the entire process of an occasion (such as a funeral or religious feast) and behaved accordingly as my status required. The other approach was to accompany my assistants while they assisted village authorities to organise the ceremonial and ritual lives of villagers. I shared my time and resources with them and tried to adapt myself into their families, ways of living and beyond in order to see the world through their eyes. I arranged and expressed my questions in the way that this process of adaptation demanded. I expressed the questions in a neutral manner in order to blunt any possible political implications and to show my indifference to or my concern for the existing issues, as every context required a different approach.

Table 22: The list of key informants

#	Name	Status, position and place
1	Anonymous	A representative of the NGO "Arbitrazh" in Shahritus district
2	Abdullo Munimov	*Imam-khatib*; Shahritus district
3	Atokhoja Hamdamov	Elder and former *kolkhozi* elite; Shuroobod district
4	Bomad Ghulomov	Elder; Shuroobod district
5	Nurullo Kholmatov	Private farmer; Shahritus district
6	Chupon Aliev	Assistant to the mahalla committee; my research assistant; Shahritus district
7	Daler Hamdamov	Teacher and head of the VO; Shuroobod district
8	Farmon Hamzaev	Teacher at the village school; Shahritus district
9	*Haji* Bobo Quliev	Private farmer and deputy head of the mahalla committee; Shahritus district
10	Halim Norboev	Brigadir; Shahritus district
11	Mahkam Boyakov	Deputy head of the mahalla committee; Shahritus district
12	Mahmad Yusupov	*Mutavalli* (guard) of the Khoja-Mashhad shrine; Shahritus district
13	Mamadzamon Eshgulov	Elder; Shahritus district
14	Mardon Saydalov	Elder; Shuroobod district
15	Marifat Ghayurova	State veteran; Shahritus district
16	Mullo Ismatov	Former *kolkhozi* elite; Shuroobod district
17	Mullo Obloqul	Principal mullah; Shahritus district
18	Munzima Saraeva	Brigadir; Shahritus district
19	Murodkhon Davlatkhonov	Elder and deputy head of the mahalla committee; Shuroobod district
20	Nasiba Nurmatova	Deputy head of the mahalla committee for women's affairs; Shahritus district
21	Nazar Numonov	Deputy head of the mahalla committee; Shahritus district
22	Nor Davronov,	Chairman of the collective farm; Shuroobod district
23	Ochil Teshaev	Elder; Shahritus district
24	Panji Alamov	*Oqsaqol;* Shahritus district
25	Polvon Kholmatov	Deputy head of the mahalla committee; Shahritus district
26	Qamar Jumaev	Brigadir and *oqsaqol;* Shahritus district
27	Rasul Nazirov	Elder and World War II veteran; Shahritus district
28	Rauf Fattoev	Brigadir; Shahritus district
29	Ravshan Eshgulov	Head of the mahalla committee; Shahritus district

30	Safarkhuja Nishonov	Deputy head of the JRC 'Dashtijum'; Shuroobod district
31	Salom Qiyomov	Brigadir of the collective farm; Shahritus district
32	Samad Ghayurov	Private farmer, former deputy chairman of the collective farm; Shahritus district
33	Saylonbi Umarova	Private farmer and cotton veteran; Shahritus district
34	Shoniyoz Eshniyozov	Deputy head of the mahalla committee; Shahritus district
35	*Sufi* Sharofiddin	*Sufi* and mullah; Shuroobod district
36	Sufikhuja Begakov	Former principal mullah and elder; Shahritus district
37	Valijon Isomatov	Private farmer and labour migrant; Shahritus district
38	Vosit Yuldoshev	Private farmer Shahritus district
39	Zamon Gulov	Teacher and former head of the DVO, former *kolkhozi* elite; Shuroobod district
40	Zubayd Salimov	Accountant for the VO; Shuroobod district

Focus groups

Focus group with 'active' members of the DVO about their perceptions of the DVO, the MSDSP and related development programmes, Devdor village; Shuroobod district (Notebook No 1-2, July 2, 2007: pages 58-59).

Focus group with members of the DVO; Devdor village; Shuroobod district (Notebook No 1-4, July 13, 2007: page 79).

Focus group with women; Devdor village; Shuroobod district (Notebook No 1-2, July 12, 2007: page 112).

Generation and integration of network maps and statistical data

In the text network maps (e.g. kinship and patron-client networks), statistical tables and figures and maps and pictures about the field research illustrate qualitative anthropological observations and case studies. However, they do not claim quantitative representativeness. They were generated through my interaction and work with key informants, semi-structured interviews and household surveys in the course and mainly at the end of my stay in each community. The surveys were feasible without any reference to sampling tools, while they covered most of the households in two village communities. Notably, the mapping and quantitative data do not infer any significant final evidence. They basically refer to qualitative conclusions in separate contexts while the dynamics may remain intact. These data are illustrative depictions of the qualitative analyses in given fragments of the thesis.

The main focus of the mapping and quantitative data was to identify personal (especially kinship and patron-client) relations among different segments of the population and at different levels. In Devdor village, I surveyed 116 families to map the *qawmdori* or personal interdependency and indebtedness of villagers (Figure 5). In Sayyod village, 633 families were surveyed to map out their kinship relations within and beyond the village, as well as to define their 23 extended families and five descent groups (Tables 6, 7 and 10). As part of the analysis in Devdor village, I identified four recipient families of *sadaqa* (Table 5) and approximately 60 families who were indebted to the elites due to their inclusion in support networks. For the same purpose, I identified 194 recipient families of the support networks of kinsmen, neighbours and villagers in Sayyod village (Tables 11 and 12).

To further understand the structures and dynamics of the support networks in Sayyod village – and thus to show their role in sustaining the cotton sector – 294 nuclear families were surveyed, which constituted 156 households (Table 13). The crucial role of personal relations among cotton elites, *kolkhozi* elites and their client farmers was also mapped out in Figure 8 and Table 15. A number of tables (Tables 14, 16, 17 and 18) generalise data about personal commitments between elites and 22 farmers and between these farmers and their subordinate workers. Since women constituted the majority of subordinate workers on the cotton farms, a number of quantitative data were dedicated to understanding their economic activities and interests. I surveyed 579 villagers, including 320 women, to identify the proportion and distribution of male and female wage labourers through 19 employment opportunities (Table 3). From among 379 cotton workers I identified 14 male and four female farmers and 30 male and 331 female workers. A total of 318 subordinate female workers were asked to categorise their economic incentives for employment on the cotton farms (Table 19). It was also necessary to categorise the family status of 414 surveyed female workers and aides, which is a crucial factor in mobilising labour for the cotton monoculture (Tables 20 and 21).